Every Individual, A King: The Social and Political Thought of Ze'ev Vladimir Jabotinsky is the second volume in the David M. Blumberg Library, a perpetual book publishing program honoring the memory of B'nai B'rith's International President from 1971 to 1978.

Manuscripts selected for publication in the Blumberg Library are outstanding literary works which seek to promote a greater popular understanding of Judaism, the Jewish tradition, and the rebirth in the twentieth century of a Jewish State in the Land of Israel.

The sponsors of the Blumberg Library are men and women who benefitted from the life and work of David Blumberg. They wish to create a living memorial which will enrich the lives of the generations to come after them. Let them know that B'nai B'rith had a leader who gave his whole heart and spirit to the welfare of the Jewish People, and with his great love of young people, he had the wisdom to know that one cannot ask a rising generation to embrace their Jewish heritage without first understanding it.

David M. Blumberg
1911–1989
זכרנו לברכה
May his memory serve as a blessing.

Patrons of the David M. Blumberg Library

Lester and Susan Crown
Joseph H. and Jacqueline Domberger
Billy B. and Rosalie Goldberg
Erwin S. and Genevieve S. Jaffe
Hon. Philip M. and Ethel Klutznick
Gerald R. and Adele Kraft
Moe and Berdie Kudler
Alan B. and Charna Larkin
Philip and Mildred Lax
Milton T. and Helen G. Smith
Jack J. and Charlotte B. Spitzer
Fred S. and Della Worms

EVERY INDIVIDUAL, A KING

EVERY INDIVIDUAL, A KING

The Social and Political Thought of
Ze'ev Vladimir Jabotinsky

Raphaella Bilski Ben-Hur

B'nai B'rith Books
Washington D.C.
Jerusalem · London · Paris · Buenos Aires · East Sydney

Translated from the Hebrew by Shifra (Charlotte) Abramson
Edited by Patrick R. Denker

Printed in the United States of America by
BookCrafters, Fredericksburg, Virginia
Typesetting: Computape (Pickering) Ltd., North Yorkshire, England
Cover design: Nina Schwartz
Photo courtesy of *The Jewish Herald*, Johannesburg
    (Jabotinsky Commemorative issue, August 3, 1965)
Index: Robert Elwood
Production Coordinator: Felice Caspar

*This book is printed on acid free paper, and meets the guidelines for
permanence and durability of the Committee on Production Guidelines
for Book Longevity of the Council on Library Resources.*

Published and distributed by
B'nai B'rith Books
1640 Rhode Island Avenue, N.W.
Washington, D.C. 20036

Library of Congress Cataloging-in-Publication Data
Bilski Ben-Hur, Raphaella.
[Kol yaḥid hu melekh. English]
Every individual, a king : the social and political thought of
Ze'ev Vladimir Jabotinsky / Raphaella Bilski Ben-Hur.
    p.   cm.
Translation of: Kol yaḥid hu melekh.
Includes bibliographical references and index.
ISBN 0–910250–24–3 – ISBN 0–910250–25–1 (pbk.)
1. Jabotinsky, Vladimir, 1880–1940 – Political and social views.
2. Revisionist Zionism.   I. Title.
DS151.Z5B4513   1993
320.5′4′095694092–dc20
        [B]   93–13605

To the memory of my parents
Devora and Zvi Bilski
who believed

Contents

Acknowledgements

I began to think about writing this book in 1980, the centennial of the birth of Ze'ev Jabotinsky, but I did not start the actual research and writing until several years after that. Unlike my other writings, where I consulted with my colleagues, this book was written in almost total self-imposed seclusion. I wanted to consolidate my thoughts by grappling solely with the thought of Ze'ev Jabotinsky.

The only one with whom I discussed the idea, with whose encouragement I undertook the task, and with whom I shared my doubts—primarily in difficult times—was my husband Nahum Ben-Hur. His contribution to the writing of the book was crucial, primarily because he became infected by my initial enthusiasm; during the entire time I was engaged in writing, he ensured that I became neither discouraged nor dissuaded from my task. His constructive criticism and the "protective wall" he built around me to provide me with the seclusion I needed helped me greatly. I appreciate his tremendous help above and beyond what my words can express.

I owe a special heartfelt thanks to Chaim Aivais, may his memory be for a blessing. During the last years of his life, he placed at my disposal the extensive library that he built and expanded over a lifetime, which included many writings by Ze'ev Jabotinsky. During his last months, we discussed various issues dealt with by Jabotinsky; I found in him a partner to my enthusiasm and to my wish to make Jabotinsky's thought available to the public. I am truly distressed that Chaim was not able to read the completed manuscript. May his memory be blessed.

My appreciation and thanks also go to Avner de Shalit for his devoted and enthusiastic assistance in collecting the material and preparing the notes for print.

I wish to express my thanks and appreciation for the helpful comments of Amnon Sasson, who edited the Hebrew version of the book.

I am grateful to Shifra (Charlotte) Abramson, who translated the book into English, and who approached the task with dedication and zeal. Once in English the manuscript benefitted enormously from the inspired editing of Patrick Denker. Wherever possible he polished and sharpened my prose, relentlessly trying to convey my analysis to English language readers. His skill, dedication, and insight have earned him a place in my heart. I am deeply grateful to my publisher, Dr. Michael Neiditch, founder of B'nai B'rith Books, who devoted countless hours to make certain that my book received every editorial attention. It was refreshing to work with someone who adheres to such high standards.

Likewise, I thank all my family and friends, who contributed to my work by respecting my desire to devote all my time and thought to my research and writing, and who waited patiently until the completion of the work.

I am deeply grateful to the Jerusalem Heritage Center and the Israeli Institute for Information and Public Relations for funding the translation of this book.

Finally, this book would not have been written without the influence and loving, long-term guidance of my mother, Devora Bilski.

To all the above, I offer my heartfelt thanks.

Preface

Rather than indulging in yet another review of the many actions of this singularly controversial man, this book instead strictly concerns itself with an examination of the social, political, and economic theories developed by Ze'ev Jabotinsky over the course of his life. Jabotinsky's fate was the same as that of many other thinkers who fathered socio-political movements: their followers translated their thought into simplified or mutated ideologies that could be used more effectively to guide political movements.

In most of these cases, we know more about the teachings of the thinker from those who considered themselves his disciples and executors of his thought and from his ideological opponents than we know from his own works.

Since an ideological movement adopts and interprets the thought in accordance with its own perceptions, it is natural that a partial, inexact, and often distorted picture emerges. Ze'ev Jabotinsky's thought has been subjected to similar (mis)interpretation.

There is more than that, however. Because he was a spellbinding and unique personality, Jabotinsky, to his misfortune, was steeped in controversy, arousing adoration or hatred. Thus, many of the books and articles on him were written by avowed enemies or confirmed admirers, none accurately representing his thought. Moreover, inasmuch as Jabotinsky was also a practical statesman and one of the most important spokesmen of the Zionist movement, many writers focused on his Zionist activities and not on his thought itself.

The purpose of this book is to acquaint the reader with Jabotinsky's thought which, to a great degree, is still relevant today. This book intentionally refrains from dealing with his Zionist activities, nor does it attempt to contest what was written about him. This discussion focuses only on Jabotinsky's thinking, utilizing the research tools and methods of political thought.

Jabotinsky's thought is scattered throughout hundreds of articles and long and short essays. In order to present his thought as one body, it was sometimes necessary to reconstruct it from bits and pieces gleaned from various writings; only then was it possible to analyze it. Jabotinsky himself did not manage to do this job although, as he testified in "The Story of My Life," he felt the urge to present his basic views as one integrated theory. Nevertheless, he did write key theoretical essays on particular subjects, notably society and economics, and nation and race.

The first section of this book deals with Jabotinsky's general philosophy, and the second with his Zionist thought. The reason for this division is not only that familiarity with his underlying theoretical structure is a prerequisite for examining and understanding his specific Zionist thought, but also that Jabotinsky's attitude in his general philosophy is different from that in his specifically Zionist thought. In the former, which deals with the entire spectrum of political, social, and economic life, Jabotinsky writes exclusively like a thinker, starting with normative basic premises, examining and analyzing phenomena, and presenting his conclusions in a general theoretical framework. In his Zionist thought, however, Jabotinsky's critical theory becomes secondary to the pragmatism and passion natural to such a statesman and activist. His foremost desire as a Zionist thinker was not merely to observe, to analyze, and to construct theory; it was, rather, to influence and fashion the history of his people.

Therefore, after presenting Jabotinsky's general theoretical thought and its analysis, the book will not only explore his Zionist thought, but will also attempt to examine the extent to which it conforms with his general philosophy. We shall try to find the reasons for any deviations, and see whether it is possible to explain them by utilizing principles of his own general theoretical thought.

I chose to include many excerpts from Jabotinsky's writings, not only in order to base my words on them, but also to enable the reader to obtain at least a taste of Jabotinsky's writing.

The English translation of the book is not identical to the Hebrew one. Many changes were introduced. A chapter (chapter one) was added, and two themes were more deeply explored: the intellectual influences on Jabotinsky's work, and the issue whether he was a fascist, pseudo-fascist, or a true liberal.

Part I

GENERAL
THEORETICAL THOUGHT

Chapter 1

INTELLECTUAL
INFLUENCES

Jabotinsky very seldom cited his sources in his writings, and thus it is generally impossible to state with certainty what the direct influences on his thinking were. What can be done, however—and shall be attempted in this chapter—is to give a brief overview of the various possible intellectual influences on him.

Jabotinsky was well-read his entire life; his reading included many of the theories published before and during his lifetime. In his youth, he consumed prodigious quantities of Russian and non-Russian literature and poetry. His favorite Russian poets were Pushkin and Lermontov; of the Russian novelists, he admired Tolstoy most, although he rejected most of the writer's moral philosophy and teachings, and opposed his desire to return to an archaic, pre-industrial society. He also greatly admired other major Russian authors such as Dostoyevsky, Gogol, Turgenev, and Chekhov, despite the fact that he found anti-Semitic elements in their works (a fact he noted in his own writings). Of the non-Russian poets and writers he preferred Shakespeare, Walter Scott, d'Annunzio, Victor Hugo, de Maupassant, Browning, Edgar Allan Poe, Mickiewicz, and the Swedish poet Tegner.[1]

After leaving Odessa at the age of 17 in 1898, Jabotinsky studied Marx's philosophy for the first time with Professor Reichesberg at the University of Berne. In the autumn of that year, he went to Rome, where he threw himself into studying. Later, he spent a year, from 1907 to 1908, reading on the problems of nationalism in Vienna.

A study of Jabotinsky's writings over the course of his lifetime reveals that the major influences on him were Western historical positivism, liberalism, and rationalism. Throughout his life, Jabotinsky was first and foremost a member of the liberal, Westernized Russian intelligentsia. Early influences

3

were of Italian and Russian origin, especially that of the liberal cultural milieu in Odessa.

Before discussing his Russian intellectual background, let us briefly consider the influences on Jabotinsky during the three years he spent in Rome, where he was systematically introduced to Marxism, and where he learned about Italian liberalism and a special brand of Italian socialism. Rome, according to Jabotinsky himself, did not as yet exhibit any sign of fascism (except for the futurism of Marinetti, with which he was not acquainted at the time). Jabotinsky was impressed by the classic Italian writers as well; in Leonardo da Vinci he saw the epitome of the ideal human being, a genius full of curiosity and creativity in a multitude of areas. He also admired Michelangelo for his approach to the human being as a unique creature. But his favorite was Garibaldi, something he repeatedly mentioned his whole life. In Garibaldi Jabotinsky saw the rare combination of a real hero and a true leader, who succeeded in combining, both in thought and action, a strong love for his nation, and at the same time, a zeal for universal humanist values. Jabotinsky also read with enthusiasm Gabriel Rossetti (an English poet and writer of Italian origin), who was inclined toward mysticism, and the aforementioned d'Annunzio, an Italian poet and playwright who claimed to be a follower of Nietzsche.[2]

It is perhaps worth mentioning that Jabotinsky was, by his own testimony, greatly impressed by Nietzsche during his youth.[3] It is possible that in later years as well he was influenced by the Nietzschean concept of the ideal man. Certainly some similarity can be found between what Jabotinsky termed the "urge for play" coupled with the "urge for domination" and Nietzsche's concept of the "will for power" of the human being, who he believed was inclined to struggle constantly and to lead a dangerous life, and who was possessed by certain noble characteristics. Some commentators have even seen the influence of Nietzsche's concept of the heroic existence in the monistic approach in Jabotinsky's Zionist theory, which required of the individual a total dedication to only one goal—the realization of Zionism—as we shall see in detail in the second part of the book.

During his studies in Rome, he learned from his teachers—who, though critical of Marx's theories, were all influenced by him to some degree—both the importance of Marxist methodology as well as the notion that man differed from other creatures in his urge for "play"—that is, in his wish to explore and dominate unknown areas. This explorative urge was accompanied by man's desire to dominate things, places and his fellow human beings. This notion may be found in Jabotinsky's late treatises on economics, as we shall see in detail later on.

In Rome, Jabotinsky came under the influence of several thinkers with different opinions and philosophies,[4] three of whom made a permanent impression on him. The first and most important was Antonio Labriola, a critical Marxist who represented a special branch of Italian socialism. From him, Jabotinsky took the notion that the rate of progress was not pre-determined, but the product of men's efforts, and gleaned as well the important idea of the crucial role played by the creative individual in history. Jabotinsky also learned from him in a systematic fashion respect for the rights of the individual, something that became a major theme in his own thinking and that inspired the title of this book.

From Enrico Ferri, whom many consider the father of sociology, Jabotinsky learned about positivism. In contrast to Labriola, Ferri did not believe in man's freedom to determine his own actions, and therefore reached the extreme conclusion that criminals might not be held individually responsible for their immoral behavior since every crime was the outcome of objective material and social factors. This view of the importance of environment on the morality of the individual was echoed in Jabotinsky's concept of morality.

From his third major teacher, Benedetto Croce, Jabotinsky learned about the superiority of the liberal economy, a concept he adopted completely in his later years. Croce was a great believer in the strength and adaptability of liberal-democratic society and government. Throughout his entire life Jabotinsky remained, as we shall see, a believer in liberal democracy and the strength of bourgeois society when accompanied by characteristics of the welfare state, as well as in its adaptability to changing circumstances.

During his one year of intensive reading in Vienna, he read about the problem of nationality (especially in regard to the building of a nation), about the rights of minorities, and about the history of national movements. He was particularly interested in the relationships and conflicts between the various nations of Austria and Hungary. In Vienna, Jabotinsky read and integrated into his thinking, to various degrees, the theories of Rudolf Springer, Karl Renner, Ernest Renan, Pasquale Mancini, Viktor Adler, Otto Bauer, and others. In all likelihood, through Adler, Bauer, and Springer he was influenced by Moritz Lazarus' psychological theory of nationhood. He was also influenced to some degree in later years by what he regarded as romantic nationalism in Poland, especially during the rule of Jozef Pilsudski.

Yet the greatest influence on Jabotinsky was that of the liberal, Westernized, Russian intelligentsia. From his youth, during his years in Berne, continuing through his stay in Rome, and after his return to Odessa—and, in particular, after his conversion to Zionism in 1903—Jabotinsky was basically a Russian liberal thinker, which he remained in many respects for his entire life. He was an ardent individualist, a fact that was reflected particularly in his earlier writings. This trait characterized him at an early stage in his thought, and was only intensified by his studies in Rome.

After his return from Rome, Jabotinsky presented an interpretation of sociology distinctly different from the Marxist interpretation prevalent in literary and artistic circles in Odessa, emphasizing the primacy of the individual, as opposed to that of the collective. While accepting particular elements of Marxism (particularly its methodology and emphasis on the importance of the forms and means of production and the imminent conflict between the industrialist and the worker), Jabotinsky completely rejected dogmatic thinking. His maxim, as expressed in his famous poem, "Schafloch," was: man is a sovereign being. His primary message in his first appearance before the literary club in Odessa was that the only goal worth pursuing is the happiness and liberty necessary for the development of the individual. "Progress" meant the liberation of the individual from the collective, since it was the individual who created progress; collectivism, in any form, was simply a new kind of slavery. Jabotinsky, who was directly influenced in this instance by anarchistic thought, and especially by Bakunin—who fought for liberty his entire life—contended that Bakunin was right in his criticism of Marx. If the proletariat succeeded in molding a "new society" according to its own concepts, it would become as tyrannical and negative as existing hierarchical, bourgeois societies.

However, notwithstanding his concurrence on certain points with Bakunin, Proudhon, and Kropotkin, Jabotinsky was no anarchist, since he acknowledged the authority of the state—only, however, in its role as supreme arbiter acting to insure the liberty of the individual. Jabotinsky indeed flirted briefly with anarchism during his youth—and read all the literature on the primacy of the individual over the state, including that by Stirner, Spencer, Lavrov, and Mikhailovski. Though in later years he developed a more complex conception of the relationship between society and the individual, he continued fervently to believe in the sacred rights of the individual as the only true measure of progress. In that sense it may be said that anarchism had a long-lasting influence on Jabotinsky's thought.

As Jabotinsky was mostly influenced by the philosophy of Bakunin, it is interesting to note that the latter, during his anarchist period, regarded himself as a materialist, an atheist, and a positivist.[5] Through him Jabotinsky also may have been influenced by Feuerbach, Comte, and Proudhon, all of whom greatly influenced Bakunin's theories. From Feuerbach, Bakunin took his notion of the alienation of man from God: that is, that man, who created God, became enslaved to Him. From Comte, Bakunin borrowed positivism; that is, the concept of the transcendence of the theological and metaphysical stages of thought, and the regard for philosophy as that which organizes the data gleaned by the various branches of science.

From Proudhon's work Bakunin formulated his idea of the transcendence of historical idealism.[6] As we shall see in this book, Jabotinsky's thought was characterized throughout by materialist and positivist elements. In his strong belief that "every individual is a king," Jabotinsky may also have been influenced by Alexander Herzen, one of the greatest Russian thinkers, who claimed that the liberty of individuals in a given place and time was an absolute value. Every human being needed, for his moral well-being, at least a minimum of freedom, one which must not be infringed upon in the name of absolute, great principles. This was a liberal attitude close to the tradition of Western libertarianism, which was characterized by von Humboldt in Germany, Benjamin Constant and de Tocqueville in France, and the radical utilitarians in England. Like early Western European liberals, Herzen emphasized liberty, and the free play of individual temperaments.[7] Like J. S. Mill, he regarded individuality and difference as desirable and opposed conformity, sameness, and thus the power of public opinion.

Generally speaking, in the debate between the Slavophiles and the Westerners in Russia that started in the first half of the nineteenth century, Jabotinsky belonged to the latter group. The indirect influence of Russian democratic and liberal Westernism can be found in his writings. At the end of the first half of the nineteenth century, Bielinsky advanced the notion—in contrast to the Slavophiles' interpretation of Russian history—that the nation's intellectual wealth was not embodied in folk poetry, but rather in the philosophical works that emerged after the reforms of Peter the Great and helped to bring about the adoption of a civilized, European way of life. In his famous "Letter to Gogol," he attacked Gogol's "Selected Passages for Correspondence with Friends," in which Gogol, departing from his earlier works, suddenly defended orthodoxy and the czarist system. Bielinksy tried to persuade Gogol that Russia's salvation did not lie in mysticism, asceticism, or pietism, but in the progress of civilization, education, and humanitarian values.[8]

Jabotinsky expressed similar opinions in his general discussion of nationhood. Yet in contrast to the Russian democratic Westerners, who emphasized the positive role of Western influences in the modernization of Russia (while simultaneously critical of capitalism), Jabotinsky was much less critical of the free economy; he favored free competition, as embodied by liberalism accompanied by a welfare state, not crude liberalism. It is not surprising that on this issue Jabotinsky differed from Russian democratic Westernism; during Jabotinsky's life, capitalism had undergone many changes and was very different from the system criticized by Bielinsky and his followers.

If Bielinsky's theory can be described as democratic Westernism, the theories of Granovski and Kavelin can be termed liberal Westernism. As an elitist, Granovski was opposed to the Slavophile's idealization of the masses, considering it a danger to progress in science and in social relations. He emphasized the importance of the autonomous personality (i.e. individualization), and considered the purpose of history to be the liberation of the individual from external determination and the creation of a society of autonomous individuals.[9] These liberal ideas found their way directly and indirectly into Jabotinsky's concepts of individualism and progress.

It is possible that Jabotinsky was also influenced by some of the Russian positivists of the latter half of the nineteenth and the early twentieth century. Russian positivism had many variations, but the majority of the positivists were influenced at least to some degree by Comte. Lavrov, for example, saw positivism as an approach advocating that all relations between all phenomena be investigated by strictly scientific methods, eliminating all reference to the metaphysical "thing in itself."[10] As we shall see, Jabotinsky indeed tried to avoid all metaphysical references, and his approach was sometimes similar to the naïve positivism that held that all problems could be solved by science. A very similar view of positivism can be found in Wyrouboff, an orthodox adherent to Comte, who did not believe that the truth could be anything other than experience verified by confrontation with previously established scientific laws.[11]

Russian positivists of that period were preoccupied with psychology, which, during that time, was often considered synonymous with epistemology. In the context of Jabotinsky's intellectual development, Kavelin's theory figures significantly. Though he continued the tradition of attacking metaphysics, Kavelin claimed that psychological processes had their own autonomous existence apart from material existence. Mental phenomena were both irreducible to material phenomena and yet, simultaneously, not independent of man's physical constitution.[12] An echo of such an approach may be found in Jabotinsky's attitude to the relationship between the physical and the spiritual in his discussion of race. The social implications of Kavelin's theory—shifting the emphasis back to the individual's personality, contrary to the contemporary trend to regard the individual as a statistic—were echoed in Jabotinsky's thought.

It is possible that Jabotinsky came under the influence of the most important branch of Russian positivism—that which dealt with sociology and was represented primarily in the works of de Roberty and Kovalevsky —being particularly affected by de Roberty's notion that in organized societies, knowledge and rational leadership played a decisive role, and action was always preceded by thought. De Roberty tried to reconcile elitism with egalitarianism, his solution being a government by an intellectual elite, combined with substantial, universal educational opportunities.[13] As we shall see, Jabotinsky was also preoccupied with the conflict between elitism and egalitarianism, although his solutions differed from those of de Roberty, if only for the simple reason than that Jabotinsky was writing in a social context fifty years after de Roberty.

The theory of Kovalevsky—who is regarded by many as the founding father of scientific sociology under the influence of Comte—differed from that of de Roberty mainly in its emphasis on empirical studies, in contrast to de Roberty's preoccupation with the philosophical side of sociology. Kovalevsky also dealt at length with the issue of progress, concurring with de Roberty's belief that the overall movement of evolution was progressive and that progress was an inexorable law of history.[14]

As we shall see, a similar naïve approach to progress was found in many of Jabotinsky's writings. Jabotinsky's definition of political progress also bore great similarity to that of Kovalevsky, who defined political progress as the expansion of individual autonomy and popular self-government, culminating in the establishment of parliamentary government.[15] Yet Jabotinsky's economic theory stood in complete opposition to that of Kovalevsky, who opposed economic liberalism and denied the importance of economic competition, seeing it as an impediment to progress. As we shall see throughout this book, Jabotinsky was not a follower of the extreme liberals, gravitating rather toward moderates such as J. S. Mill and T. H. Green, and favoring state intervention, particularly in the area of welfare. Yet in principle, Jabotinsky regarded free competition as a necessary element of progress and as inevitable, due to human nature. Again, it is possible that this difference between Kovalevsky and Jabotinsky was due to the difference in the times when the two wrote.

Looking at the overall influence of Russian positivists on Jabotinsky, one may safely conclude that he indeed did derive several elements from them, but was certainly an orthodox follower of none, developing his own distinct positivist approach.

In what is narrowly termed his Russian liberal period (from his youth until the early 1920's), Jabotinsky was also greatly taken with the British historian Henry Thomas Buckle, whose *Introduction to the History of Civilisation* exerted great influence on Russian intellectual circles in the second half of the nineteenth century. From Buckle, Jabotinsky took the idea that the fundamental characteristics of a nation were shaped by the territory—the geographic and climactic features—in which it began its sovereign existence. In the case of the Jews, this was *Eretz Yisrael*, the Land of Israel. He preferred the positivist anthropography of Buckle to organic approaches, such as those of J. G. Herder or A. Von Humboldt. We shall see in detail in our discussion of his concept of nation and race how Jabotinsky made use of Buckle's categories. Yet, in dealing with the issue, Jabotinsky also borrowed concepts from Herder, and particularly from Mazzini (whom he mentioned by name), regarding the contribution of each individual nation to humanity.

The unique contribution of each nation was its major *raison d'être*. During his Russian period, Jabotinsky also advanced the theory that religion served the Jews in the diaspora as a substitute for their lost national territory, as did the ghetto and the specific branches of the economy that the Jews chose to work in. Religion was thus the guardian of nationalism and a substitute for national territory, a notion expressed by many before Jabotinsky.

In the development of his social thought, Jabotinsky was greatly influenced, and indeed acknowledged his debt directly—something he very rarely did—by Josef Popper (whose pseudonym was Lynkeus).[16]

In *The General Right to Subsistence as a Solution to the Social Question*, Lynkeus depicted a utopian society based on humanitarian individualism. In this utopia, society as a whole took responsibility for supplying the minimum necessities of life for every individual. Beyond that minimum, each individual achieved in accordance with his work and his merit. No doubt Jabotinsky was also influenced by the ideas of J. S. Mill and T. H. Green, both nineteenth-century British liberals. Mill advocated that society provide a certain minimum, with an emphasis on education in particular, to ensure that every individual has the tools to act as a free human being—that is, to be able to make choices among alternatives. Green emphasized all the social reforms needed in Britain to provide for certain minimum human necessities. Only that way, Green maintained, could real freedom be achieved.

Special attention should be paid to the possible influence of fascism on Jabotinsky's thinking, if only because the Zionist left labeled him a fascist.[17]

Fascism, as defined by Ze'ev Sternhell, was primarily opposition to materialism. It was, from its inception in the late nineteenth century, an outcry against the legacy of the eighteenth century and the French Revolution, and thus vehemently opposed to rationalism and individualism. Fascism rejected the concept of society as an artificial creation formed by man for the sole aim of furthering the interests of the individual. Accordingly, fascism rejected a doctrine of natural rights, as well as an individualistic, mechanistic view of society. Fascism viewed the individual as merely a part of an organic whole that was the nation.

Thus fascism was opposed to both liberalism and Marxism, in which not only were the individualistic and materialistic elements dominant (although in different fashions), but which both viewed society as the arena of struggle. Liberalism considered the struggle to be among individuals in the free market, while Marxism held the struggle to be among classes and for domination of economic resources. Fascism, as it developed prior to the First World War, and in the period between the two World Wars, aimed to restore wholeness to society. As defined by Sternhell, fascism was a synthesis of organic nationalism and anti-Marxist socialism. It presented a comprehensive alternative to both liberalism and Marxism: an anti-individualistic community-based civilization, in which all individuals and classes were integrated, with the natural framework for this harmonic, organic society being the nation. The individual was but a cell in the national body.

Sternhell emphasized that this ideal type or model of fascism never in history existed, though the existence of some fascist characteristics was sufficient for a movement or a regime to be termed fascist. What united all forms of fascism was their negation of materialism. Therefore, according to Sternhell, people with entirely different backgrounds contributed to the creation of fascist ideology. The struggle against materialism in its two major forms, liberalism and Marxism, united people as disparate as Sorel, de Man, d'Annunzio, Olivetti, Barrès, Corradina, Labriola, Mussolini, Gentile, and many others.

As noted before, the two fundamental elements making up fascism, according to Sternhell, were organic nationalism and the revision of Marxism. Organic nationalism was based on the concept of the organic solidarity of the tribe. The nation was like a living organism—a closed, irrational society grounded in instinct and emotion. Such a society fought rationality in every form, and resisted individualism and intellectualism as well. Such a society was dominated by unity and harmony among individuals and classes; the proletariat class was an indistinct part of the homogeneous society as a whole. This state was achieved by the destruction of liberal democracy and reconciliation between the proletariat and the nation. Anything that divided society, such as the class struggle or free market competition, had to be eliminated. Democracy was seen as the embodiment of bourgeois interests, while Marxist socialism was regarded as the incarnation of the workers' interest. Since both were based on egoism and separatism, they were resisted by fascism. On the other hand, everything that united the nation had to be cultivated: authority, social solidarity, the readiness to sacrifice, heroic values, and the like. According to fascist belief, those elements would help destroy liberal democracy, after which a new national democracy would emerge, a form of government based on natural authority.

The second basic element of Sternhellian fascism was the revision of Marxism, in accordance with the teachings of Sorel, who discussed a revolution by and for society as a whole, including all classes. This new brand of socialism attacked the ills of capitalism, but not those of private property. It was revolutionary not in a social sense, but rather in a political, national, psychological, and moral sense. The nation was regarded as the revolutionary agent that would fight against liberal democracy rather than against the proletariat. This last notion bridged the gap between the supporters of that particular branch of Marxist revisionism and those who believed in organic nationalism. The synthesis of the two occurred, according to Sternhell, both in France and Italy, beginning in the summer of 1914. The new synthesis grew rapidly and developed as a political force. The most famous socialist who found his way to fascism through revolutionary syndicalism was Mussolini.

The First World War contributed to the flowering of fascism, according to Sternhell, primarily because it proved the ability of the state to mobilize its citizenry for a common cause, and its ability to control the economy through central planning. It also proved that the citizens were willing to sacrifice their lives for the collective. New extensions of fascist thought emerged in the period between World Wars I and II. These included, for example, the theories of Henry de Man, the new theories of Mussolini, of Marcel Deat, and of the many others who came to fascism from the right or from the non-Marxist left.

The main contributors to the new mature fascism, also according to Sternhell, were Giovanni Gentile and Alfredo Rocco. The foundation of mature fascism was the notion of totalitarianism. The collective took complete priority over the individual, who was perceived as existing in order to fulfill obligations, a mere tool with which to realize the ends of the totalitarian state. The state controlled all areas of activity (the economic activity of capitalism was controlled through corporativism), and was both the embodiment of the organic nation and the guardian of unity. It utilized every means that could strengthen it: party, propaganda, and education.

There is little doubt that Jabotinsky was familiar both with the late nineteenth-century writings which brought about the emergence of fascism, and with the mature fascist ideology of the 1930's. Jabotinsky's concept of compulsory national arbitration with regard to work relations, like his ideas about corporativism and a corporative regime, was indeed found in Italian fascism.

Jabotinsky's concept of nationalism is regarded by some as having been influenced by organic nationalism; for example, Jabotinsky valued hierarchy, obedience, and order, notions regarded as part of organic nationalism. In his Zionist thought, Jabotinsky also emphasized the monistic idea—that is, that during the realization of Zionism, the individual had to be totally committed to one ideal alone: the Zionist ideal.

Yet the question of Jabotinsky's fascism strongly depends upon the context in which Jabotinsky expressed his views—on the corporative state, national arbitration, nationhood, hierarchy, obedience, order and monism, for example. Did he borrow elements from fascism, or did he oppose fascism and what it symbolized? Was he firmly rooted in the opposing camp of liberal democracy? For instance, he emphasized that his corporatist idea did not derive from Italian fascism but from Leon Blum's "Front Populair" policy in France.

From the Jewish Zionist world, Jabotinsky was influenced primarily by the liberal thought of Herzl and to a lesser degree by Pinsker and Nordau. The influence of Jewish tradition was for the most part limited to the Bible, upon which he relied directly and mainly in his social philosophy.

The short discussion on the possible intellectual influences on Jabotinsky is intended to give the reader some idea of the broad range of his intellectual background. Only those theories which might reasonably be assumed to have influenced him to some degree were included. Yet it is possible that other theories also, not touched upon here, had some indirect influence on him.

There is a dispute as to whether Jabotinsky was an original thinker, and indeed some even claimed that he had no systematic theory whatsoever. By presenting and analyzing Jabotinsky's comprehensive thought—both general and Zionist—I hope to enable the reader to reach his own conclusion on whether or not Jabotinsky deserves to be called a social and political thinker. The reader will be able to judge whether Jabotinsky merely presented the views of other thinkers or whether, despite the many intellectual influences, he succeeded in advancing a distinct social and political theory that clearly bore his imprimatur.

Chapter 2

LIBERALISM
AND DEMOCRACY

On Morality and Truth

J abotinsky was born in 1880 in Odessa and passed away in 1940 not far from New York City. As we saw, he grew up under the influence of a variety of different world views.

However, while the majority of Eastern European Zionist leaders adopted socialist world views, Jabotinsky's thought was fundamentally liberal. His eventual adoption of a liberal-democratic world view, into which he integrated his concept of nationalism, came after a tempering process of disenchantment with Marxism and socialism. As he wrote in *The Story of My Life*, "I retained my faith in the justness of the socialist regime that was implanted in my heart, as 'something self-evident' until it was completely shattered by the Red experiment in Russia!"[1]

As an introduction to the discussion of his concept of liberalism and democracy, we shall examine Jabotinsky's attitude toward morality and truth.

Jabotinsky developed no systematic theories on the issue of morality. Thus, we must rely solely on those passages in which he specifically dealt with morality, in order to present a relatively coherent picture.

The key to Jabotinsky's corpus of general thought is the assumption that the supreme value was the individual, and after the individual, the nation. Jabotinsky's conception of "individualism," which he had evolved since his youth[2], stood in sharp contrast both to étatism, which regarded the state as the supreme value and the individual as a tool of the state, and to totalitarianism, which championed large-scale intervention by the state in the life of the individual—fascism, for example, incorporating both these elements. Thus Jabotinsky espoused:

the idea of "individualism" ... upon which, if my maker had blessed me with sufficient wisdom and knowledge to formulate a philosophical system, I would establish and construct my entire system: in the beginning, God created the individual; every individual is a king who is equal to his fellow individual—who also is a "king"; it is better that the individual sin against the public than that society sin against the individual; society was created for the good of individuals, and not the contrary; and the future end of days, the vision of the days of Messiah— is the paradise of the individual ... and "society" has no purpose other than to help whoever has fallen, to comfort him, and to raise him up.[3]

The nation, not mankind, was of secondary importance to the individual. In contrast to the universalism of Marxism and socialism, Jabotinsky maintained that in the beginning God created the nation and not humanity. Thus he averred: "I believe with complete faith that in the competition between these two, the nation takes precedence,"[4] and that "likewise, the individual takes precedence over the nation."[5]

This approach emphasized man's freedom and his mastery over his fate. Therefore, he could not morally be compelled to dedicate his life to building the state. Such a crucial decision—to subjugate one's life to the service of the nation—had to be the decision of each individual, derived from his rational conviction that this indeed was the right thing to do. When man himself decided to dedicate his life to his nation, his freedom was in no way compromised.[6] In this, Jabotinsky's view differed fundamentally from that of the early fascism of the late nineteenth century and from the mature fascism of the 1930s, which considered the individual a tool of the collective entity—that is, of the nation or state.

It was this concept of Jabotinsky's that turned his entire life into a campaign of persuasion to logically convince the Jews of the diaspora to decide freely and independently whether or not to devote their lives to the effort to resurrect the Jewish state. His speeches and articles, often constructed as Socratic dialogues, were addressed to man's reason, and attempted to logically convince his audience of the truth as Jabotinsky saw it. His failure to do so was not only a source of great disappointment to him, but was also incomprehensible. Max Nordau, to whom he confided his disappointment, responded: "These, my young friend, are the words of logic: and logic is the wisdom of Greece, which is hated by our people. A Jew does not learn from logical reasoning: he learns from tragedy. He will not buy an umbrella 'only' because clouds appeared on the horizon; he will wait until he has gotten wet and fallen ill with pneumonia ... several years passed until I discovered all the truth in these words."[7]

However, as much as Jabotinsky believed in logical persuasion, he often made decisions not on the basis of logic, but according to a deeply-rooted feeling which he described as "just because"—what we might call a "gut feeling." He defined "just because" as: "For the life of me, I do not know 'why.' 'Just because.' And perhaps there is no other explanation for the secrets of the will that will respond precisely to that term, 'just because.'"[8]

This concept of "just because" was related to his concept of morality, which he saw as an internal feeling and not something based on logic.

At first, Jabotinsky viewed morality from the point of view of its contribution to a liberation movement. In "From the Frying Pan into the Fire," he argued that one of the serious errors of the members of his generation who fought on behalf of freedom was that they defined power as economic or physical power without taking into consideration spiritual power, which Jabotinsky identified with moral power. He said of the October Revolution: "Whether it is possible or not to be victorious through moral strength, this was, in any case, the main tool—if not the only one—of the liberation movement, and thus it had to be guarded like the apple of one's eye. . . . Everything that increased and consolidated the moral strength of the masses was consistent with the goal, and whatever undermined this goal, loosened the ties, or introduced elements of separation, was inconsistent with the goal."[9]

Already at an early stage, Jabotinsky was sceptical about the possibility of achieving victory by spiritual power alone, although he saw it as a unifying element that could contribute to victory.

Around 1910, he wrote several essays specifically on the subject of morality because "it was clear that there are still things that are forbidden, and it is imperative that man have a feeling of internal abhorrence that tells him without words 'why it is forbidden.' Man comes to an understanding of moral matters not by reasoning, but rather out of an internal sense, and the person whose sense is faulty is simply handicapped."[10]

Jabotinsky concluded that there were things in the realm of morality that could not be proven. Therefore, in response to the question of why a certain act was moral, the answer was often "just because." Furthermore, even if the immoral argument was logically superior, that did not make it moral. There was no necessary connection between logic and morality, even though it frequently was possible to prove logically why something was moral.

Jabotinsky's view on this point was similar to that of many philosophers, including the famous nineteenth-century liberal, John Stuart Mill who, in his book *Utilitarianism*, not only maintained that morality was based on sensations, but actually spoke about moral sensations. He believed that a moral action was the result of an internal urge, and that man used logic only afterwards to explain why he acted as he did.

However, in contrast to the optimistic outlook of nineteenth century liberals on man's nature and morality, Jabotinsky's conclusions in a series of articles—"*Homo Homini Lupus*," "I Do Not Believe," "Right and Might" (1910 and 1911)—were gloomy and cynical.

Historical facts, he said, taught unequivocally that racial prejudice, causing persecution of the Negroes in the United States and pogroms in Russia and Poland, was deeply ingrained in the souls of the masses and existed in democracies like the United States. The thinking of socialists such as Otto Bauer and the behavior of the Russian and American proletariat also reflected prejudice. Jabotinsky considered racial prejudice "a sickness that neither general suffrage nor schools have the power to cure."[11] Moreover, racism was so strong that those afflicted with it were incapable of freeing themselves from its grip, even if they themselves had been victims in the past: "People go even farther than that. Not only does the memory of their suffering not serve as a deterrent from striking others in the same place in which they were struck, but there are instances worse than that. It happens that a people is still sighing and groaning from oppression, and crying out in despair, and at the same time shrewdly oppresses a weaker congregation of people. Just look at the Poles in Galicia, where they consider themselves masters to some degree. How they mistreat the Ruthenians!"[12]

Prejudice was one of the central ills of society not only because it led to an unfair condemnation of good things, but also because it influenced the good and spoiled it. Jabotinsky cited the stepfather as an example. Society's prejudices cast everything he did in a negative light, so that the child began to believe that his stepfather wished what was bad for him and changed his attitude. The end result was that the stepfather, who was angered by his stepson's attitude, regarded him negatively. "The problem with prejudices is not only that they unjustly denounce what is good. The main problem—and for this reason they must be wiped out—is that their influence really destroys the good and transforms it into evil."[13]

Jabotinsky's conclusion about man's attitude to his fellow man in each of these three articles was most pessimistic; Thomas Hobbes was correct, he said, in stating that "*homo homini lupus est*"—that man relates to his fellow man like a wolf.

Jabotinsky applied this pessimistic outlook on interpersonal relations to international relations. He cited the enormous injustices perpetrated throughout history—the treatment of the Indians in America by the white man being one of the prime examples—with no opposition or criticism voiced by anyone. The main point was that in all cases the conquest or the exploitation was judged by the resulting economic growth and development: "People believe that civilization is like money—*non olet* (it has no smell). The world takes into account only results, and pays no attention to the means ... before us we have simply a large, general battle of wolves in which there are no heroes and no villains and there is only a war of instincts where 'might makes right'; [it is] an open war, dirty, and wild."[15]

Though every oppressor managed to justify his conquest, these rationalizations, according to Jabotinsky, were merely lip service.

"There is nothing in the world flimsier than feeling and morality,"[16] said Jabotinsky; one could not rely on them. This view was far from, if not antithetical to nineteenth-century liberalism, which regarded man as a rational being who, with the proper form of government, liberty, and education, would also possess moral qualities; it was also in direct opposition to socialist views which held that, after revolutionary social change, solidarity in society would prevail.

Jabotinsky did not hide the fact that his opinions on this critical point differed from those of others, and he demanded that those who preached either liberal democracy or socialism not lead the public astray on this subject.

About twenty years later, in 1928, Jabotinsky addressed the question of whether a certain degree of morality was inborn or whether its development depended on man's environment:

> Man's character is neither black nor white, not good and not bad; it is the product of the relationship between his appetite and his ability. Man possesses appetites that he attempts to satisfy by following the path of "least resistance." If the resistance is too great, man tells himself that the merchandise is not worth the expense, and he forgoes his craving. However, since he sees that there is no resistance, he tells himself "here it is permissible" ... the most lethal poison to man's morality is implicit within the words: "here it is permissible." Anywhere this formula goes, morality is to no avail.[17]

This conception was based on historical phenomena. For example, the behavior of the Belgians in the Congo differed fundamentally from their conduct at home because of their feeling that "here it is permissible." Thus the moral concept of turning the other cheek—of non-response—was, Jabotinsky felt, invalid, not only because it allowed the aggressor to feel no shame, but because it stimulated the feeling that "here it is permissible." The pogroms and the persecution of the Jews in the diaspora were classic examples. Whether people were morally healthy or crippled was thus determined by accepted societal norms.

The belief that morality is fashioned by the environment (one which Jabotinsky absorbed as a student from his Italian teacher Enrico Ferri), was inconsistent with his earlier approach to morality as an innate moral sense. Since he did not deal with the subject of morality in a systematic fashion, Jabotinsky did not explain this contradiction. It is reasonable to assume from his writings that he held both these views simultaneously. He regarded moral conduct as a combination of an internal sense with which most people are born, and the influence of the environment which heightens or weakens this sense.

Is it then possible to reconcile Jabotinsky's liberal belief that "every individual is a king"[18] with his pessimistic view of actual individual and national morality, which was the antithesis of liberalism?

The answer sometimes given—that Jabotinsky abandoned his liberal world view over the course of time—is not correct. On the contrary, his liberal views intensified over the years. For example, in his article "The East" (1926), he acclaimed Western culture, which he considered an advanced stage of civilization, whereas the term "East" described a lower stage in the development of mankind. The superiority of the West was expressed, among other ways, in the constant desire for progress, that was the result of moral protest. The Jew had played a critical role in the shaping of this culture: "For the major traits of European civilization: dissatisfaction, 'wrestling with God,' the idea of progress—that entire abyss between two world views [Eastern and Western] that is expressed in the contrast between two beliefs, 'the golden generation' and 'the Messiah,' an ideal in the past, and an ideal in the future—we gave Europe those features, yet a long time before our forefathers came to Europe; we brought the Bible with us readymade."[19]

Jabotinsky immediately qualified his words: "I am speaking of course about moral Europe."[20]

He thus continued to believe in moral Europe and liberal ideals, yet reality showed him that an immoral Europe also existed, just as an immoral America existed side by side with the moral America. He believed that important events helped strengthen or weaken individual and national morality.

He considered World War I, for instance, an extremely negative catalyst that led to instantaneous moral disintegration. With scathing criticism, he noted "For a long time man had not been shown in such a conspicuous manner that 'everything is permissible': that principle, treaties, promises, tradition, dedication, freedom, humanity—are vanity of vanities, that everything is permissible; it is permitted to drown women and children, to burn people alive and to offer them as incense, to evacuate hundreds of thousands of people to the highways and to take then to the devil-knows-where, to hang, to beat, and to rape."[21]

His attitude to human morality was similar to that of the Greek sophist Thrasymacus, who argued simply that the strong always determine what is just. However, unlike other sophists like Callicles, Thrasymachus did not justify this situation morally; rather, he criticized it while noting that in reality the powerful dictate the norms.

Likewise, Jabotinsky's pessimistic description of man's immorality reflected reality, which could not be ignored. The ideal remained for him the liberal dream, "the dream of order and justice without compulsion, a vision encompassing all of mankind, made up of mercy, patience, belief in man's fundamental goodness and honesty."[22]

Jabotinsky argued that in order to progress from reality to a more ideal situation, two simultaneous types of activity were necessary. Where force reigned, there was no choice but to use force in order to survive. However, at the same time, an attempt needed to be made to eliminate the causes of immoral conduct. Those people with developed moral senses had to demarcate with clear red lines what was forbidden from what was permissible, so that those born morally defective, or whose moral sense was suppressed by society, would know how to act.

However, in several places in his works where he angrily denounced immoral situations, Jabotinsky only explained what the immediate necessary step for survival was and did not discuss the type of basic action needed in order to fundamentally change the immoral situation.

Those passages were the source of the contention that Jabotinsky stopped believing in morality altogether, causing much misunderstanding of his basic conception. This could have been avoided if he had developed a systematic outlook on morality.

It would be correct to say that sometimes Jabotinsky despaired of the morality of individuals and nations. However, after those periods of despair, he always returned to his faith in liberal ideals.

The following passages attest to the fact that Jabotinsky continued to believe in the possibility of developing man's moral sensibility even when reality indicated otherwise. The same Jabotinsky who argued that history proved that events were decided by force, which was the most universally-understood language, demanded—not in the name of power, but specifically in the name of morality—the right of a homeless people to a national homeland, despite the fact that the lands of the world were already parceled out: "When the Jewish people without a homeland demands the Land of Israel for itself, why this is immoral, because the natives find it inconvenient for them. Such morality belongs with cannibals and not in the civilized world. The world does not belong only to those that already have too much land, but also to those who have nothing."[23]

It was in the name of morality that Jabotinsky turned to the Jews in the Land of Israel in 1933 after the murder of Arlosoroff: "The sacred principle of human justice is known to every Jew who knows how to read: even an accused person standing before a court, and against whom the prosecutor is already reading his speech bringing proof after proof—even then, the accused remains, in principle, innocent both before the law and in the eyes of society.... At least wait for the verdict! ... A second sacred principle of human honesty also exists: if it happens that someone transgresses, the responsibility for the sin cannot be placed on society, which had no part in it."[24] Thus, in addressing the Jewish Settlement in the Land of Israel, Jabotinsky evoked two moral principles: that a person is innocent until proven guilty, and that collective punishment is a sin against the collective victim.

Such is not the behavior of a person who has ceased to believe in man's morality, but is rather the conduct of a person who believes in man's inherent moral capacity and who tries to enhance that capacity and to fight against circumstances leading to its atrophy. Jabotinsky's empirical approach teaches us about his attitude to morality; it also reflects the positivist influence on his thought, from that of his Italian teacher Ferri through late nineteenth and early twentieth century Russian positivism and Western positivism. His thought was largely derived from an analysis of reality. His concept of truth, which was connected to morality, was also arrived at by analyzing morality, since by "truth" he meant the justness of a particular position, and not truth in its empirical sense. Jabotinsky was aware of and preoccupied by the multitude of situations in which no single, predominating truth could be identified.

A broad knowledge of history enabled Jabotinsky to see that in many confrontations there was no one absolute truth. Reality was complicated, and in many instances both sides were right, each in its own way. "There apparently is no such conflict between groups of people in which justice is completely on the side of one group—if it is discussed impartially," Jabotinsky said in 1916.[25] About fifteen years later, in a series of articles dealing with the special situation of the blacks and the whites in South Africa, Jabotinsky analyzed the positions of both sides. While it was clear to him that the whites were faced with a great tragedy because apartheid did not provide any solution and was inherently a time bomb, Jabotinsky was able to understand the claims of both sides: that of the blacks, based on their historic right and the fact that they constituted the majority, and that of the European South Africans, based on the prosperity they had brought to South Africa, as well on as their creativity and organization as a society.

Jabotinsky concluded that only a superficial liberal could say that no tragedy inhered in this situation, and that it would be natural for the blacks to rule the land once they developed culturally because that was their right as a majority. A thoughtful liberal, in Jabotinsky's opinion, was aware of the fact that the concept of "right" was not simple. The right to land was also acquired by cultivating it. Thus, in his philosophical discussion of private property, the father of liberalism, John Locke, based the right of private ownership over land not only on acquiring it first but also on cultivating the land and using its produce.[26] Therefore, said Jabotinsky, in the struggle between the blacks and the whites in South Africa, both sides had moral validity: "This is the worst scourge in the world: in practically no place and at no time has there been one and only one truth; perhaps litigants each have their own truth, but for an impartial judge there are always two, both tragic."[27]

This distinction ran through all Jabotinsky's writing. Each party to a conflict always had his own truth, and was certain of its merit (for otherwise he would not fight for it); it was also necessary, according to Jabotinsky, that each party zealously believe in his truth without qualification.

Over the years, Jabotinsky became increasingly aware that a revolutionary leader or leadership had to cleave to *one* truth, and the fervor of his belief could galvanize an entire society. The conclusion of his article, "The Truth," in which he cited the poem by MacDonough (one of the leaders of the Irish Revolution), clearly expressed this position: "They called him their king, their leader. He guided them over a period of one year full of great things and vanquished their enemy. Afterwards, he began to ponder.... I no longer have room to transmit all his words, but their main thrust, more or less, is that everything in the world is transient, everything is relative, and there actually is no one truth. However, he would ponder, and continue to ponder, until his men grew sick of him. Then they chose as a leader a man who was severe, sure of himself, who didn't look back upon the clear desolation of the past. He fought for his land and bequeathed it peace and glory."[28]

Jabotinsky also believed that the secret of Jean Jacques Rousseau's greatness lay in his zeal. He called him a revolutionary leader who fanned the flames of revolution: "The secret of his influence ... was not in his intelligence, nor in his knowledge, nor in his clear perception, but only in his mood, his temperament, in his internal fire.... And from this man, the revolution starts, this man made history and—not those wise men who, with such a sharp eye, knew how to read the needs of the public, and so unerringly incorporated them in their own social and political ideals."[29]

The belief in one truth and internal fervor were imperative in order to rally a society to revolt and to succeed.

Might we not draw conclusions from this about the Israeli–Arab conflict? As a leader of one party to this conflict, Jabotinsky saw, because he had to see, one truth—that of the Jewish party. However, in his general thought, he acknowledged that the other side might feel equally strongly about its truth. The objective judge, who was not a party to the conflict, would generally have to come to the conclusion that indeed there was not one truth, but two, and any decision in favor of one would bring a tragedy to the other.

His general thought thus took into account that often there was no one truth. On the other hand, in our discussion of his Zionist thought, we shall have to remember that Jabotinsky was not an impartial judge on matters pertaining to the Jewish people, but rather the representative and leader of one side. According to his theoretical thought, a leader of one side had to fervently believe in only one truth—his truth—for otherwise, he could not achieve his goal.

The two central axes of Jabotinsky's general thought were liberal democracy and nationalism. In our discussion of his general theoretical concept of liberal democracy, as well as in our discussion of his nationalist concept, we shall examine how these two meshed. We shall also see whether Jabotinsky was able to deal with any tension that might have existed between them, and whether he was able to remain faithful to the maxim he presented in "The Story of My Life"—"the individual takes precedence over the nation."

Liberal Democracy: Its Virtues and its Drawbacks

One of the central issues demanding clarification in Jabotinsky's thought is his attitude toward democracy and liberalism, both of which should be defined here for the purposes of this examination.

Democracy and liberalism are not synonymous, although in recent times they have coexisted in Western countries. Democracy is defined as the opposite of an authoritarian regime, the criterion of its validity being the breadth of popular consent in which the government is based. The broader the consentaneous basis, the more democratic the government is, and the narrower the consentaneous basis, the more authoritarian it is. The democratic view thus is that the people are sovereign.

The most salient feature of democracy is the election of representatives by the people at intervals established by law. Authority for a limited period of time is granted by the people to their representatives, who are responsible to the people because their authority is given to them as a trust. A second characteristic is the multiplicity of parties—that is, the existence of real alternatives during elections. A third characteristic is the principle of the majority. Decisions in a democratic society are made according to the principle of majority rule, and the minority is obliged to accept the majority decision. There are two main types of modern democratic governments: the parliamentary-cabinet system (as in Great Britain and Israel) and the presidential system (as in the United States and France). Above and beyond the political structure—the basis of which is equality of political rights—there also exists a demand for a more equitable distribution of material resources, necessitating more state intervention in the socioeconomic sphere.

On the other hand, the liberal character of the government is determined according to one criterion: the degree of state intervention in the life of the individual, or, stated differently, the degree of state intervention in individual liberty. The less the state intervention, the more liberal the government. The greater the intervention by the state, the more totalitarian the government. Thus, a totalitarian government is the opposite of a liberal regime.

If the central value of democracy is political and socioeconomic equality, the central value of liberalism is individual liberty. Thus liberalism emphasizes constitutionality and separation of powers—judicial, legislative, and executive—including a system of checks and balances, features that lessen the government's ability to make arbitrary decisions.

There is an element of contradiction between democracy and liberalism, since democracy requires state intervention in order to reduce inequality, while liberalism demands minimal intervention so that individual freedom is preserved. Modern democracy, thus, is a combination of the democratic and liberal ideas, where an equilibrium has been achieved between equality and freedom.

It is no wonder then that the majority of Western democratic governments are also liberal, since they accept the value of both equality and liberty. Likewise, the perception of man as a rational being is a fundamental assumption common to both democracy and liberalism. Democracy holds that man is rational enough to elect, to criticize, and to be elected. Liberalism believes that man is rational enough to choose among alternatives and to bear the consequences. Furthermore, it is difficult to imagine a modern democratic government in which the scope of individual liberty is limited in areas related to freedom of thought and conscience, freedom of expression, freedom of organization, and freedom to select a profession. From this is derived the liberal nature of the modern democratic government. On the other hand, pure liberalism does not exist in a modern democracy because the state does intervene to some degree in the life of the individual, primarily with regard to distribution of resources through taxation and welfare policy.

In contrast, most authoritarian governments are also totalitarian, because an authoritarian government with a limited consentaneous basis fears granting individual liberty, lest that basis be undermined. The degree of democracy and the degree of liberalism differ from one government to another, and therefore each must be examined on its own merits.

Jabotinsky was vigorously attacked by his political opponents for his attitudes toward democracy and liberalism; there were those who even went so far as to charge that his philosophy was fascist and militaristic, and that his Zionist thought had dictatorial overtones. However, what is of more concern to us is that serious scholars also have expressed the opinion that

Jabotinsky's general political thought, as it evolved over the course of his life, was a combination of integral-nationalism and étatism; that is, that Jabotinsky viewed the nation and state as supreme values, and the individual as nothing but an instrument of the state. They also argued that he disdained the liberal belief in man's rationality and morality, and that his general theory contained elements aggrandizing the nation, the state, and the leader, and was characterized by an emphasis on militarism (which proceeded from Jabotinsky's admiration for discipline and ceremony).

In the coming chapters, we shall try to examine whether this interpretation of Jabotinsky's general thought is correct. Our discussion will focus on his attitude toward democracy and liberalism in the political, economic, and social spheres.

In "The Story of My Life," Jabotinsky stated that, were he able to, he would base a philosophical system on the premise of the supremacy of the individual—the theory of individualism. He maintained that the only consistent guideline in his writings was:

> the idea of "individualism," that same "*pan-basilia*" ... upon which, if my maker had blessed me with sufficient wisdom and knowledge to formulate a philosophical system, I would establish and construct my entire system: in the beginning, God created the individual; every individual is a king who is equal to his fellow individual—who also is a "king"; it is better that the individual sin against the public than that society sin against the individual; society was created for the good of individuals, and not the contrary; and the future end of days, the vision of the days of Messiah—is the paradise of the individual, a kingdom of brilliant anarchy, a contest between personal forces, with no law and without limit, and "society" has no purpose other than to help whoever has fallen, to comfort him, and to raise him up, and to give him the possibility of returning to that same contest. If there appear in the continuation of these volumes, the first of which is available to the Hebrew reader, my poems, "Noella" and "Schafloch," in the beautiful translation of Mr. Reichman, and the reader is amazed at their content that denies any obligation by the individual toward the nation and the public—I must admit that this is still my belief.[30]

This view is obviously diametrically opposed to étatism, in which the state is supreme; the above quotation by Jabotinsky could well be a brief statement of extreme liberal thought, or perhaps even of anarchist thought.

Jabotinsky's constant repetition of this credo in "The Story of My Life" demands that we treat it seriously. One must also remember the great influence of his Italian teacher, Labriola, with regard to the rights of the individual, and the earlier influence of anarchism (primarily Bakunin's) on his concept of the individual as the center of existence. But how did Jabotinsky apply this credo to specific issues? Did it remain a fantasy while he simultaneously developed antithetical thought, or was he indeed guided by this belief, while developing a more complex liberal-democratic conception over the course of his lifetime?

In our discussion of morality, we saw that Jabotinsky's outlook, as reflected in "*Homo Homini Lupus*," "I Do Not Believe," and "Might and Right," ran counter to nineteenth-century liberal humanism. Because of the importance attributed to these articles, we shall again cite some examples of Jabotinsky's sharp language. In "*Homo Homini Lupus*," Jabotinsky argued that the situation in which blacks were oppressed by whites in America, and Jews and other national minorities persecuted in Europe, showed that "the moral teachings of our time have no place for this slimy love of humanity."[31]

It was force, said Jabotinsky, that resolved issues and "whoever relies on fairness is a fool; fairness exists only for those who are powerful and stubborn."[32] He concluded "I Do Not Believe" in the same spirit: "No, I do not believe in a redeemer who will come tomorrow, and not in one who will come the day after that. I do believe in the club hidden in one's bosom, because I see in my neighbors' pockets, the profits that it brings them."[33] His deep disenchantment was also reflected in his third article, "Might and Right" (1911), in which he contended that morality and people's behavior have nothing in common: "What about public opinion, the press, and all other spokesmen for the fundamentals of morality? They will not bear a grudge forever; when their anger subsides, they will yet greet us with blessings."[34]

As we saw in our discussion of Jabotinsky's conception of morality, during this period of his life Jabotinsky dealt with the difference between liberal ideals and the actual behavior of individuals and nations. We noted that Jabotinsky wrote about morality on two levels simultaneously: the actual and the desired. In the cited passages, he emphasized what actually existed: immoral behavior. The source of his pessimistic outlook lay specifically in his reaction to the problem of national minorities, and particularly to the persecution of the Jews. The contention that there is nothing in these citations that impugns Jabotinsky's essential liberal-democratic outlook is reinforced by Jabotinsky's own words. He explained in these articles how his pessimistic perception of existing morality meshed with his basic outlook: *that the belief in liberalism and democracy should not blind us to the shortcomings of liberalism and democracy in everything related to minorities and racial prejudices.*

In other words, despite the cynicism and bitterness of these articles, Jabotinsky did not neglect to emphasize that he was not impugning democracy, but merely pointing out its shortcomings. He attacked the naïve liberal democrat who believed that the establishment of a liberal democracy could instantaneously destroy racial prejudices. Liberal democracy, he said, was imperative, but could not itself solve the problems of minorities, particularly the racial problems:

> Democracy in and of itself is good. We all want it, and make efforts to attain it, but there is no need to fantasize, and to promise things that will never happen. The roots of racial prejudices are ingrained first and foremost within the masses. Granting rule to the masses does not improve the situation of oppressed peoples. Of what benefit to the Jews is the constitution in Romania? What did the Jews in Finland gain by the fact that the most democratic system of elections was conducted in that country? The question of the blacks in North America sheds clear light on the sorry picture. Here, against the backdrop of an almost ideal democracy, of complete freedom, and broad rights of self-rule—here racial hatred with all its cunning operates, and in ways that arouse our horror.[35]

An extension of this idea about the virtues and shortcomings of democracy appeared in "I Do Not Believe." Here Jabotinsky developed the thesis that democracy, with all its positive elements, was not of itself a response to the oppression of one nation by the other, because in a democracy, the prejudices of the masses had greater weight. However:

> This drawback in the healing qualities of democracy in no way lessens its importance in other respects. For, apart from the national and racial minorities who fear oppression by foreigners, there exists in several places in the world, thank God, a majority which does not fear oppression by foreigners, but rather, oppression by their own people, the oppression of rule by one individual or by an oligarchy. The significance of democracy to such a majority is just about complete liberation from political oppression. And since there are incalculably more majority nations in the world than members of minorities, by right, the good of the first should be considered. And regarding the latter, the transition of the state to a democratic government also brings them relief—although not always and not in every matter. The relief is primarily in that they have a greater possibility of protesting, of organizing, of fighting. However, I do not believe that democracy, on its own, serves as a guarantee against the oppression of one nation by the other. Democracy is the most perfect form in which political expression is given to the will of the people; and therefore all the prejudices of the people are expressed most completely by actions and deeds, by the authority of the democratic government.[36]

Jabotinsky, like nineteenth-century liberals such as Mill and de Tocqueville, faced a true dilemma. On the one hand, as a liberal democrat, he regarded as essential the premise that man has rational potential (from which the principle of popular rule is derived). On the other hand, most people were full of prejudice, and democracy strengthened their power and enabled them to oppress the minority. Jabotinsky could not impugn the idea of rule by the people, because this would contradict the corpus of his thought. Thus he needed to find a solution to the problem of prejudice and oppression of one nation by another that would not compromise the essence of democracy. We shall see the nature of that solution in our discussion of Jabotinsky's thought on nation and race, mainly in his proposal for self-rule by national minorities, upon which Russian liberal ideas, such as that of Granovski, were influences.

What is certainly clear is that Jabotinsky feared the populist base of democracy, or "mob rule." Mill and de Tocqueville, who also feared the prejudices of uneducated citizens, and thus the power of public opinion, devoted large sections of their thought to this issue—Mill in *On Liberty* and *Representative Government* and de Tocqueville in *Democracy in America*. Their solutions were to increase the education of the masses, under the assumption that their inherent rationalism would be realized. The majority in society would thus become enlightened and, simultaneously, tolerance for different opinions, for minorities, for geniuses, and for anything unusual would increase. In other words, in an enlightened society, pluralism could exist in all spheres.

Mill and de Tocqueville also proposed solutions in terms of changes in the political and social structure. Mill recommended giving double weight to the votes of the educated and economically established, in the hope that this would prevent the illiterate from becoming a majority. De Tocqueville recommended an entire system of involvement by the citizens in the act of governing, primarily through different types of voluntary bodies.

The problem for Jabotinsky was that he did not believe that education was all that was necessary to eradicate prejudice and bring about tolerance in national-racial issues. Thus, he needed other solutions in addition to those proposed by Mill and de Tocqueville. We shall examine these in our discussion of nation and race.

However, it must be pointed out here that Jabotinsky adopted Mill's proposals and even expanded upon them in everything connected with the second shortcoming of liberal democracy, which he noted in "*Homo Homini Lupus*"—its inability to solve social and economic problems. To that end, he was willing, like Mill, to compromise particular liberties and to increase state intervention in order to bring about a situation where all citizens had the necessary conditions to function as free beings.

There is no question that even in the three aforementioned articles in which Jabotinsky expressed opinions contrary to the liberal belief in man's morality, he did not consider himself to be alienated from the liberal-democratic tradition, but simply emphasized the limitations and drawbacks of a liberal-democratic state. The prime example was, in his opinion, America, which was based almost completely on democratic principles (the general, direct, and secret vote; direct election of the president by the people;

near-universal suffrage), as well as on liberal principles (separation of powers with a system of checks and balances; freedom of speech, assembly, and organization), yet "nevertheless they lynch the Negroes and riot against them gratuitously for no reason, and nevertheless in the southern states the Negroes are deprived of the right to vote because of the color of their skin."[37]

The anti-liberal and anti-democratic tones of these three articles are stronger than necessary to describe the shortcomings of liberal democracy. It is likely that in addition to his sharp response to the persecution of minorities, primarily that of the Jews, these articles also expressed Jabotinsky's keen emotional disappointment with liberal democracy. Since he himself lived in a country in which, during the years when these articles were written, liberal democracy was still only a sought-after ideal, Jabotinsky's disappointment with its shortcomings in those countries where it *had* been realized brought about his extreme reaction. Over the years, his emotional reaction gave way to a more reasoned response, as reflected in his general theoretical articles. To the contrary, despite—and perhaps because of what was taking place in Europe during the first three decades of the twentieth century—his liberal-democratic outlook predominated and was crystallized.

"The Obscurantist" (1912) serves as an additional example of the exaggerated terminology he used during this period (*circa* 1910), diction engendered by his emotional fervor. Later on, Jabotinsky's responses became more moderate and were integrated into his general outlook, rather than contradicting it. "The Obscurantist" dealt with the liberator and unifier of Italy, Garibaldi, whom Jabotinsky greatly admired. Jabotinsky had Garibaldi say: "Yes, I was the champion of humanity, but I taught my countrymen to believe that there is no greater happiness in the world than the nation and the homeland, and there is no such god in the world who deserves that we sacrifice these two delightful treasures to him."[38]

This sentence on its own unquestionably absolutely contradicts Jabotinsky's declared credo: that every individual is a king, and that in the beginning man was created, while the nation, society, and the country exist for the individual. However, anyone who attempts to construct from this sentence and similar ones the theory that Jabotinsky's thought was based on the superiority of the nation and on étatism—that is, on the superiority of the state—is simply mistaken. As Jabotinsky explained in "The Story of My Life," "one's nationality was superior in significance to one's identification with the state, but" that did not negate the fact that the individual was absolutely superior to both the nation and the state. Whether or not to sacrifice his life for the nation and the homeland was the personal decision of each and every individual; such a decision was something that could not be imposed upon him. Indeed, in the sentence cited above,

Jabotinsky said in the name of Garibaldi "I *taught*" [italics mine] and not, "I compelled."

However, the terminology in "The Obscurantist" was indeed extreme, and Jabotinsky himself, some twenty years later, needed to explain his position on that issue. Thus in "The Wagon of the *Klezmer*" (1935), in response to those who accused him of fascism and étatism, he noted:

> I, too, have a blind hatred for the idea that the "state . . . is everything." And it makes no difference whether it is communist or fascist. I believe only in "old-fashioned" parliamentarianism, as inconvenient or power-less as it may seem at times. I believe in freedom of speech and organi-zation, and in almost every conflict between individual consciousness and imposed discipline, I stand on the side of the individual. And I can truly prove this with my sources and documents. . . . What we have really declared, and will always declare in the future as well, is the principle that the aspiration for a Jewish state must—among all those who acknowledge this aspiration as their ideal—stand above all class inter-ests or individual interests. Garibaldi's opinion also was that the revival of the Italian monarchy was worth more than all the sacrifices, and so Lincoln saw the ideal of the united American republic. But this does not mean that Garibaldi or Lincoln had in mind such an Italy or such an America in which the citizen was a nonentity and the state everything.[39]

Accordingly, Jabotinsky believed that it was necessary to distinguish between the period of struggle on behalf of the nation and the homeland, and the character of the state that would be established. The earlier period was a breakthrough period, in which compromise of liberal principles was permitted in order to make possible the ultimate realization of those ideals, once the state was established. (This did not constitute a true compromise because the individual himself had to decide whether or not to sacrifice his life on behalf of the nation and the state.)

The passage quoted from "The Wagon of the *Klezmer*" also contains the key to Jabotinsky's teachings on the subject of nation and race. Just as liberal democracy did not provide a solution to socioeconomic problems (and thus had to compromise the liberal principle of a non-interventionist state in order to insure a minimum standard of living for all citizens), so too was liberal democracy unable to provide a solution to the problem of oppressed nations. In order for them to achieve a liberal-democratic govern-ment, they had to first attain national self-definition and national territory, or in the case of a minority, self-rule; during the struggle for national definition, it was permissible to temporarily sacrifice liberal principles.

Before discussing Jabotinsky's fully developed liberal-democratic thought, an introductory comment is in order. At the beginning of the chapter, I distinguished between the respective characteristics of democracy and liberalism. We find such a clear and systematic distinction among nineteenth-century liberal thinkers, who emphasized liberal elements. Nevertheless sometimes, when speaking about democracy, such thinkers incorporated liberal characteristics into their discussions. Such is the case with Jabotinsky, who sometimes distinguished between the two concepts and sometimes spoke of them synonymously.

Jabotinsky's major articles on liberalism and democracy were written between 1925 and 1935. He touched upon the subject prior to 1925, but did not present a comprehensive outlook.

In his article "The East" (1926), Jabotinsky took exception to the Zionist contention that the Jews had a spiritual affinity with the East. He redefined the East, emphasizing that its central characteristics were fundamentally psychological-cultural, not geographic. The sum total of the features of what was called the "East" was inferior to that of the West—"Easternness" was simply an inferior developmental stage:

> In truth, there are no "Eastern" features and no "Western" features having a fundamental or organic nature. "East" and "West" from the evolutionary point of view are empty words. It is very true: Harun al-Rashid, or Baghdad in modern terms, was more Western than Rome in its time. It is very true: when the influence of civilization penetrates an "Eastern" land, it loses those qualities that are considered "Eastern." It is true—and that is the whole issue: what we are accustomed to calling "Easternness" is nothing but a low stage, and to a great degree, a sloppy stage, of civilization. ... And since this is retarded immaturity—for we are all the sons of Adam—now in 1926, it is necessary to heal it, to heal it with culture. Then neither the harem nor the veil nor the patriarchal sheikh nor the fatalistic surrender to fate will remain—in short, not a single "Eastern" trait. And the sooner the better.[40]

In order to describe Eastern traits, Jabotinsky had to analyze them and distinguish them from Western ones; hence his preoccupation with Western culture in "The East." According to Jabotinsky, four primary characteristics accounted for the superiority of Western culture: first, the presence in the West of moral protest against inequitable distribution of material property; second (in the political sphere), the creation of parliaments, freedom of press, various forms of supervision over the government, and public initiative; third, separation of religion from state, and clear delimitation of religious authority to man's relationship with the Divine (religion had no place in legislation, philosophy, or science, and its role in family life was largely ceremonial); fourth, a constant struggle for progress and a striving toward an ideal future society, in contrast to the East, which viewed human development as a process of retrogression from a glorious golden age that had existed some time in the past.

Jabotinsky, however, qualified his remarks about Western traits, limiting them to "moral" Europe. His attitude towards immoral Europe was displayed in some of the previously cited articles. On balance, however—as reflected in "The East"—he considered Western civilization superior to that of the East in almost every respect.

Those traits that Jabotinsky listed as characteristics of a superior West were simply liberal democracy's political, social, and cultural creations. Its salient political features included parliamentary democracy (in which the populace was sovereign and chose its own representatives—a democratic element) and various systems of popular supervision of the government (including "checks and balances" as well as a freedom for the press which allowed for constant criticism—a liberal characteristic).

The distinctive social characteristics of the West were its constant striving for progress (based on the premise of man's ability as a rational being to improve society—a liberal perception), and its constant rebellion against socioeconomic wrong (a striving toward a more equitable distribution of resources—a democratic characteristic).

The West's primary cultural characteristics were expressed in its development of all areas in which rational man could further his knowledge and creativity. Thus there was created a vital need for freedom of thought in the physical, philosophical, literary, and other sciences/arts (yet another aspect of Western liberalism).

Two of these features can be seen as predominating over all others: the West's delimitation of religion to the relationship between man and God, and its perception of history as progress.

These two super-characteristics have been the life-breath of liberalism since the nineteenth century. To Jabotinsky's mind, the delimitation of religion insured every individual's freedom to make decisions about his faith, giving full expression to the value of religious tolerance. He believed that the representatives of religion should not be permitted to interfere in various spheres of life, holding that arrangements in all spheres of social life had to be the result of rational human action and not of religious coercion. The penetration of religion into areas such as legislation, philosophy, and science restricted rational conduct and subjugated it to irrational commands, and sometimes—even worse—to prejudices. Jabotinsky thus located the superiority of the West in its liberation of human potential from the fetters of irrationality. The antithesis of this Western approach to religion was evident, according to Jabotinsky, in the status of women in Eastern culture:

> More than anything, this is revealed in the status of the women. This is, apparently, the most serious and most tragic impediment to progress in the East. Polygamy, the harem, and the veil are not only a religion and a way of life: these two institutions exert an enormous influence over the entire public atmosphere. It is no small thing when a person grows up

with the awareness that his mother is not a person of value, but only an anthropoid ... in general—she is the private property of a man and was created in order to amuse him. ...[41]

Jabotinsky, with sadness, also brought an example from Judaism on this issue:

I also know another, sadder, fact: among our people, in the lives of the Jews who maintain old-fashioned practices, many wild customs of true "Easternness" have still been preserved—hatred of free investigation, the interference of religion in life, a bewigged woman to whom a strange man will not extend his hand. However, if we believed for one moment that these features belong to the organic essence of Judaism, we would certainly despair of the ideal of perpetuating such an essence. For this purpose we had an Enlightenment, so that we might separate the tradition and the ancient laws from the essence.[42]

The second super-characteristic—the perception of history as progress —was also a foremost characteristic of liberalism. As a young man, Jabotinsky learned from his liberal Italian teacher Labriola and from the Russian positivists that progress was the creation of the creative individual. There is no question that he was later influenced by nineteenth-century Western liberalism that held that everything might be corrected by human intelligence, so long as man was liberated from tyrannical rule and was supplied with the conditions necessary to develop his rational potential. According to Mill, no man knew absolute truth. Therefore man constantly had to strive to improve his understanding and knowledge, so that he might reach a higher truth, and thus progress. Accordingly, freedom of discussion had to exist, and different opinions needed to be heard; only then would it be possible to decide which opinion had more truth. According to Mill, the search for truth—the continual striving for progress—was the prime characteristic of a normal society. To the extent that they were not trammeled by prejudice and were open to new ideas, all people played a role in striving after truth. However, the central role in human progress was played by the extraordinary people—the geniuses.

In emphasizing the element of progress, Jabotinsky clearly associated himself with the school of classic liberalism. Like Mill, he saw the extraordinary individual—the genius—as the prime architect of history, and after the genius, people with talent. In his article "Women's Intelligence," Jabotinsky distinguished between the genius and the individual of talent: "Possibly one of the differences between the genius and the talented individual is that the latter expresses the opinions of his environment and of his time, while the genius thinks his thoughts in contrast to his time and his environment."[43]

Jabotinsky expressed this opinion in many articles: the political genius differed from the talented individual in that the genius was impelled to lead society to change by an internal fire burning within him—Jean Jacques Rousseau was such a person (as Jabotinsky dubbed him in "The Igniter"); Peter the Great was a political genius ("Women's Intelligence"); and Leo Tolstoy was a genius in the realm of literature ("The Individual"). However, the role of talented individuals was also important; Jabotinsky asserted that the intelligence of both geniuses and talented people was the primary cause of human progress: "For it is the intelligence of those individuals with which they were endowed at birth that rules the world and its economy, has always ruled, must rule, and will continue to rule."[44]

Jabotinsky's thought was characterized by the elitist overtones typical of nineteenth-century liberalism; while he considered every individual a king, he nevertheless knew how to appreciate the great importance of those whose intelligence was sharper and whose thought was more original, or who had an inner flame that succeeded in igniting an entire society and changing history. In the political sphere, just as he denigrated populist democracy, he also disdained mediocre politicians who considered themselves leaders.

In both his earlier articles and in "The East," Jabotinsky repeatedly emphasized the drawbacks and limitations of liberal democracy, together with its virtues. This was expressed in "The East" in Jabotinsky's distinction between moral and immoral Europe. In other words, the existence of a democratic regime with formal liberal characteristics (such as a constitution) was not sufficient to ensure the simultaneous eradication of negative phenomena such as prejudice, persecution of minorities, mediocre rule, and the like. Jabotinsky's criticism did not differ from that of Mill and de Tocqueville, who devoted no small part of their writings to the dangers posed to the liberal foundations of society inherent in the format of liberal-democratic governments. They feared the ignorance of the masses and social tyranny, which the liberal-democratic government was not adequate to fight; changes in the social fabric were also needed.

The Principle of Majority Rule

Some of Jabotinsky's criticisms of the democratic system were more controversial; often, for example, he refused to accept the literal definition of democracy as majority rule. He challenged on both technical and moral grounds the very principle that a decision of the majority could be imposed on an entire society; this position of his is unquestionably problematic.

In his book, *Of Civil Government*, John Locke defined, clearly and unequivocally, his attitude to the issue of decision by majority:

For, when any number of men have, by the consent of every individual, made a community, they have thereby made that community one body, with a power to act as one body, which is only by the will and determination of the majority. For that which acts any community, being only the consent of the individuals of it, and it being one body, must move one way, it is necessary the body should move that way whither the greater force carries it, which is the consent of the majority, or else it is impossible it should act or continue one body, one community, which the consent of every individual that united into it agreed that it should; and so every one is bound by that consent to be included by the majority. And therefore we see that in assemblies empowered to act by positive laws, where no number is set by that positive law which empowers them, the act of the majority passes for the act of the whole, and of course determines as having, by the law of Nature and reason, the power of the whole. ... For if the consent of the majority shall not in reason be received as the act of the whole. ... Such a constitution as this would make the mighty leviathan of a shorter duration than the feeblest creatures, and not let it outlast the day it was born in .... For where the majority cannot conclude the rest, there they cannot act as one body, and consequently will be immediately dissolved again.[45]

In this famous passage, Locke explained why political society, based on the Social Contract, could operate only on the system of majority decision. However, Locke did not consider the principle of majority decision (whereby every individual, even when in the minority, had to comply with the majority) to be essential, only because the alternative—universal consent—was unrealistic. Rather, he regarded majority decision as a ruling practice best suited to logic and to the moral premises fundamental to a government based on the Social Contract. The first and most important act—the establishment of a political society—necessitated the concurrence of all. After that, the principle of majority decision had its moral foundation in the logical and conscientious concurrence of the majority of a society (or the majority of its representatives).

The principle of majority decision is undeniably a complex issue, particularly in cases where the decision of the majority differs sharply from the opinion and will of the minority.

American Federalists, who were very influential in the drafting of that country's constitution, discussed this complexity in the eighteenth century, as did Mill and de Tocqueville in the nineteenth. It was natural that liberal thinkers were disturbed by the issue of majority decision, since their fundamental premise was that the rights of the individual and the rights of the minorities needed to be protected. The central danger that Mill and de Tocqueville saw in democracy was what they termed "the tyranny of the majority"; that is, that the majority would exploit its numerical superiority to oppress the individual or the minority.

As expressed by Mill: "The will of the people, moreover, practically means the will of the most numerous or the most active *part* of the people; the majority, or those who succeed in making themselves accepted as the majority; the people, consequently *may* desire to oppress a part of their number; and precautions are as much needed against this as against any other abuse of power ... and in political speculations 'the tyranny of the majority' is now generally included among the evils against which society requires to be on its guard."[46]

Mill developed this idea in his book *Representative Government*, in an entire chapter titled "Of True and False Democracy; Representation of All, and Representation of the Majority Only."[47]

The Federalists were very concerned about the possibility of a tyranny of the majority. Their main solution was a system of checks and balances between the branches of government. They primarily feared the legislative branch, since it operated according to the principle of majority decision, and therefore they divided it into the House of Representatives (in which representation was determined according to the population of each state) and the Senate (in which all states had equal representation, irrespective of the size of their population), each serving as a check on the other. The federal system, in which governments in each state existed side by side with the central government, created another set of checks and balances. This entire legislative system came to prevent, as much as possible, the domination of the minority by the majority. Still, the Federalists' solution was based for the most part on a mere reworking of the principle of majority decision.

Mill and de Tocqueville tried to find solutions to the problem of mob rule within the democratic framework. Mill, who accepted the principle of majority decision, proposed changing the system of regional elections in Great Britain to a proportional system (as in Israel) so that the opinions of the majority would be reflected in the legislature; giving the intellectuals and the economically established a double vote so that the majority vote would not reflect the opinions of the mediocre and the ignorant; and raising the educational level of the masses and integrating them in various ways in civic activities. In addition, Mill presented his famous doctrine with regard to setting limits upon intervention by state, society, and the individual in the private sphere: "That principle is, that the sole end for which mankind are warranted, individually or collectively, in interfering with the liberty of action of any of their number, is self-protection. That the only purpose for which power can be rightfully exercised over any member of a civilised community against his will, is to prevent harm to others."[48]

De Tocqueville, who likewise accepted the principle of majority decision, proposed the strengthening of various voluntary organizations, and the encouragement of involvement by the citizens in various areas of government activity. This would limit the scope of the central government so that even if the majority decision was sometimes poor, there would be many other foci of power in society to neutralize it; it would also enhance the public's understanding of the workings of government, and thus its ability to criticize that government intelligently and effectively.

Jabotinsky went even further than the Federalists, Mill, and de Tocqueville, claiming that the very principle of majority decision—or, in his words, majority rule—was immoral and was not an integral part of the democratic idea:

> However, an important condition must first be laid down. For some inexplicable reason, democracy is identified with majority rule. This is understandable from a historical point of view—democracies were created under the banner of the struggle against different types of minority governments. This was the counter-swing of the pendulum. However, the blind identification of democracy with majority rule is not correct. The value of democracy does not depend on the feeling of subordination by forty-nine kings with equal rights to one hundred, or even of ten kings or one to one hundred. The sense of democracy must rather be sought in the theory of consent and compromise.[49]

Democracies could not allow the majority to impose its opinion on the minority; every decision had to reflect compromise and consent by all involved. Jabotinsky's opinion was due in large measure to his basic belief that "every individual is a king." For if each individual was a king, no one had the right to impose his will on another. This approach to individualism was the basis of anarchist theory and, as we shall see, one particular type of anarchy was close to Jabotinsky's heart: a vision of the End of Days with which he liked to amuse himself.

As a realist however, Jabotinsky understood that an anarchist utopia was not practicable, so as a compromise he accepted liberal democracy as the best possible solution. His attitude to majority rule, however, remained problematic. On the one hand, he stood by his opinion that the principle of majority rule was not democratic; on the other, as we shall see in his Zionist writings, he was aware of the fact that, in a democratic society, decisions were made by the majority.

His struggle with this dilemma (which remained to a large degree unresolved in his thought) was reflected in a number of articles, including his series on South Africa, "Strikes in the Land of Israel"; a series of articles, "The Truth about the Island Tristan da Runha"; and the article "Majority."

In the series regarding South Africa, Jabotinsky discussed the historical chain of events that had led to the serious dilemma for a white minority facing a tremendous black majority. Jabotinsky determined that, due to a confused and directionless policy, the existing situation was a time bomb: on the one hand, the white government's policy of apartheid forbade blacks from working together with whites anywhere, and prohibited blacks from participating in any government institution. On the other hand, blacks in South Africa had undergone a sociocultural change that severed their exclusive identity with their tribe, thus making possible their unification and revolt against the existing order. Black society was transformed under the influences of public schooling and the presence of the British, as well as that of Gandhi and the Indian movement that he inspired, leading eventually to the establishment of a black vocational organization and, finally, to a liberation movement on a national scale. The African National Congress was founded. The black national movement demanded equal rights, but its real, subconscious demand, said Jabotinsky, was to rule South Africa. The movement included people educated in England who were capable of leadership and could demand the reins of power by virtue of their being in the vast majority.

The whites were not only a small minority, but due to the lack of immigration—actually to the prohibition of immigration—were doomed to become an increasingly smaller subjection of South African society. Nevertheless, they felt that rule should by right stay in their hands because it was they who had developed and built South Africa.

As we saw in the section on morality and truth, the above situation described by Jabotinsky was typical of many historical phenomena: there were two sides to every coin, each of which was convinced of its own merit. Our concern here, however, is to examine Jabotinsky's attitude to the issue of the black right to rule by virtue of their being the majority:

> The hand of fate threatens the beautiful country; and it would be frivolous if one were to approach it with the naive criterion of superficial liberalism and ask: "What is the tragedy here? Let the blacks rule the land once they become stronger culturally—for it is their right!" It is not so simple. The very word "right" is not such a simple word. All that beauty, all that wealth in this land, is all the product of the genius of the white race—the cities and the farms, the railroads and the ports and the schools, and even the very germ of ferment in the mind of the black man. For whom and for what purpose did the white man build all this? So that in another hundred years his descendants here would be a "national minority" under the rule of dark-skinned ministers? Is it a right that the national heritage pass from people to people by the identifying mark of quantity, and not according to the identification of creative ability and organizational ability? Thus asks the "European," the South African, when he ponders the future. You will not know what to answer him. This is the worst scourge in the world: in practically no place and at no time has there been one, and only one truth; perhaps litigants each have their own truth, but for an impartial judge there are always two, both tragic.[50]

Jabotinsky could not give an unequivocal answer to the question of who had the right of ruling South Africa. However, it is clear from the above passage that he hesitated to respond that the right to rule always and in any instance belonged to the majority. In other words, he accepted the fact that in a situation such as the one that existed in South Africa, there was room to claim the white minority's right to rule on the basis of the prosperity it had brought to the country. This contradicted the cynical and bitter view he had expressed twenty years earlier in "Might and Right," where he protested against the fact that every conquerer justified his conquest on the grounds of the positive results and economic prosperity it brought. In other words, he perceived as totally legitimate the South Africans' justification of continued rule on the basis of prosperity—a position that twenty years earlier he had described as immoral. There is no question that Jabotinsky became entangled in this contradiction as a result of his attitude to the issue of the majority. If the principle of majority decision in a democratic regime had been acceptable to him, he would also have accepted the principle of majority decision regarding who should rule. And in the above instance, it is clear that the moment everyone had the right to vote—which is a basic democratic principle—the black majority would vote in favor of black rule in South Africa.

In his article "Strikes in the Lands of Israel" (1934), wherein he dealt with the issue of labor strikes and the institution of arbitration, Jabotinsky reinforced his contention that the principle of majority decision was not sacred: "In a situation where a factory owner rejects this demand, one must conclude that he is wrong, and that justice is with the workers, and is permissible to start a strike. However, when the workers refuse to submit the dispute to arbitration, the minority has the sacred right to decide on its own whether the strike that is about to break out is justified or not. When the strike is not justified, the minority has the right to continue peacefully at its work and to fill the places of the strikers."[51]

Jabotinsky's message was clear: majority decision on a matter of principle—for example, the decision of whether or not to call a strike—was not binding upon the minority. On the contrary, the minority had "a sacred right" to decide for itself whether or not the strike was justified.

Such an approach undoubtedly has numerous and dangerous implications regarding the very existence of democracy. Why should the minority have the sacred right to an opinion which brings in its wake independent action contrary to the will of the majority? Why should the minority not act similarly on issues such as the waging of war, or the withdrawal from territories? If the principle of the majority was not binding upon the minority—if the minority was entitled to arrive at independent conclusions and take action on its own—the very foundations of democracy would be undermined. The rule of law would lose all meaning. For example, a law on a matter of principle, which the minority opposed, is passed by the majority in the legislature: according to Jabotinsky's approach, as expressed on the issue of strikes, the majority would abide by the law, while the minority would not.

How is it possible to reconcile such an approach, which would obviously lead to chaos, with Jabotinsky's liberal and democratic views? It most emphatically is not. And, indeed, Jabotinsky was conscious of that. Even in the article on strikes, he proposed that, in order to avoid such situations where the minority acted against the majority decision, the majority and the minority reach an agreement and act accordingly. Similarly, in his article "Introduction to the Theory of Economics II," Jabotinsky wrote that the reason for democracy had to be sought in the theory of consent and compromise.

However, it seems that Jabotinsky was also aware that reaching an agreement between the majority and the minority was a most difficult, and sometimes impossible, task. Therefore, Jabotinsky simultaneously developed a more realistic attitude to the principle of the majority, while still adhering to his concept that majority decision was not an integral part of the democratic idea on the grounds that it was not moral, since no person—not even the majority—might impose its beliefs on someone else because "every individual is a king."

This position was clearly expressed in his Zionist writings dealing with the central goal of Zionism: the attainment of a Jewish majority in the Land of Israel. It was clear to Jabotinsky that only if the Jews were a majority, not only would they not assimilate among the Arabs, not only would they be stronger—they would achieve the moral right to demand sovereignty over the Land of Israel. Once the state of the Jews arose, the very fact of their being a majority would determine their quality of life and the laws that ruled their state. In other words, the Arab minority often would have to accept the decisions of the Jewish majority.

However, Jabotinsky often expressed the belief that the principle of majority decision was necessary, not only as a technicality without which democracy would be unable to function, but also as something positive and healthy in and of itself—in contrast to his position that the principle of majority decision had the potential to be immoral. A passage reflecting this view may be found in his series of essays on "The Truth About the Island of Tristan da Runha": "And if occasional disturbances occur, they will be met with an antidote—the healthy sense and the healthy fists of the majority, which will not need any outside guidance."[52] Jabotinsky here acknowledges that the principle of majority decision, based on the senses—on the instinctive perception of the greater number of people—is the more correct.

There existed an ambivalence on the issue of the majority in Jabotinsky's thought. Nineteenth-century liberals also feared the principle of majority decision; unlike Jabotinsky, however, they accepted it, while trying to find within its framework solutions to prevent the negative side effects likely to occur as a result of decisions made by an uneducated majority—not the least of which being the oppression of minorities and individuals.

It is reasonable to assume that the source of this ambivalence in Jabotinsky's approach to the principle of majority rule lay in the tension between his fundamental, individualistic, practically anarchistic belief that every individual was a king, that no person had the right to impose his will on anyone else—a belief that smacked of utopianism—and his realistic view that liberal democracy was essential to the peaceful continuation of human society.

A concrete expression of this conflict between Jabotinsky's utopianism and his realism is to be found in "The Truth About the Island of Tristan da Runha." This series of articles described the imaginary events on the island Tristan da Runha, a colony to which were sent people who were criminals from birth and, though incapable of living in normal society, were able to live in their own society. Since society on the island was created artificially, the island could serve as a laboratory for research into the way man's social, economic, and cultural life came into being.

The island had three features for which it was chosen: first, it was cut off from any contact with the outside world; second, before the criminals came, it was unpopulated; third, the absence of metals and coal would prevent technological development that might enable the settlers to make contact with the outside world at some future point. The first group to arrive slowly learned to cultivate the ground and to raise domestic animals. Later arrivals included people with different occupations (who were therefore warmly welcomed by the old-timers). At first, each person worried about supplying his own various needs: "the settlers gradually began to accumulate 'property,' the methods of work became more complex, and the need for a certain degree of division of labor was felt. . . . All this led to social fragmentation: on one side the simple masses began to form, while on the other were the exceptional individuals, the organizers or supervisors."[53]

This development led to the fact that people without specialties in any field were forced to create jobs for themselves:

[They] began to discuss the need for a stable organization and for a suitable bureaucracy with a specific hierarchy of ranks. If we were to use political terminology, these are the constitutionalists of the island. They wanted in essence to turn the island into a municipal, or even state, unit. . . . It would not be difficult to implant in the minds of the settlers the idea that now they are a community, a community requires order, and in order to maintain order a governmental bureaucracy must be created. ... [They] were few, not more than twelve people, but they were all united, and they of course surpassed the entire mass in education and speaking ability. They acquired many supporters, some by the promise of a secret "position," but mainly—simply by the persuasiveness of their arguments.[54]

Jabotinsky depicted this attempt by the constitutionalists as negative, while describing the leader of the opposition, Charles Lendree, in a positive fashion. Lendree succeeded in convincing the settlers that the proposed reform was not necessary, and would lead to class differences and the accumulation of power in the hands of a few:

He championed another theory. He certainly derived it from the anarchist or syndicalist pamphlets which had been in fashion during his youth; nevertheless, it reflected the true mood of most of the settlers. ... Lendree first proclaimed the principle which now is the credo of each one of them: each colony of exiles on the island of Tristan da Runha is a world better and more sublime than what remained on the other side of the ocean. Organization and a hierarchy of officialdom are only artificial remedies, that are required only by a sick or dying society, while here there is a healthy community, full of vitality. Order is necessary but it naturally takes shape on its own because that is the normal state of affairs, and the best secret to ensure it forever is not to spoil it by artificial institutions.[55]

Lendree was victorious, and the government of the colony bore his mark: "There is nothing on my island resembling general or local government. ... Their economic regime is essentially individualistic. ... The aim of the division of labor, which had evolved then, has completely vanished."[56]

Jabotinsky's sympathy for a social structure without rulers or those ruled was implicit in his words. However, lest we live in a world of dreams and attempt to establish such a society in our own countries, he said: "I would be very happy, were I able to declare, "The island of Tristan da Runha is utopia incarnate. But it is not a land of utopia at all.""[57]

In listing the drawbacks of the island, Jabotinsky emphasized the difficult life and the simple customs. However, on the other hand, in describing the positive aspects of such a society, he emphasized that the most important thing was: "that from the aspect of spiritual achievements this colony will go far, and will ascend to lofty heights at some time—despite the backwardness of their economic system, from which there is no escape and which cannot be corrected [due to the absence of copper and coal]."[58]

Jabotinsky found beauty in a certain type of anarchistic society that was isolated from the world, not only because it was built entirely on his individualistic idea, but also because its spiritual creations, being absolutely independent of the historical and cultural past of the world and of material enticements, would be absolutely pure.

It is clear that Jabotinsky was amusing himself in these articles, toying with ideas that he knew could not be realized. Thus, he spoke about colonies of criminals and about obviously unrealistic conditions (perpetual isolation from the rest of the world, the absence of metal and coal). However, one may learn from them about Jabotinsky's latent desires—that his belief that "every individual is a king," with its anarchistic conclusions, was a central component of both his utopian philosophizing and his personal emotions. The mark of anarchistic theory on him never completely disappeared, even after his youthful flirtation with anarchism had passed.

The Concept of the Leader

Jabotinsky's thought has been repeatedly criticized for its conception of the role of the leader, which, some claimed, smacked of fascism. Accordingly, we shall examine Jabotinsky's views on leadership to see whether they indeed contradict his liberal and democratic thought.

As we have already seen, in his entire life Jabotinsky espoused the principles that every individual is a king and that in the beginning God created the individual; ideally, there would be no leaders and no led. However, in real life there existed forms of authoritarian government (the opposite of democracy) based on the rule of a leader. One of those systems, said Jabotinsky, was fascism, the outstanding example of which was the regime of Mussolini (whose Italian appellation *"Il Duce"* was taken from the Latin word *dux* and was created specifically for Mussolini). Jabotinsky did not believe in the success of fascism specifically because it constantly over-emphasized the function and status of the leader.

Jabotinsky sharply criticized fascism several times, as he did commun-ism, in which the absolute ruler was the proletariat or its representatives. Let us repeat here a passage already cited: "I, too, have a blind hatred for the idea that 'the state is everything.' And it makes no difference whether it is communist or fascist. I believe only in 'old-fashioned' parliamentarianism, as inconvenient or powerless as it may seem at times. I believe in freedom of speech and organization, and in almost every conflict between individual consciousness and imposed discipline, I stand on the side of the individual. And I can truly prove this with my sources and documents."[59]

One might argue that, since Jabotinsky admired Garibaldi and Herzl (whom he considered leaders having the strength to lead peoples) his liberal-democratic thought was faulty.

Jabotinsky, however, distinguished between leadership that functioned with absolute authority (as in fascism and communism), which he totally rejected, and that which functioned within the framework of liberal democracy. He divided this second type into two categories; the first was a leader who was: "simple flesh and blood that was given a title. If he is a fool he accepts it, becomes inflated, and makes efforts to play the role; and thank God, fools are not hard to find among us. . . . Our children will be astonished when once the true biography in all countries, is read. They will be astonished when they discover that many of them all too often were actually nothing more than soft cotton rags in the hands of their circumstantial surroundings. What is particularly hard to understand is the mentality of those who long for 'leaders.' "[60]

Such "leaders" (the quotation marks are Jabotinsky's) had no natural leadership qualities. Their leadership was artificial and the result of a role that was granted to them. They did not lead in accordance with their ideas, but were influenced by those who voted for or appointed them; such people hardly merited the title "leader." Instead of the representatives of the people ruling under the supervision of the people, leaders such as these ruled under the influence of chance associates, or in Jabotinsky's words, "instead of the influence of the ballot and its results, comes the influence of chance associates."[61]

In contrast to these stood the leader with neither title nor formal role who did not impose his views on the liberal-democratic system, and often did not even belong to any party. Jabotinsky considered such a leader highly charismatic—in his words, a "conquerer of thought."

Of Herzl, whom he considered such a leader, Jabotinsky said: "True 'leaders' are born infrequently, and at times they are recognized by this specific sign that they do not come with any demand to 'lead.' Submission to them is not a question of discipline. People heed them just as they are carried away by the singing of a gifted singer—because his 'melody' expresses our own longings."[62]

Actually, Jabotinsky was speaking here about a type of genius—not in the field of science, but in the sociopolitical realm. In contradistinction to a fascist, for example, such a leader did not supplant the democratic-liberal system, which continued to exist. The natural democratic leader had a very defined role: to bring about a breakthrough and far-reaching changes, something difficult for bureaucratic representatives in a liberal-democratic government to do. Such a leader might belong to one of the parties; however, by the nature of things, his opinions and ideas spoke to the heart of the entire people. Such a leader was needed primarily at times when crucial decisions had to be made. And it is important to remember that such a leader did not want power, but rather desired to exert influence in particular fields, and was able to do so within the framework of liberal democracy.

Such a leader did not necessarily have a defined role, such as prime minister or president. On the island of Tristan da Runha, for instance, Lendree was a leader in the sense of a "conquerer of thoughts," without having any political role whatsoever—he spoke to the heart of the decision-making majority. He believed in preserving an anarchistic society without political rule; he also had no desire for power for himself, and only wanted to convince the population that anarchism was best for them. In other words, such a leader could function in a society with no government whatsoever.

Jabotinsky rejected dull, bureaucratic leaders because he considered them dangerous to the liberal-democratic system. Likewise, he considered the masses' longing for such a leader to be dangerous because, in the absence of a true charismatic leader, they granted mediocre people the prestige and the authority of "true" leaders; false leaders acted according to the interests and wishes of their immediate circles. Let us quote Jabotinsky's exact words on this matter:

> What is especially difficult to understand is the mentality of those who yearn for "leaders." The situation was completely different and better in my youth. We believed that every movement was made up of people of equal worth. Each one was a prince, each one was a king. When election time came, they chose, not people, but programs. Those who were chosen were nothing but the executors of the program. We, the masses, would follow them and listen to them, not because they were "leaders," but specifically because they were our "servants"; when you, of your own free will, chose a group of people and ordered to them to work for you, you had to help them—or remove them. Because you were obeying not their will, but only your own will, which was expressed in the election. . . . This philosophy of my youth was perhaps a complete fiction (like all human philosophies), but I much prefer it; it had more genius and more noblesse, even though it bore the name, whose prestige has declined—democracy.[63]

In this passage, Jabotinsky clearly perceives authority as a trust vested by the people in its representatives, and sees the act of voting as the making of a choice between ideological alternatives, rather than personalities. From its inception, fascism fiercely fought this concept.

By 1934 (the year that his article "The Leader" was published), Jabotinsky was already well aware of the shortcomings of democracy—which in many ways was to him a disappointing dream. He steadfastly maintained that democracy was nonetheless the best form of government. The better he came to know democracy (and its totalitarian alternatives, fascism and Bolshevism), the readier he was to reconcile himself to its drawbacks; twenty-five years earlier, Jabotinsky knew less about the weaknesses of democracy, yet was much more critical of it. It is reasonable to assume that his appreciation for democracy—despite its limitations—grew as he learned more about fascist and communist regimes.

Another point which becomes clear from Jabotinsky's idea of democracy is the significance of the concepts of *gaon* (genius) and *hadar* (noblesse) that appeared regularly in his writings, and particularly in his Zionist works. These characteristics were not associated with only a few exceptional individuals but, on the contrary, were the heritage of every person. *Gaon* and *hadar*, as we shall see in our discussion of his Zionist thought, were both internal and external qualities; the shell and the content constituted a whole. Aesthetics and ethics in Jabotinsky's view were interrelated.

In a passage from "The Story of My Life," Jabotinsky wrote about the view or "madness" that developed in him from his early youth and never left him: "I hate with a quintessential hatred, organically, a hatred transcending all reason, all logic, and being itself, any idea which hints of a difference in value between one man and another."[64] In order to guard the worth of each individual, Jabotinsky avoided addressing people in the first person. He constructed his liberal-democratic thought on the belief that every individual is a king, and thus may not be lorded over by another; the only possible government is one chosen by the individuals to carry out their will. Just as they choose it, they might oust it if it betrays their trust.

However, Jabotinsky's elitist outlook, also derived from the above belief, when accompanied by his firm belief that each person must be regarded as unique, leads to elitist conclusions: above and beyond the equality of all people qua people, each of whom is a king, there are those whose value exceeds that of others; there are kings and there are kings; there is a charismatic leader and there are counterfeit "leaders."

As we have already seen, there were strong elitist and anti-populist strains in Jabotinsky's theories regarding democracy, just as there were among the nineteenth-century liberals, whether Westerners like Mill and de Tocqueville, Russian positivists such as de Roberty, or Russian anti-Slavophiles like Bielinski.

Unlike Mill, however, Jabotinsky never translated his elitist view into a practical political proposal to give a double vote to the well-educated. Rather, Jabotinsky's elitism found expression, as we shall see, in other areas of life, primarily economic and cultural.

Discipline and Ceremony

Many people considered the great importance that Jabotinsky attributed to discipline and ceremony to be a blot on his liberal-democratic thought. The issue of discipline and ceremony occupied an important place in his Zionist thought, and was intimately connected to his concepts of *hadar*, *gaon*, and national education. However, Jabotinsky also dealt with this issue in his general thought, within the context of his discussion on militarism in two

major articles: "On Militarism" and "Turkey and the War." Jabotinsky held
that militarism was a despicable concept, and that war was evil, except when
essential for self-defense. Needless to say, his approach was fundamentally
different from fascism's attitude to war. Thus, according to Jabotinsky, it
was a crude error to build a huge army and to invest all resources in it; it was,
however, imperative to build a military capable of ensuring survival, whether
by defensive or offensive methods. Nonetheless, Jabotinsky added, that did
not mean that positive things could not be learned from military life:

> If this were the case, all of mankind, at least the liberal part, would hate
> everything reminiscent of military life. However, amazingly, even the
> most deeply committed pacifists and the most extreme leftists use clearly
> militaristic figures of speech at every step of the way. ... The "Salvation
> Army" which greatly benefits unfortunate men and women who are
> alienated from society calls itself an "army" and has "lieutenants,"
> "majors," and marches in formation on the street like a brigade of
> soldiers. ... Concepts from the lexicon of the slaughterhouse or the
> house of ill repute are not used in daily life ... but every ideological
> movement in the world draws at least half its technical terminology and
> three-quarters of its propaganda rhetoric specifically from military life.
> Apparently, it is not all that bad.[65]

The best aspect of military life, Jabotinsky felt, was its discipline:
"There is nothing in the world that will make as great an impression on us as
the ability of the masses, at particular times, to feel and also to act as one
unit, with one will, acting in a uniform tempo. Because that is the entire
difference between a 'mob' and a 'rabble' and a nation."[66]

Jabotinsky himself undoubtedly admired two aspects of military discipline: order and ceremony (which meant, in his opinion, explicit instructions
on how to stand, how to speak to superiors or subordinates, and the like).
This was clearly expressed in his book *Samson*, in which he admiringly
described the discipline among the Philistines:

> More than anything else Samson admired their organization. It is true
> that he never grasped the system on which their state was constructed:
> the precise, well-planned, intricate hierarchy, the delimitation of func-
> tions, the strict rules for every department of the administration—all
> these things were incomprehensible to him and seemed to be confused.
> But he saw clearly that out of them arose not confusion but a great
> harmony. ... One day, he was present at a festival at the temple of Gaza
> [where a festive dance was being performed] .... The whole dance
> consisted of similar movements, dictated by the baton of the priest. ...
> Samson left the place profoundly thoughtful. He could not have given
> words to his thought, but he had a feeling that here, in this spectacle of
> thousands of people obeying a single will, he had caught a glimpse of the
> great secret of the builders of nations.[67]

The passages in which Jabotinsky spoke with admiration of discipline, order, and ceremony have been cited more than once to show the great influence that early-twentieth-century integral nationalism—and thus also fascism—had on his thought. Likewise, Jabotinsky's admiration of popular unity was interpreted as an expression of his belief in the superiority of the state over the individual. Indeed, his esteem for discipline was sometimes exaggerated. Certainly, his admiration for the parade, with its marchers who strode "like a machine," is disturbing, and reminiscent of the fascist enthusiasm for parades and marching in formation. However, Jabotinsky himself was cognizant of this fact, and tried to reconcile his admiration for military discipline with his liberal outlook by saying that he was not speaking of discipline in organizations in which membership was compulsory, but rather about the discipline of soldiers who freely volunteered to serve. Thus, discipline was not imposed on them, but was instead an expression of self-discipline: "The nature of coercion whereby a person is compelled to be part of a machine, whether he wants to or not, is the same as when he is intimidated by threats of beatings or of protracted imprisonment. But the situation is completely different if the motivating factor is a particular mood, whereby a person, under no compulsion, forces himself to learn how to stand, to walk and to act, as a part of a planned mechanism. This is the ancient difference between coercion and between self-discipline: the former can be effected even with beasts of prey, while the latter succeeds only in a completely civilized atmosphere."[68]

This statement of Jabotinsky's was an attempt to construct a bridge between his democratic liberalism and his respect for discipline, a respect rarely shared by other liberal-democratic thinkers. His explanation, in short, was that man may remain free and preserve his individuality even when marching with others in perfect formation like a machine—but only if he himself had decided to be part of that formation. Whereas the orderly march of those consenting looked identical to that of those compelled, Jabotinsky maintained that the two cases were not similar; in the first instance the behavior was the result of comprehension and personal decision, while in the second it was the result of coercion, where the individual's right to control his own life was not respected.

Jabotinsky's admiration of discipline and ceremony was connected as well with his belief that form and content were identical. Walking in formation in perfect form, erect stature, and proper manners not only demonstrated to others the presence of self-respect, but also helped to strengthen that self-respect. This was particularly true of the Jewish people; and indeed, the majority of passages in Jabotinsky's work praising discipline were connected with the education of a new type of Jewish youth (as is explicit in all the essays on *Betar* and in the article "The Rigan Hasmonean," and implicit in *Samson*). However, Jabotinsky was not speaking of militaristic youth *per se*, as in mature fascism, but rather of a new type of youth who would be the antithesis of the *galuth* (exilic) Jew, youth that would be able to fulfill the minimum function of defending the implementation of the Zionist goal. Jabotinsky considered most of *galuth* Jewry to be lacking both a sense of self-respect, and a dignified external appearance, phenomena which he felt were interrelated. Strengthening one would also strengthen the other, and thus educating for discipline and teaching the ceremonial rules would strengthen the sense of self-respect.

Despite all this, there is no doubt that Jabotinsky's admiration for discipline and ceremony was exaggerated, and thus constituted a discordant strain in the complex of his liberal-democratic philosophy.

The Status of Women

During Jabotinsky's time, feminists were organizing in Russia and Germany, demanding equal rights. In England, the suffragettes were working simultaneously toward the same goal. The issue of women's rights, primarily in the political arena dominated the agenda. Jabotinsky's attitude toward the issue, which had evolved from his youth, was unequivocal; in "The Story of My Life," he stated: "I possess a trait of the northern peoples that I respect: admiration of women. I am certain that every mediocre women is an angel, without exception. If she has not revealed herself—she has not had to reveal herself, but the time will come and you shall see."[69]

Undoubtedly, Jabotinsky's personal life greatly influenced his views on this issue.[70] According to him, his mother, his sister, and his wife were strong women—"angels." But the force of his personal experience was not enough to shape his views on the roles of women in all areas of life, and there is no question that they were also deeply affected by his general liberal-democratic outlook.

In "Apropos," a 1912 article on feminism and suffrage, Jabotinsky compared the political methodology of the Russian feminists—characterized by cordiality and persuasion—with those of the suffragettes in England, whose struggle was more aggressive. He felt greater sympathy for the feminist cause, while that of the suffragettes seemed to him "masculine," undermining their femininity. His opinion, however, was different on the question of which of these movements would first achieve equal rights. As stated in his articles from around 1910—"*Homo Homini Lupus*," "I Do Not Believe," and "Might and Right," for example—here too Jabotinsky did not believe in the effectiveness of a polite struggle. In reality, the only effective method was the exertion of genuine pressure and a struggle that demonstrated strength. The English suffragettes would get their equal rights before the Russian and German feminists, said Jabotinsky, explaining: "Why? Specifically because these are courteous and polite, and the others act wildly; specifically because the former are favorably regarded both by the police and by the authorities, because they know that they are quiet and patient, that they will wait with forbearance and without scandals—while the others cause double trouble for the ministers and for the police. This world is so made, that well-mannered people are praised, the quiet are well-liked, the courteous are respected. However, only the discourteous are taken into account; concessions are made only to the rebellious. ... More strength to these [English] women; their work is already done. They know what they are doing. Because the power of reason itself will not help their cause."[71]

Already at this early stage, Jabotinsky actively supported, through his writings, women's struggle for equality. However, he was not satisfied with that; formal political equality alone was not enough. Women's abilities in all areas of life—particularly the political—had to be acknowledged in practice. Jabotinsky devoted the article "Women's Intelligence" (published post-humously) to this matter. At the beginning of the article he stated: "When a man appears in the role of an extreme feminist ... it always seems absurd. I do not know the reason for this, but it is a fact. Therefore, we, the men, attempt in such situations to speak or to write in such a tone that lightens or qualifies our words, so that afterwards it will be possible to deny it and say: 'we are not speaking seriously about this matter.'"[72]

It is difficult not to think of how little things have changed since these lines were written. He defined the issue as follows: "The debate over the right of women to attain political rights may be seen as finished. However, the debate still exists over whether they have the skill for such activity, whether they are capable of using these rights the way a man uses them. ... Here what are needed are not rational proofs, but empirical facts. And these facts are few. Equal political rights for women is something new that has just recently come about."[73]

Despite this, Jabotinsky argued, the brief experience that accumulated did not redound to women's credit since they had made only a half-hearted attempt to run for Parliament, and since those who were elected were not, in Jabotinsky's estimation, particularly outstanding. Therefore, Jabotinsky used historical examples and comparisons between the records of various kings and queens reach three basic conclusions. First, that women knew how to rule, as proved by Catherine the Great in Russia, and Queens Elizabeth and Victoria in England. Second, that women's political skills were expressed primarily in the organizational realm. Third, that "in order to be a great king, a man must be a genius; a great queen, however, may also be an ordinary woman."[74] The third conclusion was a direct result of the second. Jabotinsky believed that since women excelled in the organizational role, which did not demand genius (in contrast to the function that he called "a charge"—an introduction of drastic changes to various areas of life), and since all women possessed organizational potential (he repeatedly stated that women had greater self-discipline than men), every woman could succeed in governing in an organizational capacity.

This article was obviously not scientific, as Jabotinsky himself stated in the beginning. What is important to us is that Jabotinsky did not interpret political equality for women as merely something passive, but hoped, rather, to see many women in decision-making positions. His famous slogan— "every individual is a king"—referred to women equally as to men.

Neither was a woman's ability in other spheres of life, such as the economic, inferior to those of a man. He hoped that the formal civic equality granted to women would be translated into real involvement in all areas of life.

One may take his attitude toward women writers as an example. In his article "Women's Books" (1931), he discussed a long list of English, Italian, South African, Swedish, and American writers whom he considered first-rate. They were graced with a quality that Jabotinsky respected in writers— the ability to see life as it was and to describe it without delving too much into the depths of man's soul. He particularly noted several Jewish authors who he felt successfully described Jewish concepts as well as Jewish life and the Jewish *Weltangschauung* in their books: May Sinclair, Edna Ferber, and Fanny Hearst, to name three.

Jabotinsky's general views regarding women, their abilities, and the status they merited, was similar to those of John Stuart Mill, years earlier. The sensitive subject of women's rights was an important test of the strength of a thinker's liberalism, in Jabotinsky's time as now. It was a test Jabotinsky passed with flying colors.

The Mature Liberal-Democratic Outlook

"Revolt of the Old Men," written three years before Jabotinsky's death in 1940, summarized his liberal-democratic thinking and proved beyond a shadow of a doubt that his views were antithetical to the mature fascism of the 1930's. In this article, Jabotinsky advocated a rebellion against the period of time starting in the first third of the twentieth century. It was, in his opinion, necessary to rebel against what had been created in this period, and those suited to revolt were the "old men": "those were people whose souls were fashioned (first) yet in the nineteenth century, and to whom this anachronism (second) is dear."[75] Jabotinsky encouraged "old men" to rebel against all forms of totalitarianism and authoritarianism in the name of liberal democracy. The article was aimed at showing that there was a reason to rebel, and that old men, Jabotinsky's contemporaries, should be the ones to lead the charge.

Jabotinsky began with a sketch of the nineteenth century, the spirit of which ended, according to Jabotinsky, around 1905. The century was characterized primarily by the fact that all its great personalities had faith in the individual, and thus worked for the liberation and glorification of the individual. It was a century that believed that if man were liberated from the bonds of tyrannical rule, as well as from the fetters of poverty, his intelligence would build a new world. From its inception in the late 1900s, fascism attacked everything that this century symbolized.

Jabotinsky preferred a different definition of the common thread running through the entire nineteenth century. He had developed a theory that man was motivated by two types of urges: one connected with the need for survival (which Jabotinsky equated alternatively with necessity, bread, or hard labor), and the second connected with the desire to expand the parameters of life (which he termed play, amusements, or luxuries). People believed that the former—the need for survival—was the stronger, as did people in the nineteenth century. Jabotinsky, however, believed that subconsciously the nineteenth century thought differently: "It believed that the supreme pathos, in life and in history, was defined by the play instinct ... we all know that, aside from agriculture, man's industry is occupied, nine times out of ten, with the creation of "luxuries" (if we give the word "luxury" its true meaning: everything that is not a true necessity, that is, something without which Robinson Crusoe could have continued to exist on a deserted island). The nineteenth century subconsciously believed that this also applied to social life, to political life, and to all of history."[76]

Accordingly, this century was characterized by admiration of political freedom and the belief that every individual had to be liberated and helped to realize his rational potential in his own way and in his own sphere; the central motivation impelling individuals would be the desire to expand the parameters of their lives. Because each individual would to this in his own way, society would be pluralistic and diverse.

> Out of this chaos, a sublime world order will arise. The nineteenth century was prepared to accept and to respect "discipline" only for special needs, at exceptional moments, in times of emergency. ... as a bitter medicine. ... discipline in the form of a pervasive atmosphere of a national and public way of life, an ever-present atmosphere that penetrates everything, of the sort that today is praised everywhere. Even in a nightmare, members of the nineteenth century could not have created anything resembling that. In general, they were reconciled to statehood only with important qualifications. National government had be like a railing on a staircase—if a person's foot slipped, he could lean on it, and therefore the railing was absolutely necessary. However, there was no

need for support on every step and each stair. ... The ideal of the nineteenth century may be defined as follows: a "minimalist" state, or perhaps, in sharper terms—moderate anarchy, or in any case, "a-cracy." I do not know, whether the term "totalitarian state" was already heard in the nineteenth century. At any rate, I never heard this term nor the entire concept during my youth. A child of the nineteenth century could not have imagined anything more repellent than this odor of government leadership in every corner ... this idea of clear police-statehood, like the thickets of a tangled forest from which no one can escape. I would argue that even the nineteenth-century socialists perceived this problem specifically in this fashion. In their subconscious, they envisaged the political order in a socialist state in the form of a superbly liberal government. When their opponents claimed that socialism meant the surrender of civil liberties, they firmly denied this not only in furious anger, but also with complete innocence. ... The subconscious "pathos" of the ideal of nineteenth-century socialists was connected first with the negative side of the matter—with the elimination of want; that is, with a general humanitarian idea, or even with the idea simply of acts of charity—and not at all with the harsh organization of economic life.[77]

This passage has been quoted practically in its entirety, because in it Jabotinsky attempted to sum up the characteristics of the nineteenth century, the century that shaped his thought.

Jabotinsky's generalization was unquestionably deficient. It is true that Marx and other socialist thinkers, for example, did not describe in detail the structure of future society (Marx in fact held that the state, as a mechanism of oppression, would no longer exist in a non-alienated society); however, they did discuss intervention in the economy and in society, at least in the transition period from a capitalist society to the society of the future (to wit, *The Communist Manifesto*). Nor can it be said that nineteenth-century liberal thinkers—with the exception of extremists like Spencer or the *laissez faire* economists—sought moderate anarchy. While the centrist, dominant stream of nineteenth-century liberals, represented by Mill and de Tocqueville, considered individual liberty and the setting of limits on state intervention to be a central issue, Mill and de Tocqueville agreed, as we saw, that the state had to intervene in the socioeconomic sphere in order to expand the circle of free people. Actually, Jabotinsky himself did not perceive of the state only as a "night watchman," granting it significant amounts of authority, primarily in the social sphere.

However, despite Jabotinsky's generalities, his statement captures the spirit of the period and the aspirations of those who shaped it. There is no question that liberals and socialists alike considered liberty to be the most sublime value, and believed in the power of rational man to change their terrible reality and build a better world. The liberals and socialists differed in their proposed methods for achieving a situation wherein man would be free.

While the liberals found the solution within the context of liberal democracy, the socialists (not the Social-Democrats) formulated Utopias that first demanded the destruction of liberal democracy. Jabotinsky rejected the idea of a police state as antithetical to the concepts and values of nineteenth-century liberalism.

He therefore called the phenomenon of the totalitarian state in the twentieth century "an alien object," warning that "The regime of a police state assaults us. And worse than the fact that it in itself is terrible (who else has undergone all types of [terrible] experiences like us?) is the readiness of the "period"; the happy and smiling readiness to welcome the police state, not only without complaining, but with drums and dancing. Something invaluable has been extinguished in man's soul."[78]

More than he feared the new totalitarian state, Jabotinsky feared the change that had taken place in society. An illegitimate regime could be overthrown as long as society adhered to the principle of freedom; once it abandoned that principle, there was no remedy.

Jabotinsky explained the psychological change in society as a weariness resulting from the intensity of the nineteenth century. People were apathetic and preferred that someone else bear the burden of responsibility for their lives. This psychological weariness was expressed in two main areas. It was reflected first in the tendency to mediocrity, and in the aversion to genius. If nineteenth-century society had encouraged the exceptional individual and the genius, the twentieth century, said Jabotinsky, produced no one comparable, neither in the theatre nor in literature; not in the plastic arts nor in science (with the exception of Einstein). This weariness was noticeable primarily in Europe. It was reflected, secondly, in the tendency to "leaderism"—the search for leaders, even if they were essentially mediocre, to think for the masses: "Because of [this weariness], the cult of freedom was destroyed. It is the source of that same indifference in man's heart to his own opinion, of that same love of discipline, a hysterical love, almost sensual, of that same ability to gladly live, and even to live a pleasant life, according to a timetable set by another. Or, if we return to my terminology: the twentieth century agrees to eradicate all the elements of 'play' from life."[79]

Man surrendered his right to liberty, his right to think and to safeguard his opinions, not wanting to assume the obligation that it entailed: taking responsibility for the planning and conduct of his life. From the moment that man relinquished his right to liberty, he forwent that which differentiated him from a beast: creativity, attraction to the unknown, curiosity in all areas. In essence, he discarded everything that enabled his progress. That was the true calamity of the twentieth century—not the totalitarian state, but the weary society.

One might raise the question: how did twentieth-century man's relinquishment of the cult of freedom differ from the renunciation of individuality that was implicit in military enlistment, or in sacrificing one's life for the nation? Man did not lose his freedom in the latter two cases, Jabotinsky explained, since the acceptance of discipline or the sacrifice of one's life for the nation was the product of one's free decision, and not of coercion.

In fact, Jabotinsky's liberal view considered the compromise of liberty to be legitimate in a number of cases:

First, the establishment of a government by consent of all individual citizens was justified when this government was perceived as a trust deposited by the people in its representatives, despite the fact that their absolute freedom was thereby limited. It was justified since the function of the government was to ensure the rights of the individuals to life, liberty, and property. According to this view, the government might restrict the liberty of the individual in the event that its exercise directly harmed others. (In like fashion, Jabotinsky justified the continued existence of a government that he considered to be based on the consent of the individuals, and thus obligated to guard their rights to life, liberty, and property.)

Second, liberty might be sacrificed temporarily, based on man's rational and free decision, for the purpose of creating a society in which liberty was ensured. (Thus, for example, man's self-sacrifice in order to create a nation and a homeland in which liberal principles would be realized did not harm his liberty if he did it out of free will and understanding, according to Jabotinsky.)

Third, the liberty of particular individuals might be restricted to a certain degree in order to increase the number of people who could act as free beings. (Thus did Jabotinsky justify state intervention in the socio-economic sphere. For example: a system of taxation which took more from the rich, infringing upon their liberty as embodied in their private property, was justified in order to supply the entire society with those fundamental necessities without which they could not function as free beings.)

Thus obedience to a government that was established by consent, was perceived as a trust given by the people to its representatives, and whose function was to protect the right to liberty, was legitimate. Obedience within the military, which the individual chose to join for a defined period of time and for the purpose of protecting liberty, was also legitimate. On the other hand, government discipline that was not in the category of a trust, whose goal was to destroy liberty, was totally invalid. And that was precisely what "weary Europe" was doing: it chose a government and obeyed it despite the fact that this government was doing irreparable damage to what nineteenth-century liberals thought of as individual freedom.

And thus, in "The Revolt of the Old Men," Jabotinsky presented the two real alternatives for a social regime:

A regime in which the social life-activities of the government are determined by an order from the government of the state, or a regime in which
the determining factor in this sense is the "will" of the individual; that is
(essentially), the same regime that exists today. I placed the word "will"
in quotation marks, since I know and remember the accepted meaning of
this word: I know and remember that even a free man is not free at all in
his ability to choose; he is subject to the pressures of thousands of
circumstances, at all times and in every place; even in the most ideally
free regime, he will be subject to their pressure; aside from this, it is also
possible to intentionally introduce into the free regime all types of
semi-compulsory reforms. ... But, as long as after all the reforms, the
fundamental principle—that ultimately it is not the state that steers the
wheel of my vote—remains intact ... as long as specifically the existing
form of government remains. ... an explicit choice must be made: either
the barracks or the status quo.[80]

From a general discussion of the nature of liberalism at the beginning
of the article, Jabotinsky moved on to a presentation of liberal democracy as
the only alternative to a totalitarian regime (fascist or communist). This
liberal democracy was not a minimalist state; individual liberty in it was
limited in particular areas in order to achieve more liberty for more people
and in order to realize other values, such as social justice. Arrangements
were more complex than in the naïve stereotype of the minimalist state.
Jabotinsky described a liberal-democratic society and state which, within the
context of its liberal-democratic principles, was ceaselessly reforming
itself—primarily to contend with poverty. At the same time, it maintained its
primary characteristics: individual liberty, private property, and "free play."
Jabotinsky believed that this liberal-democratic society, the "status quo,"
was indeed capable of continuing to change itself without altering its
essence, in order to further social goals.

The early influence of Jabotinsky's Italian teacher, Benedetto Croce, is
apparent here. He believed in the ability of liberal-democratic governments
and societies to continue to exist and to adapt to changes brought about by
changing socioeconomic conditions. Jabotinsky cited Roosevelt's efforts in
the New Deal as an example of a major reorientation in a government's
approach to the attainment of social objectives which still avoided doing
damage to the essence of democracy and liberalism—an action he himself
would propose in his socioeconomic thought.

The alternative that Jabotinsky proposed to totalitarian regimes was a
liberal-democracy in which liberty remained a supreme value—a society
capable of solving its problems without resorting to communist or fascist
totalitarianism. There was, said Jabotinsky, a response to communism and
fascism; in the name of that response and for its sake, it was worthwhile—
indeed essential—to rebel against the police state.

In conclusion, there is little doubt that Jabotinsky was a committed nineteenth-century liberal who succeeded in adapting his liberal teachings to the complexity of the modern world. He did state that, had he been able, he would have composed a political philosophy based entirely on the premise that every individual is a king, and whose only conclusion would have been a practically anarchistic state. In reality however, he developed a liberal-democratic theory that was remote from anarchism, one more complex, dealing with real problems of life in the twentieth century. The contention that Jabotinsky was a liberal-democratic thinker is based on the bulk of his work, notwithstanding the two problematic points discussed above: his attitude to the issue of majority decision, and his passionate respect for discipline. While his deviation from strict liberal-democracy on these two issues may not be ignored, it is not sufficient to undermine the general liberal-democratic nature of his thought; on all other important matters, Jabotinsky's views were consistently liberal and democratic. From its inception, fascism constituted an outright assault on liberal democracy, on individualism and rationalism, and on a parliamentary system of government based on faith in man's powers of reason. Fascism negated all political culture that was anchored in the heritage of the eighteenth and nineteenth centuries, from intellectualism to a belief in continual progress; it attacked what it called the morality of merchants—the morality of bourgeois society—and the entire existing order of liberal democracy. As an alternative, the mature fascism of the 1930s offered a synthesis of integral nationalism and revolutionary syndicalism. The cornerstone of its political philosophy was totalitarianism, which saw the individual as a means to realize the goals of the state. As Mussolini defined it, the state, embracing every facet of life, was therefore obligated to intervene in every facet of life. Fascism sought a new type of man who was the antithesis of the bourgeois man; it aspired to psychological equality and to a political culture which, instead of being constructed around the rules of individual liberty and competitive exchange, would be based on a cultural, moral, and spiritual revolution, on organic unity, and an almost-transcendental obsession with heroism.

Jabotinsky's outlook was absolutely antithetical to such repressive statism. Those contradictions in his thought should not be seen as sufficient to confound this conclusion; indeed, it is precisely liberal-democratic philosophy's pragmatic concern for the realities of life and its respect for individual idiosyncrasy which make it so often peppered with contradiction. As in the man, such are the vagaries of the philosophy; the paradox is at once its flaw and its beauty—its weakness and, when viewed in the context of the thinker, often its greatest strength.

Chapter 3

SOCIETY AND ECONOMICS

Jabotinsky's economic and social theories are scattered among his many writings, the lion's share of them existing only in draft form. Nonetheless, by comparing passages from different sources, it is possible to present his socioeconomic views as a coherent whole.

Jabotinsky was highly sensitive to social and economic issues, as reflected in his writings throughout his life, his ideological struggle with Marxism and socialism compelled him, though never formally educated in economics, to offer up a viable alternative system.

His grasp of social and economic issues was influenced primarily by two sources: late nineteenth- and early twentieth-century liberalism, and the Bible. Yet despite his rejection of Marxism and Marxist socialism, Marx left a lasting imprint on Jabotinsky and his work. Jabotinsky did not make the error common to our times of separating economic and social issues, but saw them as integrally connected, and always related them to one another.

Jabotinsky's socioeconomic thought may be divided into two main sections which complement one another: theory, which he called "psycho-historic materialism" or "psycho-Marxism," and social policy, which he called "social philosophy."

Jabotinsky's Attitude toward Marxism and Socialism

Jabotinsky's social and economic views were crystallized largely during his struggle with Marxism and socialism. In his youth, as a student in Rome, he was influenced greatly by Italian socialism; his disenchantment came gradually.

His attitude toward Marxism and socialism was influenced by two factors: his observation first of Russian Bolshevism and European socialism, and later of the workers' unions in the United States. In contrast to other Zionist thinkers who clung to socialist ideas with abandon Jabotinsky believed in learning from history. When a significant number of historical facts had accumulated, he would analyze them and draw conclusions.

Jabotinsky's rejection of socialism on theoretical grounds was complemented by his advocacy—in his writings on Zionism on the struggle to establish a Jewish state—of monism (that is to say, pursuing of a single ideal—in this case, the establishment of a state of the Jews in the Land of Israel). Nevertheless, he did integrate bits and pieces of Marxism into his liberal world view. In his general theory, he tried to present alternatives to socialism in practically all areas. These differed notably from other revisions of Marxism, primarily Leninism and Sorelism.

Jabotinsky's disappointment with socialism in practice and his disenchantment with socialist theory occurred practically simultaneously. His first sharp break with socialism, in 1910, was primarily over issues of the essence and function of the proletariat. In 1904, Jabotinsky still accepted the socialist view that the function of the proletariat was to incarnate the ideals of humanity. But even then, he departed significantly from the mainstream socialist interpretation of this concept. Jabotinsky saw the development of various nations as a necessary condition for the cultural progress of mankind, inasmuch as progress demanded pluralism, and every nation brought with it a different culture. Thus he believed that a primary function of the proletariat was to stimulate the development of an individual nation:

> A class that recognized the loftiness of its universal function, that understood that it and humanity are identical, this class cannot declare that it has no interest in anything else aside from a life of satisfaction and tranquillity. Everything that is important to humanity is dear also to it. The separate development of national units helps in the advancement of mankind, and a developed and aware proletariat cannot ignore this problem, just as it cannot declare that it has no need for astronomy or the history of the ancient East ... A working man, who has developed and become fully aware cannot say: it is of no concern to me if the Israelite nation exists or not.[1]

Several years later, Jabotinsky expressed his deep disappointment not only with the socialist view of the universal mission of the proletariat—which did not allow individual nations to develop separately from one another—but also with the actions of proletariats themselves. In his article "From the Frying Pan into the Fire," Jabotinsky analyzed the activities of the proletariat from October 1905 to 1910. The "leader" of the liberation movement at that time, said Jabotinsky, was the proletariat. Its errors were enormous, the greatest being the declaration of a second general strike which failed because "such a great effort must not be repeated twice in one season. The shot missed the mark, the myth of the tremendous power of the 'leader' was shattered."[2] Still, Jabotinsky here is restrained, highlighting proletariats' tactical, political errors, while refraining from expressing moral disapprobation of their actions.

In the article, "I Do Not Believe," his criticism of the proletariat took on a new dimension. In analyzing the proletariat as he existed in reality and not according to the idyllic socialist vision of the future, Jabotinsky concluded that the workers of his time were far from the embodiment of humanity's finest moral perfection. He showed double proof, first in the attitude of the American proletarian—who had achieved class solidarity—toward his black fellow workers: "The white proletariat of southern America voted to deny the privilege of voting to its black members."[3] Prejudice, said Jabotinsky, rendered the proletariat sick. Moreover, Jabotinsky criticized the lack of solidarity among proletarians world-wide, and noted that talk of universal solidarity was not implemented in a world dominated, in reality, by the parochial interests of workers in specific countries.

Jabotinsky added that, even though his criticism of the proletariat might be premature because true socialism had not yet been reached, the seeds of such flaws as prejudice were clearly present in the writings of Austrian socialist leaders, headed by Otto Bauer. In his book *On the Jewish Question*, Bauer spoke against granting equal rights to Jews, expressed approval of anti-Semitism as a legitimate phenomenon, and suggested that Jews assimilate through intermarriage into Gentile culture.

However, despite his disappointment with major theoretical and practical aspects of the socialist parties—and with the proletariat in particular—Jabotinsky still at this stage believed in the need to nationalize the means of production. He still did not express substantial criticism of socialism as an ideal social model. While it was not until later that he changed his attitude toward nationalizing the means of production, even at an earlier stage he had reached the unequivocal conclusion that it was a task for all the classes, and not the proletariat along.

After 1912, Jabotinsky continued to relate casually to Marxism and socialism, and it was not until twenty years later that he criticized the fundamentals and essence of socialist theory. Though continuing to be influenced by socialist theory (particularly Marxism), he combined it with decidedly different principles, the result was a socioeconomic theory antithetical to socialism. Though unique, Jabotinsky's revision bore some resemblance to other democratic revisions of Marx—most particularly those of Bernstein and Jaurés—which stressed the importance of liberty and the continued existence of liberal democracy. In 1933 he wrote:

Even without being a Marxist, one may accept a Marxist principle; namely, the main cause of all historical phenomena is the condition of the means of production. But when an ordinary Marxist speaks of the means of production, he is referring only to the material means . . . and in this he is mistaken: these are not the important and true means of production. Before man made the first hammer, he had to consider what he wanted to create . . . the most important thing, therefore, is the "thinking." The supreme, the primary, and the most important of all the means of production is thus our spiritual mechanism.[4]

Jabotinsky utilized the terminology of Marxism, but revised its content. In his view materialism was replaced by what he eventually called psycho-Marxism or psycho-historic materialism. While Marxism and socialism focused on material means of production, Jabotinsky shifted his emphasis to the spiritual and intellectual apparatus of the individual. From this point on, Jabotinsky, attempted to refute most Marxist principles. Nonetheless, he admitted: "Marxism as a method of investigation—the dialectical approach of explaining history, the connection between historical phenomena and the means of production—all of this is still largely beneficial and valuable."[5]

The turn of events among the proletariat classes during the years 1910–1930, combined with Jabotinsky's developing ideas regarding technological progress and future society, finally brought about Jabotinsky's total rejection of socialism as obsolete. Jabotinsky was influenced by a futurist book about great technological discoveries, written in 1930 by Lord Birkenhead, a Conservative statesman. Birkenhead predicted in his book that one day it would be possible to create energy sources from seawater and from the atom. Tremendous changes in life styles and in the structure of society would result. Exhausting physical labor, for example, would be replaced by the press of a button; travel would be very quick. Everything that man needed, including luxuries, would be produced by a very small number of workers.[6]

Jabotinsky maintained in 1932 that the unfolding economic crisis was not a crisis of capitalism, but rather one of the proletariat. Since the time of the French Revolution, the source of problems in the developing world economy had been the proletariat, who chronically received wages which didn't reflect the value of his or her work, and whose profits were skimmed by the property owners: "In what way [is it possible] to lighten his [the wage earner's] life and work, in what manner to divide profits between him and the property owner. Would not logic dictate . . . recognizing the "whole people" as the sole possessor of all the means of production and instruments of production?"[7] The mistake, Jabotinsky claimed, lay in failing to consider the influence of technology, which was rapidly replacing physical labor and undermining the importance of the proletariat. There were masses of unemployed as a result of technological advances and he predicted that the situation would continue to worsen. "The anticipated future: a proletariat, the majority of which is gradually turning into a socially unnecessary class. This immense and powerful class, playing such an immense role in the collective life of modern humanity, is thus losing its economic usefulness, its very raison d'etre. Is not the root of the world's sickness to be found in this 'crisis of the proletariat?' "[8]

If technology continued to develop, the worker would cease to be a laborer toiling by the sweat of his brow and his work would become simple. The inescapable conclusion in that case would be that all of Marxist and socialist theory, which was based on an idealization of physical labor, dealt with what was, from a historical perspective, a passing phenomenon. There would be no need to liberate the proletariat of the future because he would already be liberated. Through social reforms which would abolish low wages, poor working conditions, poverty, and other injustices from which the worker suffered, work would cease to be essential for survival and would turn into a creative pleasure. In other words, there would be no need for a revolution, with its banner borne by the proletariat, in order to fulfill the ultimate socialist destiny. Technological progress together with social reforms would bring about the anticipated changes within the framework of a capitalist, democratic, liberal society. Indeed, experience teaches us that innovation invariably creates opportunity over the long term.

Even then, however, Jabotinsky maintained, economics as a science had to be based on four and not three factors. To nature, capital, and labor had to be added an additional, no less important factor: intelligence. As we saw in the chapter "Liberalism and Democracy," intelligence was the most important factor of all in Jabotinsky's opinion, and progress was due primarily to a handful of innovators.

Jabotinsky maintained that the socialist question of who should rule the world was foolish. However, since socialism was preoccupied exclusively with the issue of the hegemony of the working class, Jabotinsky expressed his opinion, as a democrat, that no class should rule the other. "As an old-fashioned democrat I believe that all of mankind should rule the world, as one, and with no differences."[9]

Nonetheless, if hierarchies of importance still needed to be determined, Jabotinsky's response would be clearly liberal and elitist: "The power that rules, has always ruled, should rule and will rule the world and the world economy is the intelligence of those individuals born with it, not one hundred million hammers and sickles—especially since they are gradually being replaced by buttons."[10]

We have seen that Jabotinsky's censure of Marxism and socialism evolved as a result both of his perception of its historical development (primarily in Russia), and of his conceptual and moral opposition to Marxist and socialist principles. He disliked the socialists' tendency to identify the social problem as one of hired workers, seeing it himself rather as a problem of the poor, who were not necessarily members of the working class. He also opposed the all-encompassing solutions of the socialists: "The social dreamers [with one exception—the Bible] have always made the same error. They planned how to change the entire economic structure of society, instead of considering the one, most important thing—how to eliminate poverty."[11]

Jabotinsky's final break with socialism came about as a result of his rebellion against any ideology not founded on the concept of individual liberty. His forceful opposition to the nationalization of the means of production stemmed from his belief in the sanctity of private property as the manifestation of individual liberty. He was frustrated by the analytical approach of the socialists, who placed greater emphasis on the urge for self-preservation than on what Jabotinsky called the play urge, which expanded the parameters of life beyond the subsistence level. As a liberal, his opposition to communism and to socialism (which he regarded as patient communism) proceeded from his basic antagonism to a society ruled by one class. The revolution to bring about a new world order had to be based on equality among citizens and respect for their freedoms, and the Bolshevik revolution violated the principles of both freedom and equality. Thus Jabotinsky notes:

> Both [communism and socialism] are trying to create a situation in which one of society's minorities will dominate the public, will suit the social order to its—and only its—needs and tastes—and all other parts of the public will be forced to submit. ... The class concept is connected to reaction ... it exists only with the help of the weapons of reaction. ... Equality of all citizens? Why that contradicts the essence of the class idea. Freedom of expression? Why majority opinion is against class rule, for a class is a minority and will never become the majority (especially the class of manual laborers, whose economic function, from day to day is being taken over by the machine). Freedom of assembly? Why it means the assembling of the majority of citizens against the ruling class. It is impossible.[12]

Over the course of his lifetime, Jabotinsky gradually recoiled from the socialist views he had embraced in his youth, eventually becoming one of his era's most vocal critics of socialist ideologies and regimes. Nonetheless, the influence of socialism on his thought should not be underestimated. One might say that the liberalism at the core of his social and economic theory crystallized out of his grappling with socialist ideas.

Jabotinsky's Conception of Economics: Psycho-Historic Materialism

At the beginning of his discussion on economics, Jabotinsky explained that he was indebted to Marxism for its dialectical approach to history—for emphasizing the connection between historical phenomena and the means of production. Jabotinsky, however, believed that the central creative instrument was intelligence. Thus he called his own theory psycho-historic materialism or, simply, psycho-Marxism.

Like most political thinkers, Jabotinsky began his discussion with an analysis of man's nature. His underlying assumption was: "The purpose of the activity of every living creature at every instance is the fulfillment of a particular need; however, the concept of need includes two fundamentally different and absolutely independent elements: necessity and play."[13]

Jabotinsky began with a description of infant behavior, in order to demonstrate man's inherent behavior, before being molded by environment. The infant, he said revealed by its behavior two entirely different types of needs, each accompanied by a different urge. The need for survival was linked with the urge for food and the desire for protection; the infant cried or moved in such a way as to call attention to himself when hungry or cold. Such behavior was a defense against destruction. Simultaneously, the infant made movements unconnected with necessity—he moved his limbs for no reason, gurgled, cooed. Such behavior was motivated by the need called play, and a different urge impelled this behavior:

> Without going into specific detail, it is possible to state that activity of the N [necessity] type has defensive characteristics. The organism demands a defense against the danger of partial or complete destruction. This is a form of struggle for the basic biological minimum of survival. The activities of the P type [play] are aggressive; they are not a necessary condition for survival ... here the "need" is of another kind: it is the urge to make use of the strength and possibilities contained within the organism, to broaden the parameters of life, to acquire types of satisfaction, which it is possible to forego without danger of extinction, and which can give added satisfaction to the organism above the necessary minimum.[14]

Jabotinsky considered the urge motivated by necessity the lowest form of stimulus, extant among plant and animal life alike. The urge or stimulus of play was superior, existing among many living creatures (dogs, for instance), but most highly developed among humans. Jabotinsky observed as well that the play stimulus was limited among lower animals primarily to the physical realm—that is, to amusement appealing to the senses. Human play was divided into two types; the first was associated with physical reality—for example, the eating of delicacies not essential to life, or the wearing of clothing and jewelry not necessary for survival. However, among mankind, the highest form of play was essentially spiritual, finding expression in song, prayer, philosophy, science, and the like. Man's urge for play was therefore compound, consisting both of an urge whose source was physical (for luxuries or bodily pleasure) and an urge whose source was embedded in man's soul (for spiritual pleasures).

As society progressed technologically, physical play would become more developed, bringing more complicated luxuries in food, clothing, housing, and the like. This was true also of spiritual play, which would become more commonplace as civilization (and production processes) evolved, with books, music, discoveries and inventions all becoming familiar and useful to an ever-increasing segment of the population. If necessity were the sole motivator of human action, progress would have stopped the moment man achieved minimal conditions for survival. It was the play urge, whether of physical or spiritual origin, that was responsible for human progress in spiritual and cultural respects. History, said Jabotinsky, was "the result of the reciprocal process of the two fundamental urges, independent of each other, N [necessity] and P [play] both of which are equally rooted in human nature. The two urges are interwoven and intertwined, and always act and react upon each other; likewise, there are border instances, where the stimulants are mixed and interrelated."[15]

This was the essence of Jabotinsky's psycho-historic materialism. In contrast to Hegelian idealism (which saw the idea as that which fashions history), and to Marxist materialism (which considered matter the motivating factor in historical development), Jabotinsky viewed historical progress as the result of a basic interaction between man's material and spiritual urges, between man's need to survive and his desire to expand the parameters of his life.

While Marx considered ideas and political structures to be reflections of existing economic structures, Jabotinsky posited that the former (which are a part of spiritual play) both existed autonomously and were dominant motivators in human progress. To prove his point, he cited several historical instances, the most significant of which was the spread of the religious philosophies of Christianity and Islam. These religions developed not so much as a result of material realities but as a result of the play urge—in this instance, the urge to deal in the abstract.

In his attempt to demonstrate that the interaction between necessity and play existed throughout history and indeed helped fashion it, Jabotinsky utilized Marxist analytical tools. However, he borrowed only Marx's rhetorical structure, while his content remained different, indeed antithetical to that of Marx. For instance, Marx viewed greed as the result of a purely material urge, one which brought about the alienation of both property owners (since they did not work) and workers (since the fruit of their labor did not belong to them). Workers also become estranged from the essence of their humanity since their work was reduced to a struggle for survival, completely losing its true character as a creative process linking man and nature.

In contrast, Jabotinsky saw the accumulation of wealth resulting not from a survival instinct (why did man need pearls and gold?), nor from the material aspect of the play urge, but rather from the spiritual aspect of play, "to the inconceivable spiritual recognition of happiness."[16] For example, the miser who stored up wealth but lived penuriously was motivated by a play urge stemming from spiritual, rather than physical needs. According to Jabotinsky, phenomena such as immigration or the quest for power could not be explained by material motivation, but had a very strong element of spiritual play—a lust for adventure that expressed man's desire to expand his horizons.

In all likelihood, Jabotinsky was influenced in these matters by his teachers in Italy, from whom he learned that man could be differentiated from other creatures by his urge to play. He may have been influenced as well by Nietzsche, from whom he learned of man's constant struggle for power.

Jabotinsky thus tried to prove that Marx had erred in viewing economics as the primary force behind human historical development. His case might have been stronger if he had rid himself entirely of Marxist terminology, which actually did not suit his outlook. The early influence of Marxism, however was apparently too strong.

The clear distinction he made between the subjective and objective definition of *need* is important. His objective definition was relatively simple, referring to those needs that were necessary for survival in its true sense— "the original that does not tolerate reduction."[17] This definition was not useful, however, since the real discussion of man's needs took place in a particular society at a particular time; what is essential for man in a particular context, said Jabotinsky, is not necessarily described by that objective, essential definition of need. He explained that "among the needs that are essential for man today, including those that are only material, anything in the category of real primary needs has already had its place usurped by a large class of 'luxuries.'"[18]

For example, it would not enter anyone's mind today to define basic needs as uncooked meat, raw potatoes or a piece of cloth for clothing. Clearly, the concept of "need" as a basis for formulating social policy is relative, conditioned by society's prevailing norms. This observation applies even more literally to the definition of luxury items, which, in an absolute sense, is: "Everything without which Robinson Crusoe would have been able to stay alive successfully: not only a car and shoes, but also a table, a spoon, and generally ninety percent of the things that are found in places of the worst poverty."[19]

This definition too, as the objective and limited definition of need, is not useful in determining policy. However, its importance lies in the fact that it invites us to distinguish between material needs for survival and material needs for development and play. According to this objective definition, everything in the category of luxury—even if it is unquestionably physical (e.g. gourmet foods)—stems from the play urge. For example: cooked food may seem to be an essential need and not a luxury, because it has become a physical habit (people have difficulty digesting raw meat); however, one must remember that it is a delusion that cooked meat is essential. Faced with no choice, man can survive physically on raw meat. The urge for cooked food is related in man's imagination and in his demand to expand the parameters of his life—in play.

Still, it is clear that for the purpose of developing a socioeconomic policy, one must use the relative definition of the word luxury: " 'Luxury,' in its relative sense, is a concept related to the varying conditions of place, of time, and of class. For a Negro from Botswana, a pair of shoes is a luxury and he is exceedingly proud of them, while even a car is not classified as a 'luxury' to a businessman from Chicago, and his wife demands that he buy a second car because she really can't manage without it."[20]

Jabotinsky's description of historical development was actually a description of how yesterday's luxuries become today's necessities. Most important was his emphasis that this development did not stem from man's struggle for survival, but rather from his play urge—that is, from his desire to expand the horizons of his life and to achieve more in all areas.

In Jabotinsky's psycho-historic theory, therefore, the central factor shaping history was the play instinct, and man's ultimate goal was to expand both his material and spiritual realms. According to Jabotinsky, this was made manifest in history through the technological progress that is part of economic development, and through the spiritual progress that is connected with the development of literature, science, religion, and politics. Jabotinsky called each facet of the play factor, the physical and the spiritual, a psycho-spiritual urge. Physical play was a psycho-spiritual urge (in contrast to physical necessity) since the motivating factor was not survival, but the desire to expand one's physical parameters beyond subsistence needs. In other words, Jabotinsky was addressing human activity motivated by imagination and adventurism.

Jabotinsky maintained that man's psycho-spiritual urge was expressed primarily in economic arenas (e.g. technological discoveries or the exploitation of new countries in response to commercial need) and not in spiritual activity, because economic skill was more common then literary, artistic, or scientific talent. Inasmuch as the progress of mankind was the result of the psycho-spiritual urge in all areas, Jabotinsky judged that "to the extent that human development is more advanced, it devotes a greater part of its collective creative effort to amusement and a smaller role is left in its life's activities for necessity."[21]

Did Jabotinsky consider progress to be morally positive? Or was it merely expressed in the expansion of man's material and cultural parameters, never necessarily accompanied by moral progress? It is clear that Jabotinsky was aware of the complexity of the answer to this question. Nevertheless, in his discussion of economic theory he stated unequivocally that the need for moral progress was commensurate with the degree to which human activity was motivated by the play urge.[22] His concept of progress thus described not only technological or scientific progress, but also moral development. As mentioned in the chapter "Liberalism and Democracy," Jabotinsky's views were related in this to Western liberal thinking, which viewed progress as morally positive and stood in contrast to mature fascist thinking which believed in neither the individual nor in "progress."

Jabotinsky believed that even while the play urge created new problems and difficult situations, the very existence of this strong spiritual stimulus was a positive, moral element. If the play stimulus were lessened, regression would occur. Thus Jabotinsky considered Europe's weariness in the twentieth century a source of evil. We see that at this stage already Jabotinsky looked with distaste upon stagnating societies, in which the play stimulus had disappeared. The vision of the end of days—i.e. conservative society in which the attempt to expand man's material and spiritual boundaries had ceased—was fundamentally erroneous. Nothing could be worse than the suppression of man's psycho-spiritual urge; it was that very urge that distinguished him from other creatures.

That urge might also be explained in terms of power relationships: "The motivation which is at the same time also 'the royal motivation.' ... Every amusement ... is a desire to dominate, to rule. Analyze what satisfies each man's desire: it is always expressed in 'domination.' ... There are no exceptions to this rule."[23] The very definition of the urge for amusement as an urge to expand the area of sustenance automatically assumes the desire to rule—over objects, nature, and people. (The influence of Nietzsche is obvious here.) Following from this, one might therefore also view historical development as based on man's natural desire to dominate. However, each man's urge to dominate and expand his domain was liable to conflict with that same urge among his peers; people would therefore be locked in a constant state of battle.

How then would it be possible to reconcile the urge for expansion of one's domain with the existence of a society based on the rule of law, since the existence of the latter necessitated limiting man's urge to dominate?

Rules restricting man's urges were unquestionably necessary to protect others and their right to fulfill their urges. However, restrictions had to be based on the fundamental assumption that the urge to rule was a definitive characteristic of man, and thus not only should not, but could not be regulated away.

Jabotinsky presumed that "every individual is a king," and that the number of kings in society was identical to the size of its population. Since each individual's desire was supreme, it followed that any infringement on the individual's will was a moral infringement. Thus the laws limiting the individual's urge to rule had to be the result of his own will. Any other method by which restrictive laws were imposed were unethical (e.g. the will of the king, of the ruler, or of God).

The logical conclusion of this idea was the same as that of the philosophers of Natural Rights, known also as the philosophers of the Social Contract. Thus, the theory of John Locke, father of modern Liberalism, was based on the assumption that government was the result of a social contract between all citizens. In order to preserve man's natural rights—to life, liberty, and property—individuals agreed to forego their natural right to arrest, to judge, and to punish those who harmed them, and transferred those rights to the government. This decision was reached by the individuals themselves, recognizing that, without a government, there would arise situations in which one individual violated the life, property, or freedom of another. It was therefore preferable to accept limitations (thereby reducing the areas of their freedom) in order to increase the assurance of each one that he would not be harmed by anyone else. The function of government, according to this concept, was none other than to protect the individual's fundamental rights. The moment the government abused this function, the people were entitled to rebel.

Jabotinsky's concept of the nature of the Social Contract was very similar to that of John Locke: "Law and government [are based] only on the Social Contract. This is a contract between a billion and a half kings with equal rights. They have no other choice, because without this contract, each one would intrude upon the domain of the other."[24] According to this concept, man deposited a part of his natural rights with the government as a security, in order to prevent a violation of his natural rights. The government's authority therefore was the result of the consent the individuals involved. Thus, said Jabotinsky, "state discipline must be publicized as a self-imposed discipline, reached by mutual consent."[25] This consent derived from the individuals' perception of the function of the government as the protector of the rights of life, liberty, and property. From its inception, fascism attacked this aspect of the Social Contract.

What are the functions of government? How much may the government intervene to protect the rights of individuals? Jabotinsky's view was that the functions of the state should number as few as possible, and that it should intervene only when absolutely necessary—again in contradistinction to fascism, which considered the state to be responsible for planning in the economic field as well as in other areas. Jabotinsky explained his ideas as follows: "The actual significance of this concept is the negation of the totalitarian state ... The most healthy and normal and pleasant institution for all the kings [meaning people, because every individual is a king] is the 'minimalist state,' that is, a state that acts only in case of real necessity."[26]

Jabotinsky added that the necessary minimum of state intervention nonetheless demanded flexibility; in time of war or economic or political crisis, there would without doubt be a need to expand the authority of the state—but only for the duration of the crisis. During normal times, the less the state intervention—primarily in the economic realm—the better.

The limitation upon government intervention in the economic realm in Jabotinsky's ideology was based on two fundamental premises. The first was derived directly from man's play instinct; man's urge to expand the parameters of his life was expressed in the economic sphere in his rightful desire to hold private property. The second premise derived from the universality of this fact; since everyone had the right to private property, the state might intervene only when one person's attempt to take a particular item violated another's right to private property. "Ownership of property," as Jabotinsky put it, "is the most natural form of self-expression for a normal person, and all the while there is no sharp conflict with the just demands of his peer or of society as a whole, there is no reason to disturb it."[27]

However, the implied qualification in this quotation makes it clear that Jabotinsky still defended the state's right to intervene not only in instances of conflicting claims over a particular item, but also in instances of what Jabotinsky called "the demands of society as a whole." This concession created an allowance for many kinds of state intervention (e.g. taxation, as we shall see shortly), in order to fufill general demands by society (such as a minimum income for all citizens).

That private property is a basic right, expressing something inherently human and necessary for the progress of society, is of course antithetical to Marxism and socialism. This fundamental difference is nowhere more extreme than in Jabotinsky's attitude toward the ownership of the means of production. In contrast to Marxist and socialist theorists who considered the abolition of private ownership of the means of production a necessary condition for the socioeconomic revolution, Jabotinsky maintained that the solution for social problems was unrelated to the ownership of the means of production. Individuals had the right to own the means of production; it was the right of the factory owner to own the machinery in his factory. Even if, in order to address major social problems, the state had to fulfill the material needs of some of its citizens, it had to do so through methods other than nationalizing the means of production. Nationalization of the means of production, according to Jabotinsky, contravened man's nature, and absolutely violated his right to private property: "This world view ... recognizes private property (to the extent that it is compatible with the equal rights of the citizen – kings and their claims) as the foundation, pivotal point, and impetus of the social economy."[28]

Private property was thus, according to Jabotinsky, the basis for socioeconomic policy. Jabotinsky's use of the concept of social economy was not accidental, and attests to his perception of the socioeconomic realm as a single entity.

We have seen that Jabotinsky's economic thought as presented thus far embodied the solid liberal principles with which he became imbued during his studies in Rome—particularly the views of his teacher, Benedetto Croce, regarding the superiority of the liberal economy. The first liberal principle evident in Jabotinsky's socioeconomic theory was the fundamental promise that government was the result of a Social Contract, and that the functions of the state had to be limited to the essential minimum. The second and related principle was the universal right to private property as the basis for the socioeconomic concept. One must emphasize, however, that in contrast to most nineteenth-century liberals (and in the spirit of John Stuart Mill) Jabotinsky did not refer to a society dominated by *laissez-faire*, but rather to one that was obligated to preserve the right to private property and to concern itself with the specific needs of its members; that is, to enact a social policy that would fulfill the basic needs of all citizens, even at some cost to the private property of some individuals. For example, Jabotinsky saw no contradiction between the imposition of a high tax on the wealthy in order to supply specific needs and services to the poor and the right of those same wealthy individuals to private property, believing as he did in the right of the state to intervene in property disputes among individuals and in cases regarding societal needs as a whole.

The third liberal principle central to Jabotinsky's theory was his emphasis on man's nature, in which the play urge inhered, for it was play that brought about human progress. It was the initiative, or play urge, of individuals—and particularly of especially talented individuals—that brought about human progress. Jabotinsky's thought here was very similar to that of John Stuart Mill, which placed great emphasis on the contributions of geniuses to human progress.

The difference between Jabotinsky's liberal-democratic stance, as reflected in his economic thought, and the theories of other liberal-democratic thinkers such as John Locke, John Stuart Mill, and Alexis de Tocqueville, centered on Jabotinsky's view of the democratic, rather than the liberal nature of government. The uniqueness of Jabotinsky's views was rarely more evident than in regard to the issue of majority rule.

The Federalists and later Mill and de Tocqueville pointed out that the principle of majority decision, a basic democratic tradition, was likely to violate the fundamental rights of the individual and of the minority. None of them challenged the validity of the principle of decision by majority, but each offered solutions to the problem within a democratic framework.

Jabotinsky, on the other hand, never accepted the concept of majority rule on principle:

> For some inexplicable reason, democracy is identified with majority rule. This is understandable from a historical point of view—democracies were created under the banner of the struggle against different types of minority governments. That was the counter-swing of the pendulum. Actually, the blind identification of democracy with majority rule is not correct. The value of democracy does not depend on the feeling of subjugation by forty-nine kings with equal rights to one hundred, or even by ten kings or one to one hundred. The sense of democracy must rather be sought in the theory of consent and compromise.[29]

Jabotinsky's interpretation of the individual's right freed him from the restraints or majority-rule philosophy. The alternative that he offers is reminiscent of the views of some of the Greek Sophists (particularly Protagoras) regarding the nature of the democratic process: both the majority and the minority expressed their opinions, and the decision was based on the relative strength of each. In other words, it was a compromise between majority and minority opinion. As we shall see further on, Jabotinsky's belief that decisions had to reflect a compromise among opinions was of great importance to his treatment of the fundamental socioeconomic issue of national arbitration.

Jabotinsky did not suggest a real alternative to the principle of majority decision outside of the socioeconomic sphere, and the issue remained problematic throughout his writings.

Jabotinsky saw only two alternatives for a social order: "the barracks, meaning a regime in which the social life activities of the individual are dictated by the government, or a government in which the determining factor in this regard is the 'will' of the individual."[30] Jabotinsky explained that he put the word will in quotation marks since it was clear to him that the definition of a liberal economy did not demand the total absence of state intervention; the state intervened in the free market through laws and rules in order to maintain social justice.

In his opinion, the existing government in the West already lacked a capitalist character because that government "based on liberalism and the right of property, absorbed enormous quantities of all types of antidotes, including the collective work contract, unemployment insurance, and a very large inheritance tax. It digested these antidotes and still remained the same government, although in a reformed version. The only question now is whether this regime is able to absorb and integrate additional reforms—until poverty will be completely abolished—and yet to safeguard its foundation and to continue to be a government of 'free play.'"[31]

Jabotinsky saw the abolition of poverty as a supremely important ideal and a fundamental condition of progress, because a progressive society could exist only if a solution were found for this problem. He therefore had to propose, within the framework of a democratic-liberal regime, social reforms which would solve the problem of poverty without infringing upon the liberal economic principles.

Welfare Policy and the Jubilee Idea

Jabotinsky was highly sensitive to social issues. He thus attempted to develop a social concept which would lead to the abolition of poverty, needing to find an alternative to Marxist and socialist solutions, which he rejected outright. This alternative began to take shape in 1904, in light of social legislation passed by Watson's Labour government in Australia. In his article "A Letter on Autonomy," Jabotinsky noted the latter's demands for social legislation: a compulsory arbitration law (special arbitration sessions on potentially explosive areas of disagreement between factory owners and workers, with the results binding on both sides); improved labor legislation in factories, industry, and commerce (such as the reduction of the work day to eight hours); and the establishment of a pay scale and a minimum wage. Jabotinsky considered this social legislation in Australia a step in the right direction and proof that it was possible to solve social problems within the framework of a liberal-democratic government.[32]

Over the years, Jabotinsky studied the social reforms (such as government-sponsored old-age and health insurance) that had been or were being enacted in Great Britain. Due to his argument with socialism, Jabotinsky sought to construct a uniquely Jewish moral basis for the social aspect of his socioeconomic thought. He therefore turned to the Bible, which he saw as the source of the original social message, hoping that with the establishment of a state of the Jews and conditions amenable to the creation of a Jewish social philosophy and activities, a just society would be achieved: "Perhaps specifically the rebirth of the Hebrew state, a 'social laboratory' for that same race whose idea of social reform is the product of its genius, will tip the scale and demonstrate to the world, once [the state] is established, the true model of a social regime based on justice, a regime without poverty or deprivation."[33]

Jabotinsky emphasized that a society based on the principles of social justice as delineated in the Bible would be unlike any society proposed by socialists, including those in the Land of Israel. The Bible, said Jabotinsky, was replete with social protest and solutions to social problems. The Bible's social outlook stood in complete contrast to the socialist views that sought to prevent social evil by establishing a social regime whose existence would prevent inequality in the distribution of property. Such a regime would do away with competition and economic struggle.

The Bible's social ideology was precisely the opposite, based on the premise that free initiative and competition were positive. However, since such an economic system created social injustices, the Bible established a system of safeguards to correct this evil, and not, like socialism, to prevent it.

The Bible's approach to correcting the inevitable social injustices of a free economy—in itself perceived as something positive—was based on three concepts: the Jubilee, the Sabbath, and *pe'ah* (the injunction to leave produce in the corners of the field or vineyard for the poor and the stranger).

Jabotinsky interpreted the idea of Jubilee, which appears in Leviticus 25: 7–10, as follows: "[In the Jubilee year, that is, the fiftieth year] debts are cancelled; the man who became poor through debt has his possessions returned, the servant is set free, equilibrium is restored; the game starts once again from the beginning until the next upheaval."[34] In contrast to the socialist revolution that was supposed to take place once and remain forever, the radical concept in the idea of the Jubilee year was that of cyclical revolution. Between the Jubilee years there would be a free economy, with safeguards deriving from the Sabbath and *pe'ah*; thus social injustices were continually created that would be corrected in the next Jubilee year.

Jabotinsky considered this system preferable to socialism in the long run since it was based on the belief that free economic competition was fundamental to human life:

> Men will struggle; they will lose and win. It is necessary only to pad the fighting ring with soft grass, so that the loser won't hurt himself too much when he falls. This "padding" is the Sabbath, *pe'ah* and *ma'aser* [the tithe]; all those various methods by which the state prevents exploitation to the point of blood-sucking, and poverty to the point of sheer destitution. Periodically [in the Jubilee year] the whistle of the referee is heard. The victors and the vanquished return to the places where they started in their struggle, and line up shoulder to shoulder. And therefore, specifically, the struggle will be able to continue.[35]

Because of Jabotinsky's basic view that the play urge was a defining characteristic of man and a necessary condition for human progress, the

Biblical idea captured his heart. What Jabotinsky called "padding" and what was called by the father of the British welfare state, Beveridge, a "safety network," were the same thing. Jabotinsky's idea, based on the Bible, and influenced, as he himself attested, by the writings of Popper-Lynkeus, was similar to that of the liberal Beveridge, who saw the need to turn a free economic society into a humanitarian society by creating a safety network to "catch" a vulnerable person and prevent his total collapse and destruction.

Beveridge believed in personal liberty, individualism, the encouragement of free enterprise, competition, and self-help. Yet he was able to see that the absence of humanitarianism—as evidenced by the crippling poverty affecting masses of people—was a serious blight on the liberal-democratic government of Great Britain in the 1930s. He saw unemployment as a dehumanizing phenomenon resulting in loss of self-respect. Freedom, according to Beveridge, was liberation not only from tyrannical rule, but also from social evil. As long as social evil existed, those suffering from it could not realize their human potential and function as free agents. Poverty, in his opinion, was a combination of a number of evils including want, unemployment, ignorance, and disease. Beveridge thus saw the abolition of poverty as the primary goal for all society, and not only for the poor.

A society that refused to grapple with evils of poverty lacked a social conscience. The methods proposed by Beveridge in 1942 to deal with the five evils constituted an integral social welfare policy. He demanded a minimum income for all through insurance, national health services, allocations for families, full employment, and the like. State intervention in these areas was justified and necessary in order to maintain a moral society and to enable everyone to exist at a level above bare subsistence, thus allowing them to realize their freedom.

Simultaneously, Beveridge emphasized the limits of state intervention. Competition and private initiative had to continue to exist. It was not the function of the state to eliminate gaps.

There were obviously great similarities between Jabotinsky's ideas and those of Beveridge. That is hardly any wonder: Beveridge was also a liberal thinker, and hence his basic premises were similar to those of Jabotinsky. What characterized Jabotinsky as unique were his social ideas based on the Bible, his development of these ideas, and his translation of them into modern, liberal-democratic context.

In his articles dealing with the "padding" of a free economy—"The Jubilee Idea" (1930) and "The Social Philosophy of the Bible" (1933), Jabotinsky outlined a program for a social welfare policy, broader even than that of Beveridge. It is fair to say that, despite the great influence of Popper-Lynkeus, the first integrated plan in the field of welfare policy planning was created by Jabotinsky. Beveridge is credited with this honor, since his plan was widely publicized, aroused much public discussion, and was partially implemented in Britain. Jabotinsky's plan, in contrast, received no attention, and was hardly heard of outside of Revisionist circles.

The "padding" of which Jabotinsky spoke needed to exist permanently in society, and was based on two principles. The first proceeding from the Biblical concept of the Sabbath, protected the privileges and status of the hired worker. While in its narrow sense the concept of the Sabbath limited only working hours, Jabotinsky saw it as a basis for all reforms protecting workers.

The second principle was based on the Biblical idea of *pe'ah*, and upon it Jabotinsky believed could be built an entire structure of social legislation dealing with the transfer of money from the rich to the poor: income tax, inheritance tax, unemployment insurance, and the like. It is possible to say that a broad, modern interpretation of the idea of *pe'ah* means the obligation of the state, through the taxes it collects from the rich, to supply food, medical care, clothing, education, and housing to its citizens.

Jabotinsky described his vision of a social welfare state based on principles that were laid down in the Bible, translated into modern conditions and concepts:

> A world in which the word "hunger" rings like an ancient legend, a world in which ninety percent of the tragic bitterness that today distinguishes poor from rich will disappear. A world where no one will have to worry about widows and orphans, about failure, about economic collapse—because it will be impossible for whoever has fallen to hit "rock bottom"; he will not break his head nor even a finger while falling—for society has created a soft and warm 'blanket' for everyone, making it possible to eat to satisfaction. There every man can rest and start a new life. The origin for all this was in only two short Hebrew words [*pe'ah* and the Sabbath].[36]

It was clear to Jabotinsky that, in reality, his vision could not be fully realized until wars were ended and all resources were dedicated to social ends.

Jabotinsky emphasized that through social welfare policy, gaps would lessen but not disappear. Yet, he considered this to be positive for two reasons; first a certain degree of inequality stimulated competition and developed initiative among individuals, thus fostering progress in society as a whole. Such a situation was natural in that it suited man's nature, in which the play urge—which is an aggressive instinct—impelled him to material and spiritual adventures in order to expand the parameters of his life. Thus Jabotinsky's vision of a welfare state was consistent with his fundamental thought, as presented in "Introduction to the Theory of Economics."

The second reason Jabotinsky gave as to why a certain degree of socioeconomic inequality was positive is particularly interesting. In a society without social injustice, he said, man would no longer need to struggle for social reforms, and his moral sense would become dormant. Therefore the socialist solution, which would establish the ideal egalitarian society once and forever, removed all possibility for personal initiative and personal creativity, as well as the moral incentive for social reform.

As an alternative to the socialist solution, Jabotinsky presented the vision of a welfare state based on the concept of the Sabbath and *pe'ah*, and augmented by an ongoing social revolution according to the Jubilee idea. Over a period of time, inequalities would inevitably develop, and there would be a need for readjustments so that all the members of society might again begin the race from equal starting points.

It was clear to Jabotinsky that the Jubilee idea as it appeared in the Bible was in all likelihood never realized. It was equally clear that the Jubilee idea was naïve and did not suit the complex reality of modern times. He realized that from a practical point of view, it would be easier to implement the ideas of the Sabbath and *pe'ah* as social policy than it would the Jubilee. However he was also convinced that if the representatives of the people considered the Jubilee an ideal to aspire to, it would be possible to translate its principles into concrete policy:

> I would sit down wise men and give them the task of developing the allusion in the Bible and translating it into contemporary language. I would order this commission as follows: Adapt the idea of cyclical social revolutions, which are still legal, to the economic living conditions of today. And please take note: the period of fifty years determined in the Bible is not one of the most important details. You may determine other intermediate periods. ... You may determine that the "Jubilee" takes effect upon recommendation of a specially authorized body ... The "revolutions" would thus be in effect generally in times of serious and prolonged crises—that is what is required. The main thing is that your program will once and for all sanctify the laws of that phenomenon today called a social revolution ... and likewise please consider and examine how the implementation of this principle will influence the regular economic cycle ... thus, weigh the matter in your minds, and show us the way. However, allow every man in our country to live, to create, to trade, in invent, to aspire, and to seek his goal without early censorship—but at the same time knowing that the Jubilee will come from time to time, and liberty will be proclaimed throughout the land to all the inhabitants thereof.[37]

There was a strong element of utopianism, bordering on naïveté, in Jabotinsky's belief that it was possible to develop the concept of Jubilee and adapt it to the society and economy of a modern state. His desire to instill an element of biblical vision into his socioeconomic theory was more significant than logical, and was abetted by his unassailable belief that scientific and technological developments would lead to moral progress, and thus make possible the realization of such ideas as the Jubilee.

The Jubilee ideal completed Jabotinsky's socioeconomic theory and set it apart from, that of other liberal-democratic thinkers. A free economy would exist between Jubilees, and parallel to it, a social welfare state. Jabotinsky hoped that in that way poverty would diminish or entirely disappear, but gaps would remain. Hence periodically, in order to return everyone to equal starting points, the drastic policy of a legal revolution based on the idea of the Jubilee would make readjustments. The race would start again within the framework of a free economy and social welfare policy. It is fair to assume that Jabotinsky believed that people's cognizance of periodic readjustments would bring about a different attitude in the intervening periods between Jubilees. The Jubilee ideal was the liberal democrat Jabotinsky's Jewish response to the socialist vision of the future.

Jabotinsky's social ideas constituted an integral part of his liberal thinking, and provided many parallels to the program of the British liberal Beveridge. Both assumed the continued existence of a free economy and the need for initiative and competition. The function of social welfare policy was to significantly correct the concomitant distortions created in society. Both saw a social welfare state as the third side of a triangle made up of a democratic-liberal government, a free economy, and social welfare policy. It was clear to both thinkers that without this third side, the two others could not continue to exist. Not only would it be impossible for a free economy and a democratic government to be moral without a social welfare policy, but in the absence of such a policy, destructive social turbulence would be likely to erupt, which could result in the attempt by a part of society to impose an alternative form of government—socialist of fascist, for instance —to deal with the social problems.

The importance that Jabotinsky imputed to the social welfare state policy, whether on its own merit or out of fear of a socialist or fascist alternative, was reflected in his article "Social Redemption," in which his concept of a welfare state fully crystallized. The article was constructed in the form of a dialogue that Jabotinsky conducted with a socialist about the interpretation of the concept "social revolution." The two views were contraposed, Jabotinsky's goal being to prove the socialist notion faulty at its core, starting with the definition of the problems which the social redemption had to solve.

The socialist defined social redemption as a situation where "the workers become their own 'employers'; that is, all the wealth of the country—land, factories, and machines—belongs to the state, and the citizens work for themselves; then there will be no room for the exploitation of labor and the social problem will be solved."[38]

The definition that Jabotinsky put in the mouth of the socialist was not in fact an ideal Marxist one, according to which ownership of the means of production would be in the hands of the state only in the initial stage after the abolition of capitalism, when capitalist shortcomings still existed. In the second stage, which was true socialism, the means of production would be owned by society and the state would wither away. The socialist approach that Jabotinsky presented here was not based on Marxist ideology, but rather on actual policies and events in Russia.

In contrast to the socialist definition, Jabotinsky presented his own definition of social redemption. First of all, he saw the social question as separate from the problem of the workers: "The social problem is much wider and deeper than the issue of hired workers. The issue of the wage-earner is but one part of the social problem; for a long time it has not been the most important one, and in the future its importance will continue to decline. ... The sole function of social reform or social revolution is to eliminate poverty."[39]

As we saw in our discussion of Jabotinsky's attitude toward Marxism and socialism, he believed that continued technological progress was constantly reducing the number of workers engaging in hard physical labor. The place of manual labor was being supplanted—and would be even more in the future—by the easier physical work of operating sophisticated machinery. The specific problems of the laborers would therefore no longer be relevant, and different problems would be on the agenda.

Since in a progressive technological society there would be less need for manual laborers, it would be necessary to modify socioeconomic priorities in order to avoid unemployment. Jabotinsky therefore had the socialist raise a fundamental question: in such a society, how would it be possible to realize the sacred principle that whosoever doesn't work doesn't deserve recompense from society?

Jabotinsky's concept of a welfare state stood in sharp contrast to the socialist concept. His basic principle was that every person—as a human being, and not because he worked—was entitled to receive his basic needs from the state. This might be implemented through two laws. The first determined that:

> Every person who so wants, for whatever reason, will receive a certain minimum from the state for his needs—a satisfactory minimum which will be sufficient in a particular country at a particular period of technological culture. ... "The elementary needs" ... include five elements: food, shelter, clothing, the opportunity to educate children, and the possibility of recovery in case of illness. In Hebrew, this may be noted briefly [and numonically] in five words, [each beginning with the letter *mem*]: *mazon* [food], *ma'on* [shelter], *malbush* [clothing], *moreh* [teacher], and *marpeh* [medical assistance] ... in every country and in

every era, there has existed a fair standard for each of these. It is the obligation of the state, according to "my scheme," to provide each person who so requests the "five *mems*."[40]

The second law dealt with paying for these services:

One may conclude that the state must always have the means to provide the "five *mems*" to all the citizens that demand them. How will the state secure these means? The answer to that is "my" second law. The state will obtain them by actually requisitioning them forcibly from the people just as it now collects other taxes and conscripts young men into the army. ... The government will calculate ... and the state will levy an appropriate annual tax on its citizens, or will requisition a suitable number of private factories, and mobilize an appropriate number of young people for the "social service." Although I am not a very good statistician, I am certain that the aggregate cost will be much less than the present cost of maintaining an army. In this manner they shall dispose of the entire social problem.[41]

Jabotinsky's proposed welfare state was marked by five salient characteristics. First, Jabotinsky's concept of welfare policy was not the same as what is referred to as minimal policy for the poor; that is, he did not demand a test of means. A person did not have to prove poverty in order to receive his basic requirements; it was sufficient for him to state that he was needy.

In comparing this paragraph to one on the same subject in "The Social philosophy of the Bible," in which Jabotinsky emphasized that it was the obligation of the state to supply the basic needs to each and every citizen, whether rich or poor, it is clear that he envisioned a welfare state with universal services to the entire population and not special services to the poor.[42] One may reasonably assume that Jabotinsky was guided here by his basic liberal principal that "every individual is a king," and didn't want to create stigmas by making it necessary to prove need. His proposed method was based upon a respect for fundamental human dignity.

Second, Jabotinsky specifically stated the relative nature of poverty—that is, the need to constantly redefine basic requirements as a function of society's standard of living. He expressed a similar idea in "Introduction to the Theory of Economics." It is clear that his definition of minimum or basic needs was expansive: "[The 'five *mems*' will create a situation where there is no impending fear of hunger—who can then compel me to work under bad conditions? On the contrary, the rich man will be forced to offer me conditions that are superior to the minimum of the 'five *mems*.' Otherwise, I will refuse the work."[43]

Third, the areas in which society (through government institutions) had to supply basic needs were broad, and, in modern terms, are: a guaranteed income, housing, education, and health care. Jabotinsky's welfare state was maximalist. Moreover, consistent with his concept of the relativity of basic needs, Jabotinsky stated that in all likelihood, the number of areas in which the state supplied basic needs would be enlarged over time.

Fourth, Jabotinsky repeatedly emphasized that citizens had the right to receive their basic requirements, and the state had to supply them—not out of pity or charity, but obligation.

Fifth, the necessary resources to fund the social services would be obtained primarily through taxes; that is, by transfer from those with more to those with less, because obviously more taxes would be collected from those with greater wealth.

It is worth noting that, in order to eliminate poverty, Jabotinsky was prepared to take steps that violated the principle of individual liberty, such as taxation, and even, when necessary, to take measures as drastic as the appropriation of factories and the compulsory draft of youth. He saw the war on poverty as important to a nation as defense from foreign invasion. He said that the social objectives justified this violation, just as defense needs justified the compulsory draft of young men. There was a contradiction between the legitimacy that Jabotinsky granted to the appropriation of industries in order to end poverty, and his previously quoted statements that prevention of individual ownership of the means of production might not be tolerated even for the purpose of creating consumer items. It is reasonable to assume that he saw in the "appropriation of a number of industries" a temporary and exceptional emergency measure justified only by the need to eliminate poverty.

It is clear that Jabotinsky cannot be classed with extreme liberals like Spencer or Adam Smith, but belongs rather with humanitarian liberals like Mill in the nineteenth century and Beveridge in the twentieth century. They shared the belief that the sanctity of the principle of liberty could be violated when it conflicted with a different ethical principal whose reali-zation was fundamental to the existence of liberty for all. The elimination of poverty was a necessary condition for the existence of true liberty for all. For what are we talking about, when discussing welfare policy, if not the satisfaction of basic conditions needed by all in order to function as free creatures? The person who was hungry, ignorant, and sick could not func-tion as a free individual. The essence of his humanity was destroyed in the ongoing struggle for survival, and he lacked the possibility of developing his human qualities—first and foremost, intelligence, or in Jabotinsky's lan-guage, the play urge. The "five *mems*" therefore were necessary not only from a humanitarian, moral point of view, but also as a precondition for man to function as an independent creature. Only the extreme nineteenth-century liberals defined individual liberty with such fanaticism that pre-cluded the state from assisting its citizens, aside from ensuring that the free economy was conducted without interruption. This view regarded the state merely as a "night watchman."

According to Jabotinsky, a state that would completely implement a social welfare policy as he understood it would also solve all the problems of protection of labor. Jabotinsky did not oppose legislation protecting the worker; already in 1904 he looked favorably upon labor legislation governing minimum wages, hours of work, conditions, and the like. However, the welfare state that he proposed would have engendered a situation in which there was no need to protect the worker, since the high minimum that everyone was assured by the state would obligate employers to offer a salary higher than the state minimum and to supply decent working conditions.

In a society that provided for man's basic needs, there would be a qualitative change in the content of work: it would be detached from necessity. The instinct of exertion to create new things (the play urge) was man's strongest urge, through which he expressed his personality. Man thus naturally wanted to work. Work turned into a curse only when it became essential for survival:

> It is a curse, man does not want it, man will fight against it until he is freed of the bondage of bread. However, then man will discover that work is a joy, that the pleasure of creative effort is immeasurably stronger than his fear of hunger. Assure him of the "five *mems*" and you will see how eagerly he will begin to pursue work tomorrow. What the nature of "work" will then be (taking into consideration the future role of the machine) I can not say. But no doubt future man will find channels of creative endeavor that we cannot even visualize. However, the pathos of work will be revealed in its glory only once "work" is divorced from "privation."[44]

This concept of work is one of the most interesting and important points in Jabotinsky's socioeconomic theory. It bears a certain similarity to Marx's concept of non-alienated work—work through which man expressed his humanity. But work that was not the result of the need for survival was possible, according to Marx, only in a socialist society in which private ownership was abolished, where all class differences were abolished, and the means of production belonged to society as a whole.

In contradistinction to Marx, Jabotinsky saw a purpose in work that was unconnected to necessity, in a state in which the economy was based on the free market and in which private property existed, and ownership of the means of the production was not in the hands of society, but the hands of individuals. However, a necessary condition for creative work in which man expressed his supreme urge for play—to change his material and spiritual world—was the existence of a maximalist welfare policy, and the periodic implementation of a socioeconomic policy based on the Jubilee idea.

However, with the same diligence that Jabotinsky delineated the goals of social policy, he struggled to define its limits. The function of welfare policy was to destroy poverty—not to abolish gaps. Jabotinsky brought examples of gaps in different areas: not only between rich and poor, but also between the beautiful and the ugly, between the fortunate and the unfortunate, and the like. All of these gaps brought about tragedies. The tragedy of the ugly woman who compared herself to a beauty was possibly no less for her than the tragedy of someone with less material wealth than another.

The exclusive function of a state was to ensure that the base of the socioeconomic pyramid was always rising, but that the socioeconomic structure remained in the form of a pyramid. If Jabotinsky's welfare policy was implemented, he predicted, the entire pyramid would rise (those on the bottom would have much more than they had previously) and perhaps would be less sharp; because of the satisfaction of the five basic needs on the one hand, and progressive taxation on the other, the gaps between economic classes would be smaller.

Beyond a welfare policy, "padding" a free market, the state had no authority to intervene in its citizens' social and economic life. Intervention in response to poverty was justified because poverty was a situation from which man generally could not extricate himself by his own efforts; it was in addition a situation that precluded his functioning as an independent creature.

In contrast, it was forbidden for a state to intervene for the purpose of abolishing the various gaps. These would always exist because men were not equal to one another, not in their talents, not in their industriousness, and not in their character. Fascism strongly opposed a liberal-democratic society of this sort, in which state intervention was limited to the abolition of poverty through welfare policy. For example, Proudhon's circle, established after 1914, claimed that liberal democracy constituted the greatest danger to Western civilization, while the mature fascism of the 1930's proposed "plannism," which included corporativism through which the state was able to rule absolutely over the economy.

As we saw in our discussion of morality, Jabotinsky did not see man as a naturally altruistic creature. Quite possibly the opposite was true: man's foremost concern was for himself and his desire to expand the parameters of his sustenance. This again stood in contrast to the "new man" as seen by fascism, a man who was supposed to be altruistic and work for the common good. Thus in Jabotinsky's view, every socioeconomic approach that did not allow man a wide berth for activity stemming from his natural tendencies would not be able to survive without severe repressive measures, and in the end would collapse.

Therefore, Jabotinsky's socioeconomic thought left a wide berth for man to express his competitive nature and to enlarge the areas of his sustenance. Within the field in which this competition took place, the function of the state was to ensure only the existence of rules of play. In other words, in the case of arguments among the players, the state, as an objective judge, would serve as a referee. Thus the concept of arbitration was an integral part of Jabotinsky's socioeconomic construction.

Class and National Arbitration

As we already saw in our discussion of Marxism and socialism, Jabotinsky opposed the class approach: "The law that states that world salvation (whatever that might be) will be realized only by the domination of the working class over the other classes is 'reactionary' in the utmost sense of the word."[45]

Soviet Russia served as Jabotinsky's model for his discussion of class. The government there was based on the negation of all the freedoms that were held aloft by liberalism: freedom of thought, freedom of expression, and freedom of organization.

However, Jabotinsky's opposition to the class idea was based on more than conclusions drawn in reaction to the Soviet experience. As mentioned previously, he opposed the portrayal of the proletariat as a special class. He repeatedly defined himself as a "liberal bourgeois" or as "a liberal of the classical school"; one must ask whether, beyond his opposition to the class concept insofar as it espoused the rule of the proletariat, he accepted the idea of twentieth-century society as made up of classes.

Jabotinsky preferred to view modern society as composed of different branches of human activity; his article "The Shopkeeper" (1927) clearly reflected this approach. He divided human economic activity into two basic sectors: trade and production. Initially, trade depended on production, for without it there would be nothing to trade; but after that initial point, the continued development of production depended on trade. Without trade—without the art of exchange—human history would have been radically different. Merchants were the true precursors of progress, according to Jabotinsky—those that carried the banner of civilization. The shopkeeper "turned the globe into a courtyard. ... Because the entire development of manufacture (with the exception of the era of patriarchal family life during the Flood) from A to Z is a result of the shopkeeper's achievements. Furthermore, not only would the factory be unable to gather together all the machinery and materials needed to produce the first pair of shoes without him, but without the shopkeeper, the factory—an institution which works on behalf of the masses of consumers—would not have the right to exist."[46]

Jabotinsky emphasized the powerful influence that merchants had traditionally wielded over many fields of culture. Their motivation to discover new lands to trade with stimulated the development of astronomy, geography and the like. He even made an interesting distinction between merchants and the "intelligent" vocations: doctor, lawyer, and so forth—what we today call the liberal professions. Jabotinsky considered merchants superior to professionals. His contention was simple: while the doctor, for example, had narrow professional interests, the merchant, of necessity, felt the pulse of the world and was involved in everything that took place. Said Jabotinsky: "I have personally witnessed higher intelligence, broader interest, better perception among businessmen, than among my own class of the professional intelligentsia (with the same level of education)."[47]

Jabotinsky thus preferred a division of society by occupation or major economic sector rather than by class, even though he used the concept "class" occasionally. His primary reason for this preference was that such terminology presumed the polarization of society into property owners and workers, and presupposed conflict between them. Without ignoring the fact that the interests of property owners and workers might conflict, Jabotinsky viewed society as divided into sectors and subdivided into interests within the same sector. The division was not between property owners and workers, but, for example, among industry, trade, and agriculture, with the industrial sector including both property owners and employed laborers. The same was true for agriculture and trade. This type of categorization was based not on a conflict of interests, but rather on a commonality of interests—those characteristics of the sector to which employers and workers alike belonged.

In doing so, Jabotinsky did not invalidate the division between employer and employee; this division existed naturally and cut across all the branches of the economy. However, in his opinion, such a division was losing its importance. In future society, in which technology would bring about a quantitative improvement in the character of work and the standard of living the division according to class would be even less significant.

In a modern context, Jabotinsky would have recommended dividing society into deciles according to income. Such a division was more appropriate to his way of thinking in that it related to the individual's economic situation, irrespective of whether he was an employee or independent, a property owner or a worker. The only criterion was his personal situation itself, according to which his right to welfare would be determined.

Jabotinsky repeatedly emphasized the fact that in modern society the worker was often more protected by trade unions than the shopkeeper or the professional was by any organization; therefore, socioeconomic policy based on class was likely to miss the mark of helping the weakest and poorest in society: "The fact that in time of crisis—the life of a worker in the cultured countries is nonetheless better than the lives of other 'petit bourgeois' poor is so well known that it is superfluous to discuss it. However little the support that the unemployed workers receive, the unemployed petit bourgeois doesn't receive even that."[48] Jabotinsky's attitude to strikes, and his suggested solutions—state or national arbitration—stemmed from this economic outlook.

His fundamental premise was that what was good for the nineteenth century (the period of oppression and exploitation of the workers) was not relevant to the twentieth. In the nineteenth century, all workers' strikes had been justified because "the life of the hired worker was very bad; he was the poorest of the poor; not only did the state and the law exploit him, but they were generally against him and on the side of his exploiters. The only means he had to protect himself against this inhuman exploitation . . . was a 'strike.' It was natural that in those days the strike was sacred in the eyes of every decent person, and strike-breaking was an ugly sin. This view was absolutely correct view—in those days."[49]

The situation was different in the 1930's, however. Jabotinsky talked a lot about the fact that working conditions had changed drastically, Moreover, in representative democracies, the workers had strong parties that represented their interests in the legislature. On occasion, the workers' party succeeded in becoming the strongest party which then proceeded to dominate the workings of government. He pointed out that not all strikes in the twentieth century were justified; each had to be investigated on its own merit, just like the demands of the merchants, to see whether or not it was justified.

The idea of national arbitration was based on this sort of thinking; thus, a crucial aspect of Jabotinsky's proposition was that only apolitical social arbitrators, responsible to the state, would be fair and objective, and would be able to decide which side in the strike was in the right. Jabotinsky later crystallized his thoughts on arbitration, concluding that the institution of compulsory and immediate arbitration precluded any justification for strikes.

It should be noted here that another product of Jabotinsky's division of society into professional sectors was the idea of a parliament of professions. Jabotinsky emphasized that he borrowed the idea of corporations from Leon Blum's "Front Populair," and not from Mussolini's Italian model. In the second part of the book, we shall examine in more detail how Jabotinsky applied his ideas about national arbitration and a parliament of professions to the specific instances of the state on the way and the state of the Jews.

The Uniqueness of Jabotinsky's Socioeconomic Theory

As we have already seen, Jabotinsky held human intelligence to be the first and foremost of the means of production.[50] As we shall yet see in his theory of nation and race, one of his premises was that every race had a specific form of thought, and that the "tools of each race are different from each other." Hence Jabotinsky concluded that each nation had special, unique characteristics in every area. "Perhaps the difference is more noticeable in economic than in political matters. The economy is strictly 'national'; people forget this since they see that routines of economic life are similar in every country. But underneath the similarity there are always tremendous differences in form, custom, and temperament."[51]

Each nation actualized these cultural idiosyncrasies in its economic conduct. In Jabotinsky's opinion, the Jewish nation, exiled from its homeland, engaged in economic activity as a substitute for having a geographic territory of its own.[52] In order to create a segregated economic environment in which to practice their own customs, Jews in exile engaged in trade and finance in countries whose native population did not engage in such activities. When the local population began to engage in those activities, the Jews moved to other countries, and when there too the citizens began to engage in trade and finance, the economic isolator that protected Jewish culture was destroyed. In Jabotinsky's opinion, the need of the Jewish people to achieve true isolation—a Jewish state—was one of the reasons for the rise of Zionism.[53]

Assuming that every nation developed an economy with its own unique characteristics, in its own land, Jabotinsky thus constructed his socioeconomic thought from Biblical elements dating from the time when the Jewish nation had lived in its own land, where it developed its own special social and economic models. All he needed to do was to adapt this thought, uniquely suited to the Jewish people, to modern times. The social philosophy of the Bible served as a guide for him; he felt that the social ideals therein could arouse the enthusiasm of the masses no less than the socialists' picture of a futuristic Utopia.

Jabotinsky always identified himself as "a son of that social class ... the bourgeoisie. Furthermore, many are the bourgeoisie who beg forgiveness, but my lot is not with them."[54] Thus he unequivocally defined his relationship to the social order called bourgeois or capitalist:

> In my opinion, almost all that culture that is the breath of our nostrils is
> the product of the bourgeois government and that of its earlier forms in
> Rome, Greece, Israel, and Egypt. And I believe that a government of this
> kind is infinitely flexible and elastic, and able to absorb enormous doses
> of social reforms, and at the same time to preserve its fundamental

essence. My heart is absolutely certain that the social order called bourgeois or capitalist will gradually establish a system of ways to eradicate poverty, that is, the decline of wages to a level below what is needed for sufficient food, for hygiene and self-respect. Were it not for the defense budgets, this could be realized in many countries even today. Furthermore, if it is true that, like all human beings, the bourgeois regime also eliminates all sorts of poisons, and thus periodically brings upon itself unavoidable upheavals, then I believe that it is within its power not only to tolerate these upheavals without collapsing, but even to include them within its system: to grant the examinations that is examines itself a form of legality and to introduce a permanent order in them, to ensure unlimited possibilities of improvement because of the constantly repeating social revolutions—predetermined, calculated, planned revolutions—that are, by the way, without bloodshed. In short, I believe not only in the stability of the bourgeois system, but also in the fact that objectively speaking, it contains the seeds of a particular social idea: an ideal in its usual sense, that is, a vision worth dreaming about and fighting for.[55]

Not only, in Jabotinsky's opinion, did the bourgeois system have the potential to solve true social problems, but it also served as an incentive for constant social upheaval due to its very nature—its incompleteness. In contrast to the socialist society of the future, which Jabotinsky compared to a "grazing field" in which man could live in exquisitely bored satisfaction, he saw bourgeois society as a field of activity in which man continually worked toward ever greater levels of justice.

Jabotinsky's view of human nature, with the play urge as a defining characteristic, accounts for the unavoidable aimlessness of life in a "grazing field" society which lacked all transforming, aggressive, expansive elements. In contrast, his vision of a society based on a free economy, modified by a welfare policy and regulated by the Jubilee idea, was the only suitable answer for man because: "all the sense of adventure in the game and the struggle remains, all the romanticism of the starting leap and the chase, all the enchantment that is in creative freedom. And most importantly there remains that very same thing that socialism has sworn to uproot, without which it is possibly not worth living—the eternal possibility of revolution, the volcanic foundation of society, a field of action, not a grazing field."[56]

Jabotinsky's contribution to social and economic theory was patterned after the Biblical myth of the patriarch Jacob wrestling with God—a philosophy which positively views man's eternal struggle to improve his world. He was taken with the revolutionary and utopian Biblical idea of the Jubilee primarily because in it he saw the spiritual vibrancy of the Jewish people which resonated during an era when they were able to live a normal life in their rightful homeland. The fact that the Jubilee was probably never implemented as such didn't lessen its value as a social ideal which, having inspired once before, could do so again.

Jabotinsky was aware of the central weakness of the liberal ideology *vis à vis* that of the socialist. The latter set up ideals and gave people a vision to dream (and fight) about, while to the more pragmatic liberalism, a vision had to be appended. Jabotinsky found the solution in the Jubilee, with its almost utopian vision and its potential for rousing the enthusiasm of the masses. "Sometimes I reflect in my heart: socialism has enthusiasm and dreams, that is possibly its main power. However, that same world view that the Jubilee ideal seems to me to symbolize inspires a vision whose power is even greater to attract the dreaming soul."[57]

It is appropriate to the end the chapter on Jabotinsky's socioeconomic thought with this sentence because it reflects the unique elements of his thought: a fusion of modern, Western, democratic and liberal ideas to a host of concepts derived from the Bible. The latter added a necessary dimension of social vision to Western liberal theory. In this way, Jabotinsky attempted to prove that every people—particularly the Jewish people—had special characteristics that were reflected also in their socioeconomic theory. One might say that Jabotinsky's socioeconomic theory is the unique contribution of a son of the Jewish people to twentieth-century liberal thinking.

It must be emphasized that Jabotinsky's thought was anchored in nineteenth-century Russian and Western liberalism; he himself pointed out many times that he belonged to the old-fashioned liberal school. As we have seen and shall see again, there was an interesting blend—on the surface, strange—in Jabotinsky's thought: sober realism and pragmatism with an eye toward history, accompanied by rational thought and an attempt to present utopian scientific theories which bordered on the naïve. This utopianism was reflected primarily in the belief that scientific and technological progress necessarily embraced moral progress, an approach somewhat similar to the sociological positivism of the Russian Kovalevsky. Therefore Jabotinsky believed, for example, that in the future it would be possible to translate the Jubilee idea into real policy. This interesting and strange blend characterized many nineteenth-century liberal thinkers and in this Jabotinsky's thought was no exception; on the contrary, it was a direct extension of classical liberalism.

Chapter 4

NATION AND RACE

The Relationship between Race and Nation

Jabotinsky's socio-political writings were most fervent when addressing issues of nation and race. His interest began during his studies in Rome, as he wrote in "The Story of My Life": "In the fall of that year [1888] I went to study in Rome where I spent three consecutive years. If I have a spiritual homeland, it is Italy more than Russia. ... My whole attitude toward issues of nationality, state, and society was crystallized during those years under Italian influence."[1]

Jabotinsky's articles after he left Italy included discussions on the subject of nationalism, and in 1907 he went to Vienna, where he studied issues dealing with nationalism for a year, mainly by independent reading. He attested: "I lived in Vienna for about a year. I didn't meet with a living soul; I also didn't go to Zionist meetings more than one or twice. I devoured books. In those days Austria was a living laboratory to study 'the problem of nationalities.' I spent day and night in the university library."[2]

During his year in Vienna, Jabotinsky was influenced by Rudolf Springer, Karl Renner, Ernest Renan, Pasquale Mancini, Viktor Adler, Otto Bauer, and others. Through them he was also influenced by the theory of "the psychology of nations," particularly as presented by Moritz Lazarus. At the university he studied the languages and history of many nations, primarily European, and enhanced his knowledge of Hebrew. In 1912 he presented his dissertation, "Self Rule for a National Minority," for a law degree from Yaroslavl University.

Nation and race are considered the most problematical issues in Jabotinsky's thought, seemingly in some contradiction to his liberal-democratic views. One may ask: did a liberal-democratic model, incorporating the issues of race and nationalism, dominate Jabotinsky's thought, or was it instead constructed around integral nationalism—a trait highly characteristic of mature fascism—with only liberal and democratic themes as corollaries?

In the chapter "Liberalism and Democracy," I attempted to show, through discussion of an article on Garibaldi ("The Obscurantist"), that Jabotinsky's concept of *nation* found its place soundly within liberal-democratic political philosophy. While Jabotinsky did in fact consider nationalism more crucial to human survival than humanism, he considered the individual more important than the nation. An individual's sacrifice on behalf of the nation had to be the result of his free will, and not of coercion. Moreover, the stage during which the nation came into being was a temporary, breakthrough period, when the willing sacrifice of certain liberal values was to be expected. The ultimate goal after this breakthrough period, once a people was unified in its own territory, was to fully implement liberal and democratic principles.

In the article "A Letter on Autonomy" (1904), Jabotinsky took issue with those who claimed that the solution to the Jewish problem lay in Jewish national-cultural autonomy within the countries where the Jews were a minority. It was in this article that he presented his first definition of nationalism. He started by outlining the conditions necessary for the existence of a nation: "This will [to preserve national uniqueness] must find realistic bases in the life of the nation, and must be expressed in certain needs; otherwise it will gradually decay, and the nation will be assimilated into its surroundings with no opposition."[3]

What, however, is the source of this feeling of national self-identity? At that early stage (1904), Jabotinsky gave a definitive answer:

A few years ago, I asked myself: Where does our deep-rooted feeling of national self-identity originate? ... Why is our language dear to us? ... Why does our national melody, even without words, arouse such powerful excitement? What is the source of this spiritual bond, of this cleaving to a unique national character, which is so powerful that people are prepared to undergo torture for its sake? The answer that first occurred to me was that the source lies in our individual education. ... But then I realized that this answer is wrong ... if education in itself is unable to create in us that spiritual bond with a particular way of life, and to preserve it for eternity, and if that bond is also often created outside the educational framework and even despite it, it is clear that the source of national feeling should not be sought in education but rather in something that precedes education. In what? I studied this question in depth and answered: in the blood. And I still insist upon that point now. The feeling of national self-identity is ingrained in the man's "blood," in his physical-racial type, and in it only. We do not believe that the spirit is independent of the body; we believe that man's temperament is dependent, first of all on his physical structure. No kind of education, not from his family, and not even from the environment, will make a man who is by nature calm, excitable and hasty. The psychic structure of the nation reflects its physical type even more fully and completely than the temperament of the individual. The nation shapes its essential spiritual character, in that it suits its physical-racial type, and no other temperament based on this physical type is conceivable. ... When we speak of an "essential physical structure," you and I mean, of course, something much more internal [customs or manners]. This "something" is expressed at different times by various external manifestations, according to the period and the social environment—but this "something" always remains intact as long as the physical racial type is preserved.[4]

In this paragraph, Jabotinsky unequivocally stated for the first time national identity was connected first and foremost to racial identity. He admitted that the desire to belong was important, and that education might contribute to the enhancement of nationalism by emphasizing national culture—but this was not sufficient. The crucial factor for Jabotinsky was "blood" or, in other words, belonging to a race. Race was defined primarily by physical characteristics, and each race had its own. The psychic structure of the nation was a reflection of its physical structure. Therefore an essential condition for the perpetuation of a nation was the continued existence of the physical-racial type that characterized its members. This was the source of Jabotinsky's immense fear of intermarriage between Jews and Gentiles; intermarriage would obliterate the physical, and thus the psychological, characteristics of the Jewish people, thereby spelling its demise.

Jabotinsky developed his concept of the integral, insoluble relationship between nation and race in two articles: "Race" (1913), and "A Lecture on Jewish History" (1933). He maintained that the argument over whether various ethnic groups were "pure" races was insignificant; they might reasonably be presumed to be an admixture of different races that mingled over the years. His first postulate in this writings was that the specific mixture of each race could be thought of as its "racial recipe" or "racial spectrum." If there were suitable scientific instruments, he claimed, it would be possible to determine the formula of the "recipe" that determined each race's uniqueness: "Whether there are 'pure races' or not is irrelevant in this instance. The most important point to note is that the ethnic groups differ from one another in their racial spectrums and in this sense the word 'race' acquires a defined scientific meaning."[5]

Jabotinsky's emphasis on scientific significance reflected his positivist approach. Since national belonging was connected primarily with racial belonging, every nation had its own unique "racial recipe" which characterized all its members: "From this point of view (certainly not from a political-juridical one) nation and race are almost identical."[6]

Jabotinsky's second postulate, which he posited in "A Letter of Autonomy," was that a relationship existed between a person's physical nature and his psychic activities. This, of course, was conjectural; science had yet to explain the relationship between the body and the psyche. Though unable to speak of a causal relationship, he believed strongly in the existence of one nonetheless. For example: two men with identical backgrounds and educational circumstances, living in identical conditions and distinguished only by their different physiological structures, often demonstrated different emotional responses to the same stimulus. Likewise, when given the same stimulus, two men from different ethnic groups would provide two different psychic responses.

It was relatively simple to describe the physical ingredients in the racial recipe, but to describe its spiritual components was much more difficult. Said Jabotinsky: "It is impossible to 'describe' racial spirituality. But in spite of that, there is no doubt that every racial group (in the above sense) has its own special racial spirituality which is manifested in one way or another in each member of that group (obviously besides intermediate types), despite the variations among the group."[7]

If we accept the above two postulates, we must conclude that each race, because of its specific racial recipe, develops its own unique economic and cultural life—i.e. its own literature, philosophy, religion, and laws. Thus Jabotinsky defined the ideal type of an "absolute nation" as follows:

> It must have a specific "racial spectrum," completely distinct from the racial nature of the neighboring peoples. It must have lived in its particular land from ancient times; the land must be densely populated, with clear-cut boundaries; it is best if there are no foreign minorities to undermine the national unity. It must have its own special, ancient language—not one borrowed from others. ... a language created, as it were, in the very image of the people, reflecting all the nuances of its thought and emotion. Such a nation must have a national religion, not one borrowed from others, but rather the creation of its own ancient spirit, like the religion of the Indians in India or at least of the Jews. And finally, it must have a common historic tradition, that is: a national store of historical events from previous generations. This could be an absolute, ideal nation, one whose national consciousness would be free of any divisive or separatist elements.[8]

The conditions necessary for the existence of "an absolute nation" or "an ideal nation" were many; reality, clearly, often deviated from the ideal. There were nations whose territory included national minorities; whose religion was borrowed; nations with a language that wasn't their own; nations that lacked their own country; and nations without a common history. Jabotinsky thus concluded: "Therefore we must concede, willy-nilly, that a land, a language, a religion, common history—all these are not the

essence of a nation but only characteristics of it. Although these characteristics are certainly of great value and very important for national stability,
the essence of nationalism—the first and last defense of its unique form—is
the distinctive uniqueness of its physical origin, the recipe of its racial
composition."[9] The decisive factor, as we have seen, is the physical component of the racial recipe, what Jabotinsky in "A Letter on Autonomy"
called "the blood."

Political science, said Jabotinsky, defined a nation differently—as the
existence of national consciousness. Jabotinsky did not dispute the fact that
anyone examining the issue of nations in the present, at a particular time,
might define a nation as based on the conscious will of its citizenry. In his
discussion of self-rule for national minorities, he himself used the criterion of
consciousness in order to define the nationality of every individual. This,
however, did not contradict the fact that the objective, primary factor that
defined each nation was the "racial recipe."

Jabotinsky took this approach twenty years later, in "A Lecture on
Jewish History." The significant difference between the two articles lay in the
fact that, in the later article, Jabotinsky stated unequivocally that national
identity was connected first and foremost to racial identity, and also that
race, in the sense of the physical recipe, took precedence over nation. It was
the physical recipe of race that brought a group with the same physical
characteristics to develop its own "spiritual mechanism"; therefore: "each
race with clear characteristics aspires to become a 'nation.' That is, it seeks
to create a separate society in which everything—the language, the economy,
the political structure, in short, the 'culture'—is in its own image. In other
words, everything should be in accordance with its taste, its habits, and its
virtues and shortcomings. For 'national culture' does not include only books
and music, as many imagine, but is the sum total of all the customs and
institutions and the lifestyles of all the people."[10]

There are abundant examples of such racial aspects of nationalism, one
of the most obvious being the various forms that races give to democratic
rule, and even to the parliamentary system itself. However, the primary
example in Jabotinsky's opinion is the different types of economic systems in
different countries.

It is possible to find a similarity between fascism and Jabotinsky's
concept of race only if we divorce his views from his entire corpus of thought
on the relationship between race, nationality, the individual and humanity,
and only if we ignore his concept of national consciousness as a criterion for
national identity.

It is interesting to note that in "Race," Jabotinsky did not maintain
that the existence of a separate state was a necessary condition for a nation,
while in "A Letter on Autonomy," he stated with regard to the Jewish

people what may be interpreted to apply to all nations, that "preservation of national essence is possible only if the purity of the race is preserved, and for that we need a territory of our own, in which our nation will constitute the decisive majority."[11]

In "A Lecture on Jewish History," written later, he found middle ground, emphasizing the importance of national territory more than in "Race," but less unequivocally than in "A Letter on Autonomy":

> Each race with clear characteristics aspires to become a "nation," that is to say, to create for itself a unique economic, political and spiritual environment, in which every detail originates in "forethought," and thus suits its special "taste." A race is able to create such an environment only in its own country, where it is the master. Therefore, every race seeks to become a kingdom. One race so aspires with all its might, because it has the necessary stubbornness, while another race does so more weakly, because it lacks the power of resistance, but by nature it also desires it, because it feels comfortable only in its own state whereas it feels "uncomfortable" any other way.[12]

One may understand from these words that the ideal situation for the race, and therefore the nation, in order to preserve its existence is to have its own land. However, the converse cannot be inferred: that, without a land, the race-nation cannot continue to exist.

What may we conclude about Jabotinsky's underlying attitude on this issue? His answer with regard to the Jewish nation was unequivocal—a state was an essential condition for the continued existence of the Jewish nation-race. This, however, did not apply universally. In order for a nation-race to continue to exist, it had to create a unique national culture, for that was the ultimate purpose of every nation. "For this task, the creative nation needs isolation, just as the individual creative personality is in need of it."[13] This isolation might be achieved in a territory in which the nation was at least a majority.

There were, however, other ways to achieve isolation: separate economic or geographic corners, for instance, or self-rule within the boundaries of a state in which another nation constituted the majority. None of these alternatives was as good as the ultimate solution—the establishment of a state—but historical circumstances sometimes dictated the need for compromise. Jabotinsky's general view was that a state contributed much to the continued existence and development of a nation-race, but was not an essential element. The conviction that he expressed in "A Letter on Autonomy" regarding the importance of a geographic state to the continued existence of the Jewish nation-race stemmed from the fact that he saw the alternatives to isolation rapidly disappearing. He emphasized that the Jewish people lacked even one country in which it constituted a majority; its future, therefore, was uncertain.

In his article "The Truth About the Island Tristan da Runha," Jabotinsky created an imaginary island that was inhabited by a mixture of all
existing races. Over a number of generations, intermarriage on the island
resulted in a situation where "the race of Tristan da Runha is the only race in
the world where all these races are completely integrated."[14]

In the creation of a new race, the product of the mingling of the blood
of each nation, Jabotinsky saw one of the most important assurances for the
glorious future of the imaginary island, as long as the uniqueness of this new
race was preserved.

In reality, however—as he emphasized in "Race"—this utopian vision
could never materialize. Furthermore, the ideal of an "absolute nation" or
an "ideal nation" occurred very rarely; it was therefore necessary to preserve
the fundamental elements, the *existing* racial recipe of each race. This was
the source of Jabotinsky's disapprobation of mixed marriages. In his novel
Samson, he described most picturesquely the appearances of those who had
lost their racial distinctiveness: "No Phillistines were to be seen. The rabble
of the town—labourers, artisans and beggars—was composed exclusively of
the fragments of indigenous tribes, ground past recognition between the two
conquering peoples ... The homeless dogs of the whole neighborhood had
collected outside the enclosure: all looked alike, lacking the characteristics of
any known breed, and in this they resembled the human inhabitants of the
district."[15]

Jabotinsky's racial theory, which he considered scientific or para-
scientific—an important point in light of his positivistic approach—does not
stand up to today's definition of science. Yet one must remember that in
those days scientific knowledge in that field was poor, and it was common to
use the term "race" in defining the internal psyche as well as the external
structure of a group, and in explaining the phenomena of uniqueness and
difference among the various nation-races. His theory also explained
national uniqueness without using a religious definition. However, Jabotinsky categorically denied the existence of superior and inferior races, and
his theory provided no basis for rating them. This point is important because
it makes clear that in no way may Jabotinsky be classified with the racist,
nationalist thinkers who espoused the superiority of one race over others,
and who drew practical conclusions from this fact. Because of its importance, Jabotinsky devoted a special article, "An Exchange of Compliments,"
to this issue.

Inferior and Superior Races

"An Exchange of Compliments," a follow-up to an article by A. Stolypin on
"The Inferior Race," was an imaginary conversation between a Russian and
a Jew on the subject of whose race was inferior.

The Russian attempts to prove that the races are unequal and the Hebrew race has great defects; the Jew, arguing Jabotinsky's opinion, comes to prove the opposite. "My opinion," says the Jew, is that there are no superior or inferior races. Each race has its own special qualities, its own features, and a range of its talents, but it is clear that if it were possible to find an absolute measure and to exactly gauge the special natural qualities of each race, we would discover that in general most of them are practically equal. ... All of them are by their nature equally good."[16]

The Russian contends that the Hebrew race is inferior in two respects. He attacks it from a religious-cultural standpoint, maintaining that Judaism isn't original, but borrowed from other people; that it has no tradition of plastic arts; that it doesn't speak about the next world; and that it is "dry," dealing only with mundane matters, attaching a reward to every commandment. On another level—society's attitude toward Hebrews—the Russian makes a long list of first-rate writers who did not like Jews. Reality proves, he says, that most people do not like Jews. He concludes that they cannot all be fools; if everyone, in every nation, dislikes the Jews, they must certainly be a defective race.

The Jew responds to these claims one by one: it is true, he says, that there is no specific reference to the next world in the Bible, but one may infer from it that the Hebrew people believed in an afterlife; it is true that plastic arts didn't develop because Judaism forbade them, but many colors are mentioned in the Bible; furthermore, music is highly developed among the Jewish people. The attitude of the Hebrew nation toward art can hardly be denigrated.

However—and this is the main point, says the Jew—all the Russian's claims do not prove anything about the existence of inferior and superior races. All that he has proved is that many people simply do not like Jews: "It is a matter of aesthetics. There can be no objective criterion here. ... it is a matter of taste. I do not deny the existence of races, I do not dispute the fact that there is an Aryan element and a Jewish element, which are fundamentally different from each other. But I think that any attempt to evaluate these two elements, to ascertain which of them is superior and which is inferior, is senseless. I believe that, from an objective point of view, they are both of equal value, and are both equally needed by mankind."[17]

This basic contention of Jabotinsky's shows his views to be in stark contrast to those of the racist philosophers. His liberal world view is clearly expressed in the last lines: in order for mankind to progress, it needs the pluralism of various races, each different from the other, just as a particular society needs pluralism in order to exist and progress. Therefore all elements must be allowed to develop their individual potential, and there must be room for the entire spectrum of opinions that exist in society. Racial and national variety is essential for mankind, just as a variety of personalities and opinions is essential for a specific society, and the disappearance of any nation is a loss for all humanity.

Thus, according to Jabotinsky, there are no objective criteria by which to determine the relative merit of one race as compared to the next. The only criterion is subjective—a matter of taste—what each individual likes. The Russian does not like the Hebrew race, while the Jew, in whose opinion "all nations are equal and of similar merit"[18] loves his people more than others but says, "I do not consider it 'superior.'"[19]

If a discussion of inferior and superior races is insisted upon, it is essential to determine criteria which, though subjective, are still more acceptable than other standards. The Russian's standard is the creative power and the versatility of culture. In contrast, the Jew's—and Jabotinsky's —criterion is the strength of spirit of a given race. "Superior is that race which is solid and firm, that race that may be destroyed but cannot be compelled to go against its will, that same race that even under oppression does not relinquish its inner freedom. From the beginning of our history, we have been a 'a stiff-necked people,' and now too, after so many generations, we are still fighting, we are still rising up, we have still not surrendered. We did not surrender. We are an unvanquishable race. I know no greater nobility than this."[20]

Hence, according to Jabotinsky's subjective taste, the superior race is the stiff-necked, stubborn one, and this characteristic is expressed in its self-consciousness: its feelings of national respect and pride, and its refusal to accept the authority of or to be subdued by an alien ruler. The criterion of self-consciousness is thus identical to the criterion of stubbornness: "Obviously, if we assume that there are superior and inferior races, the superior race must first have self-consciousness. It must have unvanquishable pride, which is expressed obviously not by arrogance, but in the strength of its opinion, in its respect for its spiritual values. Such a race is not suited—nor would the thought ever occur to it—to debase itself and its spirit for an alien principle."[21]

Despite the fact that the criterion of self-consciousness is fundamentally subjective, it is more important than other criteria, in Jabotinsky's opinion, because it withstood the test of history more than others. History proved that ancient races survived primarily because they had "such an awareness [of the spiritual values of their race] that they could withstand many injuries for such a long time without collapsing."[22]

Though subjective, Jabotinsky's self-consciousness test was an empirical one; all the races that survived, first and foremost the Jewish, passed the test. So did the Ukranian nation, which was characterized by a cultural national life power from which it did not deviate and which it guarded zealously.

There was, however, nothing to prevent others from determining different criteria, or to like other races and not those which met the criteria of self-consciousness. And in fact, history showed that the Jewish people was generally disliked, although it was a prime example of a race with a cultural self-consciousness that rejected mastery by foreign elements.

It automatically followed from the above, of course, that no one had the right to draw any conclusions with regard to the fate of different races.

The Individual, the Nation, and Humanity

In "An Exchange of Compliments," Jabotinsky emphasized his liberal views in calling for racial pluralism, an approach echoed in all his articles dealing with race and nationality. It is important to emphasize this point because of the overemphasis placed on another aspect of his thought: the superiority of the nation over humanity.

Jabotinsky explicitly stated in "The Story of My Life": "I believe with complete faith that in the competition between these two [nation and humanity] nation takes precedence. And likewise, the individual [takes precedence] over the nation."[23] It is important to read the entire passage and to understand it within the overall context of Jabotinsky's thought so as not to distort its meaning.

Why, in Jabotinsky's opinion, did the nation take precedence over humanity? Progressive universalism could not exist without nations, just as nations could not exist if the individuals within them were unable to realize their own potential. Jabotinsky did not believe that the future would bring the disappearance of various national cultures into a gargantuan, amorphous "humanity." That point is central to his article "Race." In that article, Jabotinsky reviewed the socialist contention that future mankind would be one race, and separate nations would disappear, being not only unrealistic but also undesirable. The amalgamation of nations necessitated mass assimilation—a surge of intermarriage—that would occur only in the event of mass immigration in all directions, and that was a logistical impossibility. The ideal future society would be quite the opposite of that envisioned by the socialists: "Therefore, when the social order heals, when the economic life is ordered in such a way that each and every citizen has a real right to work, people will not have to seek a means of support abroad. And the moment that all the factors preventing the nations from living in peace disappear, the rationale for emigration will also vanish."[24]

Moreover, Jabotinsky contended, if an organized socialist economy were indeed to arise within a democratic framework, the connection between every citizen and his national culture would be enhanced. In a socialist society, conditions would be less conducive to cultural assimilation. Furthermore, "in this entire vision of the future, there will be no possibility of the assimilation of cultures and their integration, but the contrary; a radiant flowering of original national qualities, an unprecedented flowering, while total peace exists in the world, and the mutual exchange of the products of original national creativity. Happy are those nations that will live to reach those blessed times."[25]

In his early article "A Letter on Autonomy," Jabotinsky had already emphasized that the isolation of a nation within the framework of its own state (or within another framework) was an essential condition for national creativity. Just as the scholar secluded himself during the creative process, so a nation needed seclusion in order to create: "National-spiritual creativity is the *raison d'être* of every people, and if not for the purpose of creativity, it has no reason to exist. For this role, the creative nation needs isolation, seclusion, just like the individual creative personality. And if the nation has not yet expired, its isolation will enable it to create new values, and when it creates them, it will not keep them for itself, but bring them to the common international table for the general weal—and its isolation will be considered as righteousness by mankind."[26]

This concept of national isolation did not mean isolation for its own sake, directed against humanity—as in the case of fascism—but the opposite; the result was a national creativity that was shared with all humanity. In order for mankind to grow and progress, it was imperative for its component nations to develop their own national cultures in conditions of solitude.

Furthermore, Jabotinsky added, creativity that was universal in nature was not possible. A creator was always a person, and every individual (aside from pathological exceptions) had a particular physical, emotional, and racial formula that directly influenced his creation. As Jabotinsky pointed out: "The quality of the 'spiritual mechanism' depends on the race."[27]

It was race that predominantly determined the character of a creation; thus, creativity that lacked the racial-national component was simply not feasible. Since mankind would always be differentiated into cultural-racial types, man would never be without a racial formula. Therefore, creativity not connected to race and nation was impossible. Even if all races were intermingled, and a universal race (as in Jabotinsky's fictional "Tristan da Runha") were created, the identity of any creation would stem from the racial formula of this new race. If such an unrealistic mingling of races were to occur, the benefit to mankind would be highly questionable, since the necessary basis for pluralism and diversity—a diversity of cultural-racial types—would have disappeared. What we do know, said Jabotinsky, is what happened throughout history: the cultural creations of nations that assimilated also came to an end.

Therefore, the inescapable conclusion was that national separateness had to be encouraged in order for national creativity to flourish. It was only in such a way that humanity could progress. "The [preservation of national uniqueness] both benefits and suits the spirit of progress, and is desirable, like all variety in nature."[28] Here Jabotinsky's concept of nation stood in sharp contrast to that of fascism, which emphasized precisely the opposite aspects: the closedness of the nation and the negation of progress as Jabotinsky interpreted it.

Therefore the correct understanding of Jabotinsky's statement that the nation took precedence over humanity is that the existence of races and nations was an essential condition not only for national, but also for universal, creativity and progress.

Furthermore, Jabotinsky believed that the national struggle had to take precedence over the socioeconomic struggle, because abstract, universal, socioeconomic solutions could only be partial since suitable solutions for the social problems of a particular people might be found only within a national framework. Furthermore, without a struggle for national existence, the nation would die sooner or later, and then it would be impossible to revive it. The solutions for the social problems which would be found for members of the defunct nation would not be rooted in their own psychic-racial formula, but rather imposed on them by other nations, in which they would live as individuals. The national struggle therefore could not be delayed, while the socioecomomic solutions might be postponed until after national independence. And in the case of the Jewish people, Jabotinsky said: "It is better, in my opinion, to postpone the economic liberation for a hundred or two hundred years than to die as a nation—for all eternity. But it is not essential."[29]

The last part of Jabotinsky's statement—that "the nation takes precedence [over humanity]. ... and the individual takes precedence over the nation"—is not quite that simple. It was valid when a nation had the conditions necessary for its free development. However, when a nation lacked those conditions and was faced with the danger of annihilation, the issue of self-sacrifice for the nation was equal in importance to that of individual liberty. In "The Revolt of the Old Men," Jabotinsky stated that "the goal of free development of national entities is as important and valuable as the goal of individual liberty ..."[30]

This does not necessarily constitute a contradiction of Jabotinsky's liberal principles, because the stage of attaining national liberation is an existential need. This stage may also be seen as a breakthrough period, which by nature is limited in time. Classical liberalism permitted the infringement upon liberal principles at this stage because it was only a tactical measure that was necessary for the creation of circumstances favorable to liberal ideals. When a man sacrificed his life for the nation, Jabotinsky explained, he did not yield his liberty because he acted voluntarily and for a clear goal: the creation of a national state in which liberalism would be realized.

In summary, Jabotinsky's racial and national theory did not contradict his liberal thinking and in no way resembled mature fascist thought, but constituted an integral part of his liberal thought. The state did not constitute a supreme value, but could help to create the conditions of isolation essential for the creative existence of a race–nation. In contrast to fascism, the nation for Jabotinsky constituted an existential framework for furthering the spiritual, economic, and social creativity of individuals. The primary goal was the development of the individual. This demanded that the race–nation to which he belonged (physically and spiritually) possess the isolation essential for its creative existence. The independent, geographical state was the best solution for this.

A National Minority

We now proceed to a related issue—the problems of a national minority—which was the subject of Jabotinsky's M.A. dissertation in law in 1912. Jabotinsky said that the issue of nationality had two facets: national territory and the national minority.

National territory was defined as "a land or region populated only or primarily by the members of one nationality or, in other words, a land or area in which a particular nationality has an absolute numerical majority."[31] This people would be called the majority, and the land, the national territory. The issues of majority and of national territory were key problems practically until the last quarter of the nineteenth century, and were raised by all nationalist movements of this period. The solution accepted by both politicians and political scientists was that "the supreme legal status of the majority is full self-determination—independence of the national territory."[32] The principle of territorial self-determination solved the problem for majority nations by providing the essential condition for their continued creative existence. They had a framework that distinguished them from other nations—their own independent territory that constituted a state. However, some of the social scientists of the early twentieth century thought differently. They saw the solution for a distinct population as territorial self-determination, locally autonomous but not sovereign—in place of a state, an autonomous district. Even so, the argument over the solution for a majority was only over the degree of desired autonomy, and not over the principle itself of some form of autonomy for the majority.

National majorities were the rule, and minorities the exception; Jabotinsky therefore forbade a solution for the latter at the expense of the former:

As a general rule of nature, it is possible to recognize only a nation which is a majority, and as a basic scheme for granting legal status to a nation—only the autonomy of the national territory. Only when this general principle is established, then and only then, will it be possible to deal with the exceptions, to consider, within the general territorial framework, amendments that will guarantee the rights of extraterritorial minorities. Among the two aspects of the national problem, the first—the question of national territory—is the major and the basic one; the second—the question of national minorities—has value as an addendum and a reform."[33]

For populations where territorial autonomy overlapped, the authority of national bodies was supreme. The real problem, theoretical and practical, was with the minority. Jabotinsky first dealt with this issue systematically in "A Letter on Autonomy," and later wrote about it in his dissertation.

He defined a national minority as follows: "This type of group must be seen only as a minority, because it is impossible to depict it as set apart into a special territorial region. Everywhere that it is possible to create even a small region like this, there must exist some kind of majority with its own national territory, even if it is surrounded on all sides by foreign elements and is cut off from its main national body."[34] Although such a minority might constitute a majority in a particular city, its status as a national minority was not altered. This is an important point because it limited the definition of "national minority" to those who were dispersed throughout the country without being a majority within any territorial region in the state.

Jabotinsky's first problem was: "How is it possible to maintain legal guarantees for a national group that is not in the category of a continuous and united territory, but rather, separate, alien communities which grow scattered within a foreign national field—in short—to minority peoples, in the narrow sense of the term."[35]

The first stage of the solution was to return to the principle of personal law. Parallel to law linked to the territory of a national majority, there had to exist a concurrent set of personal laws based on each individual's national identity. The difficulty with that proposition, however, was that "even if, out of necessity, in this particular case, we accept this principle of terminology [the principal of personal law], we will still be far from a solution to the problem; the more difficult part of the task will remain—to implement the principle of personal law; to establish a binding and lasting system, of extraterritorial rights, in such a way, that there will truly exist, to the extent possible, a guarantee of the national interests of the minority, that will yet be consistent with the existing circumstances in the state."[36]

Jabotinsky, dealt with this issue in his dissertation. At the first stage, the rights or demands of a national minority needed to be determined. There were two basic types of rights. The first, what Jabotinsky called "autonomous national rights," referred to the right of a people to administer its national affairs—those functions that it wished the state to surrender. "To this type belongs 'national self-definition' in its special limited meaning. The nation draws certain boundaries, within which it seeks to function autonomously."[37]

Jabotinsky called the second types of rights "civil national rights," referring to situations where the minority did not demand taking over essential functions from the state, but sought, rather, for the state always to consider the interests of the minority. The minority thus hoped to be properly represented in the various state institutions.

The assumption therefore was that the autonomous rights had to be constructed in such a way that "as large a part as possible of the national functions, specific to its essence, would be arrogated from the territorial authorities (national and local) and transferred to special national institutions."[38] The question remained of how to implement the people's will to live according to its own customs—"to define itself."

Jabotinsky divided this issue into three questions. First, if there was a need for formal organization, what should the legal sign of identity be—if not an objective sign based a racial formula—and how would it be officially registered? Second, what were the collective functions of the minority institutions, how were they defined, and how was authority divided between them and the territorial bodies? Third, what organizational form should the minority take?

Jabotinsky considered invalid two commonly accepted responses to the first question: origin and language. Origin was not enough, he maintained, to determine national identity, since there were people whose family names would indicate a particular origin, yet they saw themselves as a part of a different nation. Nor was language an adequate legal sign, since in many instances there was no overlap between language and national identity (for instance, when the native language was superseded by the language of the conquering power).

The only sign with any legal significance was national consciousness. Jabotinsky's conclusion was that "the only way, therefore, is to grant legal status to national consciousness in the theory of the only juridical sign to national belonging. The question of religious freedom must be resolved in the same manner: by a declaration, explicit or implicit, by the individual himself."[39]

There is no question that Jabotinsky was influenced here by Mazzini, the father of national liberalism. He based his opinions on Mazzini's view that national consciousness was the living soul of nationalism—that territory, origin, and language were insufficient to account for national essence. Here Jabotinsky's views differed absolutely from an integral nationalism based completely on "blood and land."

Jabotinsky proceeded to suggest that in order to give national consciousness the official sanction that was necessary for legal purposes, the individual should be permitted to declare his national identity, which would then be registered in his birth certificate. (Jabotinsky proposed another restriction: the nation with which the individual identified had to consent, but he did not detail how this would be carried out.)

After his declaration, the citizen belonged to a number of associations: his state, district, and city or town, as well as his national association. Obviously, the authority of each had to be defined. This brings us directly to Jabotinsky's second question: which aspects of personal and collective existence should and could be arrogated from the territorial associations (state, local, and city or town) and transferred to the national association, which was the only one based on a personal and not territorial element, and how was this to be done?

From examining current and historcial situations, Jabotinsky concluded that national life should not be limited to culture and language in the limited sense, as was commonly done—a concept he called educational autonomy—but ideally, should include all aspects of personal and collective national life. While this was not possible for a minority, the areas of autonomous national rights should certainly be expanded beyond language and culture.

Jabotinsky based his conclusions on his observations of the activities of existing personal national organizations, both public (e.g. the Serbian National Assembly, the highest organization of the Serbian people in Hungary) and private (e.g. the Polish banking system in Poznan, or "The Jewish Union for Colonization"). These organizations were active in many areas: religious affairs, adult education, health, internal national settlement, national judicial matters, registration of birth certificates and certificates of personal status, imposition of compulsory taxes, and even legislative matters, such as interpreting the state law or making arrangements for national elections.

Jabotinsky found these same functions essential for the self-rule of a national minority: "These are matters of religion, culture and education, public health, social assistance, job placement, and mutual assistance, conduct of immigration and internal or external settlement, registration of civil status, the right to levy taxes."[40]

With regard to national courts, there was a conflict, of course, between judicial authority based on personal status and state law based on territory. In Jabotinsky's view, there were generally no major contradictions among the attitudes of different nations, and the judge could adapt the law of the state to the lifestyle of the national minority. In exceptional cases—primarily in the area of marriage and family—national courts should have jurisdiction. He concluded that national courts had to be established, if only to clarify claims among national minorities, "and the right to act according to national custom and tradition, particularly with regard to questions of marriage and family life."[41]

The question of legislation dealt with the limits of authority and the degree of rule that should be accorded to national bodies in every branch of government. Was the rule determined to be under the authority of the national association to be legislative, or was it to be purely administrative? Jabotinsky's response was unequivocal and antithetical to several accepted views of his time:

> In today's prevailing social conditions there is no room for extra-territorial legislation. It cannot be described, it cannot be implemented. ... It is not the ill will of the majority that frustrates it, but simply, the objective impossibility. If a minority people in a cultured state were given authority with full legislative rights, they would not know which laws to pass for themselves aside from the laws of the land or the district. Because the laws of the land or the district are in their entirety an expression of those objective social and economic conditions in which the entire population of the country lives—including the national minority.[42]

Exceptions were those areas strongly connected with the national ethos, such as family life and religious ritual. The right of the minority's governing body to impose taxes should also not be seen as an attempt at legislation, since the state gave power of attorney to this independent body to act as its representative. In collecting compulsory taxes—an act with legal authority—the national body was acting as the representative of the state, and not of the race–nation. Jabotinsky's conclusion is of utmost importance:

> Therefore, even the word "autonomy" is not appropriate, since its meaning, whether linguistically or in customary political usage, is the right of independent legislation. Autonomy applies to a region, to national majorities. One can really speak only of "national self-rule" with regard to a minority people. ... The self-rule of a national minority can be expressed only in its right to establish and maintain, within the framework of its concrete legal authority, suitable institutions and bodies; to set down rules and instructions for them; to purchase and appropriate property; and to levy the needed taxes. That is—everything that is objectively possible in regard to autonomous-national rights for a minority.[43]

Since legislation was outside the authority of the national minority, the minority could not be considered to have autonomy, but only self-rule.

In response to his third question, Jabotinsky suggested a simple arrangement regarding the organization of the national institutions. First, he said, the members of any particular nationality living within a particular city or village constituted a legal-public unit called a national congregation. The congregation would choose institutions through which it would realize its rights for national self-rule. Second, the sum total of the national minority all over the state, would be one unit

> headed by a representative body, an assembly of national representatives or national authorities, bearing all the autonomous national rights of the minority people. It organizes the different communities, determines their realms of authority; supervises their activities, establishes (if necessary) regional unions of the communities and their institutions. It determines the method of election for all the national elections: for community councils, for regional conferences, for authorities. It imposes a compulsory tax for general national needs, while allowing the communities to collect taxes for local national needs. It sets general principles, which are binding on all national institutions: lower and high educational bodies, public health, economic, settlement, and the like and in particular a curriculum and language of teaching in the schools, and also an office language for national institutions and bodies. Its establishes schools of higher learning, including all types of higher central national institutions, and allocates stipends for local community institutions. It approves the budget; chooses an actions committee for the nation; supervises its activity and examines its balance books. It determines the method and the date of its convention, its location, and its internal arrangements.[44]

The organizational model suggested by Jabotinsky was a combination of a local house of representatives (which parallels what we call local government) whose representatives were chosen by the members of the minority residing in that particular city or town, and a supreme house of representatives (which parallels a central government) whose representatives were chosen by all the members of the minority living in the state. This body established a kind of executive authority which was responsible to it. It should be noted that this supreme house of representatives did not have legislative authority.

The affairs of the minority were conducted by its independent governing body in its national tongue, and it was permissible for the national tongue to be the language of instruction in its schools. The ideal solution for taxation was that the state allocate a certain amount—to be determined by set criteria—for the national minority from the taxes it collected. Any additional needs could be covered by supplementary taxes collected by the supreme house of representatives, acting as the representative of the state.

The schools, courts, and other local institutions had the same rights as other state institutions.

After defining a national minority, Jabotinsky defined how the identity of a citizen within a particular nation was determined; explored the areas in which a national minority had autonomous right; and named the institutions through which it realized these rights. Two issues still remained to be dealt with: the relationship between the national minority and the territorial association in which it resided, and the relationship between the national minority and its majority nucleus (the area or territory in which the members of that nation constituted a majority). The assumption was that most racial-national minorities were the racial-national majority somewhere in the world, and thus, somewhere, had their own geographic territory. From this point of view, the Jews—who lacked a land or a state in which they constituted a majority—were exceptional.

According to Jabotinsky, the relationship between the state and the minority—in both the territorial association and the personal association—was determined according to the following principle:

> Each one has its own sovereign area and there are no common mandatory functions. The governing responsibilities are divided in such a fashion that the state is permanently free of the duties that were handed over to the nation. Responsibility for education in its broadest sense is given to the national authority; the state provides the appropriate funds, keeping only general supervisory duties. It is the same with everything else. The national authority is a kind of state authority for all matters included in national self-rule, but an authority whose prerogatives cannot be abolished, and having unlimited, all-encompassing powers. The basic law of the state must determine that neither the central nor the regional authorities have power to legislate laws that infringe upon the rights of the national minority. Christian national institutions ... are considered like those of the state, and have the same rights as state institutions.[45]

The state obviously had every right to offer the minority nation its own competing services (e.g. educational institutions). However, these could not come at the expense of the budget that it was obligated to provide the national body for it to establish and maintain its own institutions.

The same principle had to guide the relationship between the minority community and the city or town, and between the regional authority of the state and the minority residing within the region.

Jabotinsky rejected the claim that the minority must have representation in the representative bodies of the state in which the majority nucleus of the nation lived. He believed that normal relations could be effected only through treaties by which it would be possible to coordinate activities and to exchange services. In other words, minority institutions had to have the right to make official agreements in areas of their jurisdiction with other public-legal bodies, and with the government of the state in which their majority nucleus resided.

We have seen that the issue of national minorities had to be solved according to the principle of self-rule, not autonomy, because the minority governing bodies lacked legislative authority. The law of the land was passed by state institutions and applied to its entire territory. The minority was organized as a personal, public-legal organization, as distinct from territorial, and by means of its own institutions actualized the rights of national self-government in the areas within its authority. It had no legislative powers, however, aside from the authority of the national court, and it functioned within the framework of the state law and sometimes as the representative of the state law.

"A Letter on Autonomy" deals with autonomy as a solution for the Jews in the various countries of Europe. Since this essay was composed before Jabotinsky had thoroughly researched the question of national minorities, he still used the term *autonomy* as a national cultural concept, in the sense used by European Jewish thinkers, and not *self-rule*, which he later considered the appropriate term. We shall deal with the question of self-rule for the Jews in the countries in which they were a minority in our discussion of Jabotinsky's Zionist thought.

We must also point out that Jabotinsky generally rejected self-rule for Jewish minorities. The isolated economic and religious corners that the Jews had created were disappearing as a result of economic changes and of the Enlightenment. Moreover, the Jewish minority had no majority nucleus in any territory; therefore such a solution as the isolation that would permit national creativity was nonexistent. This combination of circumstances had brought about a situation where, in the absence of a state in which they constituted a majority, solutions of self-rule to preserve the Jewish race were inadequate. Moreover, the very success of Jewish self-government would be likely to bring about a wave of mixed marriage which would threaten to destroy the Jewish race.

Jabotinsky dealt with this issue in 1906 when he was one of the main formulators of the Helsingfors Program, which he saw, he said, as the "climax of my Zionist youth."[46] The program tried to give a comprehensive answer to the issue of the character and parameters of national self-definition for the Jewish people in Russia, but Jabotinsky saw it also as relating to the universal question of self-definition for minorities.

The problems that disturbed the participants were: "Is there no contradiction between the ideal and this program,? How is it possible to reconcile the idea of creating a territorial refuge for the people of Israel in a land across the sea with their present struggle for minority rights while in exile? All were unanimous that it is necessary and possible to combine these two elements. However, how does one express the internal affinity between them? There are two points of view on this issue."[47]

One approach maintained that, even after the historical ideal was realized and a state with a Jewish majority was established, many Jews would remain in the diaspora. Though many Jews would be left in minority enclaves, one positive aspect to this approach was that Jewish culture would retain influence throughout the world. The continued existence of Judaism in the diaspora, however, also depended on the creation of a national territory that would be a workshop for the culture of Israel, and with which all Jews in the diaspora would be connected.

Regarding those Jews who would remain as national minorities in the diaspora, the Helsingfors Program proposed:

1) the democratization and liberalization of state governments, with special emphasis on the issue of equal rights without regard for religion, nationality, or sex and 2) national self-definition for the Jews: "There they will speak about a national assembly, about self-rule of the communities, of the 'right to use the national tongue and the language spoken in schools in official institutions and in community life,' the right to exchange Sunday rest for Sabbath rest."[48]

At this state of his Zionist activity, Jabotinsky grudgingly accepted the idea that simultaneous action was needed on both fronts: the establishment of a state with a Jewish majority, and the struggle for Jewish national self-definition in every country in which they were a minority. But even at this point, Jabotinsky thought that national autonomy in exile would be primarily a means "to organize the whole people with the help of the official governments ... and what will the people do once they are organized? The same things that the late Herzl wanted to arrange through a private organization: to realize the return to Zion."[49]

And in fact, as we saw in "A Letter on Autonomy," Jabotinsky claimed that the entire effort had to be focused on the main goal—self-definition in a national territory—as a result of the aforementioned unique character of the problem of the Jews.

It is likely that, at the end of his life, Jabotinsky would have said that after the establishment of a Jewish state, the solution for Jewish minorities around the world could be self-rule, with treaties linking these enclave governments to the Jewish state. The Jews were therefore an exception, to whom the conclusions in "Self-Rule for a National Minority" could apply only once the Jewish people had its own national territory.

Jabotinsky's views on a solution for the minority problem as stated in "Self-Rule for a National Minority" must be seen as definitive not only because it was his most comprehensive and basic essay on this topic, but also because it incorporated his aspects of universalist theory. Therefore, in our discussion of his Zionist thought, we shall clarify whether his ideas on the issue of an Arab national minority in a Jewish state were consistent with his advocacy of self-rule for a national minority.

The Arab National Movement

Most of Jabotinsky's examples of the universal phenomenon of nationalism drew on Europe, both because that was where many nineteenth-century nationalist movements arose, and because during his many trips to Europe, he saw history in the making. Furthermore, he had studied the subject in Vienna in 1907, when "Austria ... was a living school for studying 'the problem of nationalities.'"[50] He was well-acquainted with the nationalist problem in Turkey, where he had lived as a journalist. While he dealt less with non-European nationalist movements and knew less about them, his approach to them was the same.

Because of its importance, we shall bring as an example Jabotinsky's attitude to the Arab nationalist movements. A distinction must be drawn among three concepts he used: easternness, Islam, and Arab nationalism. In two articles, "The East" (1926), and "The Arabesque Fashion" (1927), he attempted to define the concept "east" and concluded that the "east" was not a term that defined actual nations and cultures in the East, but rather a retarded state in cultural development, a stage that Europe went through in the Middle Ages:

> The elements called eastern in the lives of those undeveloped nations are not unique to the East. Everything that people like to call "an eastern personality"—the serenity, the fatalism, the loving tolerance for punishment without considering the possibility of reforming the world by shedding the traditions—the tyranny of the patriarch, the landlord, the sheikh, the government—even when it sometimes wears the garb of benign paternalism; the effendi attitude to women which brings about the harem system, opposition to free investigation and to criticism; none of this is an Eastern monopoly, but Europe underwent all of this in the Middle Ages in practically the same way. And that is the root of the problem. Practically the entire way of life considered to be characteristic of the East has nothing to do with the soul of a people, but simply with a particular stage in the development of all people. What is called "east" in its cultural sense is nothing but retarded Middle Ages. And if they start to rid themselves of the Middle Ages—as we see happening today in Turkey—they free themselves of the "East."[51]

Jabotinsky repeated these same ideas in "The East," adding that the sooner Eastern elements disappeared from the countries in which they existed, the better it would be for those countries: "And so it will be, in my opinion, among all the Eastern countries; their national characteristics, the eternal essence of every nation will be preserved. But the "Eastern" element must and will disappear. And the quicker it disappears, the better—yes, the better—for them."[52]

Jabotinsky saw moral and educational aspects in the religion of Islam. However, as he wrote in the essay "Islam" (1925)—and in contrast to other views of his time—he did not see the pan-Islamic movement as a real political power. He opposed the view that Islamic religious zealotry blended with and even superseded national zealotry, bringing many historical examples to show that Moslem Arab nations fought one another, did not help one another, and often cut deals with non-Moslem nations. Moslem unity, about which they spoke so much, was illusory:

> And the conclusion is very simple. Two hundred million people or more believe in Islam. However, Islam as a unifying factor in international relations doesn't exist in reality. It is possible to destroy a Christian country and the other Christian people will remain neutral all the while their own economic interests aren't jeopardized. It is the same today as one hundred years ago, it is possible to bring about a serious conflict with a Moslem nation without concern about involvement by the pan-Islamic movement. Islam, like every other religion, has a high moral level and is a most positive educational element. However, we are not talking about that. As a straw man of political danger—which is how they are now trying to present it—Islam simply does not exist.[53]

What Jabotinsky said about Islam from a political point of view also applied to Christianity. World Christianity also could be seen as a political movement; political covenants were determined according to mutual interest and not common religious background, which had long ceased to be a unifying political force. Jabotinsky also maintained that a large number of Islamic countries were militarily weak, not because they had no talent for war, but because modern warfare demanded modern technology and tremendous resources: "I am not writing this in order to denigrate the Arabs or to mock them. I do not question their military attributes. Even if Leonides himself with his friends were in their place, the result would be similar. Today war is a scientific and financial matter; it is not determined by the strength of backward peoples."[54]

He did not underestimate the Arab nation. True, in his essay "Merchants of Culture" (1927), in which he argued against the thesis that Jews in the Middle Ages were mere merchants who passed on culture from place to place, he questioned whether the cultural revival of the Middle Ages was brought about by the Arabs. But it should be noted that his critique was not based on ideological grounds: "the location of this revival was in the Arab countries. However, the location itself is not proof. One of the most famous proofs is that the famous 'Moorish' architecture of Spain was almost entirely the work of Greek architects, just as the famous 'Russian' churches in Moscow were built by Italian artisans."[55] In other words, Jabotinsky questioned the authenticity of part of what was considered to be national Arab creativity, just as he questioned the authenticity of part of what was considered Russian creativity.

Jabotinsky's clearest evaluation of Arab nationalism may be found in his essay, "On the Iron Wall: We and the Arabs" (1923). Because there are different interpretations of his opinions on this issue, let us quote him exactly. He says of the Arabs of the Land of Israel: "For the Arabs of the Land of Israel, *Eretz Yisrael* would still remain not a border region but their homeland, a center and a basis for *their independent national existence.*"[56]

And again: "As long as the Arabs have even the slightest hope of in their hearts of getting rid of us, there are no sweet words nor appealing promises in the world for which they will be willing to surrender that hope—and this is precisely because *they are not rabble, but a living nation.*"[57]

Jabotinsky clearly saw the Arabs of the Land of Israel as a living nation that wanted its own state—one with all the characteristics of any other. Not only did he not denigrate the Arabs of *Eretz Yisrael*; on the contrary, it was clear to him that they saw the Land of Israel as their homeland and would be ready to sacrifice their lives on the altar of this faith. Specifically because he saw them as a living people, he concluded that it would be impossible to reach an immediate agreement with them. The demand of the Jews as a nation over the territory called *Eretz Yisrael* conflicted with the demands of the nation made up of the Arabs of that same piece of earth.

Of the Arabs outside of the Land of Israel, Jabotinsky said: "Arab nationalism set for itself the same goals that Italian nationalism aspired to before 1870: unity and political independence. The meaning of these aspirations is the eradication of every memory of British influence in Egypt and in Mesopotamia, the expulsion of the Italians from Tripoli, the removal of France from Russia—and later certainly from Tunisia, Algeria, and Morocco as well."[58]

In this chapter, we have examined the connections that Jabotinsky drew between a population's racial makeup and its national definition; we have heard his unequivocal denial of the existence of superior and inferior races; we have seen his interrelation of the individual, the race, the nation, and humanity; finally, we have glimpsed the intricate governmental structures that he proposed in an attempt to justly and peacefully weave together, into one geographic state, a myriad of races, interests, and nationalities. Though often idiosyncratic, even iconoclastic, Jabotinsky has clearly extrapolated each of these political philosophies from fundamental, liberal-democratic beliefs. If we are to retain any lesson from the political philosopher that Jabotinsky was, let it be this very process of extrapolation—that a basic belief in freedom and representation must and will mould itself to fit the political reality of the day. The alternative—inflexibility—invariably condemns a political philosophy to obsolescence and an early grave, as so many in what was once the communist world have recently and harshly experienced.

In the second part of the book, we shall examine whether, in his Zionist thought as well, Jabotinsky succeeds in remaining faithful to his liberal-democratic outlook.

Part II

ZIONIST THOUGHT

Chapter 1

THE JEWISH NATION
AND RACE

Jabotinsky came to Zionism neither through a Jewish way of life, nor through the influence of Ahad Ha'am, Herzl, or Nordau. As he related in "The Story of My Life":

> I learned to be a Zionist from the gentiles. I spent the best years of my youth in Rome and I understood the Italians very well. Italy was a pleasant and free country at the end of the nineteenth century—liberal, peace loving, without a shadow of chauvinism—just a country of Italians, in which practically all the Italians in the world lived together, and they were practically one hundred percent of all the citizens, and they didn't harm anyone and didn't oppress anyone. "So every nation should live," I said to myself, "and also we, the Jews."[1]

Jabotinsky first witnessed Jewish ghetto life in 1898 while traveling from Odessa to Berne to study, and during trips over the next three years from vacation in Odessa back to Rome. He wrote of his first encounter with the ghetto:

> I traveled by way of Podolia and Galicia, in third class, obviously, and in a train which crawled slowly and stopped at every town. Jews entered the car at every station, day and night, and I heard more Yiddish between Rasdelnaja and Vienna than I had ever heard before. I didn't understand everything, but the impression I got was strong and depressing. There in the train I had my first contact with the ghetto, with my own eyes I witnessed its paleness and its lowliness, I heard its slavish humor which contented itself with "nullifying" the strong enemy instead of rebelling. ... Now, in my old age, I know how to disclose, underneath the mask of suplication and mockery, also shadows of pride and courage. Then I did not know how to, then I lowered my head, and silently asked myself— are these our people?[2]

These sights made a deep impression on Jabotinsky. In what he called "my first Zionist speech" during a meeting of students with Nahum Syrkin in

Berne in 1898, he said: "I am a unquestionably a Zionist, because the Jewish people is a very bad people, their neighbors hate them, and they are right. Its fate in the exile will be a general 'Bartholomew Night,' and its sole salvation is general immigration to the Land of Israel."[3] During the remainder of his stay in Rome, however, Jabotinsky did not get involved nor express any interest in Zionism, although he already knew that he would dedicate his life to it.

When he left Rome in 1901, he became a sought-after journalist, sometimes writing Zionist articles. His real association with Zionism, however, dated back to his offer in 1903 to organize self-defense efforts as a result of rumors of impending pogroms. His involvement quickly intensified, and he was chosen as a delegate of the *Eretz Israel* Zionist circle to the Sixth Zionist Congress. He was 24 years old, and from then until his death in 1940 at the age of sixty, Zionist thought and activity were the focal point of his life.

From the beginning, Jabotinsky was aware of the need for a theory of Zionism that explained why the Jewish people needed an autonomous national territory in which it would constitute a majority, and why this territory had to be the Land of Israel and not another place, such as Uganda, for example. Likewise, he was disturbed by the absence of self-respect among the Jewish masses in the *galuth*, as well as by what he saw as self-contempt; in contradistinction to the ghetto Jew, he set up as an ideal what he saw as the image of the model Jew. In his early Zionist thinking—i.e. in the period from 1903 to 1913—he tried to develop a theory of Jewish race and nationality that would address the gamut of questions that preoccupied him: What were the characteristics of the Jewish race and nation? What effect did the exile have on them, and how was it possible to restore their lost self-respect and pride, both as a people and as individuals? Why did the Jewish people need a homeland, and why did this homeland have to be the Land of Israel?

Jabotinsky began to formulate his thought while defending Zionism from its critics; he continued to develop and amend his theory on the relationship between the Jewish nation and the Land of Israel, and in 1913 presented a distinct theory of the Jewish nation and race, from which he never subsequently wavered.

During a later period—1926 to 1940—he reinforced particular aspects of his concept of nation, race, and national territory, adding as well new arguments, but making no substantial changes. As part of this discussion, he also dealt with the essence and function of the Jewish religion.

Although Jabotinsky's discovery of Zionism came about through his encounter, during his years in Rome and later in Vienna, with the phenomenon of nationalism, his first articles on national problems (from 1903 to 1906) dealt with the Jewish nation, and included elements that were absent from his general political theory. His key articles on nation and race were written at the end of this period of early Zionist thought ("Self-Rule for a National Minority" in 1912, and "Race" in 1913), and his specific outlook on Jewish nation and race both influenced and was influenced by the development of his general theoretical outlook.

The Jewish Nation, the National Territory, and the Jewish Race

Jabotinsky developed his first theory of Jewish nationhood in response to critics of Zionism (primarily Kaotsky and Izgoyev—whom he respected— and Bickerman, whom he considered inconsequential). Each of them published articles in 1903 criticizing Zionism. Without going into the details of their respective philosophies (which to a large degree contradicted each other), it may be said that the main questions that Jabotinsky responded to were these: Have the Jews ceased to exist as a nation, due to the absence of a national territory for so many years? Were nationalism and Zionism reactionary, separatist movements? Was Jewish culture itself reactionary? Was it possible to create a state artificially? Finally, was Zionism indeed basically a movement that arose in response to a negative impetus—anti-Semitism?

Jabotinsky attempted to answer these questions logically and scientifically. His first premise was that "Racial-nationalist characteristics are created under the influence of many factors—among them, obviously, climate, land, and the flora of the land in which the people of whom we are speaking originally developed. ... Even under alien skies, and even after many generations, one may discern in the descendants the racial purity of their fathers' fathers."[4]

This premise, then widely accepted, was utilized by Kaotsky himself, who saw the Jewish psychology as the result of the mountainous character of the Land of Israel. According to Jabotinsky, the characteristics of a race-nation (at this stage he did not distinguish between the two) were determined by the geographic qualities of the land in which the nation had come into being, and did not disappear even when the nation lived in a foreign country over a period of years—as long as it was careful not to assimilate.

From this proposition, Jabotinsky concluded that the absence of a Jewish national territory for so many years had not destroyed the Jewish nation-race; instead, it had guarded the purity of Jewish culture. In the same positivistic argumentation, he concluded moreover that the socialist dream would not put an end to individual nations, but would effect quite the opposite; in the absence of economic motivation for immigration (and therefore assimilation), the individuality of each nation would be strengthened. In Jabotinsky's opinion, the continued existence of nations was not only logical and inevitable, but desirable. National uniqueness was an essential condition for the advancement of humanity, which needed the pluralism of different cultures in order to develop. Thus Zionism, as a national movement, was not reactionary; rather, it served, as did all national movements, to propel human advancement. In summary, Jabotinsky said: "The hopes of the honorable writers that national differences are destined to disappear have, as I tried to explain, nothing on which to base themselves, neither scientifically nor morally; on the contrary, they confute, with amazing clarity, the ethnological data and the historical processes, as well as the best interests of mankind."[5]

Significantly, Jabotinsky added that the cultural rebirth to which Zionism aspired should not be construed as a return to the ancient Jewish way of life, but rather as the development of a new culture rooted in an ancient one. Far from being reactionary, Jewish tradition and culture were progressive, and not limited to ritual laws such as the separation between meat and dairy dishes (which in Jabotinsky's opinion were a minor aspect). Central to Judaism, he said, were those "fundamental ideals which are permeated with principles of fraternity and social justice"[6] that were found in the spiritual creations of the Jewish people for forty generations. The Jewish culture contributed a great deal to the development of Western culture, and primarily to its continual sense of striving for progress. Jabotinsky repeated this argument over and over again throughout his life.[7]

In response to the criticism that Zionism sought to create a state artificially, Jabotinsky responded that Zionism had two central principles: mass immigration to a specific territory, and a guarantee for self-rule in that territory; these were among the identifying signs of all historical mass immigrations from which countries had evolved.

Jabotinsky's sharp argument against Kaotsky and Izgoyev was that they failed to use their analytical tools with regard to the Jews. Their basic premise as historical materialists was that historical events are impelled by causes; in all cases they looked for such. However, they did not relate to the history of the Jewish people

> as the struggle of a small people deprived of a land, which, for almost two thousand years, has fought for its national uniqueness, what is most amazing is that in this struggle all possible imaginable advantages tipped the scale in favor of conversion, and, nevertheless—conversion did not take place. ... [They ignore the phenomenon] which under no circumstances may be ignored, or act as if this defense of holy places and shrines over a period of two thousand years did not originate at all from a real imperative, but was almost the result of an error, of human folly. And now people have become wiser and they must prove that there is nothing to struggle for. ... It is not likely that Mr. Kaotsky and Mr. Izgoyev will fail to understand that such an outlook not only lacks the

strict scientific approach which generally characterizes their school, but doesn't approach scientific thought at all.[8]

The absence of a scientific explanation for "the Jewish phenomenon" was not accidental in Jabotinsky's opinion, but stemmed from the fact that the problem of nationalities had not yet been analyzed in scientific detail, something about which historic materialism was particularly negligent.

Jabotinsky said that Zionism also lacked a scientific theoretical basis. However:

> We all understand very well that in a scheme of the theoretical basis of Zionism, anti-Semitism and the *judennot* [the particular troubles of the Jews] are destined to play a very minor role. One may anticipate that this scheme will be something like this: every national-racial group naturally aspires to complete originality in all forms and manners of its economic way of life; the likelihood of assimilation rouses it to opposition and to war over its national preservation; this urge for national preservation brought about the fact that, with the loss of the *natural* means of isolation—the national territory—the Jewish people was forced to fence itself in *artificially* against the danger of mingling with other peoples by constructing the wall of religious dogma; now, after the economic-social circumstances of the new era destroyed the ghetto, and the culture which burst into it brought an end to dogma, and thus the *artificial* wall which had kept the Jewish people from assimilating among foreigners, toppled—this same urge for national preservation impels it to seek the revival of a *natural* means of isolation, that is, of an autonomous national territory, in order to guarantee the Jewish uniqueness comprehensive, complete liberty for all eternity for an original socio-economic way of life.[9]

This section is reprinted here in its entirety because Jabotinsky repeated this theme constantly, explaining the economic occupations of the Jews in exile, as well as the role of religion and the ghetto, as substitutes for the true isolator: a national homeland. A number of years later, in "An Exchange of Compliments" (1911), Jabotinsky maintained that the stubbornness of the Jews was a fundamental characteristic of the nation, and an important component of its national psyche. At a later stage of his thought, he insisted in 1937 that the struggle of the Jewish people to preserve its identity—and its success in not being swallowed up by its environment during the entire period of its exile—was a direct result of being "a stiff-necked," that is, a stubborn, people.[10]

However, as early as 1903, Jabotinsky had formulated comprehensive answers to critical questions regarding the character of the Jewish people and its nationalist movement, Zionism. The Jewish people, he said, continued to exist despite the fact that it had lived in the diaspora over a long period of time, lacking a national territory; this was because the Jewish racial-national uniqueness that crystallized in those countries to which Jews had first emigrated had managed to survive the destructive forces of assimilation. Jewish culture and tradition were progressive by nature since their most important elements were the ethical ideals of the Bible, and not the ritual customs that took shape in the exile in order to preserve the isolation of the Jewish people. It was indeed possible to create a state in an artificial manner; the Jews' search for a national territory at that stage of their history was a direct result of their healthy desire to preserve their national uniqueness by creating a framework for national isolation—an autonomous, national territory. After the elimination of the substitute isolators that had existed in the diaspora—the ghetto walls, the isolated, "Jewish" economy, and the rigid religious customs of Judaism—the Jewish nation naturally sought out a new framework for isolation. Zionism, like all nationalist movements, was the antithesis of reaction; it was a part of the struggle for the advancement of mankind. This rationale addresses Jabotinsky's first question—why the Jewish people needed an autonomous national homeland—but gives no answer to the second—why, specifically, must it be the Land of Israel? To this question he provided a comprehensive response some two years later.

Searching for a rational, scientific theory to explain Zionism, Jabotinsky developed a similar theory regarding the relationship between the Jewish nation and the Land of Israel. In his article "Zionism and the Land of Israel" (1905), he maintained that many Zionist groups identified the Jewish people with the Land of Israel in a vague and unscientific manner. Their willingness to view a Jewish homeland in the Land of Israel as a beautiful but non-essential dream made it possible for them to consider settling in another territory. Jabotinsky was not satisfied. The time had come, he said, "to explain that the connection between Zionism and Zion is not simply a matter of strong instinct for us which cannot be extirpated, but also a justified and weighty conclusion, emanating from purely positive considerations."[11]

If the yearning for Zion was not a romantic, historical whimsy, upon what was it then based? Jabotinsky maintained that no movement could sway the masses and continue to exist unless it reflected the collective will of the people. Relying largely on contemporary scientific theories which dealt with the analysis of history, Jabotinsky stated that existing circumstances in every period created a single will of the people that could not be changed, just as the reality that created it could not be changed. This will was not revealed supernaturally or by referendum, but rather through the perception of the geniuses of that generation. Indeed, it was made manifest to Herzl, who, even when he proposed Uganda as a national homeland, never abandoned the idea of an eventual Return to Zion. Though often persuaded by the geniuses of his time, Jabotinsky preferred to reveal the will of the people through the study of its history:

> The past lays down steel tracks for the future: if the journey of any movement left these tracks—it would fall and be destroyed. Any new stream in the life of the people must directly draw on its past: if the same fundamental motives run, like a scarlet thread, underneath the colorful events, at all times and in every place, these motives must absolutely also be found in the new stream—for if not, the new movement will not stand on a solid foundation. ... Or, when we shall be as familiar as possible with the main slogans of the people's will, which always are revealed in the different and strange events in a nation's history, we shall know with certainty if the new movement's program suits these slogans of eternity—that is, whether it emanates directly from the previous historical process or tends to deviate from the path that was set in advance by the past, and to leave the tracks.[12]

The next step thus was to locate, through analysis of the history of the Jewish exile, that which had been the driving force in the life of the disparate Jewish nation. According to Jabotinsky's analysis, the history of the Jewish people was a continuous refrain of the same tune: a community of Jews surrounded by hostile strangers who made specific demands which the Jewish community refrained from fulfilling.

"If the history of the exile is the attempt by a community of people to safeguard a treasure—what is the holy treasure that it guards with such obstinacy, and the cleaving to it, which, apparently, is the basic motivation for the whole history of this people without a land?"[13] According to Jabotinsky, it was naïve to believe that the Jewish religion was the treasure that the Jews protected in the exile. If this were indeed so, exiled Jews would have continued to develop their religion, just as they did in the Land of Israel, rather than zealously guarding it against any evolution. Jabotinsky saw all Jewish religious thought in the exile as "a barren web of glosses on glosses on glosses."[14] The religion remained like stagnant water; Judaism had stopped changing and improving since the time the people was exiled from its land. Moreover, religious thought was channeled into the preservation of the status quo. Jabotinsky's conclusion was harsh:

> Thus Judaism died; because something that doesn't develop is considered dead, even if a spark of life is hidden in its core. ... It actually died the same moment that Israel became a people without a land and started its heroic history of two thousand years of suffering for its holy treasure. If Judaism were that holy treasure, the people would have irrigated it with life-giving waters and would have enjoyed its growth and development, like before their exile. However, if the people voluntarily encased their religious consciousness within a iron frame, dried it out to the point of fossilization, and turned a living religion into something like a mummified corpse of religion—it is clear that the holy

treasure is not the religion, but something else, something for which this mummified corpse was supposed to serve as a shell and protection.[15]

This was a natural extension of Jabotinsky's concept of the function of religion in the *galuth*: a substitute for the necessary, natural isolator of a national homeland. Religion in the diaspora created a rigid, isolated corner in which the Jewish nation could continue to exist; Jabotinsky quoted the historian M. Margolin, who wrote in 1900 that "as a result of the destruction of Jewish political organization, national defense could take only a religious form."[16] In other words, religion was not the treasure the Jewish people had guarded during the years of its exile, but rather was itself the watchman over the treasure of national uniqueness. Since the function of religion was to guard Jewish uniqueness from foreign influences, it was necessary to interpret it in a fashion that would erect a variety of barriers between the Jews and their cultural surroundings.

Jabotinsky emphasized that a religion that fulfilled such a complicated function had to be strong. Out of respect, Jabotinsky attempted not to detract from religion, but it is clear that his interpretation of Judaism as a "watchman" and not a "treasure" affected his view of the function of religion once the state of the Jews was established.

Let us return to the central question under discussion. It became clear from the study of the history of the exile that "the fundamental motive of all the activities of the people without a land, Israel, was the struggle for the national uniqueness. ... We have reached the main question under controversy. What is the Jewish national uniqueness?"[17]

Jabotinsky presented a para-scientific answer based on an "environmental theory" about the identity between the people of Israel with the Land of Israel. Jabotinsky was influenced here by the theory of the English historian Henry Thomas Buckle, whose "environmental theory" was widespread among the Russian intelligentsia in the second half of the nineteenth century. According to this theory, the primary characteristics of a nation were fashioned by the geographic and climatic conditions of the territory in which the nation was created. In that spirit, Jabotinsky said that the physical and spiritual characteristics of the various nations were determined primarily by "the natural environment ... the scenery of the homeland, the climate of the homeland, the flora of the homeland, and the winds of the homeland. The psychic structure of the people is created solely by natural causes; the social causes add only secondary features, which are quickly erased under pressure of new social conditions."[18]

In contrast to the historic-materialist school (according to which people and society were fashioned primarily by socioeconomic factors), Jabotinsky held that characteristics of race were determined by the natural factors that were endemic to the land in which the race came into being.

These characteristics remained all the while the race existed. Other factors —such as economic conditions, social structure, and development of knowledge—influenced race, but were subject to change, and could not alter the fundamental stamp left by the nature of the homeland.

The architect of the Jewish nation-race was therefore the Land of Israel in the geographic sense—its climate, flora, and the like:

> Therefore, the true kernel of our national uniqueness is the pure product of the Land of Israel. We did not exist before we came to the Land of Israel. The Hebrew people was created from the fragments of other peoples on the soil of the Land of Israel. We grew up in the Land of Israel; on it we became citizens; we strengthened the belief in one God; we breathed in the winds of the land, and in our struggles for independence and sovereignty, its air enwrapped us and the grain that its land produced sustained us. In the Land of Israel the ideas of our prophets were developed and in the Land of Israel the "Song of Songs" was first heard. Everything Hebrew in our midst was given to us by the Land of Israel. Anything else in us is not Hebrew. Israel and the Land of Israel are one. There we were born as a people and there we developed.[19]

Jabotinsky adopted the atavistic view that the formative characteristics of a race were preserved indefinitely, even if foreign elements "encased" these features like husks. The development of the nation-race was possible, therefore, only under those natural conditions in which the nation was born. Only in the birthplace of the race could its fundamental characteristics be renewed and develop. Jabotinsky presented this concept, with all its implications, in saying: "Another climate, other flora, other mountains would certainly distort the body and the soul that were created by the climate, the flora, and the mountains of the Land of Israel; for the racial body and the racial soul are nothing but the product of a particular combination of natural factors, and to implant a special racial uniqueness in another natural environment means dooming it to destroy its own form and to assume a new—alien—form."[20]

Hence, the only way for the people of Israel in exile to preserve its national uniqueness was quite simply to preserve the pure uniqueness of the Land of Israel. Since only a return to the Land of Israel would make possible the development of the Jewish people, the natural will of the people was unquestionably to return to its native land. It followed that only a Jewish national movement which understood and harnessed this collective will could enlist the masses and persevere until its goal was attained.

A national Jewish movement that did not comprehend the identification by the Jewish people with the Land of Israel would not succeed. For unless the masses joined the movement and immigrated to the territory, the Jewish state would not be established. The Jewish masses would not stream anywhere but to the Land of Israel; they would not be prepared for the prolonged effort involved in the establishment of a state in any area other than the Land of Israel. According to this argument, if the national movement chose Uganda, a Jewish state would not arise in Uganda because it would fail to attract the masses. Thus any territory other than the Land of Israel would not be a second-best alternative—it would be no alternative at all.

Jabotinsky bolstered this argument with pragmatic political considerations, which, nonetheless, remained secondary to his atavistic theory, that was the linchpin of the claim. His primary pragmatic political contention was that some 80,000 Jews were already living in the Land of Israel; the percentage of Jews living in the Land of Israel was greater than in any other country. Thirty *moshavot* (private farming villages) already existed there, as did a bank with several branches, some private lands, and even industrial works. Jabotinsky maintained that all of these institutions would strengthen the Jewish claim to the Land of Israel in international diplomatic discussions.[21]

At this early stage in the evolution of his Zionist thought, Jabotinsky based his answer to the question "why specifically the Land of Israel?" on an atavistic notion because it gave him an absolutely clear response to what was then considered a scientific issue. However, it appears that, even at this stage, he recognized the weakness of this claim, and that it was open to attack from many sides. The very foundation of the claim—that physical and spiritual characteristics were influenced by natural factors—was subject to scientific criticism. There were also logical breaches in the theory. For example: why did other nations that arose in the Land of Israel not also originate spiritual creations? It is because of these doubts, perhaps, that Jabotinsky ended his article "Zionism and the Land of Israel" by saying:

> And after these things [the entire claim of the connection between the Jewish people to the Land of Israel which was brought in the article], I gladly admit that despite everything I truly *believe*. The more deeply I think, the stronger my faith grows. And for me this is not even faith, but something else. For do you really believe that after April, May will come? You *know* that, because it is not possible otherwise. Thus, for me there is no room for arguing, because by virtue of the coincidence of powerful processes, which no force can stop, Israel will be gathered together for its resurrection in its homeland, and my children or grandchildren will cast their votes for the representative assembly.[22]

These words were simply an expression of his concept of "just because"; in matters of fundamental importance—such as the question of what is moral and what is not, or the issue of the Land of Israel being the only territory for the Jewish nation—one could not always look for a logical answer, since man's knowledge of the answer was part of his very being. Its validity was often in no way compromised if the only response to the question "why?" was "just because."

The weaknesses of the atavistic claim led Jabotinsky to search for a different theory, although he never explicitly rejected his previous contention; even after he developed a new theory, the atavistic claim remained somewhere in the background.

As we saw earlier, Jabotinsky developed a theory of race in which he posited that national personality was the result of "blood"—that races were divided according to type, and that each race had a racial-physical prototype, and a unique spiritual core that derived from it. Thus "a Jew educated among Germans would be able to adopt German customs, German words, to be entirely suffused with German spirit. However, the kernel of his psychic structure will remain Jewish, for his blood, his body, his physical-racial type are Jewish."[23]

Jabotinsky's racial theory appeared throughout his life in various articles, as well as in his book *A Hebrew State: A Solution to the Question of the Jews* (1937).[24] His atavistic theory was not even hinted at in any of his racial theories. He also emphasized that the question of racial purity was irrelevant to the issue of a notional homeland. In his words: "Whether there are 'pure' races or not is irrelevant in this instance. The most important point to note is that the ethnic groups differ from one another in their racial spectrums, and in this sense the word 'race' acquires a defined scientific meaning."[25]

Jabotinsky's racial theory enabled him to expound upon the concomitant physical and spiritual uniqueness of the Jewish nation, and helped him to explain why spiritual assimilation was not likely unless preceded by a proliferation of intermarriage. "All the while we are Jews by blood, sons of a Jewish father and a Jewish mother, we may suffer from fear of persecution, disrespect, degeneracy—but the danger of assimilation in its true sense—total disappearance of our spiritual personality—is not a threat. There will be no assimilation as long as intermarriage does not occur."[26]

Jabotinsky did not mention the historical fact that for thousands of years, Jews in different parts of the world did not preserve the purity of the race, and had in fact often intermarried with the local populace. Jabotinsky pointed out the irrelevance of this fact, noting that it was clear that every race was a mixture of different races that had evolved over the years. What mattered most was that there existed different races, each unique. And indeed, the Jewish nation, despite intermarriage, had preserved its uniqueness over thousands of years in an alien environment. That observation, however, was not sufficient to dismiss Jabotinsky's claim that assimilation by intermarriage still threatened the Jewish people with cultural annihilation.

Race, for Jabotinsky, took precedence over nation. A race aspired to nationhood in order to create a separate society where everyone would be "in our image."[27] That notion was supplemented by the liberal belief that a nation needed an isolated corner in order to develop its own creativity; the most natural and the isolated corner for any nation was its own national homeland.

Local self-rule, however, was not sufficient for the Jewish nation. This was because, unlike other minorities—virtually all of which had at least one state in which their nation constituted a majority—the scattered Jewish nation lacked even one state of its own. Thus, the need of the Jewish nation for a state in which it constituted a majority was greater than that of other national minorities; for the Jewish nation it was nothing less than a matter of cultural survival or extinction.

Jewish self-rule in territories in which other nations constituted the majority would not solve the Jewish question. In the absence of a national territory, one of two things would happen to the Jewish nation. First: if self-rule for the Jews was successful, anti-Semitism would disappear; the likelihood of intermarriage would increase; Jewish culture would thus gradually disappear. Alternatively: even after self-rule for the Jews was implemented, hatred toward them would not decline; self-rule as a solution would fail; and the Jews would find themselves increasingly subjugated and oppressed. Jabotinsky's conclusion thus was that:

> The Jewish question can be solved—either completely, to the very end, with no problems remaining, or it cannot be solved at all. If autonomy is not an absolute solution—give it up. If autonomy is an absolute solution to the Jewish question, if it truly ensures us complete spiritual equality with the surrounding population that will not be dimmed by any defect, it must eventually also cause complete and absolute assimilation among the same population. Preservation of national identity is possible only under conditions where racial purity is preserved, and for that we need a territory of our own in which our people will be the decisive majority.[28]

Jabotinsky's atavistic theory provided an adequate answer to why the Jewish nation needed a national territory in which it constituted at least a majority, and explained the character the Zionist national movement must take. However, there was still nothing—once the atavistic theory had been rejected—to answer the question: why specifically the Land of Israel?

In fact, Jabotinsky never offered a full and complete alternative to the atavistic theory upon which he founded his campaign for a Jewish state specifically in the Land of Israel. His book, *A Hebrew State: A Solution to the Question of the Jews*, did not offer a scientific explanation, but did give pragmatic reasons relating to the absorptive capacity of the Land of Israel.[29] Nevertheless, his atavistic attitude to the Land of Israel even in those writings was implicit; in "The Language of the Enlightenment" (1913) he wrote: "We are Zionists and the Land of Israel is our center and the basis of all our nationalist programs."[30] In "A Lecture on Jewish History," he stated: "And today we are seeking a 'land,' and again, that very same land."[31]

Thus he always spoke about the Land of Israel as the only homeland, without attempting to give a new scientific reason for it. Over the years, he bolstered his pragmatic contentions, emphasizing geographic and geological features of the Land of Israel that would make it possible to absorb the Jewish masses. He also developed his political claim that the foothold the Jews had in the Land of Israel would make it easier to convince larger nations to grant the Jews a charter over the land.

As discussed previously, Jabotinsky considered the basis of an individual's belonging to a particular nation to be—in addition to a matter of race—a feeling of self-consciousness. We saw that in "Self-Rule for a National Minority," he proposed that the association of an individual with a particular nation be determined by his self-conscious declaration of allegiance to that nation. National consciousness did not replace race as a criterion of national affiliation, but was, rather, parallel to it.

The advantage of this theory of self-consciousness was not only that it offered a legal criterion, but also that it expressed the active side of nationalism. While the racial theory meant that man was born into a certain race, the perception of belonging to a nation as depending also on the will and consciousness of the individual turned national affiliation from something passive into something active. Jabotinsky considered the nation to be composed of individuals with identical racial formulas, *and* with self-consciousness that was continuously expressed in their desire to continue to belong to the nation. When this national consciousness weakened, the individual would not hesitate to intermarry. Hence, his children would lose the racial formulas, and thus their national affiliation. Therefore, in order to avoid assimilation, it was not sufficient for individuals to have racial formulas that associated them with a particular nation; rather, in Jabotinsky's opinion, it was imperative to strengthen their national consciousness.

Jabotinsky's concept of the nation was composed of two elements: the belonging to a race and the active consciousness of the individual. The second element distinguished his theory from integral nationalism, which later was incorporated into fascism; the latter emphasized the deterministic aspect of belonging to a race, and thereby to a nation.

Already in 1903, in his article "On National Education," Jabotinsky stressed the great importance of strengthening national consciousness among Jews through their recognition of their own national properties. A Jew had to know what it meant to be a Jew. Accordingly, he said, "first of all we must study the book of memories of our nationalism so that we may know and investigate how our people lived from the day it became a nation, how great their strength was and the power of their spirit, how much they learned to help their brethren, sons of other tribes. ... We must know the spiritual creations of our people in the past and in the present."[32]

Hence Jabotinsky's emphasis also on the importance of the Hebrew language and his continuous and stubborn struggle for Hebrew to become the language of study in school; language, in his opinion, was the strongest bond between the individual and the nation, stronger than any sense of obligation:

> With this bond from which we cannot extricate ourselves—with this poison, which has no cure, we must bind our sons to the Hebrew nation, to poison the entire texture of their souls. Language is the most important factor in national education, and content is secondary. Not that I underestimate the content—the Hebrew spirit and Hebrew knowledge; on the contrary, these are very important and without them obviously national education is deficient. But the bond—the indestructible bond, the bond which withstands every temptation and every temporary benefit, the essential bond between the individual and the nation—is the language, the language in which the individual became accustomed to think and to feel.[33]

It is hard to imagine a stronger expression of the function of language in the national consciousness of the individual. This concept motivated much of Jabotinsky's Zionist activity. The role of language in Jabotinsky's scheme of national education was not less (and was possibly greater) than that of education for self-defense and for *hadar* (a concept coined by Jabotinsky implying both internal qualities such as respect, self-esteem, loyalty and courtesy as well as the external qualities of a gentlemen. The closest translation is "noblesse.") As he says in his story "Jew Boy" (which he himself described as chauvinistic): "the student must acquire just two branches of knowledge: how to speak Hebrew—and how to give a smack in the face."[34]

Jabotinsky saw the uniqueness of the Jewish people in its developed national self-consciousness that rejected alien influences. In "An Exchange of Compliments," he emphasized that there were no superior or inferior races. All races being equal, there were thus no scientific, objective criteria by which to determine superiority or inferiority.

On the other hand, various nations could be evaluated according to personal taste and subjective criteria. Jabotinsky considered the quality of stubbornness—a developed sense of self-consciousness—to be the most important characteristic of race, a characteristic that the Jewish people possessed with a great degree of intensity:

As far as I am concerned, all nations are equivalent, all are equally good. Of course I love my people more than any other, but I don't consider it "superior." However, if we try to evaluate them according to some criterion, the result will depend upon the criterion that is used. Then, I shall insist that my criterion is the right one. Superior is that race which is solid and firm, that race that may be destroyed but cannot be compelled to go against its will, that same race that even under oppression does not relinquish its inner freedom. From the beginning of our history, we have been a 'a stiff-necked people,' and now too after so many generations, we are still fighting, we are still rising up, we have still not surrendered. We did not surrender. We are an unvanquishable race. I know no greater nobility than this."[35]

To the extent possible, Jabotinsky attempted to develop a logical and scientific theory of Jewish nationhood and race, and to integrate within it his general theory of race and concept of consciousness—both the objective, passive aspect (the individual's racial formula) and the subjective, active aspect (the individual's consciousness), respectively—of national belonging. The objective aspect (i.e. the racial formula) needed to be zealously guarded —Jabotinsky dreaded any situations that could lead to mixed marriage— but it was not possible to cultivate it because it was embedded in the blood. It was, however, possible, indeed essential, to cultivate the subjective aspect— national consciousness—hence Jabotinsky's preoccupation with national education, in developing both its substance and a framework for its implementation.

There is no question that Jabotinsky envied those whose national consciousness was organic and an inseparable part of their personalities— those who didn't need arguments, logical theories, and national education. This sentiment was reflected in his story "A Tiny Landlord," in which he described the relationship between a child living in the Land of Israel and his sense of nationalism: "I look and envy. I have never known, I shall never know that complete sense, organic, unified, and exclusive, of the feeling of a homeland, in which everything is integrated—past with present, legends with hopes, the individual with the historic. To this child belongs every step of the Jezreel Valley; every foot is populated by living and immediate figures, and he looks out upon the valley through the eyes of an owner and a veteran resident, and at every pace nods his head as if in greeting to the memories, as though he himself had lived them."[36]

The extent to which Jabotinsky's own feelings differed from those expressed above is reflected in his statement that it was a mistake to see "the essential part of national education in morality, in the creation of known sentiments (affection, closeness)—when there is nothing in the world more shaky than sentiment and morality."[37]

Because the concept of organic nationalism was alien to him—though indeed it was something he craved—he developed his Zionist thought, to the extent possible, on logical foundations. Unquestionably, a personal tragedy inhered in this conflict between Jabotinsky's desire for an organic nationalist feeling and his liberal rationalism, which at times in his life bordered on cynicism.

The integrated theory of nationalism—the racial formula merged with national consciousness—constituted the foundation of Jabotinsky's perception of the Jewish nation, upon which he added strata over his lifetime. In 1926 and 1927, Jabotinsky came out strongly against the Zionist school of thought that held that the Jewish nation was fundamentally Eastern, not only by origin but also in its psychic core. The conclusion was that a return to the Land of Israel would thus offer an opportunity for the Jewish people to develop its Eastern essence. Jabotinsky countered with the following argument:

> We Jews have nothing in common with what is called "the East," and thank God for that. The uneducated masses must be weaned from their antiquated traditions and laws which are reminiscent of the East, and this is something every proper school is doing, and the circumstances of life are achieving very successfully. We are going to the Land of Israel, first, for our national convenience, and second, as Nordau said, "to expand the boundaries of Europe until the Euphrates River." In other words, to sweep the Land of Israel clean of all traces of the "Eastern spirit." Concerning the Arabs who live there, that is their own business; however, if we could do them a favor, this would be the one: to help them free themselves from the "East."[38]

As related before, Jabotinsky considered "Eastern" characteristics inferior to those that had been developed in Western cultures. He perceived such "Eastern" traits, in fact, as actually dangerous. Despite the fact that the origins of the Jewish people were in the East, over a period of two thousand years the Jews had undergone the same process of development as had Europe, and had long since emerged from that inferior developmental stage known as "Eastern."

Moreover, the Jews were among the first to create European culture. The ideas of the Bible and of the New Testament fashioned what became known as "Western" culture. It was they who brought with them the basic concept of Western civilization: the drive for constant progress. As a nation, the Jews were pioneers in international trade and banking; as individuals, they made enormous contributions all over Europe in the fields of science, philosophy, art, and politics. Jabotinsky concluded that "Possibly, more than any other people, we have the right to say that 'Western' culture is an integral part of us. To reject 'Westernism,' to become infected with what is typically 'Eastern,' means to disavow our very essence."[39]

This perception of the Western nature of Jewish national culture was an inherent part of Jabotinsky's Zionist thought. For the liberal-democrat Jabotinsky, the ideas of progress, parliamentary democracy, separation of religion and state, and freedom of thought and expression were of utmost importance. His views stood in stark contrast to fascism, which saw in these liberal-democratic factors the imminent demise of Western civilization.

Jabotinsky believed that the Jews as a people should take much pride in the Jewish role in fashioning Western civilization; it was essential, he believed, for the Jewish national movement—and for the Jewish state, once it was established—to be based on Western elements.

Hence Jabotinsky's sharp criticism of the ancient customs and laws (e.g. intervention of religion in daily life, the position of the woman, suspicion of science) that were still found in the religious life of Jewish communities, and his perception of them, not as an organic part of the Jewish essence, but rather as shells that could be removed and discarded: "However, if we believed for one minute that these characteristics belong to the organic essence of Judaism, we would certainly despair of the ideal of perpetuating such an essence. For that was the reason for the Enlightenment, in order to separate between the ancient traditions and laws and the essence. And it was successful: the ancient traditions and laws are disappearing and the essence remains."[40]

Jabotinsky remained consistent throughout his life in his attitude toward Jewish religious customs, as well as in his basic liberal separation between religion and state. However, it is not correct to conclude that he was anti-religious; he clearly respected the philosophy of the Bible and of other traditional sources. Most importantly, he perceived the Jewish religion as an inextricable part of the national Jewish essence. He expressed this opinion very clearly in his article "Phenomena of Our Existence" (1910), in which he discussed the phenomenon of Jewish apostasy. He saw conversion as an act of moral degeneracy, of the inability of the apostate to perceive the line over which it was forbidden to cross. He said that man himself needed to understand why conversion for the sake of material gain constituted a serious violation of morality. It was not necessary to give logical proof; either a person would understand it or not. The issue of the relationship between Jewish nationhood and religion belonged in the category of fundamental things to which the real answer was "just because."

How did this attitude correlate with Jabotinsky's liberal approach which not only made separation between religion and state mandatory, but also considered religion to be a completely private issue? We can find an answer in Jabotinsky's following remarks:

> Our young people comfort us by saying that religious conversion is not national conversion, that is, that our people will still have the privilege of

counting them among its sons. That is very nice to hear, but it is simply that same sophistry which reflects gross insensitivity, an inability to feel important things that cannot be felt. The principle generally is correct: religion and state must be separate. In our days of freedom, at a time when we yet dreamed of a "national assembly" there were many even among the Zionists and the nationalists that declared that "anyone who acknowledges that he belongs to the Jewish nation, without consideration of faith and religion, is a member of the national Jewish congregation. But then we saw a different picture than that which now appears before our eyes. We saw a great independence celebration, in honor of which the Hebrew people forgave the sins of all the renegades, and from that day onward people would only abandon their religion out of complete conviction. Why this is something completely different! Conversion from one faith to one which is better in the eye of the convert— there is something noble about it . . . but when these opportunistic young people who casually, for material advantage, shirk their obligation— which involves the life and the longevity of the nation—and then they come and graciously offer to be included in the nation—why this is gratuitous generosity! No, young people, go which ever way you choose and we shall be comforted by the words of Herzl: "We only lose those whom it is no loss to lose." "Leaving the Jewish religion does not include leaving the Jewish people" . . . If those young people in all innocence truly believe that, they are mistaken. Whoever has converted up until today has also left our nation. More than that: there is a common saying in Europe—the grandfather is assimilated, the father is an apostate, and the son is an anti-Semite.[41]

This paragraph is central to an understanding of Jabotinsky's concept of the preservation of the Jewish religion. Though he advocated separation between nationality and religion, and not only between religion and state, he insisted that the Jewish nation constituted an exception for two important reasons, theoretical and empirical. The theoretical reason was that the Jewish religion (not the religious customs but the moral concept that was at the core of Judaism) was one of the fundamental expressions of the psyche of the Jewish people, serving as an alternative to a homeland by creating an isolated corner and by protecting the collective national Jewish memory. The empirical reason, based on history, was that the majority of Jewish apostates converted for material reasons (their lives would be easier if they were not identified with a religion that was so universally hated), and not out of preference for another religion. For the same reason, these converts eventually also left the Jewish nation, because the very fact of belonging to the Jewish nation was sufficient to arouse the hatred of the gentiles. As we saw in the passage quoted above, Jabotinsky added a moral reason: apostasy was simply an expression of ignobility and dastardliness, implying a treachery and a shirking of collective responsibility. The Jewish religion with its values and moral message—not the law and the commandments—was therefore an inseparable part of the Jewish nation, but in no way was it the only, or even the fundamental, expression of the Jewish national spirit. The central role it played in the lives of the Jews in the exile would end once the state was established. Jabotinsky repeated that idea in several articles, and it also appeared at later stages in his Zionist thought. In "A Lecture on Jewish History," written in 1933, he repeated the same idea that he developed in 1905 in "Zionism and the Land of Israel," according to which religion in exile was a substitute for state: "A people that lost its natural 'isolator'—its territory—makes everything an alternative to the territory, especially such a potent 'means of isolation' as the religious tradition."[42]

Jabotinsky's understanding of the Jewish religion as an expression of the Jewish psyche did not contradict his liberal concept of the separation of religion and state; he believed that a man's expression of his religious faith was solely a matter of personal conscience. Even at a later state of his Zionist activity—when, due to political considerations, Jabotinsky was more circumspect about expressing his polemical views on Jewish law and ritual—he never openly rejected the separation of religion and state, even in the state of the Jews.

Jabotinsky also enjoyed discussing the socialist philosophy of the Bible; he saw it as an ideological alternative to socialism, and clothed it in modern liberal-democratic principles, thus creating his own socioeconomic theory. He attempted to present the Scriptures as the source of the idea of progress. He devoted a short essay to this subject as part of his discussion of the socialist philosophy of the Bible, dealing with the Biblical concept that depicted man as wrestling with God: "And this is the most important part of the social philosophy of the Bible. God created the world, but man must assist in its improvement. For that purpose, he must fight, even 'declare war against heaven,' in order to extirpate what does not suit a just world order, and his weapons in this war are the knowledge of good and evil—his spirit and his mind."[43]

It was common for Jabotinsky to portray the Bible as the source of the ideas of rationalism and organization of the methods of production, and of the notion that technological progress was fundamentally positive, since it provided a way for man to dominate nature.

In the final analysis of his Zionist thought, there is no question that Jabotinsky remained faithful to his general liberal thought in his attitude to religion and its place in the collective life of the nation in a state of the Jews. Furthermore, he attributed more importance to the Hebrew language than to Judaism as a link between the individual and the people during the periods of national struggle, consolidation of the nation, and the attainment of a majority in the Land of Israel. In "The Idea of *Betar*" (1934), which included *Betar*'s program together with additional thoughts by Jabotinsky, he placed great emphasis on the role of the Hebrew language in the process of national rebirth, with not a word about religion.[44]

Jabotinsky's theory examined the character of the Jewish race and nation; explained its demand for a territory of its own; and offered reasons why that territory had to be the Land of Israel. It expounded as well upon the central spiritual expressions of the Jewish nation. He assumed that once the Jewish nation had its own national territory, it would, like every other normal nation, originate therein creations that would benefit all mankind. A Jewish national society, like any other national society, would be built in the Land of Israel only by daily activity in all fields of life—political, economic, scientific, athletic, and so forth.

Jabotinsky saw the first stage of the establishment of the state of the Jews one in which the Jews' physical hold on the Land of Israel and the national consciousness of the Jews in the diaspora would be simultaneously strengthened. He suggested consolidating and strengthening national consciousness by disseminating information on the history and the creations of the Jewish people, but not necessarily by presenting them as romantic national symbols of the past. He devoted a special article, "What Should We Do?" (1905), to this subject. He spoke about propaganda and culture, which in the following instance, were one: "Zionist propaganda means first of all speaking about the past and future of the Jewish people, about Jewish cultural values, disseminating information about our history, our language, our literature from ancient times, from the Middle Ages, and from the present. All of this is cultural work."[45]

In Jabotinsky's opinion, national consciousness had to be imbued in a multiplicity of ways. In his article he listed in detail daily activities in which every person could participate to heighten his own national consciousness and to convince others of the Zionist idea. He included such activities such as study groups, exercise classes, reading books and newspapers in Hebrew, and studying Hebrew in kindergartens and schools.

The integrated national theory presented in this chapter remained the basis for Jabotinsky's Zionist arguments throughout his life. As noted before, in Jabotinsky's later years he treated the identification of the Jewish people with the Land of Israel as something practically self-evident, not needing scientific proof. For example, as was already noted, in 1933 he wrote, "and today we are seeking a 'land,' and again, that very same land."[46] He gave no scientific explanations as to why that land had to be specifically the Land of Israel. Later on, he based his claim to *Eretz Yisrael* on the phraseology that appeared in the preface to the Mandate regarding the historical connection of the Jewish people to the Land of Israel, and sometimes he cited the Bible in speaking of the relationship between the Jewish nation and the Land of Israel.

Actually from about 1935, when he presented the Ten-Year Plan of the Revisionist Zionists, his attitude to the Land of Israel, including both banks, was essentially pragmatic, and he emphasized the land's various features suitable for absorbing mass immigration. He also cited those factors as reasons for opposing the Partition Plan of 1937.

After a period of preoccupation with the theoretical aspects of Zionism, Jabotinsky began to deal with more practical concerns; after the Balfour Declaration, he felt that the basic demands of the Zionists had come to be at least partially accepted by large portions of the public. Since the preface to the British Mandate emphasized "the historical connection of the Jewish people with Palestine," it was possible for him to devote less time to that issue because the actual problems needing to be dealt with were somewhat different. These included: convincing Great Britain and other European countries that acknowledged "the problem of the Jews" that the Land of Israel included both sides of the Jordan; that "a national home" meant a Hebrew state with a Jewish majority, and that this was indeed the intention of the Balfour Declaration; that the Land of Israel in fact had all the conditions needed to absorb millions of Jewish immigrants; that the problem of the Jews could be solved only by the establishment of a Hebrew state; and that the solution to the problem of the Jews was, first and foremost, a humanitarian, moral issue of concern to all countries having Jewish populations, and not only to Great Britain.

He articulated these issues in his 1936 lecture to the Institute for Research of National Problems in Poland; in his testimony before the Peel Commission on February 11, 1937; in his speech opposing the Partition Plan before the members of the British Parliament on July 13, 1937; in his book, *A Hebrew State: A Solution to the Question of the Jews*, published in 1937; and at a public assembly in Warsaw in 1938. Although in his lecture in Poland he admitted that there were countries that would offer the Jews an alternative homeland to the Land of Israel, he was convinced that those countries would also ultimately realize that no other territory could provide a viable solution. " ... it is clear from the start," he wrote, "that this idea about places to absorb the Jews will lead to only one place and that is: the Land of Israel. Herzl also initially presented the problem of territory, the area, and only after a while arrived at the right solution: the Land of Israel. It may be expressed in one sentence: *'The Jews need a place, and since, according to objective investigation there is only one such place, therefore give them this one place.'*"[48]

Jabotinsky needed to convince other Zionists not only that the idea of partitioning the western part of the Land of Israel was faulty, but also that the east bank should not be conceded. He began to grapple with this problem at the founding convention of the New Zionist Organization (NZO) in 1935, before he had formulated his reasons for opposing the Partition Plan proposed by the Peel Commission in 1937. Starting in 1935, Jabotinsky was occupied with the Ten-Year Plan to develop both parts of the Land of Israel as part of the concept of Greater Zionism whose ultimate goal was the return of the entire people to Zion, and "the creation of a culture which will impart its glory to the entire world, as its says 'for the Torah [in the sense of teachings] shall go forth from Zion.'"[49] Later, in a speech at the 1938 convention of the NZO, Jabotinsky attempted to define this Ten-Year Plan: "The New Zionist Organization differs from the other Zionist views in its integrality. Its goal is the elimination of *all* of Jewish suffering. The basis for that is—*all* of Land of Israel."[50] In this speech, Jabotinsky was expressing the goal of humanitarian Zionism—also known as Greater Zionism—which sought to bring to the Land of Israel not only the elite of the Jewish people, but the Jewish masses in their entirety.[51]

The goal of the detailed Ten-Year Plan was to create a Jewish majority on both sides of the Jordan within a period of ten years—that is, to create a basis for the eventual absorption of all the Jewish masses. In this plan, in his accompanying explanations, and in his speeches and appearances before gentile audiences, Jabotinsky's attitude remained essentially pragmatic. The points that he dealt with were the size of the area and the strategic, geopolitical, ecological, and geographic factors which by proper development policy could enable both sides of the Land of Israel to absorb millions of Jews.

In a series of lectures and articles starting in 1935, Jabotinsky discussed those issues, going into great detail about population density.[52] From his calculation of an average density of seventy-five to one hundred people per kilometer, he concluded that both sides of the Jordan were needed for some nine million Jews. Thus, he said, "it is important to remember that the settlement of Transjordan is more important for the Jewish future than the settlement of the western part of the Land of Israel. The size of Transjordan is three times that of western *Eretz Yisrael* and its population is only one quarter that of the latter."[53]

Jabotinsky's plan, lacking the dimension of an immediate, emotional, and organic connection to the Land of Israel, reflected the fact that most of his Zionist activities and thought transpired in a foreign country. His Zionist thought on nation and race thus was founded primarily on logical reasons. Perhaps Jabotinsky's emphasis on the need for a scientific theory to explain and justify the Jewish demand for a national territory was the result of his distance from the Land of Israel. It is likely that his detailed, almost scientific analysis of the absorption of mass immigration on both sides of the Jordan was also a result of his distance from the Land of Israel.

Nevertheless, despite the logical nature of his Zionist thought, there were romantic elements that distinguished it from his general theories on nation and race. Those romantic elements were more pronounced in his concept of the ideal Jewish nation and race.

The Ideal Jewish Race and Nation

As noted before, Jabotinsky's ideal nation was defined by a special racial formula different from that of any other nation. It had its own land, densely settled within specific borders; its own ancient language, reflecting the thoughts and feelings of its people; a national religion, the product of its spirit from early times; and a common historical tradition. According to Jabotinsky, the foremost of all of these was "the distinctive uniqueness of its physical origin, the formula of its racial composition."[54] The racial formula was expressed primarily in the physical structure of the nation, and from it was derived the national, that is, the spiritual-racial, psyche.

Jabotinsky was disturbed, from the moment he encountered the Jewish way of life in the *galuth*, by the physical appearance and the mentality of the exilic Jew. Already in 1903, in a discussion on the need to shift the Jews' emphasis from general to nationalist education, Jabotinsky presented his ideal: "the humanist Jew."[55] While the humanist side of the Jew was strengthened by the Enlightenment, his Jewish side was perceived as a heavy burden. Jabotinsky felt that the primary sickness of the Jews was their self-contempt; they tended not to recognize the glorious aspects of Judaism, but only the pathetic way of life of the ghetto. Jabotinsky described this situation in particularly harsh terms:

> We live within the narrow confines of the ghetto and see at every step the contemptible pettiness which developed as a result of oppression over many generations, and it is so unattractive. . . . And what is truly exalted and glorious, our Hebrew culture, we do not see. The children of the masses see a bit of it in the *cheder*, but there Judaism is presented in such a pathetic form and in such ugly surroundings that it cannot inspire love. It is different with the children of the middle class: these are denied even that; practically none of them know anything at all of the history of our people; they don't know about its historic function as a "light unto the nations" of the white race, its great spiritual power that all the persecutions didn't destroy; they only know the Judaism which their eyes see and their ears hear. And what is it that they see? They see the Jew who is always afraid, frightened of the sound of a driven leaf; they see that he is chased from every place and insulted everywhere and he doesn't dare to open his mouth and answer back. . . . The lad doesn't know the "Jew," but the "*Yid*;" he doesn't know "Israel," but "*S'rul*," [a typical ghetto nickname]; he doesn't know the proud Arab steed, but today's pitiful "mare." . . . Thus he carries his accursed Judaism like a disgusting blister, like an ugly hump which it is impossible get rid of, and every

minute of his life, he is poisoned by this vast space that separates what he
longs for from what he really is.[56]

The tragedy of the Jew, particularly one who was influenced by the
Enlightenment, was that he could not liberate himself from what he perceived as his intolerable Jewishness.[57] No matter how enlightened he might
be, the Jew could not extricate himself from this tragic situation.

The fact that the Jewish people were warped by life in the exile was
reflected in their external appearance, their behavior, and their thought.
They saw themselves through the eyes of the gentiles. In an imaginary
dialogue, "An Exchange of Compliments," Jabotinsky demonstrated
through a Russian's words how the gentiles perceived the Jews: "You are
definitely an incomplete race. ... You have and never had creations of your
own. ... Your range of senses is very limited and lacks shades. ... Even your
Biblical morality ... is dry ... each and every commandment is accompanied
by the promise of a reward in this world. ... The Jewish spirit is one-sided ...
everyone, in every place, and at all times has always hated and despised [the
Jews]."[58]

In the pressure of a hostile environment, many Jews lost their moral
sense and converted in order to achieve easier living conditions and to escape
hatred. The gentiles, said Jabotinsky, give "a prize for treachery, and in this
state of moral corruption our young people grow up. They know yet from
their youth—and they are not permitted to forget—that everything that is
forbidden to Jews, they will be permitted if only they betray their souls and
prostrate themselves before a foreign god. This awareness saps their strength
of character, debilitates their sources of resistance, extirpates from the heart
the feeling of moral revulsion."[59]

Because he found in Bialik's poetry complete and excellent expression
of the *Weltanschauung* of the ghetto, and of what the exile had perpetrated
upon the Jews, Jabotinsky in 1911 translated some of this poetry into
Hebrew. In the introduction to the translation he discussed the poem "A
Remote Star" (1899), in which Bialik summarized life in the ghetto:

> Life without hope, a life of rot and decay,
> Which sinks like lead, drowns in the darkness;
> The life of a ravenous dog, shackled in fetters—
> Alas, you are damned, life without hope![60]

In his long poem "The Scholar," Bialik concentrated on the single
point of light in ghetto life, the house of study; but that, too, was dark and
murky. The Jew could not taste life while in the ghetto. In Jabotinsky's
opinion, "The Scroll of Fire" was the apogee of Bialik's poetry dealing with
problems of *galuth* life; Jabotinsky explained that the poet was talking

about the defects that were decreed upon the national life of the people in the exile. From the time the people lost its independence, and then its homeland, from the moment the altar was destroyed and the holy fire that was the symbol of the colorful and complete life was extinguished —from that moment on the Jewish people shriveled up and withdrew beyond narrow and cruel iron bars. All luxuries were banned from national usage: love, joy, creativity, beauty, brightness, everything that abounds with life—everything that Bialik symbolizes in the image of woman, in the female element—were all banished. Life became like a barren wasteland. It was only in this way that the wanderer, bereft of a homeland, could guard what was left of the tribe's greatest treasure—the residue of its independent personality.[61]

In Jabotinsky's opinion, Bialik was a national poet in the fullest sense in that he described Jewish life as it was. He was a national poet also by reason of his inner rebellion, and his reproof of the Jewish people for not rising up against their suffering. Bialik demanded that the Jewish people enter the arena of history and fashion their fates with their own hands. The anger in Bialik's poetry reached its peak in "The City of Slaughter," written after the Kishinev Pogrom, in which the poet gave the masses a new feeling, one essential in order to change the fate of the Jewish people. It was the feeling of shame.

It was clear to Jabotinsky that the character of the Jew in exile— whether the ghetto Jew or the enlightened Jew—was not the true Jewish character. The physical and spiritual racial formula of the Jew continued to exist underneath the stifling layers of the *galuth*. Those layers had to be removed in order to reveal, to strengthen, and to restore the true character of the Jewish nation, as it was manifested primarily during the time it resided in the Land of Israel.

How then did Jabotinsky describe the physical and spiritual appearance of the ideal Jew? It is fair to assume that, in the image of the hero of his novel *Samson*, he saw a combination of the qualities of a true son of the Jewish race. Samson was outwardly attractive, physically strong, and full of *joie de vivre*; he was a soldier and a judge.

However, it was not Samson whom Jabotinsky pointed out as the ideal Jewish image, but Herzl. In his short article, "A Model Jew," Jabotinsky described Herzl's qualities which made him the symbol of the ideal Jew. He opened with a statement on the subject of race:

When a people leads a normal life in its land, when it lives a life of activity, that is creates, more or less successfully, its history, then true patriots are not hard to find. Then there are to be found, everywhere, people whose every trait is suffused with nationalist colors. The Jews lack such a type, and it is practically impossible for such a type to exist. From the time of Bar Kochba we have not actively participated in our history; the events that have befallen us over the two thousand years of our exile do not depend on us at all, and are beyond our power. Therefore, the Jewish image today is not the product of independent political life nor of our own activity, but is the result of various accidental events, of the vicissitudes of life caused by a foreign hand pounding away at us and crushing us. And all the familiar traits of our people—from an abased spirit to a pathetic voice of suffering—did not stem freely and naturally from its national psyche, but were imposed upon it from the outside under the heavy yoke of a hostile and unfriendly environment. Dirt and dust on the body of the wanderer. ... scars on the forehead of the injured person. Is that really his body? Is that truly his face? Those are foreign layers on him, and they are not his essence, and it is necessary to rinse them all off of him in order to reach his essence once again. ... At present, the ground from which a Jew can spring forth is missing. When we dream about the real Jew and create his image in our minds, we have no model. Therefore we are forced to use the antithesis, that is, to take as our starting point the typical Jew of our times—and to attempt to describe his antithesis.[62]

Clearly, Jabotinsky attributed great importance to the creation of the true national Jewish archetype, external and internal. True, the racial formula of a nation could be eradicated in a foreign country only through intermarriage. However, when the race was located in a hostile and oppressive environment over a long period of time, changes in its physical appearance and its spirit occurred. Though the nucleus of the racial formula remained, it was hidden from the eye by the layers which had accreted in the *galuth*.

Jabotinsky did not specifically state that the layers could be sloughed off to reveal the true Jewish core only in the Land of Israel; that was implicit, however, in his statement that the waters of European rivers could not rinse off the layers that had accumulated as a result of two thousand years of passivity. The process of rinsing or peeling away the layers was long and difficult, because it meant that the Jews had to abandon their passivity, take their fate into their hands, and shape their history for themselves. It is clear that the only way of doing this, in Jabotinsky's opinion, was through the Jewish national movement that would reclaim the Land of Israel for its own national territory. Once the state of the Jews was established, the vision of the ideal Jew would become a daily sight. This process had to start in the exile, because the majority of Jews were there, and their active national involvement would start there; its culmination, however, could take place only in the national territory of the Jewish race, the Land of Israel.

Meanwhile, Jabotinsky was able to describe the image of the ideal Jew only by contrasting him with the typical European Jew, whom he described as "homely and powerless and imageless ... cowering and degraded ... despised by all ... He loves to hide, and then he holds his breath and conceals himself."[63]

Conversely, he described the ideal antithesis of the European Jew as follows:

> Beauty, pride, energetic movements, broad shoulders, *hadar*, color. ...
> Proud and independent of other peoples' opinions. ... Full of charisma.
> ... He must, with courageous heart and strong spirit, stand up against
> the entire world, and look straight into the eyes of every person, while
> proudly declaring: I am a Hebrew! ... The special yearning—unique to
> the prophets of Israel—must be felt, together with the whimsical Jewish
> lyricism, the Jewish imagination which is the first step to anticipating
> future events; the Jewish faith in the living God; Jewish pragmatism; the
> Jewish twang, and that same love of truth of the ancient Israelite that is
> unsurpassed by any other nation.[64]

The romanticism that was missing from Jabotinsky's writings on the Land of Israel emerged in his description of the ideal Jew, whom he saw personified in Herzl, who in his outward appearance and personality embodied the racial formula of the ideal Jew: "Herzl was the perfect exemplar of a Jew from head to toe, a Jew unto the depths of his soul; he lacked even a single trait which was not impeccably Jewish. He was a sublime personality, the prototype of perfection, who evoked not the ghetto but the Bible."[65]

Not because of a defect in his personality, but because of historical circumstances, Herzl lacked one trait that Jabotinsky considered essential for the ideal Jew—the knowledge and the ability to fight. Jabotinsky found this quality in Trumpeldor, whom he also held up, in two articles written in 1920 and in 1928 respectively, as the symbol of the true Jew. To him, Trumpeldor embodied perseverance and the concept that will determines events; in his article "Tel Hai'" he compared Trumpeldor to the "dead of the desert" in Bialik's poem.[66] Eight years later, Jabotinsky wrote: "Trumpeldor as a Jewish soldier, Tel Hai as an armed Jewish fortress, are not incomprehensible, but rather are prototypes and examples for our young generation."[67]

Jabotinsky attributed importance to the quality of courage specifically because he saw it missing from Jews in the diaspora. This quality of the Biblical Hebrew would appear anew in the Land of Israel. And thus, in *The Story of the Jewish Legion*, Jabotinsky described most of the soldiers from *Eretz Yisrael* in the Jewish Legion as having the physical and spiritual qualities of an ideal Jew: "Their bravery was on a par with that which roused the imagination of the Jewish world in the defenders of Tel Hai. ... And men .. of a high order of intelligence, highly-educated, courteous, chivalrous in their conception of honor, camaraderie and duty."[68]

The bulk of Jabotinsky's efforts for a number of years was aimed at cultivating Hebrew youth in the diaspora in the image of the ideal Jew. Thus he wrote to the young Hebrew people of Wloclawek, Poland in 1927: "You are not responsible for the preservation of the language alone, but also for the preservation of the Hebrew race. The *galuth* enfeebled our bodies, undermined deeply the vital foundations of our strength—and if this generation does not return us to health, who will?"[69]

Over the years, Jabotinsky translated his thoughts about the relationship between the racial formula and the national psyche into a theory on the relationship between aesthetics, ethics, and logic. He sought to parlay that concept into a practical educational theory, through which a new Hebrew youth would be formed.

In 1933, in an article dealing with the importance of discipline and ceremony, Jabotinsky explained how the absence of suitable manners in eating, dress, walking, and speech had implications for purely spiritual matters: "Listen to the sermon of an old preacher in the synagogue; he is wiser than ten gentile philosophers, but he cannot quietly develop an idea until its conclusion. He jumps from one topic to another—and the worst thing is that his listeners particularly enjoy that. They have lost the need for order, for regularity, and they have also lost the ability to understand the importance of distinguishing what comes first and what comes last, like an army marching."[70]

Discipline and ceremony thus were doubly important: they influenced external appearances, cultivated the nucleus of the racial formula of the Jewish nation, and at the same time crystallized a form of thinking. Hence Jabotinsky's enthusiasm in 1926 for the "Rigan Hasmonean," a Jewish youth organization from Riga that had a democratic structure, but also a clear hierarchy accompanied by ceremonialism. The Rigan Hasmonean emphasized striving after the truth, and underlined the importance of creative work, justice, and liberty, but above all it stressed learning to use force for defensive purposes.

Jabotinsky wrote the anthem of the Rigan Hasmonean which came to be called "The Song of the Flag." The song was based upon what was symbolized by the three drops of the blood—whose colors were blue, white, and gold—left from the first Hasmonean. The last stanza was the most important:

> But there yet remains one drop—a drop that
> We did not recognize until today; it is not on the flag
> But in the heart—and it is red.
> When the enemy breaks through an ambush
> We shall stand up and proclaim:
> The youth endures; the sword endures; the blood of
>   the Macabbee endures![71]

There is no question that the use of arms took on an exaggerated significance for Jabotinsky, not so much because he saw the ability to fight as the most important quality for youth, but because he considered its absence to be a fundamental characteristic of *galuth* life. His entire concept of education was based on highlighting those elements that were missing in the exile. For that reason, he emphasized from the beginning of his Zionist activity the importance of the Hebrew language, as well as all forms of physical activity. He wrote many articles about the significance of the Hebrew language, and also mentioned the importance of exercise.[72] The ideology of the youth movement *Betar* was based on the concept that in order to return to the image of the ideal Jew, the layers of the exile had to be sloughed off and both the external and internal structure of the Jewish people needed to be re-formed.

"The Idea of *Betar*" (1934) included *Betar*'s declared world view plus Jabotinsky's own opinions on new questions that had arisen for which answers had not yet been given. The function of *Betar* was:

> to create that type of Jew that the people need in order to establish the state of the Jews more quickly and more perfectly, in other words, to create the "normal" or the "healthy" citizen of the Jewish nation. And indeed the great difficulty lies in the fact that since the Jewish people of today is "abnormal" and "unhealthy," the entire range of *galuth* life interferes with our ability to educate healthy and normal citizens. During the two thousand years of exile, the Jewish people stopped concentrating its collective will on one primary and foremost function; it stopped acting as a complete, unique nation; it refrained from defending itself with arms when mortal danger threatened; it became used to words and forgot action; disorder and disorganization prevailed in its life; slovenliness became the rule in its private and public life. Therefore the *Betar* education leads a very difficult, uphill struggle, and much time will pass until every member of *Betar* will attain his or her goal, both in terms of demeanor and conduct.[73]

The function of *Betar* was to fashion the archetype of the Jew from head to toe. The difficulty implicit in this goal stemmed not only from the low physical and spiritual condition of the Jew in exile, but also from the fact that it was necessary to start forming the new Jew even before the state of the Jews was established. The bulk of this process would take place in the diaspora, without the requisite conditions. Jabotinsky believed that the normal Jew would spring up almost naturally in the state of the Jews. However, until then, the process of forming the new Jew would be prolonged and difficult.

We shall now concentrate on two basic aspects of the *Betar* program aimed at fashioning "healthy" Jewish youth: the *Betar* discipline and the *Betar hadar*—noblesse—in which some people have seen the influence of fascism.

In "The Idea of *Betar*," he repeated his view that common activity, "like a machine," was not an offense to liberty but rather, an expression of each individual's ability to achieve harmony "with the personalities of others for the purpose of a common goal, to coordinate every one of his movements with the movements of all the other members. Actually, herein lies the whole concept of 'humanity' in its deepest and most refined sense: unity. Israel's redemption will come when the Jewish people learn to act together, specifically like a 'machine.' And when all of mankind learns this art, universal redemption will come, the conversion of all the quarreling factions into one world-family."[74]

Discipline and freedom did not conflict because the individual joined an organization—in this case, *Betar*—of his own volition. There was no contradiction between a hierarchy, in which discipline was implicit, and democracy, since subordination to superiors was based on the concept of the commander as "your deputy, to whom you voluntarily gave power of attorney to lead you—for otherwise you would not have joined *Betar* or you would not have remained in *Betar*."[75] This explanation reflects the difference between Jabotinsky's perception of a youth movement and that of fascism.

Undoubtedly, the criticism leveled against *Betar* led Jabotinsky to explain that it was not an undemocratic movement. He compared the hierarchic structure of *Betar*, with one commander at its head, to American democracy, headed by the president. The democratic nature of the movement would not be compromised as long as "the ultimate source of the entire *Betar* hierarchy rests with the will of the general *Betar* membership, because it freely chooses its supreme commander—the head of *Betar*."[76] In other words, *Betar* was a democratic movement because the "sovereign" was the mass membership; it chose the commander and vested authority in him, and this authority was like a trust.

Indeed, it would be difficult to say that the structure of *Betar* was formally undemocratic. The real question was whether what Jabotinsky saw as "a successful and healthy combination of liberty on the one hand and humanistic harmony on the other"[77] did not in truth create a situation in which, from a humanist point of view, individual liberty was indeed violated. We shall examine this issue in the chapter, "The Breakthrough Period—On the Way to Statehood." What is important for our discussion now is that in "The Idea of *Betar*," discipline was considered fundamental in order to fashion the ideal Jew. *Betar* discipline, said Jabotinsky, was "one of the best means of educating for '*hadar*.'"[78] And how was "*hadar*" expressed?

Hadar included "about a dozen different ideas: external beauty, pride, manners, fidelity."[79] In discussions of *Hadar*, Jabotinsky reiterated his concept of the relationship between external form to spirituality (primarily with regard to moral activity and logical thinking). In the diaspora, it was primarily the external form of the Jew that suffered; the racial formula had disappeared underneath layers of dust. As a result, there was also a lessening of the respect accorded to the Jew by others; a person who did not respect his body and whose movements and bearing were not dignified acted as if he held himself in contempt, and ultimately was despised by his surroundings. Jabotinsky maintained that a Jew's mien and comportment had to be a public declaration that he was the offspring of one of a magnificent race, one that had originated the ideas of justice and integrity. It was true that even if the Jews looked like "princes," anti-Semitism would not vanish; however, contempt for them would disappear and the world would treat them with respect. How was a generation educated for noblesse? Through discipline, but primarily, by each person's cultivating his own personality in order to simultaneously develop external and moral noblesse:

> *Hadar* is made up of a thousand seemingly meaningless things which together make up our daily lives. Eat quietly and moderately, don't stick out your elbow while you are eating, don't slurp your soup so that you make loud noises; when you walk on the street with your friend, don't take up the whole sidewalk; when you are going up the steps at night, don't talk loudly so that you wake up the neighbors; on the street, let a woman or an elderly person or a small child pass; if he is coarse, don't you be. All these and an endless list of other seemingly unimportant things create the "*Betar hadar.*" Moral "*hadar*," however, is inestimably more important. It is incumbent upon you to be benevolent: when matters of principle are not affected, don't bargain about petty rights; it is better that you make concessions than demand concession of others. Your every word must be your "word of honor" and your word of honor must be harder than flint. There must come a day when any Jew who wants to express the ultimate in personal integrity, in manners, and in respect, will no longer say "he is a real gentleman!" but instead, "He is a real *Betari!*"[80]

In one of his last speeches, on March 31, 1940, Jabotinsky spoke at a review of *Betar* members about *Betar hadar*. He gave as an example of the *galuth* mentality the passive behavior of Jewish students at an eastern Europe university: gentiles tossed a Jewish girl from one to the other and the Jewish students didn't react. Because of this *galuth* character, said Jabotinsky, there was a need "to create a new Jewish mentality—I am practically ready to say a new psychological race of Jews, a race whose character is based on *gaon* [genius]."[81]

Jabotinsky was rather extreme in speaking about the creation of a new psychological race, rather than the sloughing off of the layers to reveal the original racial core of the Jew and cultivating it. However, this sentence does not reflect a turning point in his thinking, but rather, a harsher formulation that suited contemporary events in Europe. The idea remained the same, as did the concept "that the fundamental part of Betar is *hadar*. This word includes greatness, nobility, and splendor."[82]

The *Betar* anthem, which was composed by Jabotinsky, expressed the transformation from a *galuth* Jew to an ideal Jew:

> Betar—
> From the pit of decay and dust
> With blood and sweat
> Will arise a race,
> Proud, generous and fierce.
> Captured Betar,
> Yodefet and Massada,
> Shall arise again in all their
> Strength and glory.
> Hadar—
> Even in poverty a Jew is a prince;
> Whether slave or tramp—
> You have been created a prince
> Crowned with the diadem of David.
> In light or in darkness remember the crown—
> The crown of pride and Tagar.
> Tagar—
> To all obstacles and hindrance,
> Whether you go up or down
> In the flame of revolt—
> Carry the flame to kindle;
> "Never mind,"
> For silence is despicable;
> Ownerless is blood and soul
> For the sake of the hidden glory
> To die or conquer the hill—
> Yodefet, Massada, Betar.[83]

Toward the end of his life, Jabotinsky understood that in the *galuth* Jew, too, there existed what he called "a spark of lava." Precisely because he had failed to see that spark for so many years, he valued Shaul Tchernichovsky's ability to see beyond the layers of the *galuth*. In honor of Tchernichovsky's sixtieth birthday in 1936, he wrote: "Heaven endowed Shaul Tchernichovsky with the wondrous ability which—in the words of Bernard Shaw, only one out of myriads is blessed with: normal vision. He looked at that humble Jew and discovered in him hidden reserves of 'ferment.' He discovered that aside from all sorts of 'daydreams'—dreams of glory that he will not achieve—the blood of that same poor Jew boils with a real and actual 'appetite' for glory that can be attained, that must be attained, and that is worth attaining. Let us achieve it and *gaudeamus*!"[84]

As we have seen, Jabotinsky saw the ideal Jew as a combination of the Jewish racial core and of traditional humanist values—that is, a separative element together with a universal element. Over his lifetime he developed and expanded his theory of the Jewish racial element, dealing less and less with the humanist, universal element.

Jabotinsky dealt more with the separative element since he considered the cultivation of everything uniquely and specially Jewish to be most important, particularly at the stage of struggle for national liberation and the establishment of a state. However, there was a more basic reason why he emphasized so strongly the cultivation of the physical and spiritual racial formula of the Jewish nation. As we saw in his article "The East," Jabotinsky believed that true Judaism (not the commandments and the laws, but the philosophy of the Bible) included an inherent humanistic element. Thus, the cultivation of universal humanistic values was implicit in the rediscovery of the Jewish spiritual and physical racial formula. The Jewish figures that Jabotinsky admired—Herzl and Nordau—symbolized for him the integration of true Jewish uniqueness with humanism. In this, as emphasized before, Jabotinsky's concept differed completely from the fascist conception of the "ideal new man."

In his concept of the relationship between the physical and spiritual aspects of the ideal Jew, Jabotinsky unquestionably overemphasized the former. This fact derived, however, from his belief that the racial formula was expressed primarily in physical features which in turn determined spiritual characteristics. The implication for his Zionist thinking was that, in order to construct anew the ideal Jew, it was necessary to concentrate first and foremost on his physical nature.

Jabotinsky's overemphasis on the physical, however, was not consistent with his theory that the play urge was what distinguished man from beast, and that the mind was the most important means of production. The fact that man was characterized primarily by his physical racial formula did not mean that the spiritual side was less important, but simply that the process of forming the ideal Jew, necessitated starting with the physical aspects. In order for Jabotinsky's Zionist thought on nation and race to completely correlate with his general thought, he would have had to place more emphasis on the spiritual side of the ideal Jew.

Why then did Jabotinsky so emphasize the physical nature of man as his most fundamentally important aspect? The answer may be simply that the external appearance of the exilic Jew aroused irrational feelings in him that were beyond logical explanation, and came to symbolize for him the impairment that befell any Jew who lacked a homeland.

In the last decade of his life, Jabotinsky realized that he had gone too far in his contradistinction of body versus spirit, and that he was mistaken in the meaning that he had given to the spirit of the Jewish people. For, while he considered spirit to be a prime factor in human progress, in terms of the Jewish people he considered spirit a synonym for passivity and inaction.

Jabotinsky acknowledged this mistake in his article " . . . but by Spirit" (1934), written in honor of the sixtieth birthday of Professor Joseph Klausner. He expressed his indebtedness to Klausner, whose thinking had illuminated his own error. And thus he concluded his article:

> " . . . but by spirit" . . . Please do not be angry at me that in my Zionist youth, I was gravely suspicious of this formula. It is true, that then there was talk of transplanting to Zionism the most pitiful aspect of the ghetto psychology: political passivity, admiration for the "East" with its demeanor of apathy, and customs redolent of the Middle ages and patriarchalism, and the same type of "pacifism" that indeed wants the Land of Israel to be conquered, but by others, at their expense. . . . Today we understand "spirit" differently. . . . "Spirit" contains within it the desire to rule, a conquering spirit right and left. "Spirit" wants both sides of the Jordan and political independence and the ingathering of millions of exiles. "Spirit" believes in the West, in Europe and America, in technological progress, in women's rights, and in general suffrage. "Spirit" does not fear the Jewish Legion.[85]

This amended concept of "spirit" was expressed in "Introduction to the Theory of Economics," which Jabotinsky wrote in the mid-thirties. In this seminal essay, he developed his theory on the importance of the need for play, and dealt with the spiritual urge connected with the need for play that he saw as fundamental to the desire for domination and expansion of the parameters of life, and which therefore was a central factor in shaping history. From this point, the contradiction between Jabotinsky's thoughts on the importance of "spirit" versus "body" began to disappear.

We started the discussion of Jabotinsky's Zionist thought with the subject of Jewish nationhood and race, both because of its centrality, and because this discussion clarified several of Jabotinsky's ideals. In the course of our discussion, the extent to which this subject was connected with Jabotinsky's perception of the life of Jews in the diaspora became obvious. The diaspora, with its many facets—above all, that of anti-Semitism—was a central theme of Jabotinsky's Zionist thought, and demands separate consideration.

Chapter 2

THE DIASPORA

I n his early Zionist thought, Jabotinsky grappled systematically with the gamut of issues involved in the condition of the Jewish people in the exile. He returned to this subject in 1926, and in 1937 summarized his position in his book *A Hebrew State: A Solution to the Question of the Jews*. His great attention to the diaspora stemmed from the fact that, unlike other Zionist leaders of his time, most of Jabotinsky's Zionist activity took place in the diaspora. While he spent only a short time in *Eretz Yisrael*, he was familiar with the diaspora from his many journeys to Jewish settlements all over the world over a period of some thirty-five years. These were not limited to eastern Europe; he spent about a year in Vienna, visited Turkey and Egypt among other places, lived temporarily in Paris and in London, travelled to South Africa, and made many trips to the United States, where he passed away.

The fact that he came to Zionism from "the outside" allowed him to analyze dispassionately and rationally such phenomena of diaspora Jewish life as anti-Semitism, assimilation, and apostasy. At a very early phase of his Zionist thought, Jabotinsky determined that the first goal of Zionism was to bring about a Jewish majority in the Land of Israel through immigration and the concomitant creation of an infrastructure. The first stage of Zionism necessitated activity at both the providing end—the diaspora—and the receiving end—the existing settlement in the Land of Israel.

Therefore he considered the partnership between political Zionism and the approach known as "Love of Zion" to be essential. The former was to work through political channels to obtain the consent of the great powers to establish a Jewish state in the Land of Israel, and the latter was to actually settle the land: "The 'political' method and the 'Love of Zion' method have the same value and the same degree of urgency: the second has no practical

151

value without the first, and the first is not complete and not solid without the second, and anyone who gives preference to the one at the expense of the other weakens and obstructs our business."[1]

The bulk of Jabotinsky's Zionist activity in the diaspora took place on two levels: persuading the Jews that the sole solution to the problem of the Jews was the establishment of an independent state, and diplomatic efforts aimed at the great powers, primarily Great Britain, to obtain a charter recognizing *Eretz Yisrael* as the national territory of the Jewish people.

In this chapter we shall examine Jabotinsky's perception of the diaspora, his claim that the Jews had the right to establish a state in the Land of Israel, and his conflict with the opponents of Zionism and with those who proposed alternatives to *Eretz Yisrael* as a territorial solution.

The History of the Jewish People in the Diaspora: From Zion to Zion

The essence of Jabotinsky's understanding of the diaspora is summed up in his statement that "The history of the Jewish people in the exile is not the history of what they did, but the history of what was done to them." Based on this concept, Jabotinsky built a dialectical theory whose logical conclusion was unequivocal: "the Jewish question can be solved—either completely, to the very end, with no problems remaining, or it cannot be solved at all."[2] Jabotinsky thus had to prove that Jewish history in the diaspora—including the period of the Enlightenment, and phenomena such as the bund (the Jewish worker's movement)—led to a single conclusion that would completely resolve the question of the Jews.

Already in 1903, Jabotinsky portrayed the two thousand years of exile as: "the struggle of a small people deprived of a land, fighting for almost two thousand years for its national uniqueness; and what is most amazing is that in this struggle all possible imaginable advantages tipped the scale in favor of conversion, and, nevertheless, conversion did not take place. ... It is clear that some overpowering factor of group preservation that may not be ignored is operating here"[3]. Jabotinsky's explanation for this phenomenon constituted the core of his conception of Jewish history in the diaspora. Because of its centrality, we shall repeat in its entirety the following passage from Jabotinsky's writings:

> Our movement is still very young, and it is still waiting for its own scientific theoretician—however, we all understand very well that in a scheme of the theoretical basis of Zionism, anti-Semitism and the *juden-not* [the particular troubles of the Jews] are destined to play a very minor role. One may anticipate that this scheme will be something like this: every national-racial group naturally aspires to complete originality in

all forms and manners of its economic way of life; the likelihood of assimilation rouses it to opposition and to war over its national preservation; this urge for national preservation brought about the fact that, with the loss of the *natural* means of isolation—the national territory—the Jewish people was forced to fence itself in *artificially* against the danger of mingling with other peoples by constructing the wall of religious dogma; now, after the socioeconomic circumstances of the new era destroyed the ghetto, and the culture which burst into it brought an end to dogma, and thus the *artificial* wall which had kept the Jewish people from assimilating among foreigners toppled—this same urge for national preservation impels it to seek the revival of a *natural* means of isolation, that is, an autonomous national territory, in order to guarantee the national Jewish uniqueness comprehensive, complete liberty, for an original socioeconomic way of life for all eternity.[4]

It is interesting to note the Marxist influence on Jabotinsky with regard to one crucial point: his great emphasis on socioeconomics as the means by which the nation expresses its uniqueness, and his failure to mention at all the desire of the nation for its own political or spiritual creations.

In the previous chapter, we saw that Jabotinsky at one point explained the role of religion as a means of protecting the real treasure of the Jews—the national character of *Eretz Yisrael*[5]. Religion thus became an artificial alternative to a homeland by creating a secluded corner for the Jewish nation in which it could continue to exist without assimilating into its environment.

Thirty years later, in 1933, no theoretician had yet appeared to present a scientific concept of Zionism, as Jabotinsky had expressed the hope for in 1903. There was Jabotinsky's own atavistic theory, finally consolidated in 1913, on the integral connection of the Jewish people to the Land of Israel. It was later subsumed by his theory of the Jewish race and nation. However, this was no substitute for a general scientific theory that explained the entire history of the exile as leading to one incontrovertible conclusion. It is reasonable to assume that in the absence of such a theory, Jabotinsky took the task upon himself, and in 1933 presented his scientific theory of the history of the Jewish people.

As in his theory of 1903, the Marxist influence was apparent here, too. Although Jabotinsky had long since shaken his Marxist beliefs, his fundamental premises were still formulated in Marxist terminology. He noted that "even without being a Marxist, one may accept a Marxist principle; namely, the main cause of all historical phenomena is the condition of the means of production."[6]

However, his interpretation of that principle was the opposite of the Marxism explanation: "But when an ordinary Marxist speaks of the means of production, he is referring only to the material means: a stone hammer in prehistoric times, an iron machine in the present day. And in this he is mistaken: these are not the important and true means of production. . . . The supreme, the primary, and the most important of all the means of production is our spiritual mechanism."[7]

When this theoretical premise was combined with Jabotinsky's theory that every race had its own racial psyche, the inevitable conclusion was that every race aspired to be a nation in order to create a separate society, in which everything was "in our own image."[8] This conclusion as well was antithetical to Marxism, which saw the basic means of production as material and universal. Marxism views national isolation not only as unnecessary but reactionary, since it was an obstacle on the road to the universal socioeconomic revolution. According to Jabotinsky, the opposite was true: national isolation was a precondition for the progress of humanity as a whole. A secluded environment was essential if a nation-race was to produce its own creation. "The Jews are an outstanding example of this rule, that every 'race' always seeks to live in an environment that it created in accordance with its spiritual 'means of production.'"[9]

When the Jewish people was exiled from its land, it created, through its spiritual mechanisms, isolated environments that served as alternatives to a national territory. The Jews voluntarily dealt in economic fields that their gentile neighbors did not—primarily trade, finance, and credit. Thus their spiritual means of production was able to find expression in those fields which were concentrated in the hands of Jews: "Only after many years, and for entirely different reasons were they really prohibited from engaging in other trades, but in the beginning it was done out of our own free choice: economic activity served as a means of national isolation, as an alternative to a territory of our own."[10]

The Jewish religion and tradition also created, as we saw, a secluded corner "and really a kind of substitute for a state,"[11] and therefore no changes in tradition or religion penetrated. In order for religion to serve as a means of isolation, the Jewish people needed to: "guard it against the slightest tremor. The only thing that they can do to strengthen it is to redouble their efforts to find more and more segregating elements in the tradition. They impose upon themselves hundreds of complicated dietary customs which are difficult to uphold, particularly for poor people, but they bear them like something holy because they separate the Jews from their environment, and help them create at least an illusory shadow of an environment that is their own."[12] As we already pointed out, Jabotinsky saw the creation of the ghetto, too, as the result—at least initially—of the people's will, and their desire to live together, separate from the gentiles. Thus, with the help of alternative isolating elements—exclusively Jewish economic activities, a rigid tradition and religion, and the ghetto—the Jewish nation maintained its own niche in which it successfully guarded its national existence.

Jabotinsky was certain that the economic structure of the Jewish people in the diaspora, a structure that was essential for the creation of their isolated corner, failed to help the Jews contend with rapid economic changes. Already in 1904, in his article "A Letter on Autonomy," he developed the thesis—based on an article by M. Gepstein, "The Aryans and the Semites in the Economic Arena"—that the economic structure of diaspora Jewry at the beginning of the twentieth century led to a dead end. On the one hand, occupations that had traditionally been in the hands of the Jews (trade and banking) no longer were; the gentiles were taking over those areas. On the other hand, after hundreds of years of being forced to engage in petit bourgeois occupations, the Jews were unsuited as manual laborers. Thus proletarization might have been necessary for them, but was not possible.[13] The economic process which the Western world was undergoing held another tragedy in store for the Jews as a nation: their isolated corner was being destroyed, and they had no substitute in the diaspora. In 1933, Jabotinsky wrote that "in Eastern Europe, an independent, non-Jewish bourgeoisie arose, and the Jew stopped being economically isolated."[14]

Jabotinsky had noted this phenomenon in Russia about twenty years earlier. The educated Jew, who had been excluded from trade and banking and who was not suited to be a laborer, aspired to become a professional—a doctor or a lawyer: "In Russia every poor Jew hopes to raise his son to the position of a doctor. This is in no way out of a thirst for knowledge, but rather because of the 'kindnesses' of the Russian regime. This regime has created several pathological phenomena, one of which is that the Jews, instead of aspiring to a healthy economic distribution, have begun to aspire to become a nation of paralegals."[15]

The most severe manifestation of this syndrome, Jabotinsky wrote in 1910, was the willingness of young Jews to convert to Christianity in order to obtain permission to enter university and to enter the liberal professions. Jabotinsky considered this to be moral degeneracy of the first degree, engendered intentionally by the Russian government.[16] Moreover, Jabotinsky viewed the attempts by the Jews to escape from "business," even where they were still permitted to engage in trade, as a tragic error which would distort the economic structure of diaspora Jewry. He has expressed his views on this matter earlier. At the end of his article "Dialogue," he wrote, "I would proclaim a new slogan for Jewish youth: return to the shops, return to the banks and to the stock exchange; or more accurately—not only to trade, because young people must also become actively involved in industry, workshops, and practical matters in general."[17]

He expressed that same opinion years later when writing about South

African Jewry: "But this is already a problem in Jewish life in general, not only in South Africa. The avarice for diplomas, which is unquestionably one of the most desperate forms of group frustration, is related to many of the other misfortunes of the exile; if we already can find a Jewish shopkeeper somewhere who has customers, or a tailor who is not impoverished, you can be certain that their sons will study law, and after the fathers' deaths, the business will close. So we lose the few economic footholds that we still have."[18]

This approach was completely consistent with his opinion that people who engaged in business, like merchants, were more broadly educated and were more important for progress than professionals.

His economic line was clear: both voluntarily and involuntarily, the Jews were being pushed out of their economically isolated corners, and a new economic corner for them had not been found in the diaspora. Thus, the twentieth-century economy could no longer serve as an alternative to the proper isolator of a national territory.

In the absence of a national territory and of an economically isolated corner, the economic structure of the Jewish nation in the diaspora was becoming progressively more distorted, and was losing even those positions of economic power that it had held previously. The need to live well brought about very serious moral ramifications, such as conversion. However, much more serious was the fate of the masses of Jewish petit bourgeoisie who were unsuited as industrial workers. If a Hebrew state was not established to absorb them, said Jabotinsky, they would be doomed to extinction. It was patently clear from the economic turn of events that the only solution to the problem of the Jews was a Jewish national territory. Only in such a state would the Jewish nation be able to develop a normal and healthy economic structure. Economics would assume its rightful place in the life of the individual and the nation, and would not have to fulfill a role for which it was not naturally suited—that of creating an isolated corner as an alternative to a national territory.

Parallel to his analysis of the economic situation, Jabotinsky analyzed the changes at the end of the nineteenth century in the ghetto and the Jewish religion and tradition:

> Then came the destruction of the ghetto, the closed quarter of the city, partially because of the new ideas about freedom and equality, and particularly because modern economics doesn't tolerate separate social "bureaus," and just as it breaks down the walls of the gentile "village" and attracts its residents to the city, so (and with great ease) it topples the walls of the ghetto. These two phenomena, which compelled the Jew to participate in the life and in the thought of the alien environment, also weakened the third and strongest "isolator," the fixed tradition, and particularly its dietary customs, that separated us from the gentiles—

even the close neighbors who were our partners—like an iron wall. The Jew suddenly stands as if naked, vulnerable to every foreign wind, with no protection, out in the open. At first—in the first fifty years—this even seemed good to him or he believed that it seemed good to him, but the end is that the Jew is now standing in front of the whole world and is requesting the isolator—a land.[19]

In these few sentences, Jabotinsky summarizes what he had been formulating for decades.

Jabotinsky devoted a chapter of his book, *A Hebrew State: A Solution to the Question of the Jews* (1937), to an outline of the history of the Jewish people in diaspora. The addendum to this relatively late book reflected Jabotinsky's awareness of a certain simplicity in his earlier theory:

> In this schematic overview of the history of the exile which is described here as a kind of journey to forty countries over two thousand years— from Zion to Zion—I distorted the fate of my people. I loaded upon their shoulders practically all the responsibility for the ghetto, for the mutilated economy; for the alienation from the Christian surroundings. When a person attempts to summarize, such distortion is inevitable. Obviously, there is another side to this coin—the shocking and shameful chronicles of the Aryan world, relating its cruelty and degeneracy.[20]

However, despite this realization, he was still convinced that "the fundamental root of the historical truth nonetheless is contained within this overview: I believe (and I am proud of this belief) that at the root of our two thousand years of suffering is our refusal to surrender."[21]

From the beginning of his writings on Zionist topics, Jabotinsky dealt at length with the processes that the Jewish people had undergone in the exile after the Enlightenment. He divided the people into two rough categories: those who, passed over by the Enlightenment, remained within the ghetto, and those who, subsequent to the Enlightenment, left the ghetto. The first group was left with its corner of seclusion; however, its walls were breached and its strength was diminished, as a result of the damage to the traditional branches of the economy in the ghetto, and because it ceased to be the exclusive home of the Jews. Those Jews who remained would be forced to reach Zionism by skipping the state of Enlightenment; that is, without acquiring the general knowledge and the universal ideals that it generated.

In the ghetto preserve, religious customs and observances that separated the Jew from his neighbors continued to exist, as did the constant threat of imminent slaughter. Jabotinsky tried to give the Jews of the ghetto a feeling of national pride, based not solely on those traits which characterized the Jews during the *galuth*, but rather on Jewish history, primarily during the Biblical period; on the organic connection between the Jewish people and the Land of Israel; and on the need to struggle for the establishment of a

Hebrew state. However, it is clear that from a substantive point of view, the group that interested Jabotinsky most were those who were influenced by the Enlightenment and had acquired universalist values. The problem, as defined by Jabotinsky among others, was that general education worked like a boomerang. The idea of the Enlightenment movement initially was to remove the Jew from his isolation and give a universalist dimension to his Judaism. Frequently, however, this process did not stop with the creation of a humanist-Jew, but proceeded to eradicate the Jewish character. As Jabotinsky said in 1903:

> The preachers of the Enlightenment had only one great desire in those days: to inject a humanitarian stream into the national and religious education, which was very narrow and limited. Now when this goal had been achieved, and has been achieved brilliantly, that phenomenon that always accompanies the success of every idea changed: in our panic and haste, we overran our goal. Our objective was to create a Jew who could, in addition to being Jewish, live a complete life as a human being. And now we are all infected with a passion for general culture, but, we have forgotten our duty to remain loyal Jews. Or more correctly, we have not forgotten (there are compelling reasons that do not enable us to forget) but we have half-forgotten to be Jews because we stopped having regard for our Jewish existence which we began to consider a burden. And now, on the one hand, *we are not able* to forget our Jewishness, and on the other, it is a heavy burden on us. And in this lies the primary reason for our distressing situation and thus our obligation to escape from it. There are perhaps several means of achieving this, but only *one* of them is within our power to use: we shall cease to think of our Judaism as a heavy burden and shall learn to hold it in esteem.[22]

Jabotinsky then reached the inevitable conclusion that unless the educational emphasis changed, the Jews would assimilate among the gentiles. If the slogan of the Enlightenment was "aspire to general humanity," the slogan now had to be "aspire to the national properties," with the two processes conspiring toward the creation of the humanist Jew.

The first step for Jabotinsky was that the Jews of Russia (at this stage of his Zionist thought, Jabotinsky turned to Russian Jewry) had to understand that their contempt for the Jewish identity and admiration for everything Russian was benighted. Their self-contempt stemmed from the fact that they were unaware of the national properties of the Jewish people (its history, language, and other cultural creations), and therefore identified the Jewish character with the pathetic ghetto life. Their admiration for everything Russian was, likewise, fundamentally fallacious since their only contact with the Russian people was with the intelligentsia and through Russian cultural creations:

> Unfortunately, he [the Jew] is acquainted only with the internal aspect of the Jewish world [the ghetto] and only the external aspect [the great

creations] of the Russian world. So, yet from childhood, he becomes attached, with bonds of degenerate love, to anything Russian, like the love of a swineherd for a princess. His whole heart and all his love are directed toward the other, but he still is a Jew by blood and there is no man in the world who will deign to forget that. Thus he carries his accursed Judaism like a disgusting blister, like an ugly hump which it is impossible get rid of, and every minute of his life, he is poisoned by this vast space that separates what he longs for from what he really is,"[24]

That was the tragedy of the Jewish upper and middle classes, a tragedy that in 1862, Y. L. Gordon had expressed so ably in the poem, "For Whom Do I Toil?" In it he warned of the tragedy in store for the Jewish people: the loss of the best of its sons through ideas whose objective was the opposite—strengthening the Jewish nation by adding the element of universalism.

Jabotinsky thus summarized this historical process: "The original idea, that our people adopt the culture of others so that it might afterwards develop its own culture more intensively, became an attempt to erase everything of its own and to assimilate into a foreign culture. Assimilation, which was intended to bring about national progress, became, instead, the source of national destruction."[25]

It was imperative that this process be halted lest the Jewish people remain without leadership. Jabotinsky's primary solution was to be found in his program for national education, a subject we shall discuss in the next chapter.

In the post-Enlightenment era, educated Jews firmly and enthusiastically embraced the causes of others, rather than Jewish matters and the establishment of a Jewish national movement which sought to find a normal solution for the Jewish people. The Jews, for example, took a very active part in shaping Russian history, and even tried to encourage and spread Russian literature.

In 1906, Jabotinsky demanded that the Jews who were active in Russian politics examine their contributions both to the Russian revolution and to their own people. Jabotinsky concluded that, while the Jews served the cause of the Revolution, they simultaneously also served the reactionary forces in Russia; reactionaries used the fact that the leaders of the Revolution included a large number of Jews to arouse doubts about Revolutionary ideals among the masses, in whom anti-Semitism was deeply ingrained.

However, the more important issue was whether Jewish participation in Russian events had implications for the Jewish people: "Did this Revolution, however, not bring any benefit to the Jewish people? I do not know."[26]

What Jabotinsky did know, and declared clearly and loudly, was that when Jews participated in the shaping of the history of another nation, they were destined to be pushed out of the vanguard into the second ranks. This was a natural process that those Jews who took part in shaping Russian history and who hoped to be among its leaders needed to recognize. If they wanted to be in the forefront of a national liberation movement, said Jabotinsky, let them operate within the framework of the Jewish national movement: "And we leave our places in the front lines to the members of the national majorities. We stop making unrealistic demands to be leaders. We are merely joiners, and only to the degree to that it is objectively possible for our people. In this land, it is not we who issue the call to build, and we retract our demands to create the history of a people that is not our own. The arena for our creativity is within Judaism."[27]

As he explained in an earlier article, "To the Foes of Zion: Without Patriotism" (1903), the desire of educated Jews to be active and to make changes was understandable. But the natural field of action for them was shaping Jewish history; only their own history could inspire the patriotic zeal without which action lacked an important dimension. The gentiles' reaction to Jewish activity on behalf of other people was amazement accompanied by revulsion. Jabotinsky wrote: "Things do not change with time. Centuries pass, and the new era finds us once again grazing in the fields of strangers; once again we appear like those who, with exaggerated feelings of brotherhood, latch onto people who don't want them; once again people cast us cold looks of amazement when they see us serving the alien homeland with such enthusiasm and love; again they shrug their shoulders and say, as they do now, 'it is a strange wish: to toil at any cost for matters that are not theirs.'"[28]

The same was true of the Jews' attempt to involve themselves with Russian literature and to be arbiters of Russian cultural life. In 1908, Jabotinsky came out against those Jewish writers who, instead of writing for the Jewish community, wrote for the Russians. Those writers, he said, defected from the Jewish camp for personal gain: "He goes to a place where it will be easier for him to fulfill his desires and demands, where the atmosphere is more refined, the environment is more cultured, the resonance is more intense, the ground is more solid, and in general everything is richer and more magnificent. And this is the only reason for their leaving, with nothing of the sublime."[29]

In 1909, a year after this article was written, what is called "the Chirikov Incident" took place. At an evening in a private home in honor of the performance of a new play by Sholem Ash in Russian translation, the writer Eugene Chirikov—then considered one of the most progressive members of Russian society—hinted that the growing number of Jews in Russian literature was beginning to cause hardships. Subsequent to this incident, Jabotinsky wrote a number of articles about the tragedy of the Jews' attempt to become involved with Russian literature and about the anti-Semitism of the Russian intelligentsia. He warned unequivocally that Chirikov's words faithfully reflected public opinion, and despite the fact that the initial reaction would be denial, "all those professions in Russian cultural life which are still 'full of Jews from wall to wall' will begin little by little to rid themselves of this cheap and unwanted element that loves to serve."[30]

Jabotinsky continued to warn against that phenomenon, both from the standpoint of what it taught about those Jews who had been influenced by the Enlightenment and now wanted to assimilate into a cultural environment that was not natural to them, as well as from the standpoint of what it taught about anti-Semitism. In 1912, he wrote two articles about the fact that the majority of the participants in the literary clubs in the Pale of Settlement were Jews, while the Russians frequented these clubs devoted to Russian literature less often. That process described by Jabotinsky was characteristic of the relationship of the Russian intelligentsia to the enlightened Jews. The literary club or any other intellectual circle was established initially by Russians. Jews immediately joined and their number quickly grew. As the number of Jews grew, the number of Russians declined proportionately. By the end of the process, we find, for example, a club devoted to the works of Gogol whose members are preponderantly Jewish. Jabotinsky ironically called this "a strange phenomenon," and called the Jews who were on the verge of assimilation or were already assimilated, "musicians at the wedding of strangers which the relatives have left."[31]

Jabotinsky's purpose was not to allow this absurd and pathetic situation to be hidden from the Jews. He did not deny the fact that, in reality, Jews were becoming the major purveyors of Russian culture; but this was not a function for Jews, because every nation had to create and disseminate its own culture. He felt that the Jews should leave the creation and dissemination of Russian culture in the hands of the Russians and occupy themselves with their own culture.

The existing situation was both absurd and tragic. The more the Jews exerted themselves to become the standard-bearers of Russian culture, the less successful they would be. It was specifically the assimilated Jew who, although he devoted himself unstintingly to Russian culture, would remain a second-class citizen, while a Jew living in Russia who was concerned with Jewish culture was equal in status to the Russian. All the while the Jew saw himself as a Jewish national and a Russian citizen who requested, like the Ukranians or the Poles, that the state accommodate his nationalistic demands, he was not a second-class citizen.

> All the while I see my place in Russia I am no better nor worse than others; we are all citizens of the same rank. However, if I should specifically desire to push my way into Russian society, the situation

immediately changes. By doing this I become a stranger. It is not possible to absorb, even in the space of a complete generation or even several generations, a foreign national nature, a foreign psyche, and the culture which is permeated with it. Just as an accent remains in the speech, a special imprint remains on the soul. ... I am sentenced ... to being considered an incomplete Russian, a false Russian ... And that is what it means to be second-class Russians. It is necessary to differentiate between the concepts, a son of Russia and a Russian. We are all sons of Russia, from the Amur until the Dneiper, and among this population, Russians constitute one-third. The Jew may be a first-class son of Russia, but only a second-class Russian. So other see him so, of necessity, he sees himself.[32]

This was true of assimilated Jews in Germany, in Czechoslovakia, and in Poland, indeed in every place where Jews attempted to be what they could not. Reality, said Jabotinsky, consistently proved that assimilation did not transform a Jew into a member of another nation. In all likelihood, it was already too late for the assimilated Jew to change himself and start acting like a Jew. However, it was his duty, in Jabotinsky's opinion, to acknowledge the pathos of his situation, to prevent the next generation from following in his path, and to direct them in the way of Jewish national culture. The spiritual life of the Jew as a member of the Jewish nation and as one of its architects would thus be both more intensive and happier, said Jabotinsky in 1903:

> Patriotism intensifies seven-fold the pace of intellectual activity; it adds warmth and interest. ... There is no intelligent person in the world today whose soul does not seek activity. All yearn for real action. The desolation, the Chekhovian yearning which fills the hollow emptiness of our world—all of these are nothing but the agitation of the energy which is bursting forth from within and is clamoring for productive work. ... Everyone feels that this period is coming closer, everyone says in his heart: the day is coming when you will find us suitable work. But we, the Jews, stand at the threshold of the coming century not with a sensation of joy but with a heart consumed by doubts. We also have energy and it is bursting forth from within us and we also long with all our might for work. However, we do not know for whom we must work. Shall we contribute our efforts to the land in which we live, and be content with that?[33]

Jabotinsky's answer was clear and familiar: the Jews had to work for the Jewish nation, just as members of other nationalities had to expend their efforts on behalf of their nations.

We saw that, for educated Jews, the economic isolator was disappearing, and the other two isolators—the ghetto walls and the Jewish tradition and religion—were likewise being destroyed. Such Jews were much more exposed and vulnerable than those who had remained within the breached walls of the ghetto and guarded their uniqueness with all their strength.

However, Jabotinsky did not see the metamorphasis that the middle and upper classes were undergoing as a deterministic process that necessarily terminated in assimilation; he saw it rather as a Hegelian dialectical process. In the beginning, the Jew had narrow, nationalist horizons based primarily on religious observances and laws. The Enlightenment movement was, in fact, antithetical to that situation in that it emphasized the universal as opposed to the particular. From it, the Jew attained a positive, humanitarian, universalist dimension, and the ammunition needed to confront contemporary culture. However, the Enlightenment also brought about negative phenomena—shame at being Jewish and estrangement from the Jewish people, for example.

The next stage was a kind of *Aufhebung*, a negation born of preservation and transcendence. Comprehension of the tragedy of the assimilated Jews, and the recognition of the impossibility of returning to the old corners of isolation would compel the Jews to shift their emphasis toward Jewish nationalism. The narrow concept of nationalism that had existed in the ghetto, that was based only on tradition and religion, would become the foundation upon which would be added strata of the new Jewish nationalism.

This would be implemented through Jewish national education, incorporating as well the educational attainments of the Enlightenment. The new Jewish nationalism would be based upon Jewish history and the Hebrew language, and would include all the elements of a modern national liberation movement; at the same time, it would repudiate the one-sidedness of both the ghetto and those influences of the Enlightenment that brought about assimilation. In summary, the negative aspects of the ghetto and of the Enlightenment would be abolished, and their positive aspects would be preserved and heightened to attain humanitarian Jewish nationalism. Thus Jewish history would reach its peak: the creation of the humanist Jew—the Jew who takes pride in his Judaism and engages in national Jewish creative activity and, through this, also contributes to humanity as a whole.

Jabotinsky never formulated his concept in dialectical terms, but there is no doubt that he envisioned the historical process the Jews were undergoing in such a fashion. He ended his article "A Lecture on Jewish History" by saying: "Gentlemen, just as our economic life in the exile, our dietary customs, and the ghetto itself, with their special characteristics, were various manifestations of eternal 'Zionism,' so our 'assimilation' was a stage in the development of a national resurrection, a step on the road from Zion to Zion."[34]

Jabotinsky viewed the Jewish left—the bund—in much the same way. From its inception the bund opposed Zionism as a divisive nationalist concept, and endorsed universalist, socialist ideals; still, from a historical perspective, Jabotinsky considered the establishment of the bund to have been an essential step leading to Zionism. The bund contributed significantly to developing national consciousness among the Jewish proletariat because it first had to consolidate that group. This process started by differentiating the Jewish proletariat from the general proletariat, and only at a later stage concentrated on what united them, thereby raising the matter of universal ideals.

Thus, with no such intention, and despite the struggle of the leaders of the bund against Zionism, the bund served the Zionist movement by crystallizing the national nature of the Jewish proletariat:

> The overall picture of the development of the Jewish labor movement is one of gradual and systematic "Zionization." [The researcher] will pay particular attention to one stage in this process—that in which the Jewish proletariat first differentiated itself from the others, because the separation of national forces from the "general interest" is the first step, the precondition without which independent activity by the people is inconceivable; this is the foremost principle, the basic foundation of the premises of Zionism; the actualization of this premise took on the image of the "bund." The "bund" assumed this function only because of the actual situation; neither the will of the bundists in those days—nor of the Zionists—was reflected thereby. ... It was the preparatory class in the "progressive *cheder*" of Zionism. ... This was the objective-historical function of the bund in the Jewish labor movement. The bund and Zionism are not two branches stemming from one root, but a large trunk and one of its branches. ... In the evolutionary forms of the bund, the Zionist vision developed objectively in the consciousness of the masses of Jewish workers.[35]

Everything thus led to one road: Zionism. Not only was it possible to prove, through the theory of nation and race, that there was only one way to solve the question of the Jews, but this approach was confirmed by the processes of history. What appeared to be different paths—the ghetto, the bund, the Enlightenment—were in reality nothing but offshoots of the same path, and all were destined to meet again on the main road.

Anti-Semitism

Jabotinsky discerned two types of anti-Semitism: anti-Semitism of man and anti-Semitism of things or circumstances.

Jabotinsky held racial prejudice to be a central example of a problem that liberal democracy could not solve. Furthermore, he claimed that the danger of racial prejudice was greater in a democracy, which was based on sovereignty of the people, many of whom were uneducated. Therefore, Jabotinsky sought a solution to the problem of national minorities, and presented a theory that made self-rule for every national minority imperative.

Jabotinsky considered the anti-Semitism of man to be an expression of racial prejudice, with great similarity to other types of racial prejudice, and felt that it must be fought in the same manner. Anti-Semitism of circumstances, in contrast, was not the product of prejudice but the result of the objective situation of the Jewish people—living in exile. Thus the treatment for this structural anti-Semitism was different from that for the first kind. In summing up a theme that ran through Ahad-Ha'am, Nordau, and Borochov, Jabotinsky maintained "through all these ruminations on the nature of the exile, there runs one truth among the writers: the major disaster lies not in malicious anti-Semitism, which comes out of free will, the anti-Semitism of man ... the major disaster is embedded in the 'objective anti-Semitism of circumstances.'"[36]

Jabotinsky summarized his general approach to anti-Semitism, in which he drew from the aforementioned Zionist thinkers, in his 1937 testimony before the Peel Commission:

> We are facing an elemental calamity, a kind of social earthquake. Three generations of Jewish thinkers and Zionists, among them many great minds ... have given much thought to analyzing the Jewish position, and have come to the conclusion that the cause of our suffering is the very fact of the "Disapora," the bedrock fact that we are everywhere a minority. It is not the anti-Semitism of men; it is, above all, the anti-Semitism of things, the inherent xenophobia of the body social or the body economic under which we suffer. Of course, there are ups and downs; but there are moments, there are whole periods of history, when this "xenophobia of Life itself" takes dimensions which no people can stand, and that is what we are facing now.[37]

Jabotinsky thus saw in the second and crucial type of anti-Semitism a structural phenomenon that was the result of the absence of a territory in which the Jews were the majority. Practically all other minorities had at least one state in which they constituted a majority. The major cause of structural anti-Semitism was not to be found among people, in the rabble, or in governments, but in the unique historical situation of the Jewish people. A minority everywhere, they were even stranger for their lack of a national territory; a nation without a state was like a man without a shadow. It was this strangeness that made the Jews universally hated, and this hatred could only be extirpated by establishing a state of the Jews.

Jabotinsky began to develop his concept of anti-Semitism in 1903. During the years of his study in Rome, he saw how a normal nation lived in its homeland, and he always felt that the absence of a homeland made the Jewish people foreign and strange. He was not influenced by socialist talk about nationalism being a reactionary phenomenon or about the future presaging one universal society in which national territory had no place. From early on, before he crystallized his thoughts on nation and race, he repeatedly emphasized that anti-Semitism forced people to make an attempt to be "normal." In his article "To the Foes of Zion" (1903), he says that a person without a homeland gouges out the eyes of those with a homeland: "I once read in the volumes of the philosopher Kant, that any incompleteness will not be forgiven a man. If he is missing something which is found among other creatures, this deficiency will pathologically attract people's glances, and will even anger them. Because such is the nature of man, that he does not tolerate dissonance within the general harmony."[38]

As a result of his belief that structural anti-Semitism was more significant than the anti-Semitism of man, Jabotinsky's reaction to the pogroms was different from most; many expected him to write impassioned articles and were disappointed.

In "In Days of Mourning," which he wrote in 1906, Jabotinsky admitted that he could not rouse in himself any interest in the pogroms; after the Kishinev pogroms in 1903 that made the people aware of their cowardice, there were simply no more lessons to be learned: "A tragedy must of necessity hold some hidden truth; a lesson that is learned from the suffering and that reveals to people new methods. And what did these pogroms reveal to us; what could they teach us? ... They were nothing but a great, wicked crime, brutish and without logic—and nothing more. Our lifeblood is oozing out and we do not know for what purpose, and what truth this suffering comes to teach us."[39]

None of the pogroms, said Jabotinsky, was different from any other, nor was there much reason to figure out what could be done to prevent the approaching pogroms. Experience showed that the efficacy of self-defense was limited. There was no purpose in propaganda against the pogroms because the Russian mobs would not read it. The Russian masses wanted to hear that the Jew was responsible for their suffering and troubles, and they needed the Jew as a scapegoat. They certainly were not interested in reading that the Jews were not responsible for their troubles because then they would need to search for the source of troubles within themselves, something they did not want to do. Anti-Semitism had a clear function in Russian life; it was an organic phenomenon which would not disappear even if the Russian masses all became educated.

Jabotinsky's conclusion was clear: "I learn nothing from the pogroms to our people and there is nothing that they can teach us that we did not know before. And I also do not request a balm for every separate wound resulting from the exile because I do not believe in it. I do not have a 'pogromic' philosophy nor do I have pogromic medicine."[40] For Jabotinsky there was one all-inclusive and complete solution to the question of the Jews, and that was the establishment of a state of the Jews.

Not anti-Semitism, but a historical analysis of Jewish history, on the one hand, and the theory of nation and race, on the other, inevitably led to the conclusion that a state of the Jews was the only solution. Therefore Jabotinsky opposed the thesis that Zionism was an outgrowth of anti-Semitism. The function of anti-Semitism was to arouse the people. However, once the people had awakened, the type of national resurrection they chose would be the result of the national existential urge that had been inherent within them from the day they became a nation. This urge for self-expression prevented them from acclimating to the alien environment in which they lived during the exile. If anti-Semitism were the primary motivation for behavior, the Jewish people could have found a solution by assimilating into their surroundings.

"In this scheme [Jewish history], anti-Semitism is merely a second-rate detail,"[41] Jabotinsky wrote. Indeed, Jabotinsky's theory of Jewish history described anti-Semitism as a structural phenomenon which surfaced repeatedly throughout the years of the exile. It was never perceived as a reason for the overwhelming efforts of the Jewish people to preserve their national uniqueness, just as it was not presented as a cause of the rise of Zionism.

The perception of the Jews as a stubborn and separate minority, and not as the victims of a phenomenon based on hatred and boorishness, ended any hope for the possibility of combatting anti-Semitism with partial solutions like education of the masses. Only a structural change in the condition of the Jewish people would solve the problem of structural anti-Semitism. By destroying their house of cards and their false hopes, Jabotinsky hoped to pass on to diaspora Jewry his own deep conviction that the establishment of a state of the Jews was the only solution:

> If for a moment you think you are happy, I will don clothes of mourning and will come to your party. I will make mockery of the casualness of your belief, I will ridicule your toasts; I will announce the bitter truth and I will poison every trace of pleasure, and that is the only thing which still connects me to you. I want to really gouge out your eyes, to break down your house that you built of cards, to extinguish your magic lanterns with the colorful pictures so that you would see in front of your eyes a sealed wall, and around you—the grief of despair. With all my might I will not allow you to become tranquil, I will not let you delight your souls with dreams.[42]

And indeed, in the ensuing years (1906–1912), Jabotinsky wrote cease-lessly about anti-Semitism. In his article, "Four Sons" (1911), he described the genesis of hatred toward the Jews, starting with their descent into Egypt. He contrasted the history of their wanderings with what had begun to take place in the diaspora, "how, little by little, the will of the people, which up till now was as fleeting as dust, is beginning to crystallize; how, from its fragments, a real nation is taking shape, strong in its desire, that likes itself and sees itself as the chosen people, like all healthy nations."[43]

Jabotinsky warned against the desire of educated Jews to see allusions to anti-Semitism by the leaders of the educated Russians as a passing phenomenon. "The bear," as Jabotinsky in 1909 called the anti-Semitism of the Russian intelligentsia, had peeked out of his cave. At that time, it was a quick glance, but the day was not far when the bear would burst out.[44]

Jabotinsky did not drop the subject. In that same year, he wrote "The Russian Caress," in which he described the anti-Semitic tones (which he called "caresses") that appeared in the works of such great Russian writers as Pushkin, Gogol, Dostoyevsky, and Chekhov.[45] Their opinions could not be ignored since they expressed the true sentiments and philosophy of the Russian people.

Jabotinsky continued to write about this same problem from different perspectives. In 1912, as we saw, he noted the "strange phenomenon" that the members of the Russian literary clubs were mostly Jews, while the Russians who had established the clubs were slowly and unobtrusively disappearing:

> The founders welcome them, and even are happy that they have come. After several weeks the hall is full of Jews, and then a strange thing is seen: the greater the number of Jews becomes, the number of Russians lessens proportionately. ... They leave—they do not curse, they do not become bitter and complain, and in general they do not talk, but simply disappear. And if you ask them why, they themselves could not actually explain. ... However, there is no denying that there is some kind of "rejection" that is hidden from the eye.[46]

It was important to recognize the truth, to see the sparks of anti-Semitism among the educated progressives, and to understand that the day was not far off when this anti-Semitism would become stronger. There was no refuge from it because the tragedy of the Jewish people was inherent in its abnormal condition. Jabotinsky repeated his conclusion over and over: there were no partial solutions to anti-Semitism. There was only one answer: to establish a state of the Jews. All other methods were wrong.

Jabotinsky never changed his opinions about anti-Semitism; they were only confirmed by the events which overtook Europe. In 1926 in "The Rigan Hasmonean," he described how also in Riga where there was no organized Jew-baiting, "the usual process of economic exclusion of the Jews is being conducted as usual, for this is an 'iron rule of the exile.' Except that the Jews themselves acknowledge that it develops because of the economic strength of the Latvian, and not because of the strength of malice and pressure."[47] That is, even where the individuals were not Jew-haters, anti-Semitism existed as a structural phenomenon.

The increasingly worsening condition of European Jews did not, in fact, alter Jabotinsky's basic attitude toward anti-Semitism. However, tones heard in his earlier articles from about 1910—"Right and Power," "I Do Not Believe," "*Homo Homini Lupus*"—intensified. He denounced the actions of the gentiles toward the Jews as the height of immorality and as defiance of accepted conventions of what was *verboten*. In 1927, Jabotinsky sharply attacked Petliura, who was the head of state of the Ukraine and its army during the period of more than two years when pogroms were perpetrated against the Jews. Despite his admiration for the Ukranian national party (something considered strange by many because of the anti-Semitic nature of the Ukraine), and despite the fact that Petliura did not support these incidents, Jews contended that he was absolutely responsible since they transpired during his rule. To remove all doubts, Jabotinsky made it very clear that: "Petliura's defenders will not be helped by the theory that the pogroms are, from the perspective of the philosophy of history, more the result of 'anti-Semitism of circumstances' than of the 'anti-Semitism of man.'"[48]

In other words, Jabotinsky's concept of anti-Semitism as the result of circumstances did not exonerate those who participated in it, whether actively or through speech or writing. What was taking place in Europe was a combination of the two types of anti-Semitism. In 1928, Jabotinsky was strongly convinced that the civilized world would no longer tolerate the unrestrained victimization of one group—with one exception: the Jews.[49]

In view of the events in Europe in the latter part of the thirties, Jabotinsky returned to a discussion of anti-Semitism in order to find a solution for diaspora Jewry. He once again related primarily to that anti-Semitism that was an organic part of the diaspora: "It is not the theoretical anti-Semitism that matters; much more important is the anti-Semitism of objective facts. It is an ironclad law in the history of the exile that every blow of the hammer that strikes anywhere causes severe damage, first and foremost to the landless Jew."[50]

Since Jabotinsky's purpose was to find a solution to the problem of the Jews, he now attacked the issue from a special angle. The constant search in the souls of the gentiles for anti-Semitic strains was unproductive. Even if every gentile had anti-Semitic tendencies, it did not mean that none could be found who were willing to help the Jews achieve their goal. This conclusion was tenable if one accepted that anti-Semitism was not the result of hatred for the Jews, but of an objective situation. Jabotinsky believed that even among those who did not want Jews in their state, there were people of conscience who did not want a great catastrophe to befall the Jews. It was possible, he felt, to build on this feeling and to prick the conscience of the world to bring about the establishment of the state of the Jews in the Land of Israel.

Jabotinsky based the ideas he expressed in "The Helping Storm" on this assumption. He attempted to find a positive side to the storm that had been enveloping the Jews in Europe since the beginning of the 1930's. These ideas can be found in his speeches and writings from 1936 and 1937. He wrote: "Even though this unpleasant chain of events has a harmful effect on all aspects of Jewish life, on the other hand, it increasingly makes the constructive elements and those concerned with our well-being aware that the sole answer to our tragedy is the Land of Israel. These winds, despite all their strength and intensity, are pushing the Jewish ship in the same direction that we ourselves would wish to steer it."[51]

During those years, when he developed the theory articulated in "The Helping Storm" and dealt with the evacuation program for Polish Jewry, Jabotinsky placed great emphasis on the difference between the two types of anti-Semitism, in order to clarify his approach to the problem of the Jews. He explained that while "anti-Semitism of things" was in the category of "a helping storm," the situation was different with "anti-Semitism of man": "The scientific hatred for the Jew, the desire to degrade him and to make him suffer, is kind of a 'typhoon': atmospheric shock waves with no direction. Despite every desire to do so, the typhoon cannot be converted into a wind that blows in the desired direction. The typhoon blows around and around and is capable only of destruction."[52]

"Anti-Semitism of man" was based on hatred springing deep from the emotions, something that was essential to the anti-Semite in order to continue to hate. Therefore, the awakening of that type of anti-Semitism could only harm the Zionist movement and the attempts to rescue the Jews from the exile. The world was divided between those whose anti-Semitism was based upon a moral disability bordering on sadism—to whom Jewish blood was worthless—and those whose anti-Semitism was rooted in circumstances. The latter type could be enlisted to help in the establishment of a state of the Jews. Nations such as those were liable to help the Jews, whether for reasons of conscience or in order to solve their own Jewish problem. As late as 1937, Jabotinsky believed that the conscience of the world could and had to be roused. This point is worth noting because it is the best proof that Jabotinsky was not afflicted with the feeling that "the whole world is against us"—quite the contrary, in fact.

In his testimony before the Peel Commission, Jabotinsky presented his position as an essentially humanitarian one. He had always seen the British as allies of the Jewish people, though at an early state he distinguished clearly between the British officials in the Land of Israel, whose activities he opposed, and the British people and government. In the name of morality, and in light of the lessons of history, he demanded the establishment of an independent state in the Land of Israel as the sole solution to the problem of the Jews. Only then would structural anti-Semitism completely and absolutely vanish.

We cannot end this discussion of Jabotinsky's concept of anti-Semitism without mentioning his attitude toward Nazism. In 1933, analyzing events in Germany, he concluded that the emerging anti-Semitism was not generated only by psychopathic sadists like Goebbels, but was also a structural part of Nazism: "Incitement against the Jews is an integral, objective part of the Hitlerian regime that it could not renounce even if Hitler himself suddenly became a friend of the Jews. The moment the attacks against the Jews stop, this party will crumble and its regime will disintegrate. Without hatred of the Jews, it is doomed because such hatred is the only part of its ideology and platform in which any substance at all may be found."[53]

German anti-Semitism accounted for at least half of those persons who were afflicted with racial hatred, and particularly hatred for the Jews. One-half of Germany's general population and three-quarters of the younger people had voted for Hitler. It is true that there were other Germans, said Jabotinsky, but the proportions of the phenomenon of racial hatred in Germany were so immense that concern had to be focused on Germany, and not on such extreme anti-Semites as Hitler. Thus, while German anti-Semitism was fundamentally structural, it attracted many extreme elements of "anti-Semitism of man": "It is a typical and ugly outburst of the same 'appetite' that 'increases with eating,' haste to remove the lid from that same old gluttony that was previously hidden (perhaps subconsciously) behind the sweet and accommodating diplomacy of Stresemann and Bruening. Why must we ignore this; why must the world ignore it? The Hitlerian sickness in Germany isn't a plague; it is a natural phenomenon, a poison deeply embedded with the blood of the people which manifests its signs at every appropriate opportunity."[54]

Although in his wildest dreams Jabotinsky could not have imagined that this anti-Semitism would lead to the physical destruction of millions of Jews, he warned in the strongest terms that, if world Jewry remained silent and if the world remained silent, the Hitlerian regime would deprive the Jews of their possessions, place them under quarantine, and eventually expel them. Jabotinsky understood very well that if Hitler were not stopped, the holocaust to befall the Jews would be different from anything the Jewish people had known until then, both in scope and in method.

Jabotinsky was also correct in stating that the Hitlerian regime constituted a danger not only to the Jews, but to the peace of the entire world.

However, like many others, Jabotinsky misjudged Hitler's readiness to go to war, and underestimated the amount of time that Germany needed to reestablish a large military infrastructure. This erroneous assessment was reflected in his speech before the founding convention of the New Zionist Organization in 1935: "Let us not be persuaded into believing that we are facing an iron giant, against whom acts of pressure are useless. It is not true."[55] He made a similar assessment as late as 1939 in a speech before Policy Jewry in which he said that Poland's refusal to submit to the demands of the Third Reich took the air out of the "inflated balloon" that was the Third Reich.

On the other hand, from 1935 onward, Jabotinsky was increasingly aware that the impending holocaust to German Jewry was unprecedented, and while he did not think in terms of physical destruction, he said: "The position of the Third Reich toward the Jews is expressed in a war of annihilation; it is being conducted through methods which deviate from the bounds of humanity."[56]

Jabotinsky considered anti-Semitic outbursts to be a kind of contagious disease, and feared that Eastern European countries would be infected with the vigorous and extreme anti-Semitism of the Nazis. Therefore he tried in vain to organize Eastern European Jewry into a parliament (the Zion-*Sejm*) that would be chosen in general elections and would represent Eastern European Jewry to all international factors.

Jabotinsky thus was correct in his assessment of the motives behind the anti-Semitism of the Third Reich, although he misjudged its format and its methods. However, he was adamant about the fact that all of Germany would be involved, that Nazism presented a threat to world peace, and that Hitler had to be stopped immediately. At every opportunity, he pointed out the seriousness of the situation, demanding world action in the struggle against Hitler. No normal person could have begun to imagine that physical annihilation was at stake. Certainly no one else in the Zionist movement, and perhaps in the world, gave warning about the impending catastrophe to the Jews of Europe and the fundamental nature of Nazi anti-Semitism. Jabotinsky was not content with his warnings, but considered it the function of all Jewish people to alert the world to the terrible danger from the Nazis that was lurking.

The Invalidity of Alternative Solutions to Zionism

Jabotinsky presented his position that the only solution to the problem of the Jews was the establishment of a state of the Jews in the Land of Israel in opposition to alternative solutions that were popular among the Jews at the beginning of the twentieth century. Struggling primarily against the various types of territorialists who were willing to forego the Land of Israel as the locus for the state of the Jews, and against those who espoused cultural autonomy as a solution wherever the Jews were a minority.

The territorialists' argument was simpler. Their centrist mainstream contended that a national center for the Jewish people could be established in a land other than *Eretz Yisrael*, "in which the Jews will live lives of political liberty, and in which their national uniqueness will independently become manifest when they are liberated from all oppression, and their national culture develops without obstruction from any side."[57]

In the article "On Territorialism," Jabotinsky responded in great detail to the various claims of the territorialists. To those who pleaded "just not Zion," because its land was infertile and not suitable for absorbing mass Jewish immigration, Jabotinsky's response was peremptory: it was not likely that a land which in the past had been populated by great numbers of people had undergone such a drastic geological change that it could no longer be cultivated. To the claim that, because it was the "Land of the Patriarchs," the Jews would transfer to *Eretz Yisrael* all the traditions, laws, and religious observances that had developed in the diaspora, Jabotinsky responded: "The intensification of the outward manifestations of the laws and customs served as an artificial isolator to prevent assimilation among the gentiles, and it comes as the direct result of the loss of the natural isolator—the national land. Therefore, it is clear that the very fact of living in the national land will turn the majority of laws which have become outdated—even in the eyes of the devout masses—into something undesirable and without any outside intervention, these laws will slowly be shed and disappear."[58]

The only territorialist contention which Jabotinsky considered serious was that of the centrist branch which did not reject Zion, but maintained that instead of waiting stubbornly for *Eretz Yisrael*, any land that was offered should be accepted in order to alleviate Jewish suffering. He separated this contention into two parts: first, that the Jewish people needed immediate salvation; and therefore that the land that was offered first should be accepted, and second, that it would be easier and quicker to establish the state of the Jews in a territory other than *Eretz Yisrael*.

Whoever believed that quick salvation meant the establishment of a state of the Jews in the first place that was offered did not understand that immigration to any country other than the Land of Israel was foredoomed. The Jewish nation was inextricably bound to one territory—*Eretz Yisrael*—and it would be possible to mount a mass immigration movement only to *Eretz Yisrael*.

Jabotinsky's response to the second part of the claim was that the territory

> upon which one can proceed with the utmost confidence to the building of the Jewish state. ... is the Land of Israel. ... More than 80,000 Jews are living in the Land of Israel, and they constitute eleven percent of the total population, that is, more than in any other land; these 80,000 people are now uneducated and economically backward, but by schools and organized government assistance in finding work, it will be possible within ten years to re-educate from the root the entire younger generation of these masses; the local Arab population is absolutely lacking in culture, and the Jews who, even in the most enlightened countries where they are a small group of people, know how to achieve influence, can easily acquire it here, all the more so since according to Muslim tradition, the land is destined to belong to the Jews; in the Land of Israel despite everything, we have thirty *moshavot* [private farming villages], a bank with branches, private lands in different places, and even various industrial plants; and finally, there has existed among the people from time eternity an attraction to the Land of Israel.[59]

Over the years, Jabotinsky changed his views on only one point in the above quotation; he eventually came to understand that the Arabs in the Land of Israel were a living nation who also saw in *Eretz Yisrael* their own state, and who were willing to fight for it. However, Jabotinsky clung to his central claim—that the Land of Israel was the only territory in which it was possible to establish the Zionist enterprise—even in the face of monumental difficulties on the way to building the state of the Jews there. Jabotinsky believed that his theories, with their rationalist-scientific explanations, were correct, and he used them in attempting to convince others; however, his attachment to *Eretz Yisrael* was derived first and foremost from his strong internal feeling.

Jabotinsky's position *vis à vis* autonomy was more complicated. He was among the chief formulators of the "Helsingfors Program" in 1906 which attempted to give an exhaustive answer to the question of the character and scope of national self-definition for the Jewish people in Russia. At that stage of his life, Jabotinsky was ready to work simultaneously on two parallel fronts: the struggle for the establishment of the state of the Jews in the Land of Israel, and the struggle for self-rule and equality of civil, political, and national rights for the Jews in those enclaves where they constituted a minority. At that stage, Jabotinsky did not yet see these two struggles as contradictory. However, even then he emphasized that the struggle for national self-definition of the Jews in the diaspora would allow them to live in the diaspora only until they could immigrate to the state of the Jews to be established in *Eretz Yisrael*.

Not much time passed before Jabotinsky realized that it was im-

possible to fight on two fronts simultaneously; his attitude to those support-
ing self-rule for the Jews in the diaspora then began to change. Here his
monistic outlook was expressed most absolutely: the ideal of the establishment of a state of the Jews in the Land of Israel was so important that it
was necessary to sacrifice all other ideals, lest the struggle for them interfere
with the effort to establish the state. This monistic concept characterized all
of Jabotinsky's Zionist thought relating to the breakthrough period—the
period of the struggle for the establishment of the state of the Jews.

As early as 1904, Jabotinsky wrote "A Letter on Autonomy," in which
he proved that the perception of autonomy as a permanent solution for the
Jews in the diaspora was like a boomerang; if autonomy achieved complete
equality of rights for the Jews and ended the enmity toward them, it would
also create conditions for intermarriage, thus paving the way for the eventual
but certain annihilation of the Jewish race and nation. If, on the other hand,
self-rule did not bring about the anticipated equality—what then was its
purpose? It was clear to Jabotinsky that the true problem of the Jews would
continue as long as the Jewish people lacked a state of its own. Autonomy
thus would jeopardize the future of the Jewish nation. It would be possible to
speak about self-rule for those Jews who remained in the diaspora only once
a state was established. Therefore, said Jabotinsky, "preservation of the
national essence depends upon the maintenance of racial purity, and for this
reason, we need our own territory, in which our people will constitute a
decisive majority."[60] In accordance with his general political philosophy,
Jabotinsky viewed national isolation not as isolation for its own sake, but as
a necessary condition for national creativity—which, in turn, was essential
for human progress which had to be built on a diversity of national cultures.
Thus it was in the interest of mankind that the Jewish nation have a
homeland.

Jabotinsky responded to those who opposed Zionism for socialist-
universalist reasons in a similar fashion. He believed that the progressive
proletariat, whose function it was to further the interests of humanity,
should see in the struggle of the Jewish nation part of its own struggle. Since
in this period—approximately 1910—Jabotinsky still did not oppose the left,
he pointed to the fact that, in a democratic Jewish state in which the labor
party had a majority, it would be possible to find a solution to the workers'
problems, as was done by Watson's government in Australia.

Jabotinsky's final conclusion was, as expected, that the absolute supremacy of the national ideal during the entire period of the struggle—up until
the very establishment of the state of the Jews—had to be maintained.

Chapter 3

THE BREAKTHROUGH
PERIOD: ON THE WAY
TO STATEHOOD

As we saw in the first part of the book, the breakthrough period for many liberal thinkers was characterized by significant changes whose ultimate goal was to create an ideal society and a state based on liberal principles. During this period, certain temporary, conscious breaches of liberal principles were necessary. It was also necessary to ensure, however, that at the end of this period, liberal principles would be enstated.

Jabotinsky clearly distinguished between the period that may be called "on the way to statehood" and the period after the establishment of the state of the Jews. A failure to understand this critical distinction in Jabotinsky's thought between the two periods has lead to a distortion of his theory, and to many patently false conclusions regarding his vision of the political, economic, and social character of the state of the Jews.

In this chapter, we shall examine the goals of Zionism as articulated by Jabotinsky, how they took shape, and their eventual formulation in accordance with his concept of Greater Zionism; we shall see which goals were to be implemented in the breakthrough period, and which after the establishment of the Hebrew state; we shall examine the concept of "monism" which characterized Jabotinsky's thought on the breakthrough period, and how it was translated into action in different areas; and we shall attempt to find one clear, coherent picture of goals on the one hand, and ways and means of implementing them, on the other.

Finally, throughout this chapter, we shall examine which liberal principles needed to be compromised, in Jabotinsky's opinion, on the way to statehood; whether he understood that an infringement of liberal principles was involved, and, if so, how he explained it; and whether he limited the duration of the breakthrough period.

176

The Goals of Zionism

As we saw in the chapter dealing with the Jewish nation and race, Jabotinsky felt that, in its attempt to establish a Hebrew state specifically in the ancestral homeland of the Jewish people, Zionism was the only national movement to reflect popular longing. In the terminology of his theory of nation and race, the goal of Zionism was to recreate the natural isolator of the Jewish nation and race so that they might continue, through their creativity, to contribute to human progress; in other words, to transform the Land of Israel once again into the national territory of the Jewish nation.

In an earlier period, Jabotinsky made do with a broad definition of the goals of Zionism, which he expressed in different forms. In 1903, he said that the slogan of Zionism should be "*Kadima*," based on the double meaning of the word: Eastward (geographically), and progress. During this period, he constantly emphasized that Zionism was composed of universal ideals: "In any case, it carries the noble vision of liberty and equality."[1] He considered the establishment of the state of the Jews to be a historical phenomenon— the renewed entrance of the Jewish people into history. This was a revolutionary change, because Jabotinsky perceived the history of the Jewish people in exile more as the record of what was perpetrated upon the Jews than of what the Jews had done. Zionist activity needed to take place simultaneously in the Land of Israel and in the diaspora, and had to be expressed in all spheres of life.

Later, Jabotinsky began to formulate the goals of Zionism more systematically, and from them derived proposed methods of action for different spheres of interest. His detailed discussion of the goals of Zionism was the result of his feeling that reality and action often made people forget the principles. Thus, in 1923, he said: "The first and foremost among them is: the creation of a Jewish majority has always been, is, and always will be the fundamental goal of Zionism; of *every* type of Zionism whether political or spiritual. Zionism is an attempt to give a complete answer to two questions: one of them concerns the desire for spiritual independence, the other, the palpable suffering of the Jewish masses. Any attempt to solve either question under the circumstances of a national minority is only a worthless palliative."[2]

The first and foremost goal of Zionism was therefore to bring about a Jewish majority in the Land of Israel. This goal derived directly from Jabotinsky's national concept. The tragedy of the exile lay in the fact that the Jews were a minority everywhere; the tragic situation of the Jews in the diaspora would be duplicated in the Land of Israel if they were a minority there too, under Arab rule. For the Jewish nation to develop, it needed to be able to express itself through its own government, established according to its own psyche. Thus it was necessary to have at least a majority of Jews in its own state in *Eretz Yisrael*.

The existence of a minority of Jews in the Land of Israel would mean integration and, ultimately, assimilation. Jabotinsky explained the national fervor of the Jews who at that time lived as a minority in the Land of Israel as merely the nature of the period; it was a time of transition and building, with visions of establishing a state of the Jews, a time characterized by ideological fervor; the laws of assimilation did not apply to this period.

The goal of establishing a Jewish majority in *Eretz Yisrael* was therefore an essential condition for all others: "the term 'state of the Jews' is absolutely clear: it means a Jewish majority. With this Zionism began, and this is the basis of its existence; with this Zionism will continue to function until it is realized or ceases to exist."[3]

Concomitant with the creation of a majority in the Land of Israel, it was necessary, obviously, to work toward obtaining a charter for the Land of Israel; the achievement of both would bring about the establishment of the state of the Jews. The program of the Union of Zionist Revisionists (UZR) came out in 1926; in it, the goals of Zionism were systematically defined.

First, "the primary aim of Zionism is the creation of a Hebrew majority in the Land of Israel on both sides of the Jordan."[4] The creation of a Jewish majority would make possible the establishment of a parliamentary-democratic state with a Hebrew national character. Later, it would be possible to work toward the two ultimate and loftier aims of Zionism: "finding a solution for Jewish suffering all over the world and creating a new Hebrew culture."[5]

The connection between the primary and secondary goals was clearly defined in Jabotinsky's teachings. While an Arab majority still existed, it would not be possible to establish a parliament, nor to introduce democratic principles. Under such circumstances, a democratic state would be one with an Arab national character. Nor would the Jewish nation be able to fulfill itself culturally until a Jewish majority existed in *Eretz Yisrael*, since a real corner of isolation would not yet exist. As long as the Jews remained a minority, the territory, notwithstanding that it was *Eretz Yisrael*, was not their national territory. Nor could the problem of the millions of Jews in the diaspora then be solved; an Arab majority in the *Eretz Yisrael* would never open the gates of the land to mass Jewish immigration.

In July 1931, there was an argument at the Zionist Congress about the aims of Zionism. Jabotinsky presented the Revisionist position, which, in a personal vote, was rejected by the majority. Instead, the proposal of the Labor faction to return to the agenda was accepted. Jabotinsky's position, rejected by the Labor faction, refered to three different terms by which the goals of Zionism were defined: a "secure place of refuge in accordance with open law," a "national home," and a "state of the Jews." The first two terms were intentionally vague, so as not to anger the Turkish Sultan, and later, Mandatory Britain. In contrast, the term "state" was clearer, even though it, too, had different connotations: it could refer to parts of a country (the United States, for example), but could also imply complete independence.

Nor was the term "state" sufficiently clear with regard to the question of a majority. South Africa, for instance, was the state of the Boers and the British, both of whom were minorities. Thus, while Jabotinsky chose the expression "state of the Jews," he had to elucidate its meaning. His suggested characteristics of the state of the Jews were conditions he considered essential to Zionism—an ethnic majority of Jews among the residents of the land and self-rule. The term "self-rule" was also open to different interpretations, since different levels of sovereignty were possible. This flexibility did not disturb Jabotinsky. On the other hand, he said that "one thing is not flexible; it either exists or it does not; this thing is the numerical majority of residents. The land will become a Jewish land the very instant it has a Jewish majority."[6] Jabotinsky repeatedly asserted that his was the correct interpretation of the Mandate, adding that its intent was to include both banks of the Jordan River. It was necessary, in his opinion, to thus define, explicitly and vociferously, the aims of Zionism; only such an interpretation would give a legal basis to the demand for a large immigration. There is no question that Jabotinsky's proposal was rejected, not so much because there was no concurrence regarding the issue of a Jewish majority, but because of disagreement over the tactics he suggested: using an explicit definition of the aims of Zionism rather than the vague one used in an attempt not to alienate either Great Britain or the Arabs.

This is not the place to discuss the question, interesting in itself, of which tactics were correct. What is important to bear in mind in this discussion is that by 1931 most of the Congress members still did not speak openly about a Jewish majority as the goal of Zionism. Moreover, there were important voices—among them that of Chaim Weizmann—who said in a newspaper interview that a Jewish majority in the Land of Israel was not necessary in order to create a Hebrew culture. It is therefore not surprising that Jabotinsky devoted many of his articles and speeches to the issue of a majority.

The concept of a majority, with emphasis on the ability of the Jewish nation to contribute to human progress only when it had its own state, was repeated in the *Betar* program as it appeared in "The Idea of Betar" (1934):

> The basis of the Betar viewpoint is singular and unique: the Jewish State.
> In this simple idea, however, lies a profound world view. What reason is
> there for the existence of different nations and peoples? The "reason" is

that every nation must contribute its own share to the common culture of mankind, a share that is distinguished by its own spiritual stamp. It must not be satisfied with ideas and fine suggestions to other people: it must serve as a living *example* of those ideas and ideals that it must actively carry out; to express them, not only in books, but specifically in the communal forms of life of the people. However, for the purpose every nation must possess its own "laboratory," a country wherein that nation alone is master and can freely plan its communal life in accordance with its own conceptions of good and evil. Only its own state can serve as such a "laboratory." ... What, however, is the practical meaning of a "state of the Jews?" When will we be able to say that "Palestine" has become "*Eretz Yisrael?*" Only when more Jews than non-Jews live in the land. The first condition for a national state is a national majority.[7]

Jabotinsky's repeated emphasis on the goal of a majority was the direct result of other views current among the Jews, including the Zionists; these advocated the establishment of "national positions" in the Land of Israel in the form of *moshavot* (private farming villages), universities, and the like in order to live a national life while still remaining a minority. Despite the fact that in 1934 only a few Zionists held this opinion, Jabotinsky feared that, as a result of the difficulties of achieving a majority in the Land of Israel, others would be persuaded to support it, and therefore he felt compelled to keep explaining the issue. "The Idea of *Betar*" also defined the other goals of Zionism, as delineated in the UZR program, but more clearly. After the establishment of a state of the Jews with a government based on democratic principles, would come the turn of the other two goals: the Return to Zion, and the transformation of the Land of Israel into a state that led the cultured world.

The breakthrough period—the period of transition—thus would have only one goal: "The first step ... without which there can be no Zionism, nor a Jewish state, nor a real Jewish nation, is the creation of a Jewish majority in the Land of Israel on both sides of the Jordan."[8] After its establishment, the state of the Jews, would have to grapple with two new challenges: the creation of suitable conditions for absorbing the millions of Jews who would want to immigrate, and the development of government, laws, and just social policies that would serve as "a light unto the nations."

Thus the role of Zionism would not end with the establishment of the state of the Jews; on the contrary, the realization of the goals of Zionism would occupy the state of the Jews for a long time. "Zionism is a task of tremendous importance, the limits of which our generation cannot as yet envisage."[9]

In his opening speech at the founding convention of the New Zionist Organization in 1935, Jabotinsky described the uniqueness of the Zionist

Revisionist outlook: "[The mission] is not the reform of the exile through a model strip of land in *Eretz Yisrael*, but the liquidation of the exile: an 'exodus from Egypt' for all those who thirst for a homeland—and ultimately, certainly nothing less than the end of the exile—a normalization of the Jewish people, so that it becomes normal like the large French nation or the small Danish nation. They are all in their own states; they are all free—with no exile."[10]

As in the program of the Union of Zionist Revisionists and "The Idea of *Betar*," Jabotinsky emphasized that the establishment of the state of the Jews was not a final goal but the first step toward the realization of Greater Zionism. After the establishment of the state of the Jews, the next step would be the exodus of the masses from the diaspora and their return to Zion; the question of the Jews would thus be naturally solved. Afterwards would come the final goal: "And the true final goal of Greater Zionism will not appear until the third stage—the reason for which, actually, the large nations exist: the creation of a national culture which will impart its glory to the entire world."[11]

Mass immigration to the Land of Israel was, first and foremost, a humanitarian goal, and so Jabotinsky presented it, in his testimony before the Peel Commission and in his book *A Hebrew State: A Solution to the Question of the Jews* (1937). In mass immigration Jabotinsky saw the uniqueness of Greater Zionism: if small-scale Zionism wanted to create in "the Land of Israel something singular and exemplary,"[12] something concerned primarily with the fate of the Jewish elite, "Greater Zionism" saw its function first and foremost as humanitarian: "to save from the special Jewish torments all those actual Jews who need it today or who will need it in the future."[13] A Hebrew state needed to be created as quickly as possible, so that its gates would be opened to rescue the masses of the house of Israel.

Jabotinsky's perception of the last goal—a "light unto the nations"—as the most important obviously stemmed from his liberal theoretical outlook regarding the essence the nations and their role in human progress.

At the aforementioned founding convention of the NZO, the "Ten-Year Plan" was brought up for discussion. This program went into great detail about the ways and means to achieve a Jewish majority on both sides of the Jordan within the following decade.

This Ten-Year Plan was presented by Jabotinsky on many occasions after that. He devoted a chapter in *A Hebrew State: A Solution to the Question of the Jews* to that topic. In 1938, he delivered his famous speech, "The Partition Plan Versus the Ten-Year-Plan," and wrote two articles, "The Ten-Year Plan and Trans-Jordan" and "A Precondition to the Ten-Year Plan." Jabotinsky proposed the plan as an alternative to the Partition Plan after that had failed.

The goal of a majority needed to be achieved within a breakthrough period of ten years or so, after which it would come to a close. Jabotinsky himself stated that the purpose of the Ten-Year Plan was "to create a Jewish majority in the Land of Israel on both sides of the Jordan within about ten years; that is, to conclude the first and decisive stage of Zionism."[14]

For our purposes, it is important to see whether there was anything new in Jabotinsky's presentation of the goals of Zionism in his Ten-Year Plan. An examination of the plan discloses no change from his concept of the three goals of Greater Zionism. One of the main characteristics of the Ten-Year Plan, however, was its great emphasis on the east bank of the Jordan as an integral and necessary part of the state of the Jews. The reason for that was demographic, based on Jabotinsky's calculations of population density per square meter, and his assumptions regarding the number of Jewish immigrants over the years. It is likely that if he had had other facts, he would not have insisted on the need for the east bank. The creation of a majority was the first and most important goal of Zionism during the breakthrough period, without which the other two goals of Zionism could not be realized; this outlook characterized Jabotinsky's thought from beginning till end.

Monism: Jabotinsky's Concept of Zealotry

Throughout his writings, Jabotinsky emphasized that leaders of revolutions were characterized by a fiery belief in one overriding truth. The leader of a national liberation movement had to believe in a single truth, the truth of his side, without reservation, for otherwise he would not succeed.

In Jabotinsky's Zionist thought regarding the breakthrough period, we find a passionate, unqualified belief in one truth; we see in these writings more of Jabotinsky the leader than Jabotinsky the thinker. Ideological thinking, which is unequivocal, replaced reasoned thought, which presents both sides. This was not a deviation from his general theoretical thought, because in it he discussed the fact that the thinking of a leader was basically different. Furthermore, the belief in one truth applied only during the breakthrough period. This approach is consistent with his liberal approach which permitted some infringement upon liberal principles during the transition period in order to create a political and social reality conducive to the implementation of liberal ideals. The above, nevertheless, is insufficient for us to determine whether Jabotinsky himself was aware that his thought with regard to the breakthrough period differed fundamentally from the rest of his thinking. We shall try to clarify this issue in our discussion of his principle of zealotry, which Jabotinsky often referred to as monism.

Monism as defined by Jabotinsky was the opposite of ideological *sha'atnez* (a term referring to the biblically forbidden admixture of linen and wool):

> Two ideals are absurd, exactly like two Gods, like two different altars, and like two Temples. ... Any soul which can integrate two ideals and thus be satisfied is a defective soul. Only a monistic soul is complete. The word ideal by definition can not be plural. A healthy soul which embraces an ideal can not logically accommodate another. If Zionism is an ideal, it can not possibly accommodate another independent and equal aspiration, and it is impossible to form a partnership or a cartel or any sort of "combination." An ideal removes everything peripheral, no matter how nice, pure, or sacred it might be, without impugning the attractiveness or sanctity of what has been removed.[15]

Jabotinsky maintained that it was not possible to work actively, in the full sense of the word, for several ideals simultaneously. First, there might be contradictions between the ideals, and a choice would have to be made between them. Second, even when there was no contradiction, only ideological single-mindedness could lead to complete action; anyone who believed in several ideals would have to divide his energy between the two or determine which had priority. Thus, practically speaking, he would either have to devote only part of his time to each ideal or forego the one that was less important to him.

Theoretically, a person could support several ideals at the same time and determine their order of priority; this would be true in a "normal" period, when there was no need for an overwhelming struggle to achieve a particular goal. The breakthrough period was different, however. It demanded the total commitment of all emotional resources, for otherwise the revolutionary changes would not succeed. Therefore, for example, there was no room for the simultaneous commitment to Zionism and socialism. There were many areas of conflicts between them; the idea of class warfare, for example, was contrary to the concept of national unity that was the cornerstone of Zionism.

Thus during the breakthrough period, whoever wanted Zionism to succeed would need zealously to serve that ideal alone, and abandon all others, no matter how important. In Jabotinsky's words: "The play is *We Are Building a Hebrew State*, and the name of the director is 'the National Idea.' [The true pioneer] plays the role with a hoe in his hand, tomorrow he is likely to appear as a teacher, the day after that as a member of the [Jewish] Legion; he plays the role with honesty and integrity; however, he himself is neither a teacher nor a soldier, a bourgeois nor a proletariat. He is at one and the same time everything—he is the pioneer."[16]

The concept "ideal," took on a special significance in Jabotinsky's thought. As distinct from "value," "ideal" implied a belief that demanded action. Anyone who believed in a particular ideal had to work unsparingly on its behalf: "For a perfect soul, the service on behalf of an ideal constitutes not a joke but a sacrifice."[17]

Jabotinsky called this concept "ideological prioritizing," and not "exclusivity of values." It would appear then that he was aware that an ideological concept was involved, since belief in itself was meaningless unless accompanied by action. A true pioneer had to possess ideological zeal, but not zealotry of values. The true pioneer who sacrificed his life for the ideal of Zionism might simultaneously hold other values, such as of social justice. However, he needed to be aware that those values had to take a back seat until his ideal was achieved. Only then could the other ideals be realized.

Jabotinsky generally gave as an example of *sha'atnez* the mixture of the ideals of Zionism and socialism. However, the mixture of the ideals of liberalism and the struggle for a Jewish majority in *Eretz Yisrael* was an equally valid example. And, as previously stated, he did not tolerate *sha'atnez* during the breakthrough period, when liberal ideals had to be deferred.

Jabotinsky explained the significance of ideological zealotry in "Zion and Communism" (1933). The article was a response to a letter from a young Jewish man, to whom Communism took precedence over Zionism, but who still wanted to see the establishment of a state of the Jews, after which he would devote himself again to revolutionary Communist activity. His question to Jabotinsky was: "May I, with such views, remain in the Zionist Organization? Or perhaps I should leave it? In general, what should a young man in my situation do?"[18]

Jabotinsky's answer was unequivocal: whoever could manage spiritually without the redemption of the Jewish people, whoever was satisfied with the redemption of the whole world, had no place among the Zionists: "And I say without rancor to whoever hesitates: delve into your own soul—perhaps you have made a mistake, perhaps the Zionism within your soul is not at all the only ruler, as required? If so, my dear friend, do not lose even one hour; go in peace, go and don't think of us—we will get along without you."[19]

Jabotinsky explicitly stated here that prioritizing applied to an ideal and not a view. A person might have views about many important matters simultaneously: he might be a pacifist; he might believe in socialism as the proper form of government; he might hold any social or religious views: "However, these are 'views' and not 'ideals.' The 'ideal' is the view that others *serve*, and the root of distinction between them is that in any clash between the ideal and one of the other views—the ideal is preserved and the view is sacrificed."[20]

Jabotinsky continued to emphasize the critical point that the revolutionary period was characterized by the need to sacrifice views for the ideal. Zealotry could exist for only one ideal—otherwise it would not be possible for man to sacrifice his life on its behalf: "An ideal does not tolerate any competition. Views can coexist with it without limit; however you are permitted and are able to *serve* only one view; and you must abandon the others, no matter how attractive and dear they may be to you, if this one special view demands it of you."[21]

Therefore, said Jabotinsky, it was not possible to serve the ideals of Zionism and communism simultaneously. Russian communism was directed practically and theoretically against Zionism, whether out of sympathy for the Arabs or because of its ideological opposition to capital, while the Land of Israel could not be developed without capital.

Because of the single-mindedness of zealotry, there were those who called Jabotinsky's Zionist concept monistic Zionism. Thus it is necessary to constantly reemphasize that ideological zealotry applied only during the Zionist breakthrough period:

> All the while the building process of the Jewish state continues ... their affairs—private or class [of the workers and the property owners] ... interest the Zionist "center" of our souls only to the degree that they are likely to hasten or to impede the process of creating a Jewish majority in the Land of Israel. All other goals, personal or collective, social, cultural, and the like—all of them, with no exception, must be subordinated to the single goal of the national idea. And we do not know, we do not want to know, about any other "imperatives." ... These things have no connection at all with the "solution" of the social question. That will be solved in the laboratory of the Jewish state, after this state is securely established. Today, we are in a state of construction. That construction is taking place within a bad social framework, in a bad social atmosphere, and according to the only methods and arrangements that are possible in such an atmosphere. ... The function of state Zionism is not the "liquidation" of class sentiment; its function is the "extirpation" of these sentiments and their replacement with meaningless views that lack the power to influence the economic situation in the Land of Israel all the while the process of creating a Jewish majority is not completed.[22]

Ideological zealotry thus needed to exist only until the creation of a Jewish majority in the Land of Israel; it had no place once the state was established. On this point Jabotinsky's concept of zealotry differed from that of the fascists, who held that the individual had to sacrifice his life for the collective—the nation and the state—in any situation and in any period of time.

Had Jabotinsky believed in ideological single-mindedness after the establishment of the state, there would have been an unbridgeable gap between his theoretical liberal thought and his Zionist thought, inasmuch as liberalism was the antithesis of zealotry and of the view that the individual had to dedicate his life to one collective ideal. However, liberalism demanded pluralism of opinions and beliefs, and its fundamental premise was that there was no one faith or one opinion to which others might be subordinated. Therefore it was crucial that the ideological monism posited by Jabotinsky be limited to the breakthrough period.

The creation of a Jewish majority in the Land of Israel, essential for the realization of the other two goals of Zionism, was the sole ideal that Jabotinsky served. We can see how much he consciously served that ideal from the following statement, made in reference to the aforementioned analogy: "I shall fight everything which serves as an obstacle on the way to realizing this goal. And even if it is progress itself—I shall oppose it. ... "[23] There is no better expression than this of the importance of ideological zealotry to Jabotinsky during the breakthrough period, since in his general theory, as well as that of his Zionist theory which did not pertain to the breakthrough period, he attributed supreme importance to the ideal of progress.

In Jewish youth Jabotinsky saw the reserve from whence would come the true Zionists who would devote their lives, during the breakthrough period, to one ideal. Thus the concept of monism characterized the *Betar* world view, as Jabotinsky stated in "The Idea of *Betar*": "This is the only foundation upon which the whole world view of *Betar* is based: to create the state of the Jews, that is, a state with a Jewish majority on both sides of the Jordan. The pride and glory of *Betar*, which distinguishes it from all other Jewish-youth movements, is its monism. *Betar* signifies a generation that dedicated its life to this single ideal of creating a Jewish State, without recognizing any other ideals."[24]

Later in the article he emphasized that the *Betar* member had to be conscious of the importance of other ideals, such as pacifism and social justice; however, the time for their realization would not come until after the establishment of the state of the Jews:

> First of all, however, the Jewish nation must build its state, and this undertaking is so difficult and complicated that it demands all the strength of an entire generation. Thus this present generation of Jewish youth must devote itself *completely* to this single task; all other ideas, however beautiful and noble, may influence us only as long as they do not disturb us in the work of building the state of the Jews. The very moment one of these ideas starts to become an obstacle (even indirectly) on the road to a Jewish State, it must be ruthlessly sacrificed in favor of the single ideal. ... Everything that disrupts the building of the state of the Jews—whether a personal matter or a matter of a group or "class"—any other goal must, no matter what, defer to the sole, supreme, preeminent ideal: the state of the Jews.[25]

The breakthrough period would terminate with the establishment of the state of the Jews. The present generation of *Betar* needed to dedicate itself to only one ideal—the establishment of the state. Once this ideal was realized, *Betar*'s function would be over. Another generation would arise, "and make use of the national 'laboratory' that we prepared for it, in order to test and to carry out all possible experiments to improve the social order."[26]

In the addendum to the Betar program, in which Jabotinsky expressed his opinions on problems which had not yet found solutions in *Betar*'s ideological program, he demanded a theoretical and ideological effort by the current generation to deal with social questions, emphasizing that such thought had to be accompanied by action "all the while the various speculations on the distant future do not disrupt the harmony essential to the one task of the present—the building of the Jewish State."[27]

Jabotinsky's concept of the pioneer was rooted in the idea of ideological single-mindedness. He first heard this concept from Trumpeldor in London in 1917, and publicized it in "Tel Hai" (1920). His entire philosophy may be summarized in two words: "it's nothing." In Jabotinsky's opinion these two words embraced a lofty notion: "The will is what determines; events are meaningless. From everything bitter, sweetness will go forth if only the will exists."[28] Trumpeldor was a pioneer in Jabotinsky's sense of the word—ready to do any task which served the ultimate goal of the breakthrough period.

Jabotinsky presented his concept of the pioneer in many articles, and its essential definition was clear:

It is likely that I am naïve; however, the first time I heard the definition of "pioneer" I understood it as follows: longing for sacrifices, for the most difficult sacrifices, on behalf of a great ideal. However, I am certain of one thing: that is how Joseph Trumpeldor also understood the concept "pioneer" the first time I heard about the plan for the vanguard from him in 1917, in a small room in London, and I am certain that so the first, true pioneers also understood it; and if this were not the case, what was the reason that they sang with such enthusiasm "To Eat Bread and to Wear Clothing?" ... No one is obligated to be a pioneer and to make sacrifices, but the pioneer is the only person who brings sacrifices without making calculations about numbers and without making demands for recompense for his sacrifices.[29]

Whether or not to be a pioneer was clearly a matter of free personal choice. The readiness to sacrifice one's life did not violate anyone's individual liberty because the individual chose to make the sacrifice. Thus, if his commitment was limited, he could leave the battle. Fascism, on the other hand, did not allow such a possibility because it regarded each individual as a cell in the organic whole that did not have the slightest way out of the collective body.

Trumpeldor's concept of the pioneer, which Jabotinsky adopted and developed, was as a kind of a volunteer for a particular task, the only criterion guiding him being the fact that his contribution would further one ideal: the establishment of the state of the Jews. Volunteerism involved suffering and the awareness that distress lay in store. Speaking about the Jewish worker in the *Eretz Yisrael*, Jabotinsky said: "He knows that to be a pioneer means to suffer, because in a new land, in which nothing is certain, the worker lives a much harder life than in the old normal countries. If such conditions are not acceptable to him, no one is forcing him to become a volunteer and a pioneer."[30]

This concept of pioneering necessarily involved sacrifice and suffering, and was somewhat similar to Nietzche's concept of life. Its root lay in the character of the Zionist task and was valid during any breakthrough period (a war of defense, for instance) during which personal interests had to be subordinated to the general ideal. Jabotinsky clearly saw the breakthrough period as a time of building and struggle which, in terms of the effort and sacrifice involved, was similar to war.

The concept of "conscription," borrowed from military terminology, appeared in "The Idea of *Betar*" in the section, "The Principle of Conscription." In addition to the usual meaning of the word, which in this case referred to an anticipated new Jewish Legion, "conscription" had a broader significance: "Every *Betar* immigrant to the Land of Israel, must, according to our regulations, consider himself 'enlisted for a period of two years' and he must, during his first two years in the Land, do any assigned work, in any given place, under any conditions deemed fit by the *Betar* command."[31]

The immigration of the *Betar* member to the Land of Israel had to, from the beginning, assume a pioneering character, with the sacrifice and renunciation that was implied therein. Conscription was to be compulsory; his liberty was expressed in the fact that he joined *Betar* fully aware of this condition, and was always free to leave the movement.

However, Jabotinsky limited the conscription to a period of only two years. Afterward the *Betar* member was free to plan his life in the Land of Israel. Until the establishment of the state of the Jews, however, his life had to be guided by ideological zealotry. The limitation of the term of the conscription to two years was a result of Jabotinsky's awareness of the foolhardiness of making too many demands. For while someone might be ready for sacrifice, it would be unreasonable to expect a young man to enlist for a task determined for him by others, if it demanded a commitment of more than two years. A commitment to ideological zealotry over a long period, where the individual himself decided how to realize it, was eminently feasible. But a conscription term demanding a long-term commitment was simply not realistic.

In 1928, Jabotinsky gave a philosophical explanation of his pragmatic approach. The decision to serve on behalf of an ideal must not be presented, he said, as "a duty to the nation," but as the obligation of every Jewish person to himself:

> I herewith propose an entirely different philosophy regarding the relationship between the individual and his people—its essence lies in the assumption that any "obligation" is a legend. It is impossible to prove that any man has an "obligation" to his people. A moral obligation is simply the result of voluntary acquiescence. A person is not asked whether he wants to be thrown into this world of the Holy-One-Blessed-Be-He and of the devil as a Frenchman, a Negro, or a Jew. How is it possible in this case to speak of obligation? It is absurd. Gentlemen, a people has no rights with regard to you, and thus it has no claims upon you. And if you feel like serving your people, that is your choice to become, for example, a sculptor or a pianist. You do this *for your own sakes* and not for the good of your people, and just as the people has no basis for a claim against you, you have no reason for a claim against your people. Your method of relating to your people is the embodiment of your spirit, like its embodiment in the creation of an artist; if any obligation exists, it is the obligation of the artist toward himself and not to society. If you are able to hold out until the end, all the better, and if you are not suited to this effort, if you are weary, if you are tired of the whole thing, or if it simply became clear to you that you made a mistake to begin with—that it is not your nature to be a violinist and you are attracted specifically to astronomy—that too is all right. We may wish you success in your research into the mysteries of strange heavens; the Jewish people will get along without you.[32]

This paragraph translates Jabotinsky's theoretical liberal outlook on the relationship between the individual and the collective into a concrete example of the individuals's duty to further the establishment of a state of the Jews. As a liberal, Jabotinsky refused to present the concept of conscription and volunteerism as an obligation of the individual to his nation; an individual's only obligation was to himself. As a Jew, he also had an obligation to help in the establishment of a state of the Jews, but only if he truly wanted to. The pioneer or the volunteer was internally motivated; he did not fulfill an obligation toward some abstract collective entity, but realized an ideal that was important to him and his life. The other side of the coin was that he had no right to make demands on his nation, but only on himself. That too reflected the difference between Jabotinsky's view of the pioneer and that of fascism.

Jabotinsky's notion of the pioneer was intimately connected with his concept of nationalism in general, and Jewish nationalism in particular, based on both the racial element and national self-consciousness. The racial element was passive (a person was born to a particular race), and consciousness was the active component that determined whether a person born a Jew would remain a Jew. That decision was exclusively in the hands of the individual. The real, active expression of the individual's consciousness of his Jewishness and his desire to belong to the Jewish nation during the breakthrough period was his voluntary decision to enlist in the struggle to establish a state of the Jews. The beauty of pioneering was that it has no expectation of compensation—the individual had no claims on his nation—since the reward was internal. Jabotinsky wrote: "If you have perfect pride that brings with it self-satisfaction, and does not need the esteem of others, pride whose essence lies in giving repeated expression to the natural melody of your soul, then you will remain in your place, and will continue to do your work without noticing whether the heavens take notice of you, whether the gates are open or locked, until both the gates and the closed ears open, or else you will completely disappear—proud one."[33]

Jabotinsky admired those who volunteered to serve in the struggle for the establishment of the state of the Jews, and considered their actions to be in harmony with their racial formulas. They tied their personal destinies to the destiny of the Jewish people and were prepared to sacrifice their lives in that struggle.

However, like Herzl, Jabotinsky wanted each person to make his own voluntary decision. The beauty and the strength of volunteering and readiness for self-sacrifice lay precisely in the fact that they were motivated by free will—something so powerful that no rewards from the environment were needed.

It is difficult not to notice similarities between Jabotinsky's notion of the individual and John Stuart Mill's concept of the autonomous individual. According to Mill "He who lets the world, or his portion of it, choose his plan of life for him, has no need of any other faculty than the ape-like one of imitation. He who chooses his plan for himself, employs all his faculties. . . . and when he has decided, firmness and self-control hold to his deliberate decision."[34]

And again: "If a person possesses any tolerable amount of common sense and experience, his own mode of laying out his existence is the best, not because it is the best in itself, but because it is his own mode. Human beings are not like sheep."[35]

In limiting the period of zealotry to the time until the establishment of the state of the Jews, Jabotinsky fulfilled one condition of liberalism with regard to the breakthrough period. Furthermore, his whole concept was based on the personal decision by every individual to accept the monistic view with all its practical ramifications. In other words, Jabotinsky was careful not to violate the essence of liberal belief—the autonomy of the individual and his free choice with regard to his own life—even in the breakthrough period.

We must still examine Jabotinsky's plans of action in the areas of education, politics, economics, society, the military, the attitude to the Arabs of *Eretz Yisrael*, immigration, and the attitude to Great Britain and the Mandate. When the ways and means of achieving his program encroached upon liberal principles, we must question whether the essence of liberalism was not being callously trampled.

Clearly, neither a time limitation on the breakthrough period nor the principle of free choice by individuals over sacrificing their lives for the establishment of the state was adequate assurance that the state could implement liberal principles. It was essential that the methods and means utilized during the breakthrough period itself did not seriously damage liberal principles, which would be exceedingly difficult to repair once the state was established.

We shall now discuss the degree of infringement upon liberal principles permitted during the course of implementing Jabotinsky's plans on the way to statehood, while investigating these various programs to attain a Jewish majority in the Land of Israel.

The Ways and Means to Establish the State of the Jews

Jabotinsky's slogan from the beginning of his Zionist work was: "the Jewish people must help itself." Thus he devoted much thought to the ways and means by which the Jewish people could realize the goal of the breakthrough period, the creation of a Jewish majority in the Land of Israel, which would lead to the establishment of the state of the Jews.

Such activity needed to be conducted simultaneously in the diaspora and in the Land of Israel. In the diaspora, it was necessary to convince the Jews to support Zionism and to immigrate to *Eretz Yisrael*, and to persuade the nations of the world to grant the Jews a charter over that territory. In the Land of Israel, the residents needed to develop an infrastructure that would facilitate absorption of the large numbers of anticipated immigrants. Jabotinsky's activist approach—calling for immediate action—was the result of his awareness that time was acting against Jewish interests, and a state was needed immediately. This feeling of urgency which impelled him his whole life was due to his familiarity with the circumstances in which diaspora Jewry was living which, he concluded, constituted an imminent threat. Jabotinsky could not have anticipated the physical destruction of European Jewry, but he did foresee the danger of growing anti-Semitism whose source lay primarily in the new economic circumstances in Europe, as a result of which the

Jews were expelled from their traditional occupations and were not permitted to find new sources of income. A strong combination of "anti-Semitism of circumstances" and "anti-Semitism of man" was therefore created.

Thus, impelled by a sense of urgency already in 1905, Jabotinsky wrote in "Flatten the Iron": "I want to cry out to you [diaspora Jewry living tranquilly] with all my strength: Flatten the iron! Flatten the iron! Don't let the hammer drop out of your hands, don't lose this opportunity. Because our night of redemption will also come. And then our grandchildren will come and demand a reckoning from us."[36]

However, during the same period that he coined the slogan "we must help ourselves—now," he emphasized the importance of planning. Activity in the Land of Israel and in the diaspora needed to be planned logically; all of his proposals to develop the Land of Israel were models of systematic planning.

Jabotinsky's approach was thus a combination of activism and planning. There was no contradiction in his demand for immediate action, on the one hand, and for long-term strategy of at least ten years, on the other; on the contrary, his master program—the Ten-Year Plan—proposed goals as well as ways of implementing them, and thus served as a basis both for long-range strategy and for immediate activity.

As early as 1905, in his article "What Should We Do?" he presented a brief plan for Zionist activity. The plan was made up of suggestions for the Jews in the diaspora on how to convert people to Zionism, and a range of proposals for *Eretz Yisrael*. These included removing the Arab workers from the Hebrew settlements so that the Jews would not be identified with the exploiter, and the Arabs with the exploited; exploring the nature of the land and its residents in order to prepare it for mass emigration, something that would necessitate the development of diversified industry; and providing education for the Jews, thus giving them the tools to achieve influence in the land.

Jabotinsky emphasized that each Zionist movement had to make plans and implement them and concentrate its energies on action, and not on internecine war: "Each movement must first and foremost develop and carry out its own positive and creative plans, and not pay attention to rival plans for the purpose of destructive criticism."[37]

Jabotinsky's proposed plan of action in 1905 included many elements which he expanded upon and incorporated into his later plan. It is interesting to note the combination of rhetoric, appealing to the emotions, which characterized his Zionist thought from the beginning ("Flatten the Iron!" and others), and his rational and structured approach. His rhetoric served Jabotinsky well in persuading the masses, while his rational, structured thought served as the basis for the content of his plans.

As a logical and organized thinker, Jabotinsky pondered the relation between goals and the methods of achieving them. As early as 1905, he presented his position:

> One may not acquiesce to the known Jesuit principle that the ends justify the means; nevertheless, one must remember that neither will great things happen without strong-armed methods, and such methods necessarily have an unpleasant side to them, which must not be ignored. And how much more so must the means and methods employed by a fighter be measured morally on the exclusive basis of the benefit and harm derived from them, and never according to an abstract, aesthetic fastidiousness ... a true fighter has the complete right to scornfully ignore such fastidiousness. Before choosing a goal, he will think a great deal, he will analyze and weigh it from every angle; however, after he has finally made a choice, the true fighter has only one purpose—*success*—and only one single method, *whatever happens*. ... The truth is, that no victory on earth was ever achieved or ever will be by any other method.[38]

At first glance, there is an obvious contradiction between the first part of the paragraph and the second part. The first part creates the impression that it is forbidden to employ methods which entail real damage in order to achieve the goal, while the end implies that first the goal is selected, and then the means are chosen, according to the criterion of what will further that goal, and the method is "whatever happens."

In reality, however, the contradiction was not so striking; Jabotinsky had in mind a process whereby the means of achieving a goal were considered part of the process of its selection. Whether Jabotinsky himself was able to maintain a rational method of selecting goals when later influenced by the desire for success and the method of "whatever happens" remains to be seen.

National Education

The first issue that Jabotinsky ever dealt with in earnest was national education, focusing on Jewish youth in the diaspora as well as in the Land of Israel. In 1903, he presented his principles of national education, placing teachers at the head of the battle. The idea at the root of national education was simple: the Enlightenment enabled the Jew to acquire humanism and general knowledge, but at the same time it created a feeling of scorn for Jewish culture. Therefore popular Jewish education during the early stage of the Enlightenment and the period after it were contradictory: "Then the slogan was: 'Aspire to general humanity!' ... Now our slogan must be: 'Aspire to the national properties!' ... Both these slogans ultimately lead to one goal, just as two radii lead to one center—the creation of a humanist-Jew."[39]

The purpose of national education was to educate the Jew about the history of the Jewish people in the Land of Israel, and to teach about the spiritual creations and values originated by the Jews since their exile.

That, however, was not sufficient. In the diaspora, all subjects, and not only those dealing with Jewish history and culture, had to be taught in Hebrew.

We already discussed Jabotinsky's concept of language as a central expression of the connection between the individual and his nation. He searched for the most effective methods of teaching Hebrew to the masses, particularly to the youth. His approach was pragmatic: if they studied only Jewish history in Hebrew, while learning all other, more relevant, topics in the local language, Hebrew would not become a living tongue in which they would feel comfortable conversing. In his opinion, the only way to return to the Hebrew culture was by means of the Hebrew language, and the only way of learning the Hebrew language was by using it in teaching those subjects which were of interest to youngsters. "The school implants within the souls of its students not the language they learn, but the language in which they learn—specifically general studies."[40]

Thus, Hebrew needed to become a popular language, and not merely the tongue of scholars. That meant that in the Land of Israel, the street signs, advertisements, and the like would have to be in Hebrew. For if Hebrew did not become the daily language of communication there, it would not be able to fulfill its function as a national tongue—that being, to strengthen the bond between the Jewish individual and the Jewish nation.[41]

Likewise, Jabotinsky encouraged the translation of detective stories and romances into Hebrew, no less than he supported the creation of a new Hebrew culture. In "Books" (1919), he wrote: "The generation that studies needs reading books: half of the influence of school, even in the Land of Israel, is destroyed by the absence of *interesting* Hebrew reading books for youth. However, the book must be *interesting*. Not nationalistic, but interesting. ... For if not—they will not read. And secondly, these books must be written in easy and understandable Hebrew so that they will also be appropriate for beginners."[42]

In that same article Jabotinsky went on to note which books ought to be published in Hebrew for different segments of the population—for the sole purpose of bringing the Jews to learn Hebrew out of interest in the books. He also hoped that books in Hebrew would be published to serve the student population of the Hebrew University. Jabotinsky was most enthusiastic about the translation of what he termed "action literature"; he wrote a very positive article in honor of the Hebrew translation of "By Sword and Fire," by the Polish writer Sinkewitz.[43]

As previously mentioned, he first wrote about education in the Land of

Israel in "What Should We Do?" (1905), where he presented education in the Land of Israel as the supreme goal. He demanded that teachers be brought to every place in the Land of Israel where Jews were living, and that education be made compulsory: "Schools must be provided for the Hebrew part of the Land of Israel to the point of saturation and more ... the supply of teachers must be enlarged, until it is greater than the demand, so that schools will penetrate into absolutely every segment of the population."[44] He went into a bit of detail about what should be taught, but his bottom line was that the language of instruction and schoolbooks had to be Hebrew, and the content a combination of "nationalist and general humanist spirit."[45]

All of Jabotinsky's proposals for education in the diaspora and in the Land of Israel, as well as for spreading the Hebrew language, were written as logical plans, complete with steps for their implementation. Did these plans entail any violation of liberal principles? The demand for compulsory education was consistent with the identical demand by late nineteenth century liberals. True, compulsory education constituted coercion of the parent who was forced to send his child to school. But such coercion was justified; education was imperative for the youth so that they might exercise their liberty when they matured.

Did the declared goals of national education in the Land of Israel—"to give the Land of Israel, in a few years, a young and strong group, cultured, with a sense of national identity, and remarkably united ... "[46]—and in the diaspora—"to wipe out the spirit of self-contempt and to renew the spirit of self-awareness"[47]—violate liberal principles in any way? There is no doubt that were he speaking of a normal people living in its own land, the great emphasis on "national properties," which had to be practically indoctrinated, would not have been consistent with the role of education in a liberal society. Because, instead of educating for openness and skepticism, the aspect of education that dealt with national issues provided only dogmatic answers. However, national elements were only a part—albeit a central part—of the comprehensive educational program that Jabotinsky proposed, and there was also room for open, humanist, general education.

Jabotinsky himself limited the nationalist aspects of education to the breakthrough period. Once the state of the Jews was established there would no longer be a need to teach national properties. Life in the Hebrew state, in which the Jewish psyche was expressed in all spheres, would render nationalist education superfluous.

The Settlement in the Land of Israel: The Economy and Society

Jabotinsky repeatedly and consistently emphasized that all his proposals for settling the Land of Israel were applicable only to the building phase of the state. He also called it the phase of the consolidation of the settlement, and more than one parallel may be drawn between the methods of settlement in the Land of Israel and those in other places, such as in Rhodesia and Kenya by the British. After the Ten-Year Plan was crystallized and formally adopted by the UZR in 1938, Jabotinsky limited the period of consolidation of the settlement to ten years. In other words, the construction stage would end in about 1950; there would be an economically viable Jewish majority in the Land of Israel; a charter would have been attained, the state of the Jews would arise, and the breakthrough period would come to a close.

The economic and social characteristics of the Jewish state would be different from those in the breakthrough period. The qualitative difference would be expressed by the greater involvement of the government during the period of the state on the way. Therefore, Jabotinsky always spoke about "the Settlement and the government" or about the essential "political conditions." This approach clearly contradicted the fundamental liberalism of his socioeconomic theory, in which he proposed a free economy accompanied by a maximalist welfare state and the Jubilee idea. This liberal socioeconomic concept would not exist during the breakthrough period, but would be realized once the state of the Jews was established.

As early as 1905, Jabotinsky presented his basic concept of Jewish settlement in the Land of Israel, a concept which he developed and consolidated over his lifetime. Its primary goal was to prepare the Land of Israel for mass immigration through industrial and agricultural development. This had to be done according to a detailed and specific plan.[48]

This approach of precise planning utilizing scientific knowledge and tools was rooted in Jabotinsky's liberalism—which inspired his belief in Western progress, and in the power of science and technology to give answers to economic and social questions. This approach also characterized his plans for the breakthrough period, notwithstanding the fact that a basic point—the necessity of government intervention—contravened liberal economics. However, Jabotinsky's emphasis on state intervention within the general context of his perception of this intervention differentiated it from the mature fascist concept of "plannism"—comprehensive planning by the state that had to be carried out in all spheres and at all times.

Jabotinsky was particularly interested in agricultural settlement, industry, trade, and small crafts; the infrastructure (for example, everything connected with transport); the export of industrial products; and the import of capital. Likewise, he was interested in work relations in all branches of the economy, primarily between industry and property-owners and workers; and also in the status of merchants and craftsmen. Simultaneously, he thoroughly investigated demographic calculations with a mind to the absorptive capacity of the Land of Israel.

He developed plans for all of those areas, the central component of which was what the government needed to do to make progress possible.

As we saw, Jabotinsky hoped that the Jewish people in its own state would return to those occupations in which they had not engaged during the years of their exile, and thus the economic structure of the Hebrew state would be natural and normal like those of other nations. The function of economic occupations in the diaspora was to create a corner of isolation for the Jewish people. This need would disappear in a state of the Jews. However, it was important to strive for a normal economic structure even in the period of construction. The Jews in the Land of Israel had to engage in all occupations; to be property owners as well as workers, farmers, traders, and craftsmen.

Because of the predominance of the Labor movement in the Land of Israel, Jabotinsky more than once came to the aid of the merchant or property owner. In "The Shopkeeper" (1927), he spoke of the importance of trade in society, seeing in the merchant the father of material culture: "And not only would the factory not have succeeded in bringing together all its machines and all the materials needed to manufacture the first pair of shoes without him; worse than that—without the merchant, the factory, as an institution which works on behalf of the masses of purchasers, would have no right to exist."[49] Moreover, it was historically the merchant who motivated the cultural-spiritual development of mankind. Fascism, on the other hand, saw in "merchant morality" the corrupting nucleus of bourgeois culture.

Jabotinsky's defense of the status of the merchant in the Land of Israel was consistent with his general outlook on the importance of this area of economic endeavor. Just as he warned that the youth in the diaspora were neglecting trade in preference for the learned professions, he cautioned against the anti-business ideology that existed in the Land of Israel. Nevertheless, the percentage of merchants had to be normal: "We must not accept more than a natural number of merchants, more than ten percent. However, the anti-trade ideology . . . is definitely superfluous . . . today we are searching for new and broader methods of national activity; however, that does not mean that we may abandon the shop. To abandon the shop means to evacuate our position."[50]

In 1925 Jabotinsky also came to the defense of the petty bourgeoisie that complained about "the unfriendly attitude on the part of the Zionist executive and its financial institutions and oppression by the *Histadrut*, the General Federation of Jewish Workers."[51] Aware of the complexity of the problem, Jabotinsky suggested a policy of protection for the crafts: "That same official support, which enabled the workers to establish their own bank and their own health fund, must be suitably distributed between these two branches of productive population."[52] It was clear to him that while such a change of policy would inevitably entail much hardship, it had to be effected not only out of a sense of justice and because of the importance of small industry to the Settlement, but also because discrimination might provoke a social confrontation. He concluded with a warning, which, in light of what was then taking place in Europe, does not seem at all strange: "The situation will worsen if the other side [the petty bourgeoisie], instead of organizing on the basis of economic self-help, will be forced, due to lack of alternatives, to organize on purely military foundations. Now this is called fascism and every effort must be made to prevent such a development. Therefore the time has come to declare: *Basta!*"[53]

This article, which was considered highly controversial, concluded with a warning against the development of socioeconomic conditions in the Land of Israel like those in Europe, which would be likely to lead to fascism. This point is especially ironic in that his opponents later affixed the label of a fascist sympathizer onto Jabotinsky—who himself cautioned against fascism, and suggested measures to prevent it from developing.

Jabotinsky repeatedly emphasized the importance of industrialists. His guiding idea was simple and logical: it was not possible to create places of employment in the Land of Israel without the investment of capital; there was no place for Hebrew labor without capitalists. Jabotinsky came to the assistance of industry on occasion because he felt it had been discriminated against in the allocation of resources: *Keren Hayesod* (the Palestine Foundation Fund) did not assist; the Zionist executive was not sympathetic; and even the British administration claimed that the Land of Israel was not yet ready for industrial development.

Jabotinsky's opinion, however, was quite the opposite: "It sometimes happens that a stepchild is the most beautiful of all the children, and it is likely that something like this will happen to everything connected with Hebrew industry in the Land of Israel."[54] This depended upon the existence of a specific plan and the right sort of government activity that would encourage industry. In all fairness, it is important to point out that Jabotinsky was particularly close to the subject of industry since he was a director of the Judea Insurance Company and a member of the administration of the Society of Displays and Fairs in the Land of Israel. Thus he lectured frequently on the subject of Hebrew manufacture, exports from the Land of Israel, and related topics.[55]

However, in contrast to the label that was affixed to him regarding his attitude to workers, Jabotinsky's words testify better than anything else that, just as he considered property owners essential for the development of the Settlement, he saw Hebrew workers as no less essential. In none of his articles, including those in which he engaged in sharp controversy with the left, did he underestimate the importance of the workers in the Land of Israel. In "The Left" (1925), he defended the cooperative farming village as a necessary form of settlement and discussed its achievements:

> Whatever the drawbacks of the cooperative settlement may be, one thing is clear: it will certainly occupy a preeminent position in the activities of our agricultural settlement for a long time yet, simply out of necessity, that is—the supporters of the agricultural settlement will continue to be primarily the "leftists." Up till now, since the end of the war, the entire burden was on their shoulders. They also led the way in the other branches of the economy. ... In addition, they established a network of hospitals, a number of educational institutions, a bank. Whether good or bad, it is a fact that the Hebrew *Eretz Yisrael* today is a land of workers. When those who criticize our economic method claim that this situation developed as the result of the slipshod methods of those at the head or because of "conquest by force," they are simply mistaken. The situation occurred as a result of circumstances and especially, thanks to enormous activity and dedication; all strata of society in the Land of Israel acknowledge this. I imagine that there is no other country in which the word "worker" arouses such honor in every circle, even in the "salon."[56]

This is practically a paean to the workers of *Eretz Yisrael* whom Jabotinsky affectionately called "leftists," in quotation marks, since he did not see any socialist elements in the activities of the workers: "There is no recollection here whatsoever of class warfare. What matters here is the principle of common national destiny."[57]

Jabotinsky's sharp dispute with the left centered primarily on the issue of class warfare, a subject we shall discuss separately.

Jabotinsky wanted a normal economic structure in the Land of Israel, with Jews engaged in all forms of livelihood. However, during the period of construction when the Settlement was becoming consolidated, Jabotinsky did not believe in free enterprise but rather, government intervention through a policy of encouragement.

Jabotinsky's demand for economic "adventurism" was uncharacteristic of his planned scientific approach. In 1932, he pointed out that "the spirit of adventurism" no longer characterized the activity of the pioneers in the Land of Israel, who had become prematurely conservative. His call for more adventurism was anchored in his economic theory about the importance of play as the primary cause of human progress, both material and spiritual, as presented in "Introduction to the Theory of Economics I & II." He repeated this idea in his call for economic adventurism:

> The more one examines the history of mankind, the more one law becomes clear: the fundamental part of every important step in man's progress has been in finding a means of carrying out an action which has been deemed the world over as "impossible." In truth, this is the only

meaning of the concept "progress": overcoming the "impossible." And when the world determines that something is undoable, this judgment is based on serious and basic reasons. It is generally the opinion of the greatest scientists and experts. And whoever wants everyone to believe that he is serious will listen to their opinions and not risk failure by attempting to do the impossible. What, however, despite everything, is the source of progress? Its source lies in work in which, thank God, adventurism continues to exist.[58]

With these words of Jabotinsky—the liberal who espoused progress, initiative, and the activities of exceptional people—in front of us, we shall proceed to a discussion of the programs that he proposed. There was no contradiction between Jabotinsky's planned approach and his call for economic adventurism. Economic adventurism sprang from within, and could not be planned; on the other hand, it was possible to utilize scientific knowledge in order to work out better solutions to problems. His precise plans were Jabotinsky's most important contribution to settlement efforts; as for originality, he could only point to its importance and attempt to be original himself.

In many articles over the years, Jabotinsky outlined his social and economic concepts for the period of construction. Since his fundamental views did not change, we shall concentrate on the main points as reflected in his later writings.

In 1927 and 1928, Jabotinsky wrote two articles entitled "On the Zionist NEP" (New Economic Policy). In the first, he expressed tentative ideas, but ones based on in-depth study, research, and investigation. He said:

> In my opinion, the economic problems of building up the Land of Israel are, first of all, political problems. True settlement of land that was purchased with money is, in my opinion, absurd, and also is impossible; true settlement is possible only on government land or on private land which the government appropriated and gave to the settler. So I also view the development of industry and the financial problem and every detail of Zionism: the major role is played by the government. Without that, talk about true settlement—that is, bringing masses of people to a small and poor country—is meaningless.[59]

A liberal economy thus had no place in the breakthrough period; the absorption of mass immigration to the Land of Israel could not occur without large-scale intervention by the authorities in order to develop local agriculture and industry. Infringement upon the central principle of liberalism, which demanded minimal economic intervention by the government, was justified specifically because it was a breakthrough stage. Once the state was established it would be possible to implement a liberal economy based principally on private initiative.

Actually, in our discussion of Jabotinsky's general economic thought, we saw that he supported the possibility of greater state intervention in the economy in times of emergency. Jabotinsky certainly considered the stage of the state on the way to be an abnormal period that justified deviation from liberal economic principles.

In the above article Jabotinsky discussed only those areas under the control of the Zionist movement, and his two major proposals dealt with reforms in the *Keren Hayesod* and the Jewish National Fund. He proposed that in place of distributing grants, the *Keren Hayesod* use half its money to construct houses and obtain equipment for institutions providing benefits to the public (hospitals, schools, factories, low-cost workers' housing, settlements), in return for a low rental fee. The rest of its money would serve as a "credit guarantee fund" to provide usual commercial credit for serious investment initiatives in *Eretz Yisrael*.

He also suggested that the Jewish National Fund stop buying lands which were then nationalized and could not be sold. All the while the pathological situation prevailed whereby lands for settlement purposes had to be purchased (the Mandatory government had no body that distributed government lands for settlement), the Jewish National Fund would serve as the central purchasing institution that determined land policy and prices. Jewish National Fund land would be made suitable for normal economic life with one exception: settlements of workers attempting to rehabilitate undeveloped areas.

The large amounts needed for funding key social services like education and health necessitated the backing of diaspora Jewry. Jabotinsky proposed involving private initiative in this endeavor, and pointed to methods such as adoption, along the lines, for example, of adoption of a hospital by Hadassah Women. The World Zionist Organization would offer guidance to Jewish communities abroad regarding adoptions, but without assuming responsibility.

There is no doubt that Jabotinsky's suggestions were intended to lessen the power of the World Zionist Organization, in which the labor movement was a majority, in order to prevent too large a concentration of power and authority in one body. However, one can not ignore the fact these proposals included many elements of a free economy—stimulation of private initiative—within a comprehensive economic program, whose creation and implementation were the responsibility of the government.

Jabotinsky's new and novel idea of compulsory national arbitration was similar to that put forward by Italian fascism, but was essentially different in that it would be carried out within the framework of a liberal-democratic society and government. This point, which became the source of his differences with the left and with the UZR program, appeared his article "On the Zionist NEP, Once Again" (1928).

Jabotinsky made certain basic assumptions: first, a Jewish majority meant many workers; second, creating places of work demanded capital and thus owners of capital; third, in order for the worker to survive, he must earn a reasonable salary; fourth, in order to attract capital, the potential profit must be reasonable.

He concluded that it was necessary to arrive at a balance between acceptable wages and profits. This could not be achieved through strikes or lockouts, which would harm the settlement process and hence the goals of the construction period. Since Zionist ideology had to prevail during the breakthrough period, the methods of organizing work and work relations had to be consistent with the ideal of attaining a Jewish majority. In other words, those methods could not alienate workers from employers; on the contrary—they had to strengthen that which united both sides, and thus intensify the pace of activity. Thus, he maintained: "the logical conclusion of this situation is: arbitration. Arbitration. Arbitration in all areas. Arbitration as a supreme and sole social force. Arbitration as a sacred national obligation that can not even be challenged, and violation of which is tantamount to treachery to one's people and land and self-effacement from the list of righteous people. The ten commandments of our Settlement is composed of ten lines, and each line of the same word: arbitration. The Bible of our Settlement starts with these words: In the beginning God created arbitration."[60]

It would be difficult to find a stronger statement than that, and there is no doubt that it accurately reflected Jabotinsky's attitude toward arbitration. The practical application of his proposal would be to replace the strike and the lockout with national arbitration. The authorized national bodies would choose an apolitical, permanent body, which in cases of dispute would appoint an arbitrator whose decision would be binding on both sides.

In "On the Zionist NEP, Once Again," Jabotinsky went beyond work relations and spoke of arbitration in any area in which disputes were likely to flare up. He presented his proposal for the establishment of a parliament of professions:

> If you want the method of arbitration to acquire as much and as great prestige as possible, it must be implemented within the entire structure of the Settlement, and transformed into the foundation and cornerstone of the Jewish organization in the Land of Israel. ... And this is the content of the "parliament of professions" for the Settlement: first of all, the principle of professional unionization must be implemented, that is, the organization of all the participants in one of the typical branches of Jewish economic activity in industry, trade, agriculture, banking and finance, crafts, communications, liberal professions, bureaucracy, and the like. Those branches in which there exists a noticeable separation between the three factors—the providers of work, the bureaucrats, and

the hired workers—get suitable representation. After such an organization becomes a reality, each union will itself choose from among its representatives a kind of new national council—and that is the "parliament of professions." Its function, first, is to supervise all economic life, all the problems of agriculture, trade, industry, credit, loans, claims against the government in tax matters, trade agreements, or tariffs; second—and this is the main thing—it is the "parliament of professions" that establishes the institution of arbitration from top to bottom, and among its functions is the arrangement of all relations among the various economic groups. Starting with the employment office in Safed and ending with the supreme court for arbitration of the most important matters, all the bodies of arbitration will be established as the responsibility of the "parliament of professions," and thus they will be accorded the full moral honorary status of a body which serves as a reflection of the entire productive segment of the Settlement, and a reflection not in the sense of the directions of party ideology, but in the sense of real creative interests.[61]

This paragraph was quoted practically in its entirety since various interpretations have been given to it, and it was one of the main reasons that the term fascist was affixed to Jabotinsky. Jabotinsky's words were clear and partially consistent with his general theoretical thought: it was best not to classify society in a way that emphasized that which divided (employers and employees), but rather, in a way that emphasized that which united (the branch of the economy). He proposed that occupations also be divided that way, with each occupation having its own union that included representatives of each factor: the distributors of work, the bureaucrats, and the hired workers. Each union would chose several representatives, and the representatives of all the unions would constitute the parliament of professions. Its primary function would be to regulate work relations and the organization of work, as well as to supervise developments in the economy and present demands or suggestions to the government. The parliament of professions would under no circumstances replace the traditional parliament, but would exist parallel to it, according to the bicameral system. Representation in the traditional parliament would be on an ideological-partisan basis, while in the parliament of professions, it would reflect the various branches of the economy and economic interests. Jabotinsky said of the place of the parliament of professions: "The creation of this institution does not mean the abolition of the present gathering of representatives and the national council. It is simply a kind of 'bicameral' method. ... It [the parliament of professions] must fill the role of the second house, a kind of 'senate'—as defined by the world nations—which in economic matters have a preferred status, and whose opinions must be listened to in other matters as well."[62]

It seems to me that there is enough in these two paragraphs to remove any doubt with regard to Jabotinsky's intentions for the parliament of professions, and to show, despite the similarity between his proposal and the corporative structure proposed by fascism, the substantive difference that existed between Jabotinsky's concept and that of fascism. Despite the fact that Jabotinsky was certainly influenced by the corporative attempt and by the idea itself, he attempted to turn it into an integral part of liberal democracy and not an alternative to it, as fascism proposed, and indeed, did. The parliament of professions did not come to replace the traditional democratic institutions; however Jabotinsky proposed giving it broad authority in the economic field, that would be confiscated from the government and from the *Histadrut*.

Jabotinsky stated explicitly that his primary model was the bicameral legislative system—as in the United States and Switzerland—with separate elections of representatives for each house, and an accompanying system of checks and balances. Jabotinsky's proposal differed in one fundamental way: areas of legislation were divided between the two houses. Jabotinsky maintained that he was influenced mainly by Leon Blum's "Front Populair" in this regard.

It is particularly important to emphasize that Jabotinsky's proposal related only to the period of the state on the way, and not to the period after the establishment of the state. Moreover, while the idea of national arbitration remained central to Jabotinsky's socioeconomic thought throughout his life, as reflected in the Revisionist and *Betar* programs respectively, such was not the case with the parliament of professions.

Up until now we have seen Jabotinsky's economic programs in economic areas dominated by the Zionist movement, his basic concept of compulsory national arbitration, and his idea of a parliament of professions. In his Ten-Year Plan and accompanying articles, Jabotinsky presented, some ten years later, his comprehensive program on the subjects of immigration, absorption, the economy, and society. We shall discuss immigration separately, since it was connected with plans for the diaspora, while the other issues dealt with the settlement of the Land of Israel. Jabotinsky maintained that the construction period would terminate with the implementation of the Ten-Year Plan. He based his considerations about absorption on detailed demographic calculations, the size of the territory, and the possible population density. However, his basic assumption was that no conclusions about the settlement of the Land of Israel might be drawn from other settlements, not only because of the difference in objective conditions (such as fertility of the land), but also because the one most important factor affecting the capacity for absorption was "the character of its citizens or settlers ... the decisive factor in success is not the existence of raw materials, but man's spirit of initiative. ... man himself, his talent, his perseverance, his will power, his capital, his world connections."[63]

The possibilities of settlement in the Land of Israel were greater first and foremost because the settlers were Jewish; their will power and initiative over the past decades had proved to be much greater than that of other settlers:

> But among the Jews specifically, and particularly with regard to the Land of Israel, huge stores of pioneering capacity for sacrifice were revealed, and together with that, an increasing readiness to invest large sums of money in the Land of Israel. To that must be added other special factors, which distinguished the Jew as a settler—his expertise in the superb achievements of European and American techniques; his traditional stubbornness, perhaps racial stubbornness, that became a byword; his world connections, trade and cultural, that promise to transform the Land of Israel into a recognized crossroads of international trade.[64]

To this had to be added the location of *Eretz Yisrael* at the intersection of two anticipated great world trade routes.

Jabotinsky thus concluded that the potential population of the Land of Israel, including both its banks, could reach more than ten million. The number of Jews in the world at that time (1937) was about sixteen million, and Jabotinsky estimated that emigration would reach between one-third and three-fifths of that amount. Thus the Land of Israel could solve the problem of the Jews, and it would be possible to say: "Give us the Land of Israel and in a few generations it will have eight million Jews and two million Arabs—and plenty of room will remain, and all will be well with the world."[65]

Absorption of the immigrants would necessitate significant government economic activity: first, a protective tariff to stimulate local industry; second, investigation of the potential of the uncultivated land, followed by agrarian reform, land distribution, and price control; third, a system of taxation to ease the immigrants' first years; and finally, a transport policy which would facilitate transfer of merchandise from the factory to different places in the Land of Israel. Jabotinsky noted that the Mandatory administration, which he termed "a typical anti-settlement government,"[66] had done practically nothing in all these areas.

Nonetheless, the number of Jews reached 420,000 in 1937 versus 83,974 in 1922, constituting about one-third of the population; at the same time the number of Arabs rose from 570,057 in 1922 to 871,726 in 1935.

During this time, the number of farming villages quintupled, the area of orchards increased two and a half times, and the number of factories and workshops was multiplied by two and a half. Imports and exports both grew by three and a half, although imports were four and a half times as great as exports.[67] All of this was attained despite the anti-settlement character of the government—which hampered the economy with too little investment of capital into industry and agriculture.

Realizing the goal of the breakthrough period thus necessitated "a change in the structure of government from top to bottom."[68] The first change proposed by Jabotinsky was the institution of national arbitration which would exist until a Jewish majority was achieved: "The institutions of national arbitration, when they come to decide what are the conditions of work that they must set in a particular factory, in a particular place, and a particular time, must first of all take into consideration one interest: the interest of the establishment of a state. . . . Only one factor must be taken into consideration: the development of the Jewish Settlement, the increasing number of places for absorbing Jewish settlers, and the Jewish majority."[69]

In order to hasten the pace of building the Zionist enterprise—and in light of the worsening plight of Eastern European Jewry in the thirties—the Ten-Year Plan was born. Its stated goal was "to create over a period of approximately ten years a Jewish majority in the Land of Israel on both sides of the Jordan, that is, to complete the first and decisive stage of Zionism."[70]

For that purpose it was necessary, according to Jabotinsky's calculations, to bring in some 150,000 Jews annually—a number that was within the realm of possibility. From data of 1932, Jabotinsky concluded that for every two thousand immigrant laborers, no less than two million liras in personal capital also entered. The Ten-Year Plan needed to include master plans for both the settlement of immigrants in the Land of Israel and for their exodus from the most important lands of the diaspora.

The first scheme, which dealt with settlement in the Land of Israel, proposed the following: first, working toward a "settlement government"; in other words, adapting the administration and laws of *Eretz Yisrael* to be conducive to further settlement. This included the reappropriation of uncultivated lands; agrarian reform; the creation of a national land fund; reform of the system of tariffs and taxation; the institution of a quota of Jewish soldiers in the British standing army; and the authorization of Jewish self-defense. Moreover, the principle of cooperation between the British authorities and world Jewish institutions had to be strengthened constitutionally, and attempts to establish "representative" institutions in the Land of Israel had to be deferred until the Jews constituted a majority there.

Second, all these reforms had to apply also to the east bank of the Jordan; it was crucial that the east bank be opened to Jewish settlement according to the same principles as in western *Eretz Yisrael*.

Third, the share of public capital relative to private capital in funding settlements had to be drastically increased. This would be possible if the Jewish National Fund and the *Keren Hayesod* were replaced by a source of world Hebrew loans, secured by the government and backed by the real value of the developing Hebrew economy. The flow of private capital and its exploitation needed to be improved, and the first step had to be the creation of a reserve to assure private credit.

Fourth, the government treasury had to contribute to the funding of Hebrew construction in an amount relative to the takes paid by the Jews. The treasury also had to establish an independent bank for the Land of Israel.

Fifth, Zionist economic policy had to be based on the full development of the economic potential of the Land of Israel, including Transjordan, in all areas: agriculture, industry, crafts, trade, transportation, tourism, water resources, and so forth.

Sixth, Zionist social policy had to be based on the organizational plan of national compulsory arbitration of disagreements between labor and property. Moreover, the weak elements of immigration had to be protected by assistance to their economic enterprises during their critical stages, as well as by the construction of housing with the aid of social welfare institutions.

Seventh, Arab interests needed to be assured that current Arab residents and their descendants would not be expelled from *Eretz Yisrael*, and guaranteed that complete equality of rights between the two peoples would be maintained.[71]

In his speeches and articles on the Ten-Year Plan, Jabotinsky emphasized that its implementation would be impossible without a suitable government policy. In other words, the government would have to intervene in the economy in a very real fashion during the breakthrough period. Simultaneously, Jabotinsky stressed that political intervention in the economy had to end with the termination of the construction period. And even during this period, Jabotinsky encouraged the strengthening of private initiative within the framework of a planned economy and an interventionist government.

It is immediately obvious that in his entire discussion of social problems, Jabotinsky's only explicit practical proposal was the institution of national arbitration. He touched upon the questions of budget for the educational and health-care systems and assistance to weak settlements in their early stages, but none of this constituted a well-formulated plan of social policy. This deficiency was particularly glaring in light of Jabotinsky's intricately detailed economic programs.

Jabotinsky was well aware of this shortcoming; at the Third Revisionist World Conference in 1928, he said: "The Revisionist Zionist concept of the method and the process of building the land socially is based on 'monism.' During the period of settlement, all class interests—even if on their own justified—must take second place and defer to the interests of building up the Hebrew state, because they alone must be the preeminent and decisive interests. A uniform method of national arbitration must replace class-warfare in cases of disputes between classes, and it must be implemented by a complete network of regional and local arbitration institutions."[72]

Social issues—most importantly, defining the essence of a just society and how to achieve it in the Land of Israel—had to be deferred during the breakthrough period, until after the establishment of the state of the Jews. Thus, the only social policy mentioned in the program of the Zionist Revisionists (1926) was compulsory national arbitration, in the section headed "Class Warfare."

"The Idea of *Betar*" (1934), emphasized the special character of the breakthrough period in everything connected with social problems:

> A settlement period has its own social laws, which are fundamentally different from those that perhaps govern well-established countries. Here are several social laws as interpreted and embraced by *Betar*: a) one hundred percent Hebrew labor in all Jewish enterprises ... b) decent working conditions for the Hebrew worker; otherwise, he will be unable to emigrate to the Land of Israel, which will then never become a state of the Jews c) a normal opportunity for profits for private investment; otherwise the flow of capital will stop and the building of the state of the Jews will cease d) compulsory national arbitration in all social disputes in the Hebrew economy, and a taboo against the two national crimes: the strike and the lockout.[73]

In "The Socialism of *Betar*," which included thoughts on issues not resolved in the *Betar* program, Jabotinsky discussed the function of *Betar* during the breakthrough period: to create a national "laboratory" in a securely established state of the Jews. Once the state was established, the time would have arrived to "try to carry out all possible experiments in order to improve the social order."[74] Until then, however, monism would have to prevail, social issues would have to wait. Here, however, Jabotinsky added a new element: during the breakthrough period, the members of *Betar* should ponder social problems and develop a policy based on Jewish values; it was in this context that he proposed the adoption of his welfare policy and Jubilee idea.

A summary of Jabotinsky's position that the breakthrough period was not the time to really deal with social issues during may found in *A Hebrew State: A Solution to the Question of the Jews*, in the chapter "The Class Question in the Settlement." There Jabotinsky presented his well-known view that national arbitration was a direct outgrowth of ideological monism, and was essential to further the goal of the breakthrough period: the creation of a Jewish majority. He explained that only in such a way would it be possible to maintain a balance between the interests of workers and of owners of capital; to thus give both sides the incentive to remain in the Land of Israel; and to thus provide motivation for other workers and owners of capital to immigrate. Moreover, national arbitration prevented damage to the economy because work continued as usual during the arbitration period. Neither his book, the *Betar* program, nor other late writings mentioned the parliament of professions.

After presenting his views on national arbitration, Jabotinsky summarized his approach to social issues during the breakthrough period: "These things have no connection at all with a 'solution' of the social question. That will be solved in the laboratory of the Jewish state, after this state is securely established. Today, we are in a state of construction. That construction is taking place within a bad social framework, in a bad social atmosphere, and according to the only methods and arrangements that are possible in such an atmosphere."[75]

These lines capture the essence of Jabotinsky's social policy. One will not find any plans dealing with social issues in his Ten-Year Plan, or in other plans relating to the breakthrough period; the place for those, he felt, was in the state of the Jews. To this previously mentioned goals for the state of the Jews—the Return to Zion and the transformation of the state into the standard-bearer of progress—Jabotinsky added a third goal, related to the second: the implementation of a just social policy. The most just social theory possible, which would provide solutions to social problems, would emanate from the Hebrew state because it would be based on the social philosophy of the Bible, in which the most lofty ideals of social justice are expressed.

Monism Versus the Class Approach in the Settlement: the Argument with the Left

In the twenties and early thirties, Jabotinsky was engaged in a heated debate with the left in the Land of Israel over the relationship between workers and the owners of capital during the period "on the way to statehood." The views Jabotinsky espoused in this argument were no different from his usual outlook, but their formulation was more extreme, like that of the opposite side.

His starting point was that the boycott of Hebrew labor and the employment of Arabs was treacherous to Zionism, since the goal of the breakthrough period was the attainment of a Jewish majority. If Hebrew labor were limited, industrial and agricultural workers would not immigrate, and those already living in the Land of Israel would not even be able to survive.

In "Petach Tiqva and 'Company'" (1928), Jabotinsky argued that the employers were the guilty party in the boycott of Hebrew labor. The root of the problem, however, lay in the preference for Arab labor, not because of lower wages, but because of his different attitude toward his employer. Since the average Jewish laborer was, in Jabotinsky's opinion, "the most intelligent individual in the Settlement,"[76] with more education generally than his employer—and since he didn't excel in diplomacy—he behaved arrogantly toward his employer. Moreover, in contrast to class warfare in countries where the worker was weak, Jabotinsky noted that in the Land of Israel:

> It is specifically the worker who is the pet of the World Zionist Organization, of the *Keren Hayesod*, of the Jewish National Fund. A very large part of all budgets go to it, and its stalwarts get the most important positions in the Zionist bureaucracy. At the time of the great immigration and growth in the building industry, the movement assumed control of economic life from both ends: from below, through the union, and from above, through *Solel Boneh* [a government construction company]. ... It controls schools, three-story workers' homes in cities, rest homes.[77]

In other words, discrimination was exercised in favor of the workers in the Land of Israel, and the labor movement actually had a hegemony in the Settlement. The crucial factor, however, was that all the aforementioned were attained thanks to the various funds whose money was donated by middle-class Jews. According to Jabotinsky, "under such circumstances, the theory of class warfare takes on a totally different character. People may accept the fact that they are treated like enemies, but in this situation, the middle-class feels that it is regarded as dirt, from which gold and silver are extracted, and afterwards is trod upon."[78]

Jabotinsky maintained that the left in the Land of Israel was not a real left since all its money came from the bourgeoisie. The *k'vutzah* (a form of collective settlement), for example, was an "endearing" bourgeois enterprise, like all the enterprises and programs of the Labor movement.[79] The rhetoric was socialist, but the actions were bourgeois. Since they denied that, however, they used money raised from the middle-class, on the one hand, and on the other, treated the local middle-class as inferior.

The middle-class was aware that it was exploited and despised at the same time. The employer, whether a factory owner or a farmer, responded by using the same terminology of class warfare as the workers, but from the opposite vantage point: if the workers constituted a class, so did the farmers; if the interests of the workers as a class were sacred, so were those of the employers. Thus, according to Jabotinsky, the worker himself gave the employer a reason to employ Arab workers without feeling any embarrassment.

This did not mitigate the fact that those employing Arab labor were traitors, because the pace of creating a Jewish majority was thus slowed down. The danger was very clear. The solution, said Jabotinsky, using very moderate language in this article, was for the workers to change their socialist ideology about class warfare in favor of what Jabotinsky called "economic diplomacy"—the acceptance of national arbitration during the breakthrough period. During the course of his controversy with the left, Jabotinsky added another argument: politics by majority must be forbidden in the Land of Israel, and the workers should not exploit the fact that they constituted a majority in the various institutions. Said Jabotinsky:

> A new type of Jewish life is being established in the Land of Israel, based on cooperation and compromise. And even if there is a majority of workers in a local Jewish body, majority politics should not be conducted: that because I have twenty-one votes to your twenty I don't have to take you into account at all. The Settlement is a voluntary society. It can not be governed by a majority. It may be governed only by continuing compromise. Actually, the National Council should be turned into a large council of arbitrators—and I shall return to this subject another time—however, the spirit of arbitration at least must penetrate every cell of Settlement life. This spirit is the only one which suits a nation of settlers. Its external wars are sufficient; it can not fight both internally and externally.[80]

Democracy in the breakthrough period—and in that period only—had to be based on compromise among the various bodies, and not on majority decision. We saw in our discussion of Jabotinsky's general political thought that at a certain stage he presented a concept of democracy not based on majority decision, but on compromise between different views. We pointed out that in this Jabotinsky differed from the major nineteenth-century liberals who, despite the dangers inherent in the principle of majority rule, accepted that principle, and attempted, within that framework, to find solutions which would minimize the negative results likely to arise from the principle of decision by the majority.

In the paragraph quoted above, however, Jabotinsky did not present his view on compromise–democracy as an alternative principle to be replaced by the principle of majority rule, but rather as a principle which was pragmatically essential during the breakthrough period when it was imperative to concentrate on that which united and to minimize divisive elements.

Jabotinsky's attacks on the class concept and its concomitant weaponry of strikes, as well as on the principle of majority decision in the Settlement, grew stronger over time. In "With Two Sticks" and "A Warning," both written in 1929, he blamed the labor movement for not fulfilling its obligation to the Jewish soldiers, who received no assistance whatsoever from any institution. He accused the workers of violating the social equilibrium in the Settlement: "This equilibrium was disturbed, disturbed in a manner unprecedented in any community in the world apart from Russia. A limb was created in our public body that swelled to seven times its natural size and weight."[81]

The equilibrium was disturbed, Jabotinsky claimed, because the *Histadrut* was concerned only about the working class. The hegemonic labor movement that flourished on bourgeois wealth disdained and discriminated against the other classes—small craftsmen, businessmen and industrialists.

Jabotinsky's warning in 1929 was reminiscent of the one issued in his 1925 article "*Basta!*" There he warned that if the inequality between classes continued in the Land of Israel, the situation could degenerate into fascism, something which had to be prevented at all costs. He repeated this caution in "A Warning," without using the term *fascism*. Instead, he emphasized once again that the government's open preference for the working class, coupled with a double standard that allowed the worker what was forbidden to the other classes, would "poison the Zionist enterprise."[82]

One of the most blatant expressions of this pathological situation in the Settlement was the use of the weaponry of strikes, which often caused damage to the economy. In several articles, Jabotinsky came out against any class concept based on divisive elements (property owners versus those without property; employers versus employees), and therefore antithetical to the proper ideology for the Settlement: unity. We have come to the Land of Israel, said Jabotinsky, in order to build, and not to be built. Thus he said, "When we protest against the class idea, the least offensive matter is the issue of wages. ... Hopefully they will increase ... we are speaking of something much more important: 'why, oh why did the soul descend?'. ... Or, on the contrary, why did it ascend in the sense of ascent to the Land of Israel? For what purpose is our *avant garde* going to Zion—to 'build' or to 'be built?' To build a state for other Jews to help realize the prophecy of the Return to Zion—or to build a comfortable life for themselves?[84]

In "The Left," Jabotinsky maintained that "the cult of the cow, the tractor, and the budget ... have taken root ... " among the Jewish workers, particularly among the "leftists."[85] Jabotinsky contrasted his own ideological monism—the self-sacrifice of each individual, whether worker or employer, for the sake of an ideal—with the concept of class warfare, in which the ideal would improve the status of the working class alone, and could thus not be pursued universally.

Jabotinsky did not believe in ideological *sha'atnez*, which in this instance meant the combination of socialism with Zionism, because every such ideological admixture necessitated the sacrifice of the lesser ideal. Monism posited a single ideal—the establishment of a state of the Jews—and any other concept or goal had to be subordinate.

The labor movement, on the other hand, attempted to graft the goal of Zionism onto the concept of class warfare, sacrificing Zionism in the process. Jabotinsky's conclusion was simple: class warfare had no place in the breakthrough period; compulsory national arbitration had to take the place of strikes. In Jabotinsky's thought, arbitration symbolized the fundamental difference between the ideological monism of the Revisionists and what he considered the ideological *sha'atnez* of the left. Therefore constant references to national arbitration appeared in his articles, speeches, and letters, and in the UZR and *Betar* programs.

With that, Jabotinsky emphasized in a significant number of articles, that ideological monism was legitimate only during the breakthrough period. In summarizing the subject, he stated:

> None of this in any way constitutes an attempt to solve our class problem, not completely and not partially even to a very small degree. ... It would be an error were we to assume that we could wipe out the spirit of class sentiment in the Land of Israel. The laborer and the employer will never feel comfortable with each other, like two lambs grazing in one field. On the contrary—it is certain that each of these two groups will always think and claim that it, specifically, and not the other group, is the "salt of the earth" and the foundation of the world economy.[86]

It was not Jabotinsky's intention to solve the class problem or to destroy class sentiment. These would by the nature of things continue to exist, and the time to grapple with the problem would be after the establishment of the state. However, he said, during the construction period "the function of state Zionism is not the 'liquidation' of class sentiment; its function is the 'extirpation' of these sentiments and their replacement with views that lack the power to influence the economic situation in the Land of Israel, *all the while the process of creating a Jewish majority is not completed.*"[87] It is important therefore to remember that Jabotinsky limited ideological monism, together with his views on the class issue and his proposed temporary solution of comprehensive national arbitration, to the breakthrough period, until a Jewish majority in *Eretz Yisrael* would be attained.

Such is the case also with his concept of democracy in the Settlement as a compromise instead of as a majority decision. In "Yes, to Break," in which he proposed breaking the monopoly of the workers' union by establishing a second union made up of Revisionist workers, and in "Strikes in the Land of Israel," Jabotinsky maintained that until national arbitration was accepted as a method, the workers in any place where a strike had been declared by the majority were not obligated to obey the decision if they did not feel the strike was justified. The principle of majority decision did not apply when the minority had its own position on an issue of principle, and had proposed an alternative approach of resolving the crisis (national arbitration). Such behavior by the minority was just and moral since it would prevent damage to the economy of the Settlement.

The socialist had to put away his socialist belief until after the establishment of the state:

> Even the socialist understands that building a Hebrew state today is possible only within the present social framework. There is no possibility of construction without private capital; and such capital, naturally, goes where it is likely to achieve profits. It may be that this feature of private capital is very bad, but it is a basic, intrinsic, immutable feature, which must be acknowledged if we do not want to delay the beginning of building the Land and the realization of Zionism until another social order prevails in the world.[88]

No principles were sacrosanct besides the attainment of a Jewish majority in *Eretz Yisrael* and the establishment of the state of the Jews. It must be said, to Jabotinsky's credit, that he made no demands on the left that he did not also make on himself: he sacrificed, as we saw, some of his own economic principles during the period of the state on the way, and put off their implementation until after the establishment of the state.

The controversy between Jabotinsky and the left included many other issues which boil down to the class question. However, Jabotinsky's argument with the left is not the topic of this book. We probably would not have even raised the subject at all, were it not for the fact that this controversy highlights the difference between the two approaches toward the goals of the breakthrough period, and sharpens the picture of Jabotinsky's ideological zeal.

The Army, Militarism, and the Exercise of Force

The label of someone who espoused militarism and the use of force, which has been affixed to Jabotinsky, helped those who claimed that he was nothing but a fascist. If, in fact, Jabotinsky's Zionist thought was characterized by militarism and the use of force, its liberal character would be severely compromised.

Jabotinsky struggled for two years to establish the Jewish Legion, until he finally succeeded in 1917, and a significant part of his book *The Story of My Life* was devoted to this effort.[89] And once the Legions were disbanded, he continuously demanded their reestablishment.[90] Moreover, military education occupied a central place in *Betar*, the youth movement which Jabotinsky helped found, and whose world view he played a dominant role in fashioning. In about 1910 (when he wrote "Right and

Might," "*Homo Homini Lupus*," and "I Believe") Jabotinsky was overridden with a sense of pessimism about the future of morality. He concluded from the persecution of the Jews and other minorities that since the whole world had adopted violence, the Jews must do so also in order to survive. He also admired the ceremonial aspects connected with military discipline. It was those elements that led to Jabotinsky's reputation as a sworn militarist, as someone who believed that the solution to the problem of the Jews was to be found in force.

A thorough perusal of Jabotinsky's thought, however, reveals an approach with no admiration for the use of force and no worship of war. Rather, he engaged in a practical and pragmatic discussion on the exercise of power as one of the necessary methods to implement the goal of attaining a Jewish majority in the Land of Israel.

Jabotinsky developed his central thesis on militarism in "The Court Jews" (1922). His main contention was that the Jewish Settlement in the Land of Israel, like all other settlements in history, was naturally threatened by the opposition of the natives (the Arabs), and therefore needed military defense. This function of protection was assumed by the British Mandate, and the tragedy lay in precisely that fact, because the fate of the Jews was identical with that of the court Jews in the diaspora. The Arabs actively threatened the Jews any time they did something of which they did not approve. In practical terms, that meant that the British army had to intervene to protect the Jews. The soldiers killed or injured in defense of the Jews were British soldiers; the blood spilled was British blood, and the money needed to maintain an army was British money. Moreover, the British soldiers stationed in the Land of Israel found it difficult to identify with the Jewish interests they were supposed to protect, for *Eretz Yisrael* did not belong to the British Empire, and the British, as a mandatory power, were merely appointees of the League of Nations.

Likewise, said Jabotinsky, one might easily understand the sympathy of the British soldiers for the Arabs, who had been living in *Eretz Yisrael*, while the Jews, in their eyes, were new settlers who were depriving the Arabs of what was theirs. Jabotinsky quoted from a letter of a pro-Jewish, Christian British officer: "We must play the role of the official who executes the orders year after year—and the end is still far. This is a very difficult moral test."[91]

Jabotinsky said he could understand this feeling among the British soldiers, but the Arabs exploited the situation by threatening active resistance that would result in bloodshed in which the British would be involved. Thus over the years, the British became the enemies of the Jews and undertook methods to satisfy the Arab population and prevent clashes. The conclusion, said Jabotinsky, was clear:

First of all, Britain's standing army can truly protect us only on the condition that it is made up primarily of Hebrew soldiers. Second, only under such circumstances would it be possible to reform the method of administration of the Land of Israel, which will pave the way for carrying out the Mandate—first of all, toward mass immigration and settlement. Just as we cannot demand money from England to support Zionism, so we may not demand her blood. If there are casualties to the standing army, the list of killed and wounded must not include the names of Peter and John but the names of Moses and Isaac. If the standing army must take upon itself the function of scattering the riots by force, then neither must this work be done by John and not by Peter for whom it involves a serious moral sacrifice, but by Moses and Isaac, who believe in what the League of Nations believed, that Zionism is a just matter, and that certainly driving away its enemies is also a just matter.[92]

Jabotinsky's demand to establish Jewish legions within the British army was thus purely pragmatic, and based on a cold analysis of what it was possible to demand of the British. Since the goal was to create a Jewish majority in the Land of Israel, a continuation of the situation where British soldiers were being killed would lead to a continuation of the anti-Jewish Mandatory policy. That meant closing the gates to Jewish immigration in order to appease the Arabs and avoid a confrontation with them. Only Jewish soldiers within the British army could protect the Jewish Settlement properly, and would almost certainly be able to prevent clashes. In all likelihood, the very fact of having Jewish soldiers would serve as a deterrent to the Arabs, and thus the bloodshed would at least be lessened. In summarizing his article, Jabotinsky said: "The question of whether we favor militarism or not is not relevant here. We face a logical series of premises and conclusions that cannot be appealed: we are settling the Land of Israel against the will of the natives; the opposition of the natives is unavoidable; therefore settlement is possible only under conditions of armed and active surveillance. England does not want such surveillance and cannot put it at our disposal; thus, the standing army must be composed of Jews; if not— Zionism is not feasible."[93]

There is no question that Jabotinsky was disturbed by the image that was painted of him as a war-monger. In an article to commemorate the anniversary of Trumpeldor's death, he portrayed Trumpeldor as the symbol of the Hebrew soldier, afterwards discussing the issue of militarism. Passivity and lack of response simply intensified people's feelings that "here it is permissible," said Jabotinsky. Not everyone was blessed with an internal sense that enabled him to know where the lines that could not be crossed were. Many took the path of least resistance, and did not hesitate to conquer and exploit where they did not encounter any resistance. The first function of the ability to fight was thus to prevent a situation that invited exploitation.

For many years Jews did not bear arms or display active resistance, thereby exacerbating their vulnerable situation. The time had come to replace passivity with activity. There was no trace of militarism in the capacity for self-defense, said Jabotinsky, because:

> Militarism means a regime in which the state has too many soldiers. That is the only proper use of this Latin word. However, no person of clear mind has yet demanded that a people remain totally without armed forces. ... We, the Jews, lack even this minimum although, as God is our witness, we very much need any means at all to "keep order" around Jewish areas. I understand when those who are not satisfied with the minimum are called militarists. But to hang this collar around the necks of those who have nothing and who want to obtain at least one tenth of the minimum is simply meaningless talk.[94]

Eleven years later, in 1933, Jabotinsky wrote an entire article on militarism, in which he unequivocally elucidated his opinion on war: "War, the killing of young, innocent souls, is evil ... And the truth is that only war is ugly: military life 'in and of itself' is distinguished by many fine aspects. ... Hatred for war is the spiritual heritage of our people: our prophets were the first who protested against mass killing, and we are all faithful to their teachings."[95]

What Jabotinsky liked about the army were discipline and ceremonialism. Since we already discussed this matter at length in the chapter "Liberalism and Democracy," it is sufficient to state here that the reason for his admiration of discipline and ceremony was his desire to use these as a means of straightening the Jew's bent posture—external and internal—to invest him with external and internal *hadar*. Military life, as a result of discipline and ceremony, could also serve as a unifying factor and turn the Jews from a multitude into a people.

Therefore, in *Betar* Jabotinsky strove to educate for military discipline, order and ceremony. In that way, the youth would learn to act in an organized fashion, and would also develop respect for external form, which would enhance their sense of self-respect.

Jabotinsky was aware that the military education of youngsters who were not previously acquainted with the military was likely to result in exaggeration as a result of their over-enthusiasm: "The cult of physical preparedness can sometimes bring, especially early on, to lightheaded quickness to use hands when it is unnecessary and totally unjustified. The cult of ceremony is likely to create in the beginning, unnecessary and purposeless boasting over all types of 'coats of many colors.' And this can be also unpleasant. But one does not judge a general phenomenon by its youthful errors. ... One must gird oneself with patience particularly with regard to youth."[96]

The purpose of military education thus was not to educate a generation to love war, but to develop organization and self-respect, both of which were so lacking in exilic Jewish life. Military training was also necessary for the youth to be able to defend themselves.

As someone who tried to learn from an analysis of history, Jabotinsky concluded that the passive response of Jewish youth to the idea of the Jewish Legion in 1914–1918 was responsible for missing the historic moment when it would have been possible to establish a Jewish army of tens of thousands. Their reaction was completely opposite to that of normal youth; instead of being a stimulating and energizing factor, they were obstructive. Youth who preferred calm were likely to cause the loss of another historic moment; therefore it was necessary to imbue them with "war readiness." Jabotinsky did not fear that training Jewish youth for the military would fashion a generation that enjoyed battle and would bring about war. The objective situation of the Jewish people was such, he said, that: "We Jews can not cause war or military provocation. Because of that, the concept of 'readiness' has a totally different meaning to us—essential, beneficial, holy. Its meaning is: 'In the event that a tragedy such as a war occurs, our youth must be ready to dedicate their live in such a fashion that will bring us closer to our national goal.'"[97]

Jewish youth had to have sufficient military knowledge to be victorious if war was forced upon them in the process of the establishment of the state of the Jews. Jewish youth had to be educated for military activity, because by nature they opposed it. Hatred of war was a credo for the Jew. Therefore it was necessary to bring the youth to a point where they were prepared to make sacrifices and to lay down conditions if there was another war in the Middle East.

From an analysis of the situation in the Middle East in the early 1930s (primarily the Arabs' desire to be rid of Europe), Jabotinsky concluded that there was a great likelihood of a war in the region. In such a case, the Jewish youth must not act as they did at the time of the first Jewish Legion.

It is in this context that his famous article, "*Affen Prippachek*, the New A B C" (1933), must be understood. Anyone reading the following sentence out of context might well see in it a slogan of extreme militarism: "For the generation growing up now and upon whose shoulders responsibility for the greatest turning point in our history will apparently be placed, the A B C has a very simple sound: young people—learn to shoot."[98] However, within the general context—Jabotinsky's analysis of the need for Jewish soldiers to protect the Settlement in the Land of Israel, and his analysis of the natural behavior of Jewish youth in the past—the sentence obviously was simply a translation of theory into action; the Jews had accepted the Mandate knowing that a Jewish settlement would not be possible without military protection. As early as 1922, Jabotinsky analyzed what had transpired in *Eretz Yisrael* during the time that the Jews were like "court Jews," but he presented this analysis once again in 1933. The existing situation in the Land of Israel only strengthened his earlier analysis and its inevitable conclusion that: "Without armed power to physically prevent any possibility of disturbance to the settler, settlement is impossible. Not 'difficult,' not 'dangerous'—*impossible*. ... Zionism is settlement and therefore its entire destiny depends on armed force. It is important to plow, it is important to produce, it is important to speak Hebrew. To our sorrow, there is nothing more important than knowing how to shoot, otherwise we shall have to forego the game of settlement."[99]

Learning to fight was a basic condition without which the goals of the breakthrough period could not be realized. While in 1922 Jabotinsky spoke about Jewish soldiers within the framework of the British army, in 1933 he raised the question of whether there was reason to cooperate with a mandatory power that in the previous decade had lost some of its prestige, and thus its backing for that limited force that it had been ready to exercise in the Land of Israel.

The problem was that there was no assurance that the British would make it possible for Jewish youth who had received military training in the diaspora to use arms. This did not change Jabotinsky's opinion about the need to be emotionally and physically prepared to fight. Youth "who long to shoot" and in the time of need would be ready and trained to fight were preferable to young people with a passive psyche that shrank from a just war, like at the time of the first Jewish Legion. Jabotinsky said: "You can tell me countless times that this is spiritual militarism, and I will defend my position: it is the healthy instinct of a people who are in situation like ours."[100]

Jabotinsky's views were translated in a simple and clear form into the *Betar* program in 1934:

> *Betar* stands like a firm rock on the foundation of the Legion: it demands of its members and of all Jewish youth thorough training in the use of arms, and to be ready at any time to respond personally to every call, whether for defense or, when the time comes, for a new Jewish legion. For *Betar*, a pioneer who has not been trained for this function is a bad pioneer and is useless for *Eretz Yisrael*; and this "training in self-defense"—that is, military experitse—is, for *Betar*, the first and most important type of training for pioneers.[101]

The pioneer, in Jabotinsky's sense, saw defensive military training as the most important of all training. However, the fact must not be overlooked that the same program called upon the pioneer with similar fervor to fulfill every task that was requested of him. Fighting was only one of the pioneer's many tasks; and the criterion by which the importance of a task was evaluated was its success in furthering the goal of achieving a Jewish majority in *Eretz Yisrael* and establishing a state of the Jews. Since Jabotinsky explained many times that settlement was not feasible without military defense, it is clear why military training was so important.

Since Jabotinsky was aware of the criticism leveled against *Betar* as a militaristic movement, the following paragraph appeared in the program:

> Its opponents will call it "militarism." Do not be afraid of the Latin word. . . . If a state that is not threatened begins to arm itself in order to attack its peaceful and secure neighbors, that is bad militarism. However, if we Jews, who are beaten practically all over, and whose places of residence apart from *Eretz Yisrael* are threatened with forceful destruction and violence—if we arm ourselves in order to protect our lives, our property, our future, that is good militarism, and we are proud to be such militarists.[102]

It is clear that military training referred to here was for the purpose of a defensive war.

The UZR program of 1928 did not emphasize military training, but rather the idea that it was necessary to increase the amount of Jewish support for the defense of *Eretz Yisrael*, because the British could not be asked to supply the defense or the funds. The program called for a Jewish Legion of 3000 men, to be funded by the *Keren Hayesod*, as an essential condition for the survival of the Settlement and for mass immigration, as well as for the existence of Zionism.

Jabotinsky fought for his entire life for Jewish soldiers in the Land of Israel, and for the military training of Jewish youth in the diaspora at an early stage. Among all the Zionist leaders, it was Jabotinsky who insisted upon the immediate establishment of a Jewish Legion. He did not then call for a Jewish army, because that was clearly impossible without a state.

Jabotinsky succinctly reviewed his entire position on this issue in his book *A Hebrew State: A Solution to the Problem of the Jews* (1937) in the chapter, "The Court Jews and the Legions." In the conclusion of that chapter, he addressed the British contention that in a land inhabited by two peoples, justice did not permit the arming of one while leaving the other unarmed. His response was based on the principle that, in times of peace, the exercise of armed force had to be prohibited. Existing circumstances, however, were not peaceful; one side had made and continued to make numerous attempts on the lives of the others. Therefore, those who came under attack had to be able to defend themselves. Granting the victim permission to use force for defensive purposes did not mean that the same permission had to be granted to the aggressor. This was not a case of granting equal rights to ensure a just distribution, but the opposite; justice would be achieved only if the attacked party was able to defend itself against aggression.[103] Throughout his life, Jabotinsky repeatedly emphasized that he called for use of force only for defensive purposes.

Thus in 1921 he opposed arming the general population. "I caution against giving arms to young people who have not been trained in discipline. Arms may be distributed only to designated people, who are under strict supervision."[104] He pointed out that the only solution was to reestablish the Jewish Legion, whose function was clearly defined as "prevention of violence," "so that the Arabs may understand that they may protest, write, vote against us, but may not use violent measures against us. If this is achieved, the door will have been opened to the beginning of mutual understanding."[105]

About fifteen years later, in 1936, Jabotinsky summarized his concept of the need for a Jewish Legion for defense purposes:

> There is no way out—we live in this world and we cannot be free of its influence. The main problem that we, like other nations, have is: are you able to defend yourself against attack? And if not, every effort is futile, certainly talk, because there is nobody to help you and you must accept everything: a legislative council, cantons, Abdullah's state, and so forth, without end. So that with us, like with other people, our national future depends upon "arming ourselves" in the Land of Israel, and we are forced by circumstances to place security demands first in our political fight.[106]

An analysis of Jabotinsky's concept of the army, militarism, and power shows that his considerations were most pragmatic, and, unlike fascism, lacked any attempt to glorify or exalt war. His discussion focused on defining the important role to be played by the army in defending the Settlement in order to achieve the primary goal of the breakthrough period. Did Jabotinsky deviate from liberal principles in his attitude to militarism and the exercise of force? Perhaps he exaggerated his enthusiasm for discipline and ceremony, but this too must be seen against the backdrop of his desire to forge the image of the ideal Jew as an instrument for fashioning external and internal *hadar*.

The Arabs of the Land of Israel

Jabotinsky's attitude to the Arabs of *Eretz Yisrael* was an outgrowth of his liberal world view on nationalism. That attitude was reflected in his general theoretical thought, primarily in "Self Rule for a National Minority," and in his concept of the creation of a Jewish majority in *Eretz Yisrael* as the central goal of the breakthrough period. Was he indeed able to bridge between his liberal views and his concept of the need to alter the reality of the Land of

Israel, whereby the Arabs would be transformed from a majority into a minority?

Already at the beginning of his Zionist thought, Jabotinsky considered the question of the Arabs of the Land of Israel to be of primary importance. Then he did not yet speak of them as a nation with nationalist aspirations of its own for *Eretz Yisrael*, but rather as settlers or natives who constituted a majority in the land. One of his proposals in 1905 included replacing Arab labor in the farming villages with Jewish labor. The reasons for this were multifold: so that the Jew should not assume the image of an exploiter and the Arab of the exploited; to reform the distorted economic structure that existed in the diaspora where the Jews did not engage in agriculture; to make work more efficient because the Jew was more honest and diligent; and in order to increase the security of the farming villages in case of clashes between the Jews and the Arabs.

Jabotinsky did not mince words nor attempt to whitewash the implications for the Arabs of the attainment of a Jewish majority in the Land of Israel:

> In that same cultural vanquishment that is before us, it will be the victor who will achieve the most influence. But achieving influence means first of all investigating all the minute details of the character of the land and its residents. ... For that purpose we must first achieve one thing: our settlers there must turn from a collection of boors who lack economic independence, are fragmented, and have a weak identity—to educated people, independent by virtue of hard work, and united in a stable national consciousness. Otherwise, they will simply achieve a position of primacy among the other culturally backward groups in the population of the land.[107]

One of the ways of obtaining the necessary influence in *Eretz Yisrael* was to attract the Arabs to the Jewish schools that were being developed:

> The children must become accustomed to the thought that everything comes to them from the Jews: both physical and spiritual culture. ... In general, we must, methodically, win over the Arabs. ... It seems to me that the bad habit of acting boorishly towards the Arabs has developed among the settlers. This must be strictly avoided. We must treat the Arabs with strength and friendliness, without violence, without any injustice whatsoever; we must impress them with our external and internal culture, because that is what subdues wild people.[108]

The Jews had to treat the Arabs justly and correctly, but at the same time, they needed to cultivate a sense of affection toward themselves based on a feeling of dependence, together with elements of patronage. Jabotinsky's view of the Arabs, as people with an inferior culture—that same "Eastern" culture that was inferior for reasons he explained in his general thought—and as natives who were indeed connected to the Land of Israel, but who did not constitute a living nation, changed fundamentally in his later thought. Without question, he was also mistaken from a tactical point of view in his initial approach to the Arabs because affection is not achieved by creating dependency. Quite the opposite; a feeling of dependence accompanied by a sense of inferiority provides fertile grounds for the growth of hatred.

Over time, as a result of his closer acquaintance with the situation in the Land of Israel, Jabotinsky changed his attitude to the Arabs living there, and began to consider them a "living nation" with nationalist ambitions focused on *Eretz Yisrael*, prepared to struggle for domination of the Land. The tactics of arrogance, implicit in his earlier remarks, disappeared, although he continued to believe in the inferiority of Eastern culture. Thus in "Majority" (1933) he maintained: "Arab culture is impoverished and undeveloped."[109]

However, in that same article Jabotinsky said that any attempt to delude the Arabs into believing that the goal of Zionism was not to turn them into a minority in the Land of Israel was doomed to failure.

> There is no possibility of deceiving the Arabs—or anyone else—on this question. Every *fellah*, who can neither read nor write, and who perhaps is not even familiar with the terms "majority" and "minority," nevertheless understands very well what the Jews hope to attain. He expresses it in innocent words: "They want to slowly become stronger than we in the Land of Israel." ... And as for educated Arabs, they have heard not only of "majority" and "minority," but also of the book, *The State of the Jews*. Therefore, all Arabs, whether educated or illiterate, see any attempt to distort the ultimate goal of Zionism as a clear attempt to deceive them.[110]

There were those in the Zionist movement who accused Jabotinsky of ascribing too much importance to the Arab movement. Therefore, in a speech before the Zionist Actions Committee in Prague in July 1921, Jabotinsky said: "The Arabs, too, are good Zionists like us, and the land is full of Arab memories. ... I do not believe, as a matter of principle, that it is possible to bridge the gap between us and the Arabs in words, through gifts, and through bribery. I have been accused of attributing too much significance to the Arab Movement. Sokolov believed that I place too much value on it; however, this movement exists ... and do not think that it is possible to bribe the Arab movement.[111]

Jabotinsky's attitude to the Arabs of the Land of Israel became one of respect, such as is accorded an open enemy. However, he did not see the Pan-Islamic movement as a political force which should deter Great Britain from granting a charter over the Land of Israel to the Jews. That was because, according to Jabotinsky, history had proven that neither Islam nor

Christianity constituted a basis for a real political alliance, and because the technological backwardness of the Islamic countries would not enable them to become military powers.[112] Nevertheless, he understood that it would be necessary to contend to a certain degree with the Arab nationalist movement (particularly with the Arabs of Syria, Iraq, Saudia Arabia, and Egypt) and first and foremost, the Arabs of the Land of Israel.

Jabotinsky's starting point in his later attitude to the Arabs of the Land of Israel was that they were a living nation with nationalist aspirations. "For the Arabs of the Land of Israel, the *Eretz Yisrael* would still remain, not a border area, but their homeland, the center and foundation of their independent national existence.[113]

Jabotinsky's reactions to the various proposals put forward would be based on this view; in 1931, he formulated a Zionist approach to the Arabs of the Land of Israel, including what their status should be in the state of the Jews:

> All of us, all the Jews and Zionists of all streams, want the good of the Arabs of *Eretz Yisrael*. We do not want to remove even one Arab from the east or the west bank of the Jordan. We want them to thrive both economically and culturally. We envision the government of the Land of Israel in this way: the majority of the population will be Hebrew, but not only will equal rights for all Arab citizens be promised, they will also be realized; the two languages and all religions will have equal rights, and every nation will receive broad rights of cultural self-rule; the question is, however: will this be enough for the Arabs?[114]

This and similar passages elucidate Jabotinsky's view of the status of the Arabs in the state of the Jews. The Arab minority in *Eretz Yisrael* would have self-rule, as Jabotinsky advocated for all national minorities. Their status as a minority in the state of the Jews would in no way conflict with their liberal rights as a national minority. Jabotinsky repeatedly emphasized this point:

> The writer of these lines is considered an enemy of the Arabs, someone who wants to have them expelled from the Land of Israel, and so forth. There is no truth in that. My feelings for the Arabs are the same as for all other peoples—polite indifference. My political attitude to them is determined by two principles. First, I consider it absolutely unfeasible to expel the Arabs from the Land of Israel; two peoples always lived in the Land. Second, I am proud to belong to that same group that once drew up the Helsingfors Program, the program of national rights for all nationalities living in one state. In drawing up that program, we had in mind not only the Jews, but all peoples, wherever they might be, and its basis is absolute equality of rights. I am prepared to take an oath binding ourselves and our descendants that we shall never abrogate this equality, and shall not make any attempt to expel anyone. As the reader can see, this is a fairly peaceful credo.[115]

In a speech before the British Parliament in 1937, Jabotinsky said: "There would be no need for the Arabs to emigrate: it would be the condition of any normal country where there is a majority and a minority."[116] Within the framework of the Ten-Year Plan, the interests of the Arabs of the Land of Israel and their descendants were assured; however, Arab immigration, like any large non-Jewish immigration, would not be allowed. One outstanding example of the protection of Arab interests in the Ten-Year Plan was in the field of agriculture: the plan proposed that the national land reserves be utilized on the basis of equal rights for both peoples. Property would be distributed to both Jews and Arabs under the same conditions. Jabotinsky rightly pointed out that the economic changes in the Land of Israel would affect the structure of the land: "The Arabs will have to become accustomed to it (while deriving tremendous benefit to themselves). However, in the process of acclimation to new economic conditions, a certain percent are always removed from their positions. This step is essential: it is noted in all textbooks of political economics; and will occur also in the Land of Israel."[117]

However, talk and action during the breakthrough period were based on the fact that the Arabs, then the majority, wanted to remain the majority. Jabotinsky described the goals and desires of the Arabs in the early 1930s and analyzed their implications. First, the Arabs demanded the right of supervising Jewish immigration. Second, they demanded the creation of a larger Arab federation that would include, in addition to the Land of Israel, Transjordan, Syria, Iraq, and possibly other Arab countries. Third, they wanted to free themselves from European domination. Thus did the Arabs seek to insure that the demographic relationship in the Land of Israel was not altered by Jewish immigration—that is, that the Jews remained a minority. Moreover, they hoped that the establishment of an Arab federation would make the percentage of Jews in the Land of Israel marginal. All this would happen while ties with Europe were cut. In simple language, the purpose of the Arab demands was patently clear: to preclude the establishment of a state with a Jewish majority in any part of *Eretz Yisrael*. Peace with the Arabs necessitated giving in to their demands. Zionism could, under no circumstances, accept those demands because they meant foregoing the establishment of the state of the Jews.

Jabotinsky ridiculed those who held that the Arabs could be bribed with minor civil rights and economic appeasements, calling such an attitude one of "endless scorn for the Arab soul, with no basis for it. It is possible to buy single Arabs, but no one will succeed in tempting an entire people to give up, of its own good will, its nationalist aspirations in return for 'economic advantages.'"[118]

Jabotinsky repeated this view in a later article:

To imagine that they will voluntarily consent to the realization of Zionism, in return for the cultural and economic advantages that we can grant them—the source of this childish notion among our "Arabophiles" is a feeling of scorn for the Arab people. It seems that in their opinion ... the Arab people is nothing but a mercenary mob that is ready to sell its patriotism for a developed network of railroads. There is no basis for such a belief. Certainly it is possible to bribe individual Arabs, but that does not mean that all the Arabs of the Land of Israel are prepared to sell that patriotic fervor, which even the Papuans will never sell.[119]

The sharp turnabout in Jabotinsky's attitude to the Arabs of *Eretz Yisrael* over the years is obvious. His later attitude was precisely the opposite of his early notion (1905) that it would be possible to befriend the Arabs and persuade them by making them economically and culturally dependent on the Jews. This radical change in his attitude was no doubt rooted in his later view of the Arabs as a living nation, while earlier he had not realized that they had nationalist aspirations.

In his later thought he maintained that the conflict between the two peoples could not be resolved by negotiations: "It is impossible to even dream of a voluntary agreement between ourselves and the Arabs of *Eretz Yisrael*. Not now, nor in the prospective future. ... There is no hope, however slight, of obtaining the consent of the Arabs of *Eretz Yisrael* to convert 'Palestine' into a country with a Jewish majority."[120] This was the source of his "iron wall" policy. Citing historical examples, Jabotinsky explained that new settlements always encountered hostility by natives, irrespective of the behavior of the new settlers. Such hostility was natural, he said, because every nation wanted to be sovereign in its own national territory, and would never consent to someone else's sovereignty. Even when the new settlement brought economic growth, the natives would not agree to surrender their national territory: "No people in the world ever sold its national aspirations for the price of a piece of bread with butter."[121]

The behavior of the Arabs of the Land of Israel was normal in every way. Thus, no explanations that they would be granted equal rights and self-rule in the state of the Jews would avail; Arabs would never consent to becoming a minority in the Land of Israel.

The tragedy in the Land of Israel lay in "the nature of things," and could not be changed. Two nations wanted one territory—the Land of Israel—as their national territory, in which they would be a majority. This conflict could not be resolved by negotiations. Jewish settlement spoke for itself and there was no reason to delude the Arabs: "Every native population in the world resists colonists as long as it has the slightest hope of ridding itself of the danger of the foreign colonization. That is what the Arabs in the

Land of Israel are doing, and what they will persist in doing as long as there remains a spark of hope in their hearts that they will be able to prevent the transformation of 'Palestine' into the 'Land of Israel.'"[122]

Nor did Jabotinsky believe in an agreement with the Arab states because they all would make demands which undermined the very existence of Zionism. Furthermore, even if it were possible to reach an agreement with the Arab states regarding the future of the Land of Israel, such an agreement would not be accepted by the Arabs in *Eretz Yisrael* itself, who would continue their struggle to maintain their status as a majority.

The inevitable logical conclusion therefore was that either the Jews forego their goal of becoming a majority in *Eretz Yisrael*, or continue mass immigration and absorption "under the protection of a power that does not depend on the local population, from behind an iron wall, which the local population will not have the power to break through."[123] This, in Jabotinsky's opinion, was the function of the Mandate until the Jews became a majority, and that was the meaning of the Balfour Declaration. If the Mandate was unable to provide the "iron wall," the British would have to leave, Jabotinsky said; as he captioned his testimony before the Peel Commission: "fulfill your promise or give back the mandate!"[124]

Any agreement with the Arabs would be possible only once they understood that they had no hope of "getting rid" of the Jews. Only then would it be time for negotiations. Jabotinsky wrote: "And only then will the moderates appear, with proposals for mutual concessions; and only at such a time will they begin to negotiate with us on practical matters such as guarantees against expulsion of the Arabs, equal civic and national rights. My hope and my faith are that indeed then we will give them satisfactory guarantees and the two peoples will be able to live in peace as good neighbors. ... The only way to reach an agreement in the future is to abandon all efforts to seek an agreement at present."[125]

Jabotinsky was aware of the moral criticism leveled against the philosophy of the iron wall, and explained the moral foundation for his position by saying that the stage of moral decision occurred when it was determined that Zionism was moral. If Zionism and its goals were moral, then Jabotinsky's iron wall policy—which was the only way to achieve results—was also moral.

Turning the Arabs into a national minority by creating a Jewish majority in the Land of Israel was moral, said Jabotinsky. It is true that both nations laid claim to the same territory, but while the Arab nation had many other states where it constituted a majority, the Jewish nation lacked even one. The moral claim of the Jewish people was stronger than that of the Arabs. To contend that the moral position of the Arabs was stronger simply because they were already a majority was to sanctify the existing situation. The Jewish claim had strong humanitarian aspects as a result of the structural tragedy of the Jewish people, inherent in their life in the exile.

Jabotinsky's response to the rejection of the Jews' moral claim to the Land of Israel was:

> That is a free-for-all and not morality. Human society is based on mutuality; remove mutuality and justice turns into a lie. That same person who is taking a walk on the street has a right to live only because, and to the same degree that, he recognizes my right to live; but if he has in mind to kill me, he has not, in my opinion, any right to exist—and this rule also applies to nations. ... The world must be a place of mutual surety. If we are speaking about life—all have the right to live, and if destruction is destined, it must apply to everyone. But there is no such morality which permits the glutton to eat to his heart's content, while allowing the abstemious person to die of hunger under the fence.[126]

The abstemious person in this analogy obviously refers to the Jewish people, who sought only one state in which they were a majority, while the glutton is the Arab people who, in addition to the existing Arab states in which they were a majority, wanted yet another state. Jabotinsky's claim of mutuality, and the fact that every right depends upon the obligation of others to honor it, is a well-known argument put forth by the father of liberalism, John Locke. Locke, however, espoused this position with regard to individuals, while Jabotinsky applied it to interstate relations. He maintained that international relations—like relations between individuals—had to be based on morality, and not on power; where justice was on the side of the weak countries, they had to be helped through mutuality. Thus, it was the moral obligation of all nations to help the Jewish people, who lacked a homeland, to establish its own state. For otherwise,

> if there exists in the world a people without a land, why its very yearning for a homeland is immoral. Those without a home must remain without a home for all eternity; every plot of land on the face of the earth is already distributed and is gone. Those are the conclusions of "morality!" ... The place of such morality is among cannibals, and not in the cultured world. Land belongs not to those who already have too much territory, but to those who have no territory at all. If one plot is confiscated from a people with large estates in order to give it to an exiled people—that is a just act. If the landed people objects to this—and that is a most natural thing—measures must be taken so that they do not under any circumstances cause disruptions by murders and assaults.[127]

There was no symmetry between the two claims to the Land of Israel. Both were natural, normal, and legitimate. However, since both could not possibly be satisfied, the more just claim—that of the Jewish people—should be supported.

In our discussion of Jabotinsky's thought we pointed out that, despite his earlier cynicism about the morality of individuals and nations, his fundamental approach was that society and nations had to exist according to the laws of morality. Thus it was in the name of morality that he demanded a homeland for the persecuted Jewish people; that was the approach he took in testifying before the Peel Commission. In that testimony, he dealt with the Arab question:

> What I do not deny is that in the process, the Arabs of Palestine will necessarily become a minority in the country of Palestine. What I do deny is that that is a hardship. It is not a hardship on any race, any nation, possessing so many National states now. ... One fraction, one branch of that race, and not necessarily a big one, will have to live in someone else's State: well, that is the case with all the mightiest nations of the world .... [most have] a branch living in someone else's State.[128]

Did Jabotinsky exaggerate in maintaining that the Jewish claim was the more just of the two conflicting claims, or that the Arabs of *Eretz Yisrael* would not find it a hardship to become a minority? While these remarks might be criticized as insensitive, there is nothing in them to justify the contention that he was unaware of the tragedy implicit in the situation. Quite the contrary; later on in his testimony before the Peel Commission, he spoke about "the decisive terrible balance of Need."[129]

He repeated that there was practically never an instance in which justice was on one side—that in most cases, there was merit to the positions of both sides, and a decision in favor of one was inevitably tragic. So it was in this case. However, one side had more justice to its claim; the potential hardship caused to the Arabs of *Eretz Yisrael* by becoming a minority was dwarfed by the suffering of the Jews in the diaspora, which would worsen immeasurably if a state of the Jews were not established. To mitigate the hardship to the Palestinian Arabs, Jabotinsky repeatedly emphasized that the Arabs of *Eretz Yisrael* had to be granted equal rights and self-rule in the state of the Jews.

Immigration to the Land of Israel and the Evacuation Plan

The subject of immigration to the Land of Israel was integrally connected with the goal of creating a Jewish majority there on the one hand, and on the other, with Jabotinsky's analysis of the situation of the Jews in the diaspora. Thus, early on in his Zionist thought he dealt with the issue of Jewish immigration from Europe to the Land of Israel.

He divided immigration into two periods. During the period before the establishment of the state, a certain number of Jews would be brought in. These would preferably possess traits that would help in creating suitable conditions for the Return to Zion—mass immigration—during the second period, after the establishment of the state.

Jabotinsky called for an open declaration of the first goal—the attainment of a Jewish majority—in order to justify the demand for mass Hebrew immigration. He calculated that one and a half million Jews needed to immigrate in the earlier period, and later, after the establishment of the state, multitudes.

Since we are discussing the breakthrough period, we shall concentrate on Jabotinsky's plans for Jewish immigration from the early 1930s, since they were the most relevant and significant.

When immigration to the Land of Israel was prohibited in February 1932, Jabotinsky spoke out in favor of illegal immigration in his article "On Adventurism," in which he developed the theory that, under unusual circumstances, an activity that seemed like an adventure had more likelihood of success. He thus justified illegal activity against the British rule in the Land of Israel. He did not stop with mere support of illegal immigration, as did the Revisionists and *Betar*, but went on to provide a moral foundation for such activity. The British government, by forbidding immigration, had performed an immoral action, "a cynical act of injustice lacking any moral justification."[130] The British government had destroyed its own moral foundation, and therefore any activity against the British rule was morally imperative, while submission to such laws would be complicit with immorality.

In 1932, Jabotinsky proposed a plan for creating immigration cooperatives in the diaspora in order to facilitate the emigration process, as well as absorption in the Land of Israel. In his fashion, he presented a detailed and logical program, with clear goals and clear means of implementing them.

However, the uniqueness of Jabotinsky's thought on immigration can best be seen in his Ten-Year Plan, both in terms of the development of his concept and its interconnection with the evacuation plan for Polish Jewry. Even earlier, Jabotinsky had made precise calculations; the UZR program of 1926 stated: "In order to create a decisive Hebrew majority on the west bank of the Jordan alone during the next twenty-five years, we need an annual immigration of approximately 40,000 Jews. And if we also take into consideration the east bank, this number will reach 50,000–60,000 Jews annually.[131]

Jabotinsky presented immigration to the Land of Israel as a Zionist principle, and considered the Revisionist demand for mass immigration as one of the fundamentals of Greater Zionism. However, as it clearly stated in the above excerpt, he envisioned a gradual immigration process during the breakthrough period; the time for mass immigration would not come until after the state was established. Jabotinsky's emphasis on gradualism and selectivity during the breakthrough period was not the result of constraints, but a matter of principle and an extension of his structured way of thinking. This did not prevent him, however, from demanding free immigration to the Land of Israel.

At the founding convention of the NZO in 1935, when presenting the Ten-Year Plan for discussion, he said:

> The details of the plan need to be worked out by experts, mainly in the Land of Israel itself. It will be based on the assumption that approximately a million and a half Jewish immigrants will settle in the land; this number will have to be divided among the various lands of the diaspora, so that each one of them may enjoy the beginning of the large evacuation. Once the Ten-Year Plan is accepted by the authorized bodies, it will be necessary to get ready by enlisting the world conscience; and that is what all those who are politically sophisticated see in what is inadequately termed, the "petition movement." All civilized people and their governments, and particularly those from the countries to be evacuated, must be included in the effort. ... The plan of action will obviously include other areas also: we are concerned with the distribution of immigration permits, and the training and choice of the immigrants.[132]

In that very year, subsequent to the death of the Polish ruler, Marshal Pilsudski, Jabotinsky began to view the fate of Polish Jewry with serious concern. As we saw in our discussion of his attitude to anti-Semitism, he feared for diaspora Jewry already at the beginning of the twentieth century, when he saw anti-Semitism as a structural phenomenon that would not disappear all the while the diaspora existed. We saw also that his concern for diaspora Jewry intensified as the temporary isolators that the Jewish people had created for themselves in the diaspora disappeared, his prime worry being that the basic economic changes that Europe was undergoing would destroy the sources of income of the Jews, increase anti-Semitism, and bring a holocaust upon the Jews.

He foresaw that this holocaust would reach maximum pitch in Poland, because he did not believe that the new government had the power to forestall the translation of institutional anti-Semitism into virulent, personal anti-Semitism. Therefore he decided that it was necessary to develop, with the help of the government of Poland, a structured plan for the evacuation of Polish Jewry to the Land of Israel. Jabotinsky believed that through pressure by the Polish government and the Jews, it would be possible to arouse British public opinion to influence the British government to change its policy and open the gates to the Land of Israel.

It was for this purpose that he organized the "petition" effort. In our discussion of anti-Semitism, we saw that he believed that it would be possible to utilize, for Zionist purposes, the storm threatening eastern European Jewry. Reality proved his hope to be false, and Great Britain did not change her policy. It is of interest to us, however, that since the discussions of the Ten-Year Plan were under way, and it was officially adopted by the Revisionists in 1938, Jabotinsky combined his plan for the evacuation of Polish Jewry with the Ten-Year Plan. Since the holocaust that he envisioned did not involve immediate physical destruction, he presented a detailed plan for the organized emigration and absorption of Polish Jewry over a period of ten years, within the broad framework of the settlement and building of the Land of Israel.

The Ten-Year Plan and its interconnection with the Evacuation Plan reflect Jabotinsky's typical comprehensive planning: "The purpose of the Ten-Year Plan is to serve as a basis for stages of activity, whose goal is to transform all of the Land of Israel, that is the Land of Israel on both sides of the Jordan, into a Hebrew state with a Hebrew majority, by creating the political, economic, and social conditions for the settlement of a million and a half Jews within the next ten years."[133]

The Ten-Year Plan dealt with the problems of both absorption and exodus from the diaspora. Based on the number of immigrants in 1935, Jabotinsky calculated the number of immigrants needed and that could be absorbed at around 150,000 annually.

Since the Ten-Year Plan placed greater emphasis on absorption, Dr. Jan Bader conducted research on the influence of the plan on the lives of Polish Jewry. Jabotinsky considered this study important, and in "A Pre-condition to the Ten-Year Plan" (1938), he discussed the need for similar research into all centers of Jewish emigration in Europe.

Since unlimited immigration would be unrealistic because of the problems of absorption—even if the gates of the land were opened to mass immigration—one of Jabotinsky's main concerns was which age groups be permitted to immigrate first. Jabotinsky pointed out the uniqueness of the Ten-Year Plan specifically on that point:

> However, the most important aspect of the Ten-Year Plan is the equi-librium between the absorptive capacity of an undeveloped land, and the number of residents that the land can gradually "digest." This capacity grew with the help of capital and experience. It necessitates a constant choice between various types of candidates for immigration, and there will be a need to quickly reach a compromise over the issue of age. We shall have to place the emphasis, not on adolescents, but on young adults. I am not an expert on demography; however, I have been told that the most fertile age for Eastern European Jews is between 25 and 27 for men, and between 23 and 30 for women. These criteria must also be considered in calculations connected with the Land of Israel: people of those ages are still suited for lives of starting settlers.[134]

This rational and logical paragraph explains the essence of the Ten-Year Plan. It speaks of planning, both in the Land of Israel and in the diaspora, over a period of several years. Each stage was dependent on the one that preceded it, and a very logical connection existed between the specific, detailed arrangements for absorption and the evacuation arrangements. The Ten-Year Plan detailed the development of the Land of Israel in all areas, while the Evacuation Plan, in complete coordination with the development plan, outlined the process of evacuating Polish Jewry, including the methods of liquidating property.

It is the function of the historian to determine how realistic were the assumptions on which the Ten-Year Plan and the Evacuation Plan were based. Much has been written on this sensitive subject; opinions are divided, and certainly more will yet be written. From the point of view of political thought, it is interesting to analyze the type of thinking disclosed in the combination of the two plans. From the aspect of internal logic, it was a model program.

Still, a critical question arises: how is it possible that Jabotinsky, who spoke with a sense of supreme urgency about the holocaust hovering over Polish Jewry, was able to propose a solution that would take at least ten years? Even if his hopes were realized that Great Britain would open the gates to the Land of Israel, that Poland would assist in the Evacuation Plan, and that the development of the Land of Israel would proceed at the pace anticipated in the Ten-Year Plan, how could he have spoken about an impending catastrophe, and yet have proposed a detailed and logical plan whose realization would take ten years? In view of the holocaust he foresaw for Polish Jewry, would it not have behooved him to abandon his logical and structured method, and to insist upon mass immigration, however disorganized, and however bad the absorption arrangements might be?

Jabotinsky himself supplied the answer to that question. Wherever he spoke about the holocaust hovering over Polish Jewry, he was not referring to mass physical destruction that demanded an immediate response. Rather, as we saw in our discussion on anti-Semitism, he was referring to the deprivation of Jews of their work and livelihoods, and to manifestations of active anti-Semitism; neither process would be complete in only a year or two. Moreover, Jabotinsky based his Evacuation Plan on the supposition of cooperation with the Polish government. He presumed that if the Poles knew that the evacuation of the Jews was underway and that Poland would within a short time be practically "free of Jews," they would wait patiently.

His fundamental assumption thus was that the anticipated holocaust was neither immediate nor physical, but rather an intensification of the "anti-Semitism of things" as a result of economic changes; thus, despite the seriousness of the situation, there would still be time to evacuate the Jews in an organized manner. This assumption was reflected in the petition which more than a quarter of a million Polish Jews signed in 1934. Addressed to the

Polish government, the petition stated, among other things, that "The difficult conditions of our life and our desperate situation, which are primarily the result of the tragedy of the Jewish exile, are not, as the exalted government knows, temporary circumstances for its Jewish population. ... It is understood that, because of those circumstances, it is not likely that our fate, which is too difficult to bear, would remain without any influence on the interests and welfare of the state. Settling in the Land of Israel offers our only hope of salvation, whereby we may arrange our lives and those of our families on a healthy foundation."[135]

Words in a similar spirit were addressed to the King of England in a petition: "This request does not include anything that might be construed as damaging to that state of which we are citizens, its government, or its sovereign people; because the situation which forces us to turn to His Majesty with this request, which is made with complete esteem, is first of all, the result of the historical tragedy of the Jewish exile."[136]

Emphasis was placed on the fact that the terrible situation of the Jews was not the fault of a particular government, nor the result of malicious anti-Semitism of man, but rather of an institutional anti-Semitism which could be remedied only by the liquidation of the exile. Solving the problem of the Jews was also in the interest of those countries that had Jewish populations that they wanted to be rid of. This approach was the basis of Jabotinsky's appeal to the government of Poland and his speeches before Polish leaders. His lecture "Poland Will Assist and Will be Assisted by the Evacuation Plan" in Warsaw in 1937 reflected this view. After logically explaining the main points of the Ten-Year Plan and the preconditions necessary for its implementation, he turned to the question of emigration from Poland, including the issue of the liquidation of the property of the emigrants and the transfer of money: "This issue needs to be dealt with sensitively and with great care, and needs concessions from both sides. The state will not be able, on the one hand, to declare that some of its citizens feel the objective need to emigrate, and that the possibility of their emigration will bring relief to the state, and on the other hand, to take away from them the ability to use this relief."[137]

The above quotation refers to a proposed plan, to be made in cooperation with the government of Poland, dealing with the property of the Jewish emigrants. Certainly no sense of imminent physical destruction of the Jewish people is evident in it.

In his article "Two Warnings" (1936), Jabotinsky stated: "They are all convinced that the fewer the Jews who remain in the diaspora—and for God's sake [may that be] at the earliest possibility—the better."[138] However, "at the earliest possibility" meant in accordance with the Ten-Year Plan. Similar strains echoed from his words in 1938; his article "A Precondition to the Ten-Year Plan" shows that he continued to think in terms of evacuation and absorption as construed in the Ten-Year Plan. He even discussed the political conditions necessary for the implementation of the Ten-Year Plan, including a change in the Mandatory policy and immediate changes to be made by the Jews, mainly regarding the reinstitution of voluntary Zionist taxes and the establishment of institutions of compulsory arbitration. Likewise, another essential condition was that the Mandatory power change its hostile attitude to a friendly one. Jabotinsky summarized: "These are essential conditions on which no compromise is possible. The Ten-Year Plan will stand or fall with its political progress."[139]

We must conclude that by 1938 the only solution that Jabotinsky offered was still the Ten-Year Plan with all its rational planning and gradualness. Despite his emphasis that its implementation was contingent upon the fulfillment of certain political conditions, he did not present any alternative plan.

It is clear from all of this that Jabotinsky, who in the 1930s sounded the loudest warnings about the situation of the Jews in exile, and who meticulously planned their gradual and complete evacuation, simply was unable, in his wildest imagination, to conceive of the Nazi holocaust.

Like many others, Jabotinsky miscalculated the power of Nazi Germany, and thus could never have anticipated the fate of the Jews. In his address at the founding convention of the NZO in 1935, he said: "In the Jewish press, we have read hopeful things that one of these days the 'Third Reich' will permit or encourage a comprehensive evacuation of German Jewry by an organized exodus to the Land of Israel, including both people and property. I want to emphasize here, that there is no such talk, except by those Jews that want it. And likewise, of the renewal of the normal conditions of economic life for those who remain."[140]

It seems to me that there is nothing to add to this quotation, which clearly expresses the tragic difference between Jabotinsky's widely-shared perception of what was transpiring in Germany and what actually took place there a number of years later. In May 1939, in his last speech to Polish Jewry, Jabotinsky expressed his belief that a world war would not break out, and that Poland's absolute refusal to submit to the demands of the Third Reach would remove the air from the German balloon: "Until a few months ago, world opinion held that there was one great fist which could destroy everything—and *basta*. And here, one country arose, and not necessarily the largest of countries, one country—and this will certainly be recorded with praise and glory in the annals of history—and said: 'We shall go to war.' And by that word, the fist was finally burst. And then the world was convinced that the fist was not full of power, but full of air!"[141]

Despite his fundamentally mistaken evaluation of Nazi Germany,

Jabotinsky did emphasize that Eastern European Jewry faced a terrible holocaust, worse than what had been previously imagined. The political regimes were likely to prevent the emigration of Jews to the Land of Israel in the near future. And for the first time, he conceded: "the Ten-Year Plan, about which I already spoke, no longer suits the present circumstances. A plan for today must include a response to the basic problems of our existence."[142]

But even in face of urgency, which was heard with greater intensity in his words, Jabotinsky was not willing to forego the "Plan." Of the three major objectives that he defined—resistance, a plan, and consolidation of the forces of the nation—preparation of a plan was imperative: "The second command is—there must be a plan. There are doubters who walk about among the Jews and ask: why is a plan necessary, for, in any case, everything is a free-for-all? Is it that you do not know that the day will come and you will bitterly regret that you have no plan. If the world forgets you, when it is being rebuilt, you will be truly lost."[143]

A plan had to be ready so that it might be produced at the appropriate moment. In other words, a plan was needed under any circumstances, whether or not it was used, so that if conditions for its implementation were created, the opportunity would not be lost for lack of a plan. However, whether because of the outbreak of the Second World War or because he passed away in 1940, Jabotinsky did not succeed in developing a replacement for the Ten-Year Plan.

We have spoken of Jabotinsky's personal tragedy deriving from the absence of an organic national feeling. A far greater tragedy for him and for the Jewish people lay in the fact that Jabotinsky—the Zionist leader par excellence, who recognized the condition of the Jews in Europe and understood that a terrible tragedy was about to take place, who time and again sounded the alarm about it, and who prepared a logical and structured plan for the evacuation of the Jews from Eastern Europe—did not succeed in significantly influencing the course of events. This was mainly because his views were at least partially rooted in erroneous political concepts. However, the main reason was that it was impossible to anticipate the true nature of the Holocaust, a violent, revolutionary nightmare which the liberal measure and balance of the Ten-Year Plan could not hope to withstand.

Nonetheless, one may by no means minimize the influence of the urgent warnings and alarms to eastern European Jewry that Jabotinsky sounded with ever-increasing frequency during the thirties. From that point of view, he certainly did more than any of the other Zionist leaders.

Did the ways and means of encouraging immigration that Jabotinsky proposed for the breakthrough period in any way violate liberal principles? Aside from his support of illegal immigration, which might also be justified morally, he proposed acting in legal, legitimate ways. And it was precisely in his approach to the painful subject of the escape of the Jewish people from the diaspora that Jabotinsky's basic liberal confidence in the world conscience and his belief in the efficacy of morality was expressed.

Jabotinsky's liberal belief in science and progress was also well expressed in his rational, structured approach, and in his attempt to utilize the science of demography as much as possible. This was reflected in his precise definition of goals, as well as the ways and means of achieving them, even on such a sensitive subject as the evacuation of eastern European Jewry. Sometimes we sense naïveté in the conflict between Jabotinsky's faith in the possibility of mass evacuation and immigration through logical planning, on the one hand, and his belief that the values of science and progress would impel the West toward greater morality, on the other. For that reason undoubtedly, his logical plans were sometimes unrealistic.

Great Britain and the Mandate

Jabotinsky distinguished between his relationship to Great Britain and his relationship to the British in *Eretz Yisrael*. While until his last day he considered Great Britain a partner and an ally, his criticism of British rule in the Land of Israel grew more pointed as the Mandate continued. Though it was sometimes difficult to maintain this distinction, Jabotinsky rationalized it by contending that the actions of the British administration in the Land of Israel did not accurately reflect the attitude of the British government and British public opinion, which supported Zionism.

From the beginning of the Mandate, Jabotinsky believed that the British, in whom he saw a nation with a developed sense of morality, recognized and would continue to recognize the justness of the Jewish demand for their own state in the Land of Israel, as long as the Jews continued firmly and clearly to insist upon that right. His letter of resignation from the Zionist Actions Committee and the World Zionist Organization averred: "Whoever stands up stubbornly and is not deterred from fully executing his right will meet only with concurrence and respect among the English people and its government, and also—even after a protracted struggle—just recognition."[144]

His attitude toward Great Britain stemmed from his basic view that the Jews in the Land of Israel were a branch of Western culture in the East, and thus shared common interests with the British. Since he did not regard Pan-Islam as a significant political or military factor, he assumed that Britain concurred in that evaluation, and viewed neither Islam nor the Arabs as a potential threat. The clearest expression of Jabotinsky's view of the commonality of interests between the Jews and Great Britain can be found in the Revisionist program of 1928, in the section "England: Mutual Loyalty":

> Our attitude to the Mandatory government is determined by two factors: we believe with complete faith in the recognition of justice and righteousness by the British people; we are absolutely certain that every just demand will be fulfilled by it only on condition that the petitioners themselves will be prepared to take upon their shoulders the burden of supplying the human material and the financial means. However, there is a second factor, which is commonality of interests. It is not true that England does us a kindness without deriving some benefit from it. England greatly benefited from our assistance, and stands to gain more in the future. There is only one land today among all the European colonies which is developing and growing at an unparalleled pace ... British public opinion as well as the British government understand this very well, despite attempts by the diplomats to ignore this truth, or of our enemies, to deny it. And more than that, along the eastern and southern shores of the Mediterranean Sea—England's corridor to the East—where anti-European designs are lurking, the Jews are building the only outpost which from a moral point of view belongs to Europe and always will. The Jew derives much from England and gives much to her. The account evens out. And both sides have equal rights. Mutual loyalty on the basis of mutual benefit—that is the only foundation upon which Zionism must base its relationship to the Mandatory government. This perception in no way impugns the historical sense of gratitude that the Hebrew people feels and will forever feel for the Balfour Declaration.[145]

Mutual loyalty on a foundation of mutual benefit was thus the basis of the relationship between Zionism and Great Britain. To this had to be added the gratitude of the Jewish people for the Balfour Declaration, which Jabotinsky from the beginning interpreted as consistent with the demand to establish a state of the Jews. It was this interpretation of the Balfour Declaration and of the Mandate, together with an analysis of the texts and of additional proofs, that Jabotinsky presented in his testimony before the Peel Commission in 1937.

In his analysis of the British administrative activities in the Land of Israel, Jabotinsky said that the Jews felt "terribly disappointed." He did not see British activity in the Land of Israel as the result of planned anti-Jewish policy, but rather, of "the absence of a system and a plan." However, he said, "we were even more disappointed by the absence of the second requirement: clarity. The Arabs were never told what the Balfour Declaration was meant by Lord Balfour and all the others to mean."[146] He thus criticized the British government on two fundamental issues. First, that they failed to prepare a plan of action to implement the Balfour Declaration, to translate into fact "'placing a country under such administrative, economic, and political conditions as might facilitate the establishment' of ... the Jewish national home."

Second, Britain did not explain to the Arabs the purpose of the trust it had received; on the contrary, the goal of the Mandate was intentionally obscured in order to placate the Arabs. Jabotinsky also criticized the fact that the British did not supervise what was taking place in the Land of Israel; worse, they allowed the ruling system to become filled with people with no sympathy for Zionism or for the Jews. The British were unable to fulfill their role of providing military defense, decreasing the number of legions to below what was needed. Jabotinsky repeated his central thesis that the British should not shed their blood in defense of Jews, and again demanded the reestablishment of the Jewish Legion: "I do not demand a 'Jewish Army' before there is a Hebrew State; we want the Jewish Regiment just as it existed during the War, rendering decent service. ... if blood has to be shed by the defenders of Palestine, let it be our blood and not English blood. But that suggestion has always been turned down."[147]

Jabotinsky proposed that the British investigate who was guilty for the uprisings; then, plan how to carry out the intentions of the Balfour Declaration, announce the plan publicly, and take all necessary steps to assist in its implementation.

At the end of his testimony, Jabotinsky asked what would happen if Britain could not grant the Jews their request, that is, if they could not create the conditions for the establishment of a state of the Jews. He answered that question by saying that in such a case they had to return the Mandate but not without prior consultation with the Jews to find an alternative. However, he concluded his testimony by saying: "I hope that time will never come. I am fully convinced that it will not be necessary. I believe in England just as I believed in England twenty years ago when I went against nearly all Jewish public opinion, and said: 'Give soldiers to Great Britain!' because I believed in her. I still believe. But if Britain really *cannot* live up to the Mandate well—we shall be the losers; and we will sit down together and think what can be done."[148]

In 1937 Jabotinsky still expressed the hope that under the pressure of public opinion and after clarification of the facts, Great Britain would change its policy in the Land of Israel and it would be possible to continue cooperating with her. However, even if Britain were unable to implement the Mandate in the spirit of the Balfour Declaration as Jabotinsky understood it, he did not suggest an absolute severance of relations, but a joint attempt at finding an alternative solution.

Jabotinsky began a campaign against the Partition Plan recommended by the Peel Commission in 1937. His rationale was pragmatic: the east bank of the Jordan was too small an area in which to settle all the Jews who needed to immigrate to Israel; as an alternative, he presented his Ten-Year Plan. In 1938 when the Partition Plan was already on its way out and it was clear that it would be rejected, Jabotinsky still did not place the entire responsibility on the British government: "But the truth must be told: a large part of the blame for England's violation of her promise must be placed on the fact that they are swept along after their Jewish advisors."[149]

At that time, Jabotinsky called for a violation of the policy of restraint, but under no circumstances did he call for a revolt again British rule. He emphasized the importance of military defense, without which it would be impossible to continue the Zionist enterprise and establish the state of the Jews. He supported demonstrations against the Mandate, but not illegal activities. His poems from that period spoke about revolt—not in the sense of revolution against the British Empire, but rather, in the sense of renouncing passivity, restraint, non-reaction. "It is All Mine" (1938), was a revolutionary poem, similar in its concept of revolt to Bialik's poetry. The fourth stanza reads:

> For their end—they shall either rot in a pit
> Or rebel against their heritage of shame.
> We shall call a revolt—and they will come
> With this vale—to redemption.

He called upon the Jews to rebel against their "heritage of shame," to revolt against the world view that had guided Jewish life for two thousand years, to develop all that was the antithesis of the exilic Jew, to turn a new page.

Under no circumstances may one conclude from this poem or from other writings in which he used the term revolt, that Jabotinsky was referring to concrete action against British rule. At no point in his testimony before the Peel Commission did he say that the British failure to implement the aims of the Mandate removed the legitimate basis for their retention of the Mandate. Rather, he stated that the British would have to give back the Mandate. In other words, their departure from the Land of Israel would be the direct result of a legal process. Moreover, he requested that they not leave until after consultation with the Jews about an alternative.

Parallel to his concept of the coincidence of interests between the Jews and Great Britain, Jabotinsky's criticism of the Mandatory actions in *Eretz Yisrael* grew. This was reflected in many speeches and articles such as "On the Uprisings of 1929" (1929), "The Sum Total" (1935), and the articles that we already discussed on the role of the British in providing military defense.

However, together with his criticism of British military activity in the Land of Israel, Jabotinsky also presented the British point of view. Likewise, he agreed that the Jewish Legion be made up of Jewish soldiers and a British command: it was clear to him that the formation of an independent Hebrew army would not be possible until the establishment of a Hebrew state, and he realized that British backing was needed; hence the establishment of Jewish legions within the framework of the British army.

In his book, *A Hebrew State: A Solution to the Question of the Jews*, Jabotinsky summarized Mandatory activity and its various proposals as a web of failures and omissions in all areas. For example, he maintained that "everything that it was possible to do to prevent the Hebrew economy from really taking root—all this was done, all this continued from the first day of the British conquest until today, and this was done then and is done now by the administration of *Eretz Yisrael* and under the authority of the Colonial Office in London."[150]

However, in the same breath as this scathing criticism of the British Mandate, Jabotinsky went on to say: "Together with that, I do not believe that in the beginning this was done intentionally, with malicious intent, by premeditation. Worse than that: it was done without any thought; out of the British habit of never anticipating the future, of operating without any plan, of relying on the 'power of improvisation,' on 'the sense of reality,' on the person on location; that is, on the district governor. The English refer to this method by the honorable name of 'empiricism.' I would call it frivolousness."[151]

The guilt thus lay in the British system, that operated in a similar manner all over and not only in the Land of Israel. There was no malicious intent against the Jewish settlement in the Land of Israel. Jabotinsky concluded with the hope that Britain had learned its lesson not to use the system of improvisation. "Therefore, together with her mighty partner, Zionism also must make the effort—to present a final question, and to demand a clear and absolute answer."[152] Jabotinsky also presented this position in a moving speech at the founding convention of the NZO in 1935, and, as we saw, in his testimony before the Peel Commission in 1937.

Despite his great disappointment with the British rule in the Land of Israel, it is clear that, in his heart of hearts, Jabotinsky continued to have faith in Britain's good will, and believed that ultimately it would change its policy and open the gates to mass immigration. But Jabotinsky's belief in the unity of interests of the Western world and his faith that technological progress was necessarily accompanied by moral progress prevented him from accurately perceiving reality in the 1930s. Had he been as pessimistic then as he was in 1910, his attitude to Great Britain would probably have been different. Only in this was is it possible to explain how Jabotinsky did not understand Britain's true intentions, and always sought to separate Mandatory policy in *Eretz Yisrael* from British policy, even when there was no basis for such a differentiation.

Democracy as the Rule of the Majority and Democracy as a Compromise

Jabotinsky's belief in the absolute primacy of the Zionist program was reflected in all his plans for the state on the way; everything during the breakthrough period was aimed at the single ideal of creating a Jewish majority in the Land of Israel. In the event of a conflict with any other ideal, implementation of that ideal had to be deferred until after the state of the Jews was established. Because Jabotinsky's thought on the breakthrough period was characterized by the belief in one truth, it was more like an ideology. The ideology of the breakthrough period was composed of primary goals and the methods of realizing them, and Jabotinsky placed great emphasis on the methods.

Jabotinsky's plans were inherently logical and, to the degree possible, had a scientific basis. The fact that some of them were not realized—e.g. those connected with the Ten-Year Plan and the Evacuation Plan—had nothing to do with an absence of internal logic.

Jabotinsky's difficulty in believing that the West could degenerate morally derived in large measure from his liberalism, and from his belief that scientific progress was naturally accompanied by moral progress. This approach no doubt impaired his ability to interpret the political and historical map of Europe in the thirties. Moreover, despite his insistence that a leader needed to see only one truth, because of his liberal approach he himself also tried to see the truth of the opposition, the Arabs of *Eretz Yisrael*.

Likewise, his fundamentally liberal-humanitarian make-up was expressed in his ideology of the breakthrough period and the ways and means of carrying it out. Although he sacrificed liberal principles, he did so within set bounds, and also limited the duration of the breakthrough period. He always had in mind the next stage—the state of the Jews—which he wanted to see built on liberal ideals. None of this, however, prevented Jabotinsky's detractors from claiming that his thought was merely a form of fascism and étatism. Those attacks were primarily the result of the fact that they lacked a comprehensive overview of his thought, and lifted particular details out of their general context.

Unquestionably, the emotion-laden atmosphere of controversy between the left and Revisionism contributed to this situation, clouding the logic of both sides. It is difficult to explain in any other way how it was possible, for instance, to accuse Jabotinsky of wanting to expel the Arabs from the Land of Israel, or of demanding sacrifices only from labor, and not from owners of capital.

However, the greatest error of Jabotinsky's enemies stemmed from the fact that they did not distinguish between his thought on the breakthrough period of the state on the way and his concept of the permanent state of the Jews. Anyone who saw in Jabotinsky's plans for the state on the way a plan for the state of the Jews grossly distorted his Zionist thought. Only such a distortion—which probably was as often due to political motives as to a lack of understanding—could lead to the contention that the state was everything and the individual nothing in Jabotinsky's thought.

In "The Wagon of the *Klezmer*" (1935), Jabotinsky himself, in response to the sharp criticism leveled against him, pointed out the mistake in attributing the character of the breakthrough period to that of the state of the Jews. It is appropriate here to review Jabotinsky's remarks, part of which were already quoted in the first part of the book:

> I, too, have a blind hatred for the idea that the "state is everything." And it makes no difference whether it is communist of fascist. I believe only in "old-fashioned" parliamentarianism, as inconvenient or powerless as it may seem at times. I believe in freedom of speech and organization, and in almost every conflict between individual consciousness and imposed discipline, I stand on the side of the individual. And I can truly prove this with my sources and documents. ... What we have really declared, and will always declare in the future as well, is the principle that the *aspiration* for a Jewish state must—among all those who acknowledge this aspiration as their ideal—stand above all class interests or individual interests. Garibaldi's opinion also was that the revival of the Italian state was of greater value than all the sacrifices, and so Lincoln saw the ideal of the united American republic. But this does not mean that Garibaldi or Lincoln had in mind such an Italy or such an America in which the citizen would be a nonentity and the state everything. When effort and thought precede speech, this difference is apparent.[153]

Jabotinsky's writings themselves are the best testimony to his views. However, as pointed out in the first part of the book, Jabotinsky's views on one central issue were problematic from a liberal-democratic point of view; we are speaking, of course, about his attitude to the principle of majority rule, and his strong advocacy of an arbitration system that was to operate within the framework of a democratic government.

We have already discussed the problems of this concept of democracy. However, the question remains of whether this view was an integral part of his general political philosophy, or whether it applied only to his Zionist thought on the breakthrough period.

In his Zionist thought on the breakthrough period, Jabotinsky opposed the establishment of a parliament in the Land of Israel as long as a Jewish majority did not exist there because he knew that a parliament with an Arab majority would prevent the creation of a Jewish majority. While he strongly opposed the establishment of the parliament, it was not out of opposition to this democratic institution; rather, he opposed a situation where representation would be determined by the relative population of Arabs and Jews in the Land of Israel during that period. The size of the Jewish population should be determined not by the number of Jews living in the Land of Israel, he felt, but by the number of Jews whose homeland was the Land of Israel and who were temporarily prevented from reaching it. Such a calculation would, of course, have given the Jews a majority. Only such a calculation was just and the establishment of a parliament would have to be delayed until it could be based on such a calculation:

> Where is democracy, where is the sacred principle that a majority must rule? We are responding to that question, because democratic principles were created for countries whose residents already are in their place; and after that happens, the majority will also rule in the Land of Israel (and then too perhaps there will be a need to reconsider as, for example, in the cases where mass insanity like Hitlerism breaks out); however, when the whole world has acknowledged that the Jews have a right to settle in the Land of Israel—that is, has acknowledged that not all the "residents" of the Land of Israel are yet there—a parliament may not be established and Jewish immigration ended.[154]

Not the slightest anti-democratic tone is evident in such a position, nor is there any denial of the principle of majority decision. Quite the contrary, precisely because he acknowledged the principle of majority decision as binding in a democracy, Jabotinsky attempted to delay the establishment of a parliament all the while the Arabs constituted a majority, knowing that this will be the end of the dream to establish the State of the Jews. Important is his reference to the serious issue that sometimes majority decision fundamentally violates the basic principles of democracy, as it did with Hitler's rise to power, is also important.

At the Fifth Revisionist World Conference, Jabotinsky initiated a number of decisions with regard to leaving the World Zionist Organization. Subsequent to this conference, and as a result of differences with Jabotinsky over this issue, Meir Grossman was expelled from the Union of Zionist Revisionists and established the Party of the Jewish State. Due to differences among the Revisionists over the respective positions of Jabotinsky and Grossman, the Would Council of the UZR met in Kattowitz in 1933. Jabotinsky did not succeed in enlisting a majority to his side, nor to his demand that both sides of Revisionist thinking be represented on the executive on a parity basis. The meeting ended without arriving at a clear position, and a day later Jabotinsky notified the members of the movement that, in view of the situation, he was dissolving the executive and personally assuming authority. At the same time, he announced a plebiscite so that the movement could decide in which direction (and thus with whom) it was going. The result was 31,000 in support of Jabotinsky and 2,000 against him.

As a result of the "Kattowitz Incident," Jabotinsky was asked by members of his movement how he could unilaterally dissolve the executive while lacking a majority at the conference. Close friends like Israel Rosov and Dr. Michael Schwartzman questioned Jabotinsky about his attitude to the principle of democracy. Jabotinsky answered that his action might indeed be seen as a putsch; he conceded that the legality of his action might be challenged, but his goal was specifically to establish a leadership of the majority. In a letter dated October 8, 1933 to Dr. Michael Schwartzman he wrote:

> The question of the democratic principle caused me, more than any-thing, great personal pain. For me, democracy, particularly equality of all—has been an *ideé fixé* from my youth. ... My conscience is clear. I am convinced that you are all confusing two concepts: democracy and legality. I was certain of that already in Kattowitz when the elections gave us 96,000 votes and the opposition 12,000. It turned out that only one person represented such a majority on the world executive, versus four representatives of such a small minority, and that those four absolutely refused to allow a change even to fifty-fifty. And that is democracy. I was in all honesty completely certain, and I am certain today too, that my putsch was a kind of *reestablishment* of the principle of democracy. And not the opposite, if only democracy is a precise concept connected with the relation between the majority and the minor-ity. I do not see with what reason it is possible to complain ... about the legality of my action. I am also ready to insist that justice is on my side, on the basis of all customs and traditions ... any rebellion or revolution must of necessity be extra-legal. Their meaning is also almost always included in the fact that the "legal" situation led to the absurd, which goes against intelligence and justice (in this instance—directly contrary to the principle of democracy); thus there is a need to turn everything over and to start afresh. Therefore, the "rebellion" cannot be measured by the degree of legality according to the charter, but only in accordance with the goal: was the goal to decide to establish a leadership of the majority or of the minority?[155]

It is clear that Jabotinsky's behavior and its justification in this instance were similar to his attitude to the establishment of a parliament in the Land of Israel while there was no Jewish majority. A chance majority of delegates representing a minority could not be allowed to make decisions; the Arab majority in the Land of Israel was temporary, and thus the establishment of an institution in which this temporary majority would make decisions was forbidden. It is notable that Jabotinsky justified the revolution that he brought about after the Kattowitz conference by defending the democratic principle of the majority in its truest sense: that the represen-

tation reflect the positions of the represented, and that decisions be determined in accordance with the principle of the majority. In a letter to Israel
Rosov of November 11, 1933, Jabotinsky clearly stated:

> Do not believe the fiction that I conceded the democratic principle. In
> Kattowitz I fought against the hegemony of the *minority*—against the
> fact that those who represented ten percent wanted to choke the repre-
> sentative of ninety percent; and the elections to the Congress proved that
> my conclusion was correct. It is possible to argue about whether the
> method of the putsch was correct; however, one may not deny that I
> struggled on behalf of the right of the majority, that is for the basic
> principle of democracy. ... If tomorrow, I receive one vote less than my
> colleague, without any sense of injury, I will join him as his assistant or I
> will go over to the ranks of simple soldiers. You *can not* believe that in
> my old age I would forego the principles on which we grew up, and
> would be swept after the title of leader, which I scorn to the point of
> nausea.[156]

There is no question that Jabotinsky was very disturbed by the criticism leveled against his attitude to democracy subsequent to the Kattowitz
conference, just as there is no doubting the sincerity of his words stating that
he fought for the principle of the majority.

It is interesting that Jabotinsky repeatedly emphasized his faith in the
principle of the majority, in absolute contradistinction to his position
against democracy as the rule of the majority in his articles "Introduction to
the Theory of Economics II" and "Strikes in the Land of Israel," written
some two years later. To elucidate the sharp contrast between Jabotinsky's
stance in his letters and that expressed in his articles, we shall repeat a
passage already quoted at the beginning of the book: "For some inexplicable
reason, democracy is identified with majority rule. ... Actually, the blind
identification of democracy with majority rule is not correct. The value of
democracy does not depend on the feeling of subjugation by forty-nine kings
with equal rights to one hundred, or even by ten kings or one to one
hundred. The sense of democracy must rather be sought in the theory of
consent and compromise."[157]

The concept of democracy as government based on agreement and
compromise appeared in a significant number of articles that Jabotinsky
wrote between 1928 and 1935, generally within the context of arguments
against class warfare, and in opposition to the principle of majority decision
with regard to staging a strike. Jabotinsky considered the class approach and
strikes to be factors that fragmented society in the Land of Israel and
delayed achieving the goal of a Jewish majority.

Thus in 1928 he wrote: "A new Jewish life is being established in the
Land of Israel on the basis of cooperation and compromise. And even if
there is a majority of workers in a Jewish local government, the politics of

the majority should not be conducted: because he has twenty-one votes and you have only twenty, he does not have to take you into consideration at all. The Settlement is a free society. It may not be ruled arbitrarily by a majority. It may be ruled only by constant compromise."[158]

Arbitrative democracy was thus the correct operative interpretation of democracy for the Settlement during the breakthrough period, when a Hebrew state with a Jewish parliament still did not exist.

In "Strikes in the Land of Israel," Jabotinsky called for non-compliance by the minority with the decision of the majority in the event of a strike which the former felt was unjustified, and when the striking workers had rejected in advance the idea of national arbitration. He even defined the right of the minority to defy the majority decision in such a case as "a sacred right to decide for itself whether the strike about to break out is just or not."[159] In the continuation of the article, Jabotinsky explained why he spoke of the sacred right of the minority: "Continuation of work and non-participation in a strike when it is considered unjust not only is not a Zionist sin, but is a clear obligation of Zionist consciousness."[160]

As in the previous passage, it is patently clear here that Jabotinsky was speaking of a moral criterion that was valid only during the breakthrough period of the state on the way. The "Zionist sin" of which he spoke referred to the yardstick by which every action had to be measured during the breakthrough period—whether it furthered the ideal of a Jewish majority or hindered it. An examination of Jabotinsky's attitude to democracy as it related to labor during the breakthrough period shows that he considered the concept of majority decision to be harmful during the period of construction because it placed a wedge between the main partners in the building effort: the workers and the employers.

That Jabotinsky accepted the principal of majority decision in times other than the breakthrough period is supported paradoxically by his explanation of why the Revisionists had to leave the World Zionist Organization and form a new Zionist organization. Jabotinsky maintained that, since the Union of Zionist Revisionists could not remain in the Zionist Organization and still maintain its right of independent action against the will of the majority, and since the opinion of the UZR often differed from that of the majority, there was no moral alternative other than to secede.

Jabotinsky considered this decision to break away from the WZO—viewed by many as an unwillingness to accept the majority decision, and interpreted as undemocratic behavior—as the only way to act if the principle of majority decision was in fact to be respected:

> The situation is clear. The Zionist Organization does not want people in its midst who maintain the right to act independently against the will of the majority. Obviously it is possible to deceive the Zionist Organization

with no difficulty: to purchase *shekalim* [a coin that signified membership in the Zionist movement] with a commitment to [abide by the
movement's] discipline, to sign and to promise to do everything requested, to go to Congresses—and afterwards to disregard all of these.
... The [World Zionist] Congress lacks the power of governmental
coercion, and here, there is no purpose in "deception": it is not for such
methods that we tried to teach the young generation the concepts of
hadar ... However, they too [the majority in the Zionist organization]
have the right to demand that we be honest with them, if they present
clear conditions. We are faced with the choice: either to agree to the
conditions or to leave; and because we shall not accept the conditions,
we shall leave.[161]

Jabotinsky's concept of democracy and majority decision as expressed
here, like that regarding *Betar*, was that when a person joined a particular
group that functioned democratically, a sense of honesty and propriety
obligated him to adhere to the decision of the majority. If that decision went
against his conscience, he had to draw conclusions and perhaps, resign.

How then would it be possible to maintain law and order in a democracy if the minority left every time the majority rejected its views? In a
democratic regime, resignation and splits were legal and legitimate in voluntary organizations such as parties, youth movements, and the like. It was
specifically a democratic-liberal government that permitted minority groups
in the party (or in other voluntary bodies) to leave for ideological or other
reasons and to establish a new party. The situation was different, however,
with regard to official government institutions. There, the law forbade
members of national institutions and bodies from seceding for the purpose
of establishing alternative bodies; thus, for example, members of parliament
who did not like the decisions of the majority might not break away and
form a new parliament.

The World Zionist Organization, like all bodies that existed before the
establishment of the state, was in Jabotinsky's and other people's opinions, a
free and voluntary body and not a governmental institution. This view was
at the core of his attitude that resignation from the WZO and the creation of
a new Zionist organization was not only legal but also moral.

Jabotinsky apparently considered the principle of the majority to be an
integral part of democracy in a normal state, and presented the alternative
democratic concept of compromise with regard to the special conditions of
the state on the way. However, something became problematic in his thinking as a result: the concept of democracy as a compromise became close to
his heart because it so suited his essential view that "every individual is a
king" and that no one had the right to impose his will on the other. The view
of democracy as a compromise was expressed in "Introduction to the Theory
of Economics II," although it did not deal with the breakthrough period.

However, as we saw, because he was a realist, Jabotinsky continued to simultaneously believe in the concept of democracy as decision by the majority.

Was Jabotinsky aware of this duality in his approach to the principle of majority decision? On the one hand, we have reason to believe that he was not, for if he had been in his later years he would certainly have developed one clear, unified theory. On the other hand, it would seem likely that he was aware of his ambivalence and preferred not to make a clear-cut decision because of doubts about the principle of majority decision resulting from the rise of the Nazis. Yet, because he believed in democracy with his whole heart, despite all its weaknesses—and the more he learned about authoritarian and totalitarian alternatives, the more he valued democracy—he simply could not in his later years deny the principle of majority rule. Despite the fact that this principle occasionally had dangerous results, it would be impossible in an established state to implement democracy as a compromise at the level of political action without destroying democracy. In the reality of democratic politics it would not be feasible for every decision to be a compromise between the opinions of the majority and the minority; sooner or later it would result in a paralysis of the political system. Like John Stuart Mill, Jabotinsky was forced to accept the fact—although he did not explicitly admit it—that, while it was possible to hope for a situation where in other areas of life, material and spiritual, the different sides would listen to each other—and in many cases reach a compromise that would express the truth existing in each opinion—the democratic political process was based on the principle of majority decision. Which of these assessments—or perhaps another one—is correct remains an open question. What is not subject to debate is that Jabotinsky's concept of democracy during the breakthrough period was of a regime whose decisions were based on compromise between majority and minority opinion. At the level of theoretical principle, as we saw in the first part of the book, his views remained ambivalent. However, in the majority of cases, reality dictated that he accept the principle of democracy as majority decision, but his approach to that principle was and remained ambivalent, while the idea of democracy as a compromise remained close to his heart.

Chapter 4

THE STATE
OF THE JEWS

A s we saw in greater detail in the chapter "The Breakthrough Period—On the Way to Statehood," the ideological single-mindedness that Jabotinsky preached for the period preliminary to a state was expressed first and foremost in his own thought. He devoted the lion's share of his Zionist thought to defining the goal of the breakthrough period, and formulating plans for its implementation. He did not discuss the character of the state of the Jews once it was established in any exhaustive or organized manner. The absence of methodical thought on this issue was not coincidental. As we saw, he considered the attainment of the one ideal of the construction period a goal that demanded the total enlistment of all resources for a significant period of time. Therefore, as a Zionist leader, he harnessed all his energy to the process of planning and convincing the Jews and the nations of the world that a state of the Jews had to be established. Fashioning the character of the state, he believed, was a separate task that could not be dealt with until after its establishment. This view was expressed clearly in a letter to Ben-Gurion dated May 2, 1935:

> My friend Ben-Gurion ... just one "philosophical" paragraph: I am certain that there is a certain type of Zionist to whom the social tone of the "state" does not matter: I am like that. If I were convinced that the only path to a "state" is socialist or even that it would bring about the creation of the state more quickly, within one generation—I would readily accept it. More than that: I would agree to a state of pietists in which I would be forced to eat *gefilte* fish from dawn till dusk. ... Even worse: I would acquiesce to a *Yiddishist* state, which for me means the end of all the charm in the matter. And I would leave a will to my children to make a revolution; but I would write on the envelope: open five years after the birth of the Hebrew state. I searched my soul several times to ascertain that these were truly my feelings, and I am certain that they are.[1]

Without that being its intention, this letter explains why Jabotinsky did not deal in a systematic fashion with the desired image of the state of the Jews. His life was dedicated to the single ideal of establishing the state of the Jews as early as possible. With that, the letter implies that Jabotinsky had his own view of how the state should take shape. Indeed, it is possible to glean enough material from his various writings to form a general image of his ideal state of the Jews.

In discussing Herzl's book *Altneuland*, Jabotinsky indicated that the state of the Jews could be written about in either of two ways: as a utopia or as a design for the near future. The state as envisioned by Herzl related in Jabotinsky's opinion to 1923 (twenty years after the book was written), and was not a utopia because, he said: "We call an ideal regime by the name utopia—a government in which the writer sees the realization of all his sociopolitical dreams. Thus, the authors of utopias have the courage to be carried away to eras hundreds and even thousands of years off. But Herzl never intended to write about a utopia, that is, to depict the embodiment of his civic dreams. The purpose of *Altneuland* was completely different: Herzl wanted to show what the *Judenstaat* is like, which, under favorable circumstances might be established within a very short period, really practically 'next year.'"[2]

Jabotinsky did not want to deal with utopian writings, and in place of writings based on realistic considerations like *Altneuland*, Jabotinsky preferred a theory of Zionism that would interpret Jewish history from Zion to Zion: the essence of anti-Semitism, and why it could be combatted only by the liquidation of the exile; the character of the Jewish race and nation, and their right to their own territory, the Land of Israel; and the image of the ideal Jew. Together with a theory of Zionism, Jabotinsky focused on a definition of the aims of Zionism. He also discussed an operative definition of the objective of the period of the state on the way, and prepared logical and detailed plans for its implementation.

Through his discussions of these plans, Jabotinsky disclosed, generally unintentionally, his vision of the government, society, and economy of the state of the Jews. The main source of information, however, about the character of his model state of the Jews is his general socio-political writings. There, he discussed ideal forms of government, economy, and society. Since Jabotinsky hoped that the state of the Jews would be "normal" in every way, those attributes that he considered desirable would certainly have been incorporated in the state of the Jews. Unquestionably he was influenced also by *Altneuland*, which described a liberal, bourgeois state.

The image of Jabotinsky's ideal state of the Jews, according to the characteristics presented in his general and Zionist thought, was as follows: it had to be "healthy" in every respect, and its character should not be clouded over or influenced by the trauma of the exile. The ghetto mentality—that "the whole world is against us"—should not be allowed to permeate the state. This position was expressed unequivocally by Jabotinsky at the Fifth Revisionist World Conference in 1926:

> The ghetto awaits revenge. The creators of Zionism rejected it and cursed it, and now the ghetto wants to take revenge upon us. ... Of the many types of poisons poisoning the soul of the ghetto, the most lethal is the concept of the world around us as a world of robbers. Such a concept is the product of the two thousand year old nightmare of Jewish history, and like every nightmare, this concept, too, is distinguished by its essential fallaciousness. We reject this view. The collective name of the "goy" is Socrates and Plato, Dante and Beccaria, Garibaldi and Rousseau, Voltaire and Hugo, Lincoln, Wilson, and Balfour. The "goy" has the same greatness and the same sense of justice as we. He learned much morality from our prophets, but also had his own prophets, pure and noble like ours. And if we are now cultured people, we owe this to the "goy." He created the modern state, which is conducted according to the will of the nation; he made the French Revolution; he abolished slavery; he freed us from the ghetto—he is equal to us, he is both our student and teacher. It would be a disgrace if we forgot all this, just to satisfy our suspicious inclinations, that can lead us only to despair and disintegration.[4]

The establishment of a state of the Jews would bring about "*a normalization of the Jewish people,* so that it becomes normal like the large French nation or the small Danish nation."[5]

Life in exile forced the Jew to create corners of isolation as alternatives to national territory, in the form of the ghetto, religion, and uniquely Jewish means of livelihood. The establishment of the state of the Jews would end the need for separation and isolation, because the Jewish nation would be able to achieve self-realization in its national territory. The state of the Jews would gradually give rise to the proud Jew possessing internal and external noblesse, according to Jabotinsky, and the shells and the scars of two thousand years in exile would disappear. The mentality of the *galuth* Jew, who humbled himself before prominent people, and yet saw a foresworn enemy in every gentile, would disappear. The existence of a national territory would make it possible for the Jewish nation to develop its own psyche in all material and spiritual fields and, through its national creativity, to help further all humanity. The state of the Jews had to be based on a world view antithetical to that of the ghetto; it had to interact with the nations of the world as an equal among equals, and not with constant suspicion. Eventually, Jabotinsky hoped, as national creativity in the state of the Jews flourished, it would indeed carry the banner of progress to other nations.

With the establishment of the state of the Jews, the breakhrough period would come to an end, as would the stage of the absolutist colonist imperative. However, the birth of the state would not mark the end of Zionism, but rather, its beginning; Jabotinsky perceived the state as a "laboratory" in which the Jewish nation would create political, economic, and social values and institutions in accordance with its special psyche.[6]

Jabotinsky defined the first Zionist goal of the state of the Jews (like his concept of Greater Zionism) as "not the reform of the exile through a model strip of land in Palestine, but the liquidation of the exile: an 'exodus from Egypt' for all those who thirst for a homeland—and ultimately, certainly nothing less than the end of the exile. . . . The state of the Jews is nothing but the first step in the process of the materialization of Greater Zionism. Afterwards, the second step will come: the return of the people to Zion, the exodus from the exile, and the solution of the question of the Jews."[7]

Jabotinsky estimated that approximately one-third to three-fifths of the Jewish people would immigrate to the state of the Jews after its establishment. During the breakthrough period, the economic infrastructure for only about a million and a half Jews—who would turn the Jews into a majority on both banks of the Jordan—would be set up, and thus the Hebrew state would need to plan the absorption of the other millions of Jews.[8]

Jabotinsky did not deal directly with the question of how those Jews who remained in the diaspora would live. However, from his writings on self-rule for national minorities, we may infer that he favored a framework of self-rule within the various countries that they lived. That means that they would have to demand both civic-national rights and autonomous-national rights. Thus the Jew would be a citizen with equal rights, but the specifically national aspects of his life would be conducted through national bodies, with the supreme national body a kind of national parliament whose representatives were chosen by all the Jews in the country. The authority of this national parliament would be administrative rather than legislative, and it would deal with specifically defined national issues.[9]

Hebrew had to be the language of instruction in the schools within the framework of self-rule, and Jabotinsky no doubt would have recommended that part of the agenda be devoted to the history of the Jewish people, and to its past and present spiritual creations. The relationship between the national parliaments of the Jews in their respective countries of residence, to the state of the Jews might take in the form of a covenant.[10]

Jabotinsky's position in the argument that existed from the time of the Helsingfors Program over the desired relationship between the state of the Jews and the diaspora was always that it was insufficient for the state of the Jews to be the only spiritual center and capital of Judaism, nor was the continued existence of the Jewish diaspora a positive goal. However, as a realist he understood that the diaspora would continue to exist after the establishment of the state, and thus it was necessary to insure that it would be "economically and culturally strong, possessing national consciousness, organized on a solid foundation, and enjoying full civil, political and national rights."[11]

The very definition of the "Return to Zion" as the primary Zionist goal of the state of the Jews indicates the direction of Jabotinsky's thought, also typifying his concept of Greater Zionism; he believed that the state of the Jews had to strive to concentrate within it the majority of the Jewish people. Since he considered immigration to the Land of Israel to be the paramount fulfillment of Zionism, he undoubtedly would have considered one of the functions of the Hebrew state to be convincing diaspora Jewry to immigrate. However, as he often and explicitly stated, he would have left this decision to each individual's free choice.

The second goal of the agenda of the state of the Jews was the third goal of Zionism: "the ultimate and true goal of Greater Zionism is ... the creation of a national culture which will impart its glory to the entire world, as it says 'because the Torah [in the sense of teachings] will go forth from Zion.'"[12] Or, as expressed slightly differently in "The Idea of *Betar*": "Afterwards we will face the third task, but the most important one of all: to turn the Land of Israel into a state that leads the entire civilized world—a country whose customs and laws will serve as a model for all the countries in the universe."[13]

This goal united Jabotinsky's Zionist thought with his general liberal thought, in which the existence of a nation in its own national territory was not an end in itself, but a precondition for the existence of national creativity whose importance lay in its contribution to the progress of all mankind. National creativity was expressed in all areas: political structures, economic methods, social policies, and scientific and cultural advances. Thus Jabotinsky defined the Hebrew state as a "laboratory" in which the Jewish nation would "experiment" with its various national creations. In contrast to the view that the Jewish people could best fulfill its "mission" if it was scattered among the nations, Jabotinsky believed:

> This is a crude mistake. As already stated, one cannot "guide" others with advice: the world learns only from tangible examples even if speaking only of new ideas. England, for instance, has enriched the world with a valuable social idea: self-rule of free citizens, that is, the parliamentary government. However, how did the English nation teach other peoples to understand and run such a government? Certainly not be being scattered among the nations and convincing them; just the opposite. The English were in a position to "teach" the others only because they established and developed a parliamentary system in their native country. And thus they became a living example from which the world learned. ... We believe that mankind will yet learn from us many

truths, truths still unknown to it. However, the only way to achieve that is by creating a state of the Jews. ... We strongly hope that it will be specifically the Jewish State that will show the world the true path to eternal peace and social justice.[14]

Despite the weaknesses and limitations of a parliamentary democracy, Jabotinsky still considered it the best possible form of government, and one which should be adopted by the state of the Jews.[15] Therefore, after the termination of the breakthrough period, there would be various political parties with different world views and plans for their implementation. These parties would conduct ideological struggles within the framework of a liberal-democratic pluralistic society. Jabotinsky's model was the parliamentary-cabinet system of Great Britain.

Although in his Zionist thought Jabotinsky presented the idea of a parliament of professions during the breakthrough period, one may not assume that he favored such a parliament in the state of the Jews. Actually, even during the period of the state on the way, he was not adamant on this point.

On the other hand, it is likely that he would have welcomed a bicameral system, such as exists in the United States, in order to strengthen the system of checks and balances, primarily because of his ambivalent attitude toward the principle of majority decision upon which the democratic system is based. In the absence of an operative alternative to the principle of majority decision to preserve the democratic character, Jabotinsky grudgingly accepted that principle. However, like outstanding liberal thinkers such as John Stuart Mill and Alexis de Tocqueville, Jabotinsky was aware of the dangers to the rights and freedoms of the minority sometimes present in the system of majority decision. Therefore, it is reasonable to assume that he would have adopted any means, within the framework of a democratic system and a principle of majority, which could have minimized or weakened the dangers present in the power of the majority.[16]

The state of the Jews thus would have to be a liberal democracy, and Jabotinsky would have strengthened its liberal elements as much as possible. From his concept of a liberal-democratic government derive such arrangements as separation of powers through checks and balances between the legislative, the executive, and the judicial branches; a bill of rights as part of a constitution or a system of basic laws, with emphasis on freedom of thought and expression; freedom of religion and conscience, and freedom of organization; equal rights for minorities; and a strong legal system that preserves law and order and also defends the citizen from the government. He devoted special attention to equal rights for women, in the hope that this equality would be expressed in all areas of life.

Jabotinsky maintained that liberal views also needed to be expressed in the sensitive area of the relationship between religion and state. As we saw, he considered values and individual faith, and not laws and observances, to be the essence of Judaism. In his political thought, he spoke about the clear need for separation between religion and state; the penetration of religion into different spheres of life was the sign of a backward culture.[17] In his Zionist thought, on analyzing Jewish history, he elaborated upon the important function of religion in the exile as an artificial isolator, an alternative to a state, and saw this communal function coming to an end with the establishment of a state of the Jews. In the thirties, he was forced to be circumspect on the subject of religion, primarily because many of the supporters of Revisionism were Orthodox. However, he never explicitly retracted his basic position with regard to separation of religion and state. Even in his address to the founding convention of the NZO in Vienna in September 1935, in addressing the religious question specifically—apparently because of the participation of an organized group of Orthodox people from Poland—he mentioned his liberal views on "removal of the religious element from the essence of society and state," while explaining that he had been referring to religious institutions; the result, however, was "the removal of God. And that is quite another matter."[18] Because of the negative and unintentional ramifications of the "removal of God" issue, Jabotinsky raised the question of whether the liberal position of the 1890's suited the twentieth century. His answer was:

> Religion is a private matter, having to do with my emotions; whether I believe or doubt, whether I reject or accept, is indeed a private matter, and I must not ever be permitted to suffer or to be punished because of that. However, if there still exist in the world houses or worship and sanctuaries, it is not a private matter, and the state must express its opinion on whether religious celebrations can continue to exist, and whether the eternal flame will continue to burn in the houses of worship and the sanctuaries, and whether the word of the prophets lives on in the life of the community or it has become an embalmed body preserved under glass. This must be prevented, and it rightly becomes a matter for the state.[19]

These words in no way contradict his fundamental position of separation between religion and state on the institutional level. All Jabotinsky said—and that was the only change in his stance versus his previous opinions—was that even after the establishment of the state of the Jews, the universal religious values would retain their importance, and it would be the function of the state to see to it that they were preserved. He did not detail how this would be done, remaining intentionally vague. Because of his basic belief in the need to separate between religious institutions and the state, Jabotinsky was careful throughout his life to speak of a "state of the Jews" or a "Hebrew state," refraining as much as possible from using the term "Jewish state."

With the establishment of the state of the Jews, the period of significant economic intervention by the state would also end. A liberal economy, as presented by Jabotinsky in his economic writings, would replace a planned economy, whose purpose was to allow the Settlement to become economically established and to facilitate the absorption of a Jewish majority in the Land of Israel.

Moreover, the emphasis during the period of the state on the way was on the economy, with the central goal being economic stabilization and the creation of places of employment and sources of income. In contrast, the social aspect, based on a just division of resources, was deferred so as not to create ideological *sha'atnez*. Jabotinsky's Zionist ideological exclusivity did not permit the existence of a second ideal, such as the creation of a just society. Thus the only social policy proposed by Jabotinsky during the period of the state on the way was compulsory national arbitration. The goal of the latter was not to achieve social justice, but to attain a state of "peaceful coexistence" between workers and employers during the breakthrough period to prevent strikes and lockouts, which harmed the economic effort. Jabotinsky consciously and explicitly deferred the discussion on attainment of a just society to the period after the establishment of the state of the Jews. He took this position in many places, and we shall bring two examples. In "The Idea of *Betar*" he stated:

> For we decided, once and for all, that if we are building a state, we must do so according to our means, whether on new or old, good or bad foundations, as dictated to us by reality—as long as the result is a Jewish majority. Afterwards, a new generation will arise and make use of the national "laboratory" which we prepared for it in order to carry out all possible tests to improve the social order. And this is a sound principle, on which depends the sacred principle of "monism" of our practical deeds.[21]

He expressed similar ideas in his book, *A Hebrew State: A Solution to the Question of the Jews*: "These things [national arbitration] have no connection at all with the 'solution' of the social question. That will be solved in the laboratory of the Jewish state, after this state is securely established."[22]

Jabotinsky believed that the Jewish nation had a special message, specifically in the areas of social justice, whose source was in the social philosophy of the Bible. He felt that the Jews could serve as a model for other nations only if they implemented their ideas; if they originated social theories and developed policies, other nations would emulate them. Jabotinsky felt that the establishment of a just society had to occupy a central place on the national agenda of the state of the Jews, and was actually a crucial part of the broader goal of being a "light unto the nations."

Jabotinsky was well aware that since ideological single-mindedness would terminate with the establishment of the state, an ideological debate on the concept of social justice would ensue, and that the labor movement would propose its socialist program ideology based on class warfare. The function of state Zionism during the breakthrough period, he said, "is not the 'liquidation' of class sentiment; its function is the 'extirpation' of these sentiments."[23]

The extirpation of class feeling was only temporary, and it was obvious to Jabotinsky that, after the establishment of the state, the class issue would arise. "The laborer and the employer will never feel comfortable with each other, like two lambs grazing in one field. On the contrary—it is certain that each of these two groups will always think and claim that it specifically, and not the other group, is the 'salt of the earth' and the foundation of the world economy."[24]

This approach was propounded in the *Betar* program which explicitly stated: "We see in class warfare a healthy and essential phenomenon."[25]

Issues of class warfare, however, had a place only after the establishment of the state of the Jews: "Classes exist only in a 'completed,' 'built-up' society: in a place where the process of settlement is taking place. That is, in the beginning of a new society, classes are not classes, the proletariat is not a proletariat, the middle class is not considered a middle class. These are all only 'pioneers,' each of whom participates in his own way in a joint enterprise which is immeasurably difficult."[26]

In contrast to the socialism of the labor movement, Jabotinsky proposed for the state of the Jews the socioeconomic concept that he evolved in his general theory, and which we discussed in detail in the chapter "Society and Economics": a free economy, a maximalist welfare policy, and the revolutionary Jubilee idea.

He felt that liberal-democratic society was strong enough to adopt his socioeconomic view, and that it would be able to reform and repair itself in the direction of greater social justice with the ultimate goal of eliminating poverty and lessening the economic gaps between classes—but under no circumstances eliminating them. Gaps had to remain so that there would be a purpose to initiative, excellence, and originality, because ultimately the critical contributions to progress were rooted in the original thought of geniuses and talented people.

It is fair to assume that Jabotinsky would also have included compulsory national arbitration within the above socioeconomic framework as long as there remained a conflict of interest between workers and employers.

Jabotinsky was aware that, in a state of the Jews, his concept of a just socioeconomic policy would have to vie with the socialist alternative proposed by the workers' movement, and that the voters would determine at the polls which was the more just. In any case, Jabotinsky hoped that a "light unto the nations" would emanate from the state of the Jews, specifically with regard to a just society and the social policy deriving from it. As stated in his general theory, he considered it the goal of every normal nation to contribute to human progress. He felt that the state of the Jews could best make a contribution in the important area of social justice if it adopted his proposed social policy, with its roots in the social philosophy of the Bible.

The issue of military defense of the Settlement in the Land of Israel by Jewish soldiers occupied a central place in his thought on the breakthrough period. In the previous chapter, we also saw that, during the period of the state on the way, Jabotinsky attributed great importance to the discipline, order, and ceremony that were part of militarism, in order to help form and nurture the ideal Jew.

The military, according to Jabotinsky, had to be big enough only to defend the state of the Jews. Remember, Jabotinsky defined "bad" militarism as the keeping of an army that was larger than necessary. War must never become an independent goal, as it is decidedly contrary to Jewish and liberal values, and the state of the Jews should aspire to establish peace with its neighbors; only then will it be possible to spend fewer resources on security, redirecting them instead to social ends.

Jabotinsky did not see military personnel as having any special status in the state of the Jews. In accordance with his general theoretical view, he envisioned a situation in the state of the Jews like that in any normal democratic, liberal, Western state: the army needed to be under strong supervision by the civilian authorities. Even the military elements—discipline, order, and ceremony—would lose their fundamental significance in the state of the Jews. These would still be positive elements; however, from the moment the Jews became a normal people with its own state, the ideal Jew who had internal and external *hadar* would naturally and gradually evolve, and the importance of such aids as military education would diminish.

As we saw earlier, Jabotinsky dealt at great length with the question of national minorities, proposing self-rule for a national minority scattered throughout a land in which another nation was the majority. In his thought on the breakthrough period, Jabotinsky had to fashion a policy toward the Arabs of *Eretz Yisrael* in light of the existing situation in which they where a majority. At the same time, he had to consider the goal of the breakthrough period, which meant turning them into a minority. Thus, he explicitly dealt with the issue of the future situation of the Arabs of *Eretz Yisrael* after the establishment of the state.

Jabotinsky believed that, once Arabs understood that they lacked the power to stop the process of transforming the Land of Israel into the state of the Jews, it would be possible to begin negotiations over their future status. Jabotinsky did not foresee the War of Independence, and the state of the Jews with an Arab minority about which he spoke should have resulted from a discussion process facilitated specifically by the "iron wall" policy.

As we saw in the previous chapter, Jabotinsky eventually considered the Arabs of the Land of Israel a living nation with nationalist aspirations. He perceived the situation that was created as a tragedy in which two nations demanded—in both cases legitimately—the same territory. Both demands were just but that of the Jews was more just, since the Arabs had many states in which they were a majority, while the Jewish nation lacked even one. In comparison with the tragedy to the Jews, the potential tragedy to the Arabs if they became a national minority would be dwarfed.

However, the state of the Jews had to ensure the interest of the Arab minority, made up of those Arabs who lived in the Land of Israel at the time and their descendants. How would this equality of rights express itself? Did Jabotinsky have in mind civic-national equality? That is, would the state, fulfilling its authorized functions *vis à vis* its citizens, take into consideration the nationality of the Arab minority by, for instance, using their national language? By ensuring that they had suitable representation in the parliament, in the government, and in administrative institutions? Or did he mean that, in addition to civic-national rights, the Arabs of *Eretz Yisrael* would also be given autonomous-national rights which they would realize through self-rule? Would specific areas in which they would conduct their national affairs be defined?

Complete consistency with his general political philosophy would necessitate that Jabotinsky demand both civic-national rights and autonomous-national rights for the Arab minority that would exist in the state of the Jews. Let us examine the paragraphs in Jabotinsky's writings that dealt with this issue. In "A Round Table with the Arabs" (1931), Jabotinsky said: "We envision the government of the Land of Israel in this way: the majority of the population will be Hebrew, but not only will equal rights for all Arab citizens be promised, they will also be realized; the two languages and all religions will have equal rights, and every nation will receive broad rights of cultural self-rule."[27] In "The Iron Wall" (1932), he stated: "Two peoples have always lived in the Land of Israel ... I am proud to belong to that same group that once drew up the Helsingfors Program, the program of *national rights for all nationalities living in one state. ...* In drawing up that program, we had in mind not only the Jews, but all peoples, wherever they might be, and its basis is absolute equality of rights. I am prepared to take an oath binding ourselves and our descendants that we shall never abrogate this equality."[28]

In the first passage Jabotinsky emphasized autonomous-national rights for the Arab national minority, and in the second he stressed equal civic-national rights. It is thus obvious that he did indeed maintain that in the state of the Jews the Arab minority should receive equal rights in both areas, and the autonomous-national rights would be implemented by a gradual degree of self-rule. He defined the area of autonomous-national rights as "cultural," but in his theoretical writings, primarily "Self-Rule for a National Minority," he expounded upon the fact that the term "cultural" should be interpreted broadly and not in the sense of "popular education."

And indeed, the same idea appeared in the Revisionist program, more clearly articulated: "Complete equality of rights for both races, for both languages, and for both religions will exist in the future Hebrew state. *National self-rule for each of the races living in the Land on matters of communities, education, culture, and political representation must be perfected to the broadest and fullest degree.*"[29]

Jabotinsky repeated these ideas many times in speeches and articles; the basis for his concept of the status of the Arabs of the Land of Israel as a national minority in a Hebrew state was: "the same situation will exist there as in any normal country with a majority and a minority."[30]

In reference to the situation of the Arab minority in the state of the Jews, however, Jabotinsky did not explain in detail what he meant by "a normal" situation, and explained his idea of "national self-rule" only slightly. What he did say was amplified by his clear presentation of this issue in his general political theory; we may conclude that he indeed did intend for the Arab national minority to enjoy complete equality of rights in the state of the Jews, as well as self-rule in specifically national areas.

In his opinion, the autonomous-national rights that a minority nation needed to realize included religious matters, higher education, schooling, health, social aid, distribution of jobs, mutual aid, the administration of internal settlement, registration of certificates of civic status, and the right to impose taxes for the specific national functions.

He saw the organized national minority as a personal, public-legal association, with its own governmental bodies (that had only administrative authority), headed by a kind of national parliament under which there would be regional conferences and community councils. He also called for national courts to adjudicate claims among the members of the national minority; these would have the right to act according to their national customs and traditions, especially with regard to matters of marriage and family life. The national parliament would determine the official language of all the bodies and institutions of the national minority. Schools at all levels that would be set up by the national bodies would have the same rights as parallel state institutions. The state government would be responsible for the implementation of all legal decisions by the national bodies and the rights of the national minority would be determined by the law of the land and would apply to all its territory.[31]

The terminology that appeared in the Revisionist program of 1928 referred to a gradual process leading to perfected system of national self-rule. The principle was the same as that in Jabotinsky's 1912 essay "Self-Rule for a National Minority." The Revisionist program did not go into detail about specific autonomous-national rights for the Arab minority, nor about the national bodies authorized to implement these rights; the principle of national self-rule was determined, but its precise character (the areas and methods of implementation) was left to be determined jointly in the state of the Jews by the Arab minority and the Jewish majority.

We have seen that Jabotinsky anticipated that part of the contribution of the state of the Jews would be expressed in its unique concept of social justice and social policy: "And the state of the Jews will take pride in the fact that it will serve as a laboratory for this Hebrew spirit of social reform and will serve as a model of a new social image for the entire universe."[32]

Apart from this, Jabotinsky envisioned as the unique contribution of the state of the Jews the development of additional ideas and ideals. He saw the Jewish concept of man struggling with God as the source of the constant striving for progress that permeated Western culture. He considered pre-exilic Jewish culture glorious and special. Jabotinsky unquestionably believed that with the establishment of the state of the Jews, an era of cultural renaissance in all areas would arise. This cultural life would be based on originality, curiosity, and the untiring striving for progress.

Jabotinsky's state of the Jews was not a Messianic vision that was incapable of realization. On the contrary, Jabotinsky intended, first and foremost, that the state of the Jews would be normal like other nations, and belong to the family of progressive, Western, liberal-democratic nations. "The seal of the special spirituality" of the Jewish nation would be imprinted in its laws, institutions, and ways of life, in the Hebrew language and in the culture that would take shape in the state of the Jews, exactly as the special seal of every nation is imprinted in its cultural creations. He attributed special importance to the revival of the Hebrew language because he saw in language a central means of connection between the individual and the nation, and a prime expression of the national psyche. The Hebrew language had to be a living tongue in the state of the Jews, "the only language which dominates all aspect of the lives of the Jews."[33] Jabotinsky hoped that the pluralistic national Jewish creations would be of interest to all humanity.

Jabotinsky perceived of the era of the state on the way as an emergency period, and his Zionist thought on this period had all the attributes of an ideology focused on achieving the goal of a breakthrough. In contrast, the period after the establishment of the state of the Jews would be normal and Jabotinsky's attitude to the state of the Jews was the same as to any progressive liberal-democratic Western state. Thus, Jabotinsky's Zionist thought achieved complete harmony with his general liberal-democratic theory in his ideal image of what would one day become the state of the Jews.

EPILOGUE

During the course of my research and writing of this book, I would occasionally ask myself what Jabotinsky would say, were he alive, about the State of Israel as it exists today, and about the Israeli Jew that was formed in it. What would his attitude be to the central characteristics of Israeli society as they took shape—among them the existing foci of tension, whether between Jews and Arabs, the religious and the non-religious, different ethnic groups, or weaker and stronger classes? What would be his opinion of Israeli culture, including political culture, or of Israel's national policy in different areas? What, if anything, of the national culture created by the Jewish people in the State of Israel, would he consider the unique Jewish contribution to humanity?

Like everyone who lives in the State of Israel, I was not able to cut myself off completely from contemporary events during the time I was writing the book, and thus I often wondered how Jabotinsky would have reacted to specific issues that came up on our national agenda.

Because I hope that I have succeeded in understanding Jabotinsky's thought and his internal world, I was occasionally tempted to interweave strands of relevant issues in the book through such conjectures as : "If Jabotinsky were alive today, he would think this and that and he would propose such and such."

I have refrained from speculative writing of that sort, which is neither scientific nor legitimate. I have scrupulously tried to preserve the character of the book whose concern is the "reconstruction," presentation, and analysis of Ze'ev Jabotinsky's thought as it is, and not as presented by either admirers or detractors.

After my writing was finished, it became clear to me that, despite the fact that I had not raised speculations on Jabotinsky's possible reactions if

264

he were with us today, an understanding of his thought in its entirety enables any reader who is interested, to learn what he can from Jabotinsky's general and Zionist thought, while relating it to practical, current issues. In my humble opinion, Jabotinsky's thought still has tremendous relevance for the Jewish people in Israel and in the diaspora.

That Jabotinsky's thinking from decades ago can still serve as a source of inspiration and thought in our time is perhaps the best testament to the quality and value of his thought. Jabotinsky himself distinguished between a publicist, no matter how talented, and a thinker. The writings of a publicist lose their value with a change in social conditions, while the writings of a thinker, which relate to essential questions of human existence, do not deteriorate with the passage of years.

Although Jabotinsky himself did not believe that he left an organized body of thought, and expressed sorrow over the fact, there is no question that there was enough in what he did write so that we may see him not only as a Zionist ideologue and leader, but also as a thinker whose work is worthy of scrutiny and discussion.

Notes

A General Note Regarding Quotations from Jabotinsky's Writings:

Apart from *Exile and Assimilation*, which is the first volume of *Selected Writings*, published by S. D. Salzman, Tel Aviv, 1930, and *A Hebrew State: A Solution to the Question of the Jews*, published by T. Kopp, Tel Aviv, 1930, works cited are included in the eighteen volume *Writings* by Ze'ev Jabotinsky. These volumes are: *Autobiography, Nation and Society, On the Way to Statehood, In the Tempest, The Five, First Zionist Writings, Speeches 1905–1926, Speeches 1927–1940, Stories, On Literature and Art, Feilletons, Poems*, and *Samson*, published by Eri Jabotinsky, Jerusalem. The volumes, *Sparticus, Memoirs of My Contemporary, Letters, A Foreign Land*, and *Notes* were published by Eri Jabotinsky and Amichai Publishing, Tel Aviv. Unless otherwise indicated, all references herein are to the writings of Ze'ev Jabotinsky.

All citations, except those from John Locke and John Stuart Mill, refer to the works in Hebrew, unless otherwise noted. All quotations herein have been translated from Hebrew by the translator of this book, unless noted otherwise.

PART I: GENERAL THEORETICAL THOUGHT

CHAPTER I: INTELLECTUAL INFLUENCES

[1] For more about Jabotinsky's reading, see Joseph Schechtman, *The Life and Times of Vladimir Jabotinsky*, 2 vols. (Silver Spring, Maryland: Eshel Books, 1956), in English, especially Vol. I, chap. 1; Corney Chukovsky, "Jabotinsky and his Generation: Four Letters to Rachel Margolin," introd. M. Gilboa, *Ha'uma* (April 1975); Joseph Nedava, ed., *Ze'ev Jabotinsky: The Man and His Thought* (Tel Aviv: The Ministry of Defense, 1980), introd. Part I; Ze'ev Jabotinsky, *Autobiography*, "The Story of My Life," especially pp. 21, 22, 28.

[2] Jabotinsky, "My Life," p. 29.

[3] L'Amerique a un Metre, *On Literature and Art*, p. 189.

[4] "My Life," p. 30.

[5] For a discussion of Bakunin's theory and of general Russian thought, some of which influenced Jabotinsky, see Andrzej Walicke, *A History of Russian*

Thought from the Enlightenment to Marxism (Stanford, California: Stanford University Press, 1981). See also Isaiah Berlin, *Russian Thinkers* (London: The Hogarth Press, 1978); V. V. Zenkovsky, *A History of Russian Philosophy* (London: Routledge & Kegan Paul Ltd., 1953). These are all in English.

[6] Walicke, p. 273.

[7] Berlin, p. 87.

[8] Walicke, p. 141.

[9] *Ibid.*, pp. 147–48.

[10] *Ibid.*, p. 350.

[11] *Ibid.*, p. 351.

[12] *Ibid.*, p. 359.

[13] *Ibid.*, p. 366.

[15] *Ibid.*, p. 368.

[15] *Ibid.*

[16] Yaakov Shavit, *The Mythologies of the Right* (Tel Aviv: Emda, 1986), p. 211.

[17] Jabotinsky, "The Social Philosophy of the Bible," *Nation and Society*, pp. 189–90.

[18] A lengthy discussion of this issue, in English, may be found in Y. Shavit, *Jabotinsky and the Revisionist Movement 1925–1945* (London: Cass, 1988), chap. 12.

[19] Ze'ev Sternhell, *"Fascist thought and its Variations"* (Tel Aviv: Sifriat Poalim, 1988) especially pp. 9–45. See also: Ze'ev Sternhell, *Neither Right Nor Left* (Tel Aviv: Am Oved, 1988), especially pp. 27–63.

[20] I chose to rely on Sternhell's definition and analysis, but the reader may wish to use other sources to become acquainted with fascism. For example: E. Nolte, *Three Faces of Fascism, Action Française, Italian Fascism, National Socialism* (New York: Holt, Reinhart and Winston, 1966), in English, or Y. Talmon, *The Myth of the Nation and the Vision of Revolution* (Tel Aviv: Am Oved, 1985). Each of these includes bibliographies.

[21] For example, Shavit claims on pps. 30 and 110 that Jabotinsky was not an original or systematic thinker while Shlomo Avineri in *Varieties of Zionist Thought* (Tel Aviv: Am Oved, 1980) maintains that Jabotinsky was unquestionably a great thinker.

CHAPTER 2: LIBERALISM AND DEMOCRACY

[1] *Exile and Assimilation*, "The Story of My Life Part One," p. 34.

[2] *Ibid.*, p. 25.

[3] *Ibid.*, p. 44.

[4] *Ibid.*, p. 45.

[5] *Ibid.*

[6] *Ibid.*

[7] *Autobiography*, "The Story of My Life Part Two," p. 113.

[8] *Exile*, "My Life I," p. 30.

[9] *Exile*, "From the Frying Pan Into the Fire," p. 172.

[10] *Exile*, "Phenomena of our Existence," p. 235.

[11] *Exile, Homo Homini Lupus*, p. 199.

[12] *Ibid.*

[13] *Notes*, "On Fathers and Sons," p. 120.

[14] *Exile, Homo*, p. 202.

[15] *Exile*, "Might and Right," p. 217.

[16] *Exile*, "The Language of the Enlightenment," p. 297.

[17] *Memoirs of My Contemporary*, "Trumpeldor's Anniversary," p. 107.

[18] *Exile*, "My Life I," pp. 25, 44, 45.

[19] *Notes*, "The East," pp. 282–83.

[20] *Ibid.*, p. 283.

[21] *Notes*, "Solveig," p. 104.

[22] *Exile*, "My Life I," p. 35.

[23] *On the Way to Statehood*, "Ethics of the 'Iron Wall,'" p. 266.

[24] *In the Tempest*, "Cold and Firm," pp. 94, 96.

[25] *Feuilletons*, "The Truth," p. 203.

[26] John Locke, *Of Civil Government* (London: J. M. Dent & Sons Ltd.), pp. 129–141.

[27] *Notes*, "In South Africa—the Negroes," p. 239.

[28] *Feiullitons*, "Truth," p. 204–05.

[29] *Notes*, "The Ignitor," p. 17.

[30] *Exile*, "My Life I," pp. 44–45. Emphasis the writer's.

[31] *Exile, Homo*, p. 199.

[32] *Ibid.*, p. 202.

[33] *Exile*, "I Do Not Believe," p. 209.

[34] *Exile*, "Might and Right," p. 219.

[35] *Exile, Homo*, p. 198.

[36] *Exile*, "I Do Not Believe," pp. 203–04.

[37] *Ibid.*, p. 204.

[38] *Exile*, "The Obscurantist," p. 278.

[39] *Statehood*, "The Wagon of the *Klezmer*, pp. 271–22.

[40] *Notes*, "The East," p. 280.

[41] *Ibid.*, p. 279.

[42] *Ibid.*, pp. 281–82.

[43] *Notes*, "Women's Intelligence," p. 131.

[44] *Ibid.*, "The Crisis of the Proletariat," p. 314.

[45] Locke, pp. 165–166.

[46] John Stuart Mill, "On Liberty," in *Collected Works of John Stuart Mill*, ed. I. M. Robon, Vol. XVIII. (Toronto: University of Toronto Press, 1977), p. 219.

[47] Mill, "Representative Government," in *Collected Works*, Vol. XIX, pp. 448–466.

[48] Mill, "On Liberty," p. 223.

[49] *Nation and Society*, "Introduction to the Theory of Economics II," p. 219.

[50] *Notes*, "In South Africa—the Negroes," p. 239.

[51] *Notes*, "Strikes in the Land of Israel," p. 292.

[52] *Nation*, "The Truth About the Island of Tristan da Runha," pp. 281–82.

[53] *Ibid.*, p. 280.

[54] *Ibid.*, pp. 280–81.

[55] *Ibid.*, p. 281.

[56] *Ibid.*, p. 284.

[57] *Ibid.*, p. 283.

[58] *Ibid.*, p. 285.

[59] *Statehood*, "The Wagon of the *Klezmer*," p. 271.

[60] *Memoirs*, "Leader," pp. 215–16.

[61] *Ibid.*, p. 215.

[62] *Ibid.*, pp. 216–17.

[63] *Ibid.*, p. 216.

[64] *Exile*, "My Life," p. 25.

[65] *Statehood*, "On Militarism," pp. 41–42.

[66] *Ibid.*, p. 43.

[67] *Samson*, pp. 196–197, quoted from the translation in English, *Prelude to Delilah* (N.Y., B. Ackerman: 1945), pp. 200–01.

[68] *Statehood*, "On Militarism," p. 43.

[69] *Exile*, "My Life I," p. 19.

[70] *Autobiography*, "My Life II," p. 149.

[71] *Feuillitons*, "Apropos," (about the feminists and suffragettes), pp. 180–81.

[72] *Notes*, "Women's Intelligence," p. 127.

[73] *Ibid.*

[74] *Ibid.*, p. 134.

[75] *Nation*, "The Revolt of the Old Men," p. 226.

[76] *Ibid.*, p. 228.

[77] *Ibid.*, pp. 229–30.

[78] *Ibid.*, pp. 231–32.

[79] *Ibid.*, pp. 232–33.

[80] *Ibid.*, pp. 234–35.

CHAPTER 3: SOCIETY AND ECONOMICS

[1] *Exile and Assimilation*, "A Letter on Autonomy," p. 158.

[2] *Exile*, "From the Frying Pan Into the Fire," p. 174.

[3] *Exile*, "I Do Not Believe," p. 207.

[4] *Exile*, "A Lecture on Jewish History," p. 334.

[5] *Nation and Society*, "Introduction to Theory of Economics I," p. 196.

[6] *Notes*, "Reflections On a Provincial," p. 93; "The Crisis of the Proletariat," p. 311.

[7] "The Crisis of the Proletariat," pp. 309–10.

[8] *Ibid.*, p. 311.

[9] *Ibid.*, p. 314.

[10] *Ibid.*

[11] *Ibid.*, "Social Redemption," p. 299.

[12] *Nation*, "Class," pp. 239, 241, 242.

[13] *Nation*, "Economics I," p. 197.

[14] *Ibid.*

[15] *Ibid.*, p. 205.

[16] *Nation*, "Economics II," p. 213.

[17] *Ibid.*, p. 209.

[18] *Nation*, "Economics I," p. 203.

[19] *Ibid.*, p. 204.

[20] *Ibid.*

[21] *Ibid.*, "Economics II," p. 211.

[22] *Ibid.*, p. 216.

[23] *Ibid.*

[24] *Ibid.*, p. 217.

[25] *Ibid.*, p. 218.

[26] *Ibid.*
[27] *Ibid.*, p. 220.
[28] *Ibid.*, p. 221.
[29] *Ibid.*, p. 219.
[30] *Nation,* "The Revolt of the Old Men," p. 234.
[31] *Ibid.*, p. 235.
[32] *Exile,* "Autonomy," p. 163–5.
[33] *Nation,* "Class," p. 244.
[34] *Nation,* "The Jubilee Idea," p. 176.
[35] *Ibid.*
[36] *Nation,* "The Social Philosophy of the Bible," p. 191.
[37] *Nation,* "Jubilee," pp. 177–78.
[38] *Notes,* "Redemption," p. 295.
[39] *Ibid.*
[40] *Ibid.*, pp. 297–98.
[41] *Ibid.*, p. 298.
[42] *Nation,* "Social Philosophy," p. 190–1.
[43] *Notes,* "Redemption," p. 301.
[44] *Ibid.*, pp. 301–02.
[45] *Nation,* "Class," p. 240.
[46] *Statehood,* "The Shopkeeper," pp. 103–4.
[47] *Ibid.*, p. 106.
[48] *Notes,* "Strikes in the Land of Israel," p. 288.
[49] *Ibid.*, p. 287.
[50] *Exile,* "Jewish History," p. 335.
[51] *Ibid.*
[52] *Ibid.*, p. 337.
[53] *Ibid.*, p. 339.
[54] *Nation,* "Jubilee," p. 178.
[55] *Ibid.*, p. 179.
[56] *Ibid.*, p. 180.
[57] *Ibid.*

CHAPTER 4: NATION AND RACE

[1] *Exile and Assimilation,* "The Story of My Life Part One," p. 34.
[2] *Ibid.*, pp. 81–82.
[3] *Exile,* "A Letter on Autonomy," pp. 141–42.
[4] *Ibid.*, pp. 142–43.
[5] *Exile,* "Race," pp. 288–89.
[6] *Ibid.*, p. 289.
[7] *Ibid.*, pp. 289–90.
[8] *Ibid.*, p. 291.
[9] *Ibid.*, pp. 291–2.
[10] *Exile,* "A Lecture on Jewish History," p. 335.
[11] *Exile,* "Autonomy," p. 153.
[12] *Exile,* "Jewish History," pp. 335–36.
[13] *Exile,* "Autonomy," p. 154.
[14] *Nation and Society,* "The Truth About the Island of Tristan da Runha," p. 292.

[15] *Samson*, pp. 12–13, in English translation, p. 13.
[16] *Exile*, "An Exchange of Compliments," p. 220.
[17] *Ibid.*, p. 225.
[18] *Ibid.*, p. 229.
[19] *Ibid.*
[20] *Ibid.*, pp. 229–30.
[21] *Ibid.*, pp. 226–27.
[22] *Ibid.*, p. 226.
[23] *Exile*, "My Life I," p. 45.
[24] *Exile*, "Race," p. 294.
[25] *Ibid.*, pp. 295–96.
[26] *Exile*, "Autonomy," p. 154.
[27] *Exile*, "Jewish History," p. 334.
[28] *Exile*, "Autonomy," p. 157.
[29] *Ibid.*, p. 166.
[30] *Ibid.*, p. 159.
[31] *Nation*, "Self-Rule for a National Minority," p. 15.
[32] *Ibid.*, pp. 15–16.
[33] *Ibid.*, pp. 24–25.
[34] *Ibid.*, p. 18.
[35] *Ibid.*, p. 19.
[36] *Ibid.*, pp. 221–22.
[37] *Ibid.*, p. 26.
[38] *Ibid.*, p. 27.
[39] *Ibid.*, p. 37.
[40] *Ibid.*, pp. 51–52.
[41] *Ibid.*, p. 71.
[42] *Ibid.*, p. 57.
[43] *Ibid.*, p. 58.
[44] *Ibid.*, p. 61.
[45] *Ibid.*, pp. 67–68.
[46] *Exile*, "My Life I," p. 76.
[47] *Nation*, "The Helsingfors Program," p. 140.
[48] *Ibid.*, p. 142.
[49] *Exile*, "My Life I" p. 70.
[50] *Ibid.*, pp. 81–82.
[51] *On Literature and Art*, "The Arabesque Fashion," pp. 220–21.
[52] *Ibid.*, p. 220.
[53] *On the Way to Statehood*, "Islam," p. 213.
[54] *Ibid.*, p. 219.
[55] *Literature*, "Merchants of Culture," p. 239.
[56] *Statehood*, "The Iron Wall: We and the Arabs," p. 257. Emphasis the writer's.
[57] *Ibid.*, pp. 259–60.
[58] *Ibid.*, p. 258.

PART II: ZIONIST THOUGHT

CHAPTER 1: THE JEWISH NATION AND RACE

[1] *On Literature and Art*, "But by Spirit," p. 363.

[2] *Exile and Assimilation*, "The Story of My Life Part One," pp. 31–32.

[3] *Ibid.*, p. 33.

[4] *First Zionist Writings*, "The Critics of Zionism," pp. 35–36.

[5] *Ibid.*, p. 42.

[6] *Ibid.*, p. 45.

[7] For example, see *Exile*, "Four Sons" and "A Lecture on Jewish History"; *Notes*, "The East"; *Nation*, "The Social Philosophy of the Bible."

[8] *Writings*, "Critics," p. 46.

[9] *Ibid.*, pp. 53–54. Emphasis the writer's.

[10] *A Hebrew State: A Solution to the Question of the Jews*, "Why We Do Not Want the Exile" (Tel Aviv: M. Kopp, 1930), p. 25.

[11] *First Zionist Writings*, "Zionism and the Land of Israel," p. 111.

[12] *Ibid.*, pp. 113–14.

[13] *Ibid.*, p. 115.

[14] *Ibid.*, p. 116.

[15] *Ibid.*, pp. 117–18.

[16] M. Margolin, *Basic Streams in Jewish History*, p. 21, quoted by Z. Jabotinsky in *Writings*, "Zionism," p. 118.

[17] *Writings*, "Zionism," p. 120.

[18] *Ibid.*, pp. 121–22.

[19] *Ibid.*, pp. 123–24.

[20] *Ibid.*, p. 124.

[21] Jabotinsky developed these pragmatic political reasons in *Writings*, "On Territorialism," which is a continuation of "Zionism."

[22] *Writings*, "Zionism," p. 129. Emphasis the writer's.

[23] *Exile*, "A Letter on Autonomy," p. 144.

[24] A slight emendation in his theory of race is found in *A Hebrew State*, "Why We Do Not Want the Exile," p. 24. Here he does not insist that the spiritual apparatus differs among all groups, and maintains that it is likely that there are groups which, for whatever reason, have similar psyches.

[25] *Exile*, "Race," pp. 288–89.

[26] *Exile*, "Autonomy," p. 145.

[27] *Exile*, "A Lecture on Jewish History," p. 335.

[28] *Exile*, "Autonomy," p. 153.

[29] *A Hebrew State*, "The Absorptive Capacity of the Land of Israel," pp. 7–15.

[30] *Exile*, "The Language of the Enlightenment," p. 312.

[31] *Exile*, "Jewish History," p. 336.

[32] *Exile*, "On National Education," pp. 103–04.

[33] *Exile*, "Enlightenment," pp. 298–99. Emphasis the writer's.

[34] *Stories*, "Jew Boy," pp. 200–01.

[35] *Exile*, "An Exchange of Compliments," pp. 229–30.

[36] *Stories*, "A Tiny Landlord," p. 216.

[37] *Exile*, "Enlightenment," p. 297.

[38] *Notes*, "The East," p. 276.

[39] *Ibid.*, p. 283. Jabotinsky expressed the same views a year later in *Literature*, "The Arabesque Fashion."

[40] *Notes*, "The East," pp. 281–22.

[41] *Exile*, "Phenomena of our Existence," p. 238.

[42] *Exile*, "Jewish History," p. 338.

[43] *Nation*, "The Social Philosophy of the Bible," p. 185.

[44] *On the Way to Statehood*, "The Idea of *Betar*."

[45] *Writings*, "That Should We Do?" p. 182.

[46] *Exile*, "Jewish History," p. 336.

[47] *Speeches: 1927–1940*, "To Die or to Conquer the Mount," p. 314.

[48] *Speeches: 1927–1940*, "Poland Will Help and Will be Helped by the Evacuation Plan," p. 218. Emphasis the writer's.

[49] *Speeches: 1927–1940*, "Greater Zionism," p. 180.

[50] *Speeches: 1927–1940*, "In Place of the Partition Plan—the Ten-Year Plan," p. 293. Emphasis the writer's.

[51] Also see *A Hebrew State*, "Small-Scale Zionism and Greater Zionism," pp. 17–19.

[52] See *In the Tempest*, "A Helping Storm" (1936), and "Transjordan and the Ten-Year Plan" (1938); *Speeches: 1927–1940*: "On the Evacuation Plan" (1936), "Poland Will Help and Will be Helped with the Evacuation Plan" (1937), "Fulfill Your Promise or Give Back the Mandate" (1937), "In Opposition to the Partition Plan" (1937), "In Place of the Partition Plan, the Ten-Year Plan" (1938), and "To Die or to Conquer the Mount" (1937-8); in *A Hebrew State*, "The Absorptive Capacity of the Land of Israel" (1937).

[53] *Tempest*, "Transjordan and the Ten-Year Plan," p. 231.

[54] *Exile*, "Race," p. 292.

[55] *Exile*, "On National Education," p. 98.

[56] *Exile*, pp. 100–01.

[57] *Exile*, p. 104.

[58] *Exile*, "Compliments," pp. 221, 222, 223.

[59] *Exile*, "Phenomena," p. 240.

[60] Quoted by Z. Jabotinsky in *Literature*, "An Introduction to the Poems of Bialik," p. 101.

[61] *Ibid.*, p. 107.

[62] *Memoirs of My Contemporary*, "A Model Jew," pp. 221–22.

[63] *Ibid.*, p. 222.

[64] *Ibid.*, pp. 222–23.

[65] *Ibid.*, p. 223.

[66] *Statehood*, "Tel Hai," pp. 15–17.

[67] *Memoirs*, "Trumpeldor's Anniversary," p. 105.

[68] *Autobiography*, "The Story of the Jewish Legion," p. 284. Quoted from the English translation by Samual Katz (N.Y.: B. Ackerman, 1945), p. 161.

[69] *Letters*, "To Jewish Youth in Wloclawek, Poland," p. 363.

[70] *Statehood*, "On Militarism," p. 44.

[71] *Notes*, "The Rigan Hasmonean," p. 196.

[72] *Writings*, "Regular Work," pp. 194–95.

[73] *Statehood*, "The Idea of *Betar*," p. 308.

[74] *Ibid.*, pp. 319–20.

[75] *Ibid.*, p. 320.

[76] *Ibid.*

[77] *Ibid.*, pp. 320–21.

[78] *Ibid.*, p. 322.

[79] *Ibid.*, p. 321.

[80] *Ibid.*, pp. 322–23.

[81] *Speeches: 1927–1940*, "On the *Betar Hadar*," p. 347. Emphasis the writer's.

[82] *Ibid.*, p. 348.

[83] *Poems*, "The *Betar* Anthem," p. 205. Quoted here from Moshe Giloni, *Statesman, Soldier, Man of Vision* (NY: Jewish National Fund), p. 19. As he relates in his article, "Tel Hai," Jabotinsky borrowed the expression "it's nothing" from Trumpeldor who used it to express the idea that it is necessary to transcend life's difficulties, and to remain steadfast in one's goal.

An interesting point that Jabotinsky relates in "The Story of My Life" is that he was guided phonetically by his love for the Hebrew letter *resh* in composing the *Betar* anthem. He was influenced by Edgar Allen Poe, whose famous poems, "The Raven," and "Annabel Lee," he translated superbly into Hebrew.

[84] *Literature*, "The Poet of Ferment," pp. 381–83.

[85] *Literature*, "But by Spirit," pp. 368–69.

CHAPTER 2: THE DIASPORA

[1] *First Zionist Writings*, "Zionism and the Land of Israel," p. 129.

[2] *Exile and Assimilation*, "A Letter on Autonomy," p. 153.

[3] *Writings*, "The Critics of Zionism," p. 46.

[4] *Ibid.*, pp. 53–54.

[5] *Exile*, "Zionism and the Land of Israel."

[6] *Exile*, "A Lecture on Jewish History," p. 334.

[7] *Ibid.*

[8] *Ibid.*, p. 335.

[9] *Ibid.*, p. 336.

[10] *Ibid.*, p. 337.

[11] *Ibid.*, p. 338.

[12] *Ibid.*

[13] *Exile*, "Autonomy," pp. 160–61.

[14] *Exile*, "Jewish History," p. 339.

[15] *Exile*, "Dialogue," p. 268.

[16] *Exile*, "Phenomena of Our Existence."

[17] *Exile*, "Dialogue," p. 270.

[18] *Notes*, "The Jews in South Africa," pp. 269–70.

[19] *Exile*, "Jewish History," p. 339.

[20] *A Hebrew State*, "Why We Do Not Want the Exile," pp. 27–28.

[21] *Ibid.*, p. 28.

[22] *Exile*, "On National Education," pp. 97–98. Emphasis the writer's.

[23] *Ibid.*, p. 98.

[24] *Ibid.*, p. 101.

[25] *Ibid.*, p. 108.

[26] *Exile*, "The Jewish Revolt," p. 117.

[27] *Ibid.*, p. 118. Emphasis the writer's.

[28] *Writings*, "To the Foes of Zion" (Without Patriotism), p. 15.

[29] *Exile*, "The Jews and Russian Literature," p. 169.

[30] *Exile*, "The Chirikov Incident," p. 179.

[31] *Exile*, "A Strange Phenomenon," p. 244.

[32] *Exile*, "The Wrong Way," pp. 248–49.

[33] *Writings*, "Foes," pp. 13–14.

[34] *Exile*, "Jewish History," p. 340.

[35] *Writings*, "The Bund and Zionism," pp. 274–75.

[36] *A Hebrew State*, "Anti-Semitism of Man and Anti-Semitism of Circumstances," p. 32.

[37] *Speeches: 1927–1940*, "Fulfill Your Promise or Give Back the Mandate," pp. 226; in English, Evidence Submitted to the Palestine Royal Commission, February 11, 1937 (Tel Aviv: New Zionist Organization), p. 7.

[38] *Writings*, "Foes of Zion," (Without Patriotism), p. 15.

[39] *Exile*, "In the Days of Mourning," p. 119.

[40] *Ibid.*, p. 123.

[41] *Writings*, "The Critics of Zionism," p. 54.

[42] *Exile*, "Your New Year," p. 128.

[43] *Exile*, "Four Sons," p. 135.

[44] *Exile*, "The Bear From his Lair."

[45] *Exile*, "The Russian Caress."

[46] *Exile*, "Phenomenon," pp. 243–44.

[47] *Notes*, "The Rigan Hasmonean," p. 190.

[48] *In the Tempest*, "Petliura and the Pogroms," p. 276.

[49] *Memoirs of My Contemporary*, "Trumpeldor's Anniversary," p. 108.

[50] *Tempest*, "A Helping Storm," p. 223. The same view is expressed in *A Hebrew State*, "A Helping Storm, A Typhoon, and Evacuation."

[51] *A Hebrew State*, "A Helping Storm, a Typhoon, and Evacuation," pp. 111–12. *The Tempest*, "A Helping Storm" expresses the same ideas.

[52] *A Hebrew State*, "A Helping Storm, a Typhoon, and Evacuation," p. 112.

[53] *Tempest*, "No Until the End!" p. 190.

[54] *Ibid.*, p. 194.

[55] *Speeches: 1927–1940*, "Greater Zionism," p. 187.

[56] *Ibid.*

[57] A section of the article by G. Stein, "Controversial Points in the Zionist Program," quoted by Jabotinsky, *Writings*, "Zionism and the Land of Israel," p. 110.

[58] *Writings*, "On Teritorialism," p. 138.

[59] *Ibid.*, pp. 145, 151–52.

[60] *Exile*, "Autonomy," p. 153.

CHAPTER 3: THE BREAKTHROUGH PERIOD: ON THE WAY TO STATEHOOD

[1] *First Zionist Writings*, "To the Foes of Zion" (*Kadima*), p. 21.

[2] *On the Way to Statehood*, "Majority," p. 197. Emphasis the writer's.

[3] *Ibid.*, p. 203.

[4] *Statehood*, "What the Revisionist Zionists Want" (the *Betar* Program, 1926), p. 283.

[5] *Ibid.*

[6] *Speeches: 1927–1940*, "On the 'MacDonald Letter' and on the Goals of Zionism," p. 117.

[7] *Statehood*, "The Idea of *Betar*," p. 308–10. Emphasis the writer's.

[8] *Ibid.*, p. 311.

[9] *Ibid.*

[10] *Speeches: 1927–1940*, "Greater Zionism," p. 179.

[11] *Ibid.*, p. 180.

[12] *A Hebrew State*, "Small-Scale Zionism and Greater Zionism," p. 17.

[13] *Ibid.*, p. 18.

[14] *A Hebrew State*, "The Ten-Year Plan," p. 97.

[15] *Statehood*, "*Shaatnez Lo Ya'aleh Alekha*," p. 74. Emphasis the writer's.

[16] *Ibid.*, p. 75.

[17] *Ibid.*

[18] *Statehood*, "Zion and Communism," p. 61.

[19] *Ibid.*, pp. 62–63.

[20] *Ibid.*, pp. 63–64. Emphasis the writer's.

[21] *Ibid.*, p. 64.

[22] *A Hebrew State*, "The Class Question in the Settlement," pp. 91, 93–4. Emphasis the writer's.

[23] *Speeches: 1927–1940*, "On the Evacuation Plan," p. 200.

[24] *Statehood*, "*Betar*," p. 312.

[25] *Ibid.*, pp. 312–14.

[26] *Ibid.*, p. 332. (This is the second section of "The Idea of *Betar*," in which Jabotinsky expressed his opinions on the yet unresolved ideological problems of *Betar*.)

[27] *Statehood*, p. 333.

[28] *Statehood*, "Tel Hai," p. 16.

[29] *In the Tempest*, "Sweeter Than Honey," p. 79.

[30] *Tempest*, "Yes, to Break!" p. 51.

[31] *Statehood*, "*Betar*," p. 323.

[32] *Statehood*, "When Immigration Was Stopped," p. 57. Emphasis the writer's.

[33] *Statehood*, p. 58.

[34] Mill, *On Liberty*, pp. 262–263.

[35] *Ibid.*, p. 270.

[36] *Notes*, "Flatten the Iron!" p. 186.

[37] *Writings*, "What Should We Do?" p. 212.

[38] *Writings*, "Doctor Herzl," p. 88. Emphasis the writer's.

[39] *Exile and Assimilation*, "On National Education," p. 98.

[40] *Exile*, "The Language of the Enlightenment," p. 301.

[41] Jabotinsky dealt with this general issue in *Exile*, "Popular and National Language."

[42] *On Literature and Art*, "Books," pp. 170–71. Emphasis the writer's.

[43] *Literature*, "Sinkewitz."

[44] *Writings*, "What Should We Do?" p. 209.

[45] *Ibid.*

[46] *Ibid.*

[47] *Exile*, "Education," p. 98.

[48] *Writings*, "On Territorialism," pp. 142–44.

[49] *Statehood*, "The Shopkeeper," p. 104.

[50] *Ibid.*, pp. 106–07.

[51] *Tempest*, "Basta!" p. 23.

[52] *Ibid.*, p. 28.

[53] *Ibid.*, p. 29.

[54] *Statehood*, "Industry in the Land of Israel," p. 111.

[55] See *Speeches: 1927–1940*, "The Manufacturer and the Merchant" (1929); *Statehood*, "Of the Choice Produce of the Land" (1932).

[56] *Tempest*, "The Left," p. 16.

[57] *Tempest*, p. 17.

[58] *Statehood*, "More on Adventurism," p. 170.

[59] *Statehood*, "A Zionist NEP," p. 123.

[60] *Statehood*, "On the Zionist NEP, Once Again," p. 134.

[61] *Ibid.*, p. 138.

[62] *Ibid.*, p. 139.

[63] *A Hebrew State*, "The Absorptive Capacity of the Land of Israel," p. 10.

[64] *Ibid.*, p. 11.

[65] *Ibid.*, p. 13.

[66] *A Hebrew State*, "The Settlement and The Government," p. 44.

[67] *Ibid.*, "Building the Land and its Problems," pp. 47–48.

[68] *Ibid.*, p. 52.

[69] *A Hebrew State*, "The Class Question in the Settlement," pp. 92–93.

[70] *A Hebrew State*, "The Ten-Year Plan," p. 97.

[71] *Ibid.*, pp. 97–104. This appeared in summary a year later, in 1938, in *Speeches: 1927–1940*, "In Place of the Partition Plan, The Ten-Year Plan," pp. 299–302. Transjordan was emphasized in *The Tempest*, "Transjordan and the Ten-Year Plan," pp. 231–37, written in 1938. *The Tempest*, "A Precondition to the Ten-Year Plan," pp. 241–47, emphasized the political conditions necessary to implement the Ten-Year Plan.

[72] *Speeches: 1927–1940*, "On Independent Policy the Social Program," p. 41.

[73] *Statehood*, "*Betar*," p. 317.

[74] *Ibid.*, p. 332.

[75] *A Hebrew State*, "The Class Question and the Settlement," p. 93.

[76] *Tempest*, "Petach Tiqva and 'Company,'" p. 36.

[77] *Ibid.*, p. 37.

[78] *Ibid.*, p. 38.

[79] *Tempest*, "A Social Profile," pp. 57–62.

[80] *Tempest*, "Petach Tiqva," p. 41.

[81] *Tempest*, "A Warning," p. 72.

[82] *Ibid.*, p. 74.

[83] The most notable of the articles are: *Notes*, "Strikes in the Land of Israel," and *A Hebrew State*, "Class Question."

[84] *Tempest*, "Sweeter than Honey," pp. 78–79.

[85] *Tempest*, "The Left," p. 19.

[86] *A Hebrew State*, "Class Question," p. 93.

[87] *Ibid.*, pp. 93–94. Emphasis the writer's.

[88] *Tempest*, "Yes, to Break!" pp. 50–51.

[89] Also see: *Speeches: 1905–1926*, "In Favor of the Establishment of a Jewish Legion in the British Army," pp. 59–77, propaganda among Jewish immigrants in England in 1916.

[90] See for example: *Speeches: 1905–1926*, "A Jewish Legion in the Local Garrison," pp. 183–88, and "The Security of the Settlement—the Fundamental Question of Zionism," pp. 191–207; "The Political Offensive and the Legion," p. 267, and "After the Establishment of a Border Guard," pp. 294–305.

[91] *Statehood*, "Court Jews," p. 192.

[92] *Ibid.*, p. 194.

[93] *Ibid.*

[94] *Memoirs of My Contemporary*, "Trumpeldor's Anniversary," p. 108.

[95] *Statehood*, "On Militarism," pp. 41, 42, 45.

[96] *Ibid.*, pp. 44–45.

[97] *Statehood*, "The Legion," p. 34.

[98] *Statehood*, "*Affen Prippachek:* The New A B C," p. 89.

[99] *Ibid.*, pp. 92–93. Emphasis the writer's.

[100] *Ibid.*, p. 94.

[101] *Statehood*, "*Betar*," p. 318.

[102] *Ibid.*

[103] *A Hebrew State*, "The Court Jews and the Legions."

[104] *Speeches: 1905–1926*, "A Legion or Arming the Population," p. 192.

[105] *Ibid.*

[106] *Tempest*, ". . . and There is no Peace," p. 208.

[107] *Writings*, "What Must We Do?" p. 208.

[108] *Ibid.*, pp. 209–10.

[109] *Statehood*, "Majority," p. 199.

[110] *Ibid.*, pp. 109–10.

[111] *Speeches: 1905–1926*, "The Role of the Legion in Preventing Violence," p. 198.

[112] See *Statehood*, "Islam," pp. 207–21; *A Hebrew State*, "The Danger of Islam."

[113] *Statehood*, "The Iron Wall; We and the Arabs," p. 257.

[114] *Statehood*, "A Round Table With the Arabs," p. 245.

[115] *Statehood*, "Wall," p. 253. The same ideas formulated a bit differently appear in *A Hebrew State*, "The Arabs of the Land of Israel."

[116] *Speeches: 1927–1940*, "An Address to the Members of the British Parliament," p. 284.

[117] *A Hebrew State*, "The Arabs of the Land of Israel," p. 104.

[118] *Statehood*, "Round Table," p. 247.

[119] *Statehood*, "Wall," p. 255.

[120] *Ibid.*, pp. 253–54.

[121] *A Hebrew State*, "Arabs," p. 74.

[122] *Statehood*, "Wall," p. 255.

[123] *Ibid.*, p. 259.

[124] *Speeches: 1927–1940*, "Keep Your Promise or Give Back the Mandate!"; in English, "Evidence Submitted to the Palestine Royal Commission, February 11th 1937 (Tel Aviv: New Zionist Organization.

[125] *Statehood*, "Wall," p. 260.

[126] *Statehood*, "Ethics of the Iron Wall," pp. 264–65.

[127] *A Hebrew State*, "Arabs," pp. 78–79.

[128] *Speeches: 1927–1940*, "Keep Your Promise," p. 229; in English, p. 13.

[129] *Ibid.*, p. 230. In English, p. 13. Emphasis the writer's.

[130] *Statehood*, "On Adventurism," p. 26.

[131] *Statehood*, "What the Revisionist Zionists Want," p. 284.

[132] *Speeches: 1927–1940*, "Greater Zionism," pp. 182–183.

[133] *Tempest*, "Transjordan and the Ten-Year Program," p. 231.

[134] *Tempest*, "Precondition," p. 242.

[135] *A Hebrew State*, "Petition I," p. 126.

[136] *A Hebrew State*, "Petition II," p. 127.

[137] *Speeches: 1927–1940*, "Poland Will Help and Will be Helped by the Evacuation Plan," p. 219.

[138] *Tempest*, "Two Warnings," p. 254.

[139] *Tempest*, "A Precondition," p. 247.

[140] *Speeches: 1927–1940*, "Greater Zionism," p. 188.

[141] *Speeches: 1927–1940*, "Zion *Sejm* for Self-Preservation," pp. 343–44.

[142] *Ibid.*, p. 340.

[143] *Ibid.*, pp. 339–40.

[144] *Speeches: 1905–1927*, "Why I Resigned," pp. 240–41. (In 1925 Jabotinsky agreed to return to the World Zionist Organization as the head of the opposition; he broke finally from it in 1935.)

[145] *Statehood*, "What the Revisionist Zionists Want," pp. 297–98.

[146] *Speeches: 1927–1940*, "Keep Your Promise," p. 236; in English, p. 19.

[147] *Ibid.*, p. 242; in English, p. 23.

[148] *Ibid.*, p. 249; in English, pp. 28–29.

[149] *Speeches: 1927–1940*, "To Die or to Conquer the Mount," p. 311.

[150] *A Hebrew State*, "Building the Land," p. 51.

[151] *Ibid.*, pp. 51–52.

[152] *A Hebrew State*, "The Tractate of the Mandate," p. 62. In *Speeches: 1927–1940*, "Greater Zionism," Jabotinsky emphasized that despite everything, his faith in Britain remained firm: "I know the splendor of the nobility of England, and also its weaknesses, and perhaps more than any of my Zionist contemporaries, I have seen the shadows in the English character. Despite everything, as someone who believes at midnight that the sun will yet shine, so I have faith in the ultimate decision of this people of knights and judges" (p. 184. Emphasis the writer's.).

[153] *Statehood*, "The Wagon of the *Klezmer*," pp. 271–72. Emphasis the writer's.

[154] *Tempest*, "Yes, to Break!" p. 47.

[155] *Letters*, "To Dr. Michael Schwartzman," pp. 300–01. Emphasis the writer's.

[156] *Letters*, "To Israel Rosov," p. 286. Emphasis the writer's.

[157] *Nation and Society*, "Introduction to the Theory of Economics II," p. 219.

[158] *Tempest*, "Petach Tiqva and Company," p. 41.

[159] *Notes*, "Strikes in the Land of Israel," p. 292.

[160] *Tempest, Ibid.*

[161] *Tempest*, "Pro and Con," pp. 145–46.

CHAPTER 4: THE STATE OF THE JEWS

[1] *Memoirs of My Contemporary*, "A Letter to David Ben Gurion," p. 21. Emphasis the writer's.

[2] *First Zionist Writings*, "Doctor Herzl," p. 79. Emphasis the writer's.

[3] The quotations in this chapter are taken mainly from the writings of Jabotinsky that specifically discuss the state of the Jews in order to show that his general theoretical thought on the desired form of government, society, and economy indeed applies also the the state of the Jews.

[4] *Speeches: 1905–1926*, "The Roots of the Crisis," p. 323.

[5] *Speeches: 1927–1940*, "Greater Zionism," p. 179. Emphasis the writer's.

[6] See for example, *A Hebrew State: A Solution to the Question of the Jews*, "The Class Question and the Settlement," pp. 89–91; *On the Way to Statehood*, "The Idea of *Betar*," pp. 308–09, 312–13.

[7] *Speeches: 1927–1940*, "Greater Zionism," pp. 179–80. A similar definition was given in the respective programs of the UZR (Union of Zionist Revisionists) and *Betar*.

[8] For an example of Jabotinsky's considerations see *Hebrew State*, "The Absorptive Capacity of the Land of Israel," pp. 9–13, and "Small-Scale Zionism and Greater Zionism," pp. 17–19.

[9] For a detailed discussion of this issue see the section "A National Minority" in the chapter "Nation and Race" in the first part of this book.

[10] Jabotinsky made this proposal in his general thought dealing with self rule for a national minority. See *Nation and Society*, "Self-Rule for a National Minority," p. 70.

[11] *Nation*, "The Helsingfors Program," p. 142.

[12] *Speeches: 1927–1940*, "Greater Zionism," p. 180.

[13] *On the Way to Statehood*, "The Idea of *Betar*," p. 311.

[15] *Ibid.*, pp. 309, 310, 312.

[15] For a detailed discussion of this subject see the chapter "Liberalism and Democracy," in the first part of this book.

[16] For a detailed discussion of this subject see the section "The Principle of Majority Rule" in the chapter "Liberalism and Democracy" in the first part of this book, and the section "Democracy as Majority Rule, and Democracy as a Compromise," in the chapter "The Breakthrough Period—On the Way to Statehood," in the second part of this book.

[17] Mainly in *Notes*, "The East."

[18] *Speeches: 1927–1940*, "Greater Zionism," p. 191.

[19] *Ibid.*, p. 192.

[20] For a detailed discussion of this subject see the chapter "Society and Economics" in the first part of this book.

[21] *Statehood*, "*Betar*," p. 332.

[22] *A Hebrew State*, "The Class Question in the Settlement," p. 93.

[23] *Ibid.*, pp. 93–94.

[24] *Ibid.*, p. 93.

[25] *Statehood*, "What the Revisionist Zionists Want," p. 299.

[26] *Statehood*, "*Betar*," p. 314.

[27] *Statehood*, "A Round Table With the Arabs," p. 245. Emphasis the writer's.

[28] *Statehood*, "The Iron Wall: We and the Arabs," p. 253. Emphasis the writer's.

[29] *Ibid.*, "Revisionist Zionists," p. 298. Emphasis the writer's.

[30] *Speeches: 1927–1940*, "In Opposition to the Partition Plan," p. 284.

[31] See the details of the discussion in the section "A National Minority," in the chapter "Nation and Race," in the first part of this book. Jabotinsky discussed this problem in depth in *Nation*, "Self-Rule for a National Minority."

[32] *Ibid.*, p. 185.

[33] *Statehood*, "*Betar*," p. 311. For a detailed discussion of the issue of the Hebrew language in particular and the popularization of the language in general see *Exile and Redemption*, "The Language of the Enlightenment" and "Popular and National Language."

Appendix

KEY DATES IN THE LIFE OF ZE'EV JABOTINSKY

This list is based on "Important Dates in the Life of Ze'ev Jabotinsky," compiled by Solomon Gepstein and Yohanan Pograbinsky, which appears in *Memoirs of My Contemporary*, pp. 293–323. The dates were compared with those in Joseph Schechtman's book, *The Life and Times of Vladimir Jabotinsky*. In the few instances of discrepancy, additional sources were consulted.

1880   Ze'ev (Vladimir) Jabotinsky was born to Yona and Chava Jabotinsky in Odessa, Russia.

1898   He discontinued his high school studies and went to Berne, Switzerland to study law. Simultaneously he began to write for the *Odessky Listok* under the pseudonym "Altalena." In the autumn he left Berne for Rome where he continued as a correspondent for liberal Russian newspapers.

1901   He left Rome and returned to Odessa where he began to work as a journalist for the *Odesskiya Novosti*.

1902   Before Passover, following rumors of impending pogroms, Jabotinsky, together with student groups, helped organize self-defense efforts in Odessa, although in the end no pogroms took place there.

1903   A bloody pogrom took place in Kishinev. Jabotinsky went there as a correspondent for the *Odesskiya Novosti*, where he first met Zionist leaders J. M. Kogan-Bernstein, M. M. Ussishkin, Y. Y. Tiomkin, Dr. J. B. Sapir, and C. N. Bialik.

       That year Jabotinsky was chosen as the delegate of the Zionist circle *Eretz Yisrael* to the Sixth Zionist Congress. There he met

Theodor Herzl for the only time in his life. Jabotinsky was among the opponents of the Uganda Proposal.

At the end of the year he moved to St. Petersburg where he began working on the editorial board of the Zionist monthly *Yevreyskaya Zhisn*. He also began writing for two large Russian newspapers, *Nasha Zhisn* and *Rus*.

1906   He took part in the preparation of the Zionist program, *Gegenwartsarbeit* (national and political activities in diaspora countries), which was presented in November at the Helsingfors Convention.

He ran unsuccessfully as a candidate for the Duma in the province of Volhynia. (In 1907 and 1912 he ran again in the province of Odessa, and was again defeated.)

1907   He married Johanna (Anna) Galperin.

1908   After the outbreak of the Young Turkish Revolution, he was sent to Constantinople as the correspondent for the St. Petersburg paper *Rus*. In Constantinople, he was involved with Zionist information activities.

In the fall, he visited the Land of Israel for the first time.

1912   He received a law degree from the University of Yaroslavl.

1914   He was appointed roving correspondent to Western and Northern Europe for the Russian newspaper *Russkiya Vyedomosti*; in that capacity he visited Spain, Africa, and Egypt. While in Madrid, he visited Max Nordau and raised the idea of the establishment of a Jewish Legion.

1915   He met for the first time with Joseph Trumpeldor in a camp in Gabbari (Alexandria) for those who had been expelled by the Turks from the Land of Israel. He discussed the establishment of a Jewish Legion with him.

1917   After a struggle of years, on January 21 he signed a memorandum regarding the establishment of a Jewish Legion which was presented to the British War Cabinet; he immediately enlisted as a volunteer in the British army.

1918   He reached the Land of Israel with the second Battalion. There he joined the Zionist Commission and served as its chief political officer until the beginning of 1919.

1919   He participated in a conference in Petach Tiqvah of the representatives of volunteers from America and *Eretz Yisrael*, which discussed the future of the Jewish Legions.

1920   On February 24 he participated in a meeting of the *Vaad Zemani* where he opposed defending Tel Hai. He contended that the available means of defense were inadequate, and that adequate defense could not be sent in time; therefore, any such attempt would inevitably result in tragedy for the defenders of Tel Hai.

In the spring he resigned from the Legion and joined the editorial staff of *Haaretz*. Shortly thereafter, his mother, sister, and wife arrived in the Land of Israel.

With the outbreak of riots in Jerusalem during Passover, Jabotinsky became head of the defense efforts; on the third day of the riots he was arrested by the British authorities and sentenced to fifteen years of hard labor. After the verdict was handed down, he was sent to Kantara, and after a number of days was returned to the Acre prison. On July 8, the High Commissioner, Sir Herbert Samuel, granted amnesty to Jabotinsky and his friends. Jabotinsky demanded an acquittal.

At the Zionist Conference in London in July, Jabotinsky was chosen as the representative of all the Zionist factions, who placed him at the head of their lists; he left for London on August 18 in order to take part in the work of the World Zionist Organization; he was also chosen as a member of the executive of the Keren *HaYesod* (Palestine Foundation Fund).

1921 In August, he was elected by the Twelfth Zionist Congress to the Zionist Executive.

1922 Together with Chaim Weizmann, he signed the first White Paper of Churchill-Samuel in July. He began to write for the Berlin newspaper *Rasswyet*. His first articles later served as a basis for his revisionist teachings.

In September he made a short secret visit to the Land of Israel, for a meeting with Sir Herbert Samuel.

1923 At a meeting of the Zionist Actions Committee in Berlin on January 18, he resigned from the executive and left the World Zionist Organization, because he considered its stance toward Britain to be excessively lenient and compromising. Under his guidance, *Betar* (*Brit Trumpeldor*) was established in Riga on December 27.

1924 He moved to Paris and also moved the newspaper *Rasswyet* from Berlin, and became its chief editor. He lived in Paris until 1936, except for the years 1928–1929 when he lived in Jerusalem.

1925 He established a new party, the Union of Zionist Revisionists (UZR). Its first World Conference took place in Paris. In accordance with the Conference decision, Jabotinsky returned to the World Zionist Organization.

1926 In October he visited the Land of Israel, where he gave several lectures, organized the Revisionists and *Betar*, and participated in the

First National Revisionist Conference in Tel Aviv. In Tel Aviv he met for the last time with Ahad Ha'am. At the end of the year he returned to Paris and convened the Second Revisionist World Conference. The Conference decided to turn *Betar* into the world union of Revisionist youth and Jabotinsky was elected as head of *Betar*.

1927 He was elected as the head of a faction of ten to the Fifteenth Zionist Congress.

1928 He agreed to head the Judea Insurance Company in the Land of Israel, and arrived in Israel on October 5. He became the chief editor of the daily newspaper *Doar Hayom* and put together an editorial board of Revisionists. He went to Vienna to participate in the Third Revisionists World Conference.

1929 The tension between Jabotinsky and the left intensified. In the elections to the Sixteenth Zionist Congress, three Revisionist representatives from the Land of Israel were elected. During the Congress, bloody riots took place in the Land of Israel. In November Jabotinsky returned to the Land of Israel and lectured about the riots.

1930 He went to South Africa to raise money, as well as for Zionist informational purposes. During this time, the British administration in the Land of Israel prohibited his return.

In Prague, he convened the Fourth Revisionist World Conference in which, as a result of the shaky relations between the Revisionists and the left, a last attempt at cooperation at the Seventeenth Zionist Congress was decided upon.

1931 The Revisionists came to the Seventeenth Zionist Congress with fifty-two representatives. After the Congress rejected Jabotinsky's demand to openly declare the ultimate goal of Zionism, Jabotinsky tore up his delegate's card, and left the Congress together with the other Revisionists. However, the faction returned to the Congress without Jabotinsky and elected Nachum Sokolov as Weizmann's successor to the Presidency of the World Zionist Organization. Their return caused a rupture between Jabotinsky and his faction. Jabotinsky sought to leave the Zionist Organization and to establish a new Zionist organization. He refrained from participating in Revisionist activities.

1931 At the end of the year he returned to the Central Committee of the UZR.

1932 The Fifth Revisionist World Conference convened in Vienna, and as a result of Jabotinsky's demand to separate from the World Zionist Organization, a split ensued between him and Meir Grossman.

1933 As a result of the dispute between Jabotinsky and Grossman, the world party council was convened at Kattowitz. It ended on March

21 without taking a clear stand. On March 23, Jabotinsky left for Lodz and on March 23 he issued a statement to the members of the movement announcing that as a result of the situation he was suspending the World Executive and personally assuming authority. Simultaneously, he called for a plebiscite so that the members could choose between the two sides.

The result of the plebiscite was 31,000 in favor of Jabotinsky and 2000 against him. Jabotinsky began campaigning for the Eighteenth Zionist Congress.

On June 17, Chaim Arlosoroff, head of the Political Department of the Jewish Agency was murdered, and three Revisionists including Dr. Abba Achimeir were arrested and accused of the murder. Jabotinsky threw himself single-mindedly into the defense effort in various ways until the accused were declared innocent in 1934.

At the same time, he continued his campaign for the elections to the Congress. A faction of forty-seven was chosen. In Paris, Jabotinsky organized the Revisionist Executive Committee.

1934   After negotiations, Ben-Gurion and Jabotinsky signed a pact for the normalization of relations both in the Zionist Organization and between the *Histadrut Ha'Ovdim* (the General Federation of Jewish Workers) and the Revisionist National Labor Federation.

1935   The Jabotinsky-Ben-Gurion agreement was ratified by the Sixth Revisionist World Conference in Cracow; however, in a referendum, the member of the *Histadrut* in the Land of Israel rejected the agreement.

Jabotinsky proposed that the Revisionists leave the Zionist Organization and establish a new Zionist organization. He called a plebiscite among the members of the movement and about ninety per cent voted in favor of leaving the World Zionist Organization.

On September 7, the Founding Congress of the New Zionist Organization (NZO) opened in Vienna, and Jabotinsky was chosen as its president. He moved to London where he opened the NZO's main office.

1936   The NZO Council met in Vienna in November and demanded the establishment of a Hebrew military unit and the end to the policy of restraint in the Land of Israel. During the period of the riots in 1936–1937, Jabotinsky called for retaliatory action against the Arabs and determined the basic direction of the *Irgun Zvai Leumi* (IZL) during those years.

1937   On February 11, he appeared before the Peel Commission; after the declaration in July of a Partition Plan, he launched a struggle against it. In September, he opened negotiations with the government of Poland for a voluntary evacuation plan.

1938 The British government abandoned the Partition Plan. Jabotinsky refined his Ten-Year Plan, and concentrated on furthering his policy of treaties, through which he hoped to pressure Great Britain, with the help of other states who were eager to solve the question of their Jewish minorities.

1939 For what turned out to be the last time in his life, he visited the Jews in Poland, Lithuania, Latvia, and Estonia. He was shocked by the German takeover of Poland and the outbreak of the Second World War.

　　　　He developed a plan to raise a Jewish army to fight against Nazi Germany and began a campaign for British public opinion.

1940 He made a trip to the United States to convert people to his ideas. Toward the end of his visit, on August 4 he went to the *Betar* camp near New York and passed away suddenly.

　　　　His will, written in Paris on November 3, 1935, included the following instructions: "It is my desire to be buried or to be cremated (it is the same to me) in the same place where I happen to die; and my remains (should I be buried outside of the Land of Israel) may not be transferred to the Land of Israel unless by order of that country's eventual Jewish government." (Will, *Memoirs*, p. 18). Jabotinsky was buried, in accordance with his instructions, in Long Island, near New York. On the twenty-fifth anniversary of his passing (29 *Tamuz* 1965), at the instruction of the late Prime Minister of Israel, Levi Eshkol, and thus in accordance with Jabotinsky's last will and testament, his remains and those of his wife Johanna were reinterred, in a state funeral, on Mount Herzl in Jerusalem.

Writings by Ze'ev Jabotinsky:
A Selected List

1. *Writings*, published by E. Jabotinsky, 1947. The 18 volumes include:
    Autobiography: "The Story of My Life Part Two" (1936); "The Story of the Jewish Legion"* (1926); "Twenty-four Hours: An Interlude in the Life of the Acre Prisoners"* (1929); Index.

    Nation and Society: "Self-Rule for a National Minority"* (1912); "On Languages and Other Things" (1911); "Constituencies" (1911); "The Obscurantist" (1912); "Greater Albania" (1913); "Race"* (1913); "The Helsingfors Program" (1912); "An Exchange of Compliments"* (1911); "A Lecture on Jewish History"* (1933); "The Jubilee Idea"* (1930); "The Social Philosophy of the Bible"* (1933); "Introduction of the Theory of Economics I & II"* (1936); "The Revolt of the Old Men"* (1937); "Class"* (1933); *Homo Homini Lupus* (1910); "The Truth About the Island of Tristan da Runha"* (1925); Index of Sources and Notes.

    Sparticus and Other Stories: "Raphael Giovanioli: Sparticus" (translated from the Italian by Ze'ev Jabotinsky); "Two Traitors" (1905); "Fat Pepino" (1903); "The Yellow Gloves" (1902); "Berne" (1898); "Knight Gofredo" (1902); "The Mytholody of Canaan" (1931); "The Prospero Maliglioli Affair" (1933); Notes.

    On the Way to Statehood: "Tel Hai"* (1920); "On Adventurism"* (1932); "The Legion"* (1933); "On Militarism"* (1933); "When Immigration Was Stopped" (1928); "Zion and Communism"* (1933); "Shaatnez Lo Yaalah Alekha"* (1929); "His Children and Ours"* (1930); "*Affen Prippachek*: The New A B C"* (1933); "The Shopkeeper"* (1927); "Industry in the Land of Israel" (1927); "A Zionist NEP" (1927); "On the Zionist NEP, Once Again" (1928); "Of the Choice Produce of the Land" (1932);

---

* available in English. This is not a complete listing.

"Immigration Cooperatives" (1932); "More on Adventurism" (1932); "Class Problems" (1927); "Court Jews" (1922); "Majority" (1923); "Islam" (1925); "On the Eve of the Last Step" (1928); "Small-Scale Zionism"* (1930); "A Round Table With the Arabs" (1931); "The Iron Wall: We and the Arabs"* (1923); "Ethics of 'The Iron Wall'"* (1923); "The Wagon of the *Klezmer*"* (1935); "What the Revisionist Zionists Want" (1926); "The Idea of *Betar*"* (1934); Index of Sources and Notes.

In the Tempest: "The Left" (1925); "*Basta!*" (1925); "Petach Tiqvah 'and Company'" (1928); "Yes, To Break!" (1932); "A Social Profile" (1929); "With Two Sticks" (1929); "A Warning" (1929); "Sweeter than Honey" (1925); "According to the Muskovite Example" (1933); "Cold and Firm" (1933); "Our Position Thus Far"* (1935); "On Unity" (1935); "A Disruption of Disciplines" (1933); "The Danger of Flooding" (1933); "A Test of Our Statehood" (1933); "No, Until the End!" (1933); "On The Brink of The Precipice"* (1937); "... and there is no Peace" (1936); "Amen"* (1939); "A Helping Storm" (1936); "Transjordan and the Ten-Year Plan"* (1938); "A Precondition to the Ten-Year Plan" (1938); "Two Warnings" (1936); "Between the Sixth and the Eleventh"* (1931); "Petliura and the Pogroms" (1927); "The Prohibition of Entry in the Land of Israel" (1930); "Noah's Ark" (1930); "Pro And Con" (1935) Index of Sources and Notes.

Memoirs of My Contemporary: "A Letter to his Wife" (1918); "Will" (1935); "A Letter to Ben-Gurion" (1935); "Memoirs of My Contemporary" (1933); "The Alexandrian Battalion" (1915); "The Mule Drivers" (1919); "So Were the Banners of the Legions Passed On" (1925); "Trumpeldor's Anniversary"* (1928); "Commander Patterson" (1929); "Turkey and the War"* (1917); "Leader"* (1934); "A Model Jew" (1904); "That Max Nordau" (1933); "Abraham Idelson" (1925); "A Conversation with Zangwill" (1939); "Tiomken" (1928); "Daniel Pasmanik" (1930); "H. Sliosberg" (1933); Important Dates in the Life of Ze'ev Jabotinsky.

*The Five** (a novel).

First Zionist Writings: "To the Foes of Zion" (1903); "The Critics of Zionism" (1903); "Hebrew Education"* (1903); "Doctor Herzl"*(1905); "Zionism and the Land of Israel" (1905); "On Territorialism" (1905); "What Should We Do?" (1905); "The Bund and Zionism" (1906); Index of Sources and Notes.

Letters: a) Personal Letters; b) Letters to Newspapers and to Public Institutions; Index of Sources and Notes.

Speeches 1905–1926.

Speeches 1927–1940.

"A Foreign Land" (a play).

* available in English. This is not a complete listing.

Stories: "Diana"* (1910); "Territory for Students" (1901); "Via Montelelb 48"* (1930); "Bichetta" (1902); "The Acacias" (1911); "A Description of Switzerland"* (1911); "Edmee" (1912); "The Hun" (1914); "The Conquerer" (1915); "The Story of Mr. A. B." (1916); "A Tale of the Dark Ages"* (1925); "Squirrel" (1925); "Virginia" (1930); "Jew Boy" (1931); "A Tiny Landlord" (1911); "A Galilean Romance"* (1926).

On Literature and Art: "The Ten Books" (1905); "Causeries" (1910); "The Wandering Goddess" (1930); "The Jews and Russian Literature" (1908); "The Chirikov Incident" (1909); "An Introduction to the Poetry of Bialik"* (1911); "Literature" (1912); "The Lessons of Schevchenko's Anniversary" (1911); "Herzl's Feuilletons" (1912); "The Honest Vampuka" (1912); "Sinkewitz" (1919); "Books" (1919); "Pearls of Food" (1925); "L'Amerique a un Metre" (1926); "At Abel Pann's Exhibition" (1927); "The Arabesque Fashion" (1927); "About Disraeli" (1927); "Merchants of Culture" (1927); "Emile Zola" (1927); "Bialik is Silent" (1927); "The New Adventures of Reb Yisrael" (1928); "Habima Festivities" (1928); "The Sleeping Poland" (1929); "The Poet of the Pioneers" (1931); "What People Read and What They Think" (1929); "Women's Stories" (1931); "When the World Was Young"* (1931); "Once Upon a Time ..." (1931); "For the Sixtieth Birthday of Bialik" (1933); "But by Spirit" (for the sixtieth birthday of Prof. Joseph Klausner) (1934); "After the Death of Bialik" (1934); "The Poet of Ferment" (for the sixtieth birthday of Shaul Tchernichovsky) (1936); Index of Sources and Notes.

Feuilletons: "Apropos" (1902); "Lists Without Titles" (1905); "In the Days of Mourning"* (1906); "The Jewish Punishment" (1906); "Your New Year"* (1908); "The Light of the Sunset" (1910); "Phenomena of Our Existence" (1910); "I Do Not Believe" (1910); "Right and Violence" (1910); "In Place of A Defense" (1911); "Four Sons"* (1911); "Apropos—As an Impartial Observer" (1912); "Dialogue" (1912); "A Strange Phenomenon" (1912); "In the Way of Falsehood" (1912); "Apropos" (about feminists and suffragettes) (1912); "Old Odessa"* (1913); "The Truth"* (1916); "The Muse of Fashion" (1916); "The Mountainous Province" (1928); "The Brigadeer Luba Gola" (1930); "An Hour in Madeira" (1931); "Lulu My Friend" (1931); "The Riddle—Yavnu Azaf" (1932); Index of Sources and Notes.

Notes: "The Ignitor" (1912); "The Individual" (1911); "On Muna and Anna" (1902); "On Feuchtwanger's Novel" (1933); "Rude" (1900); "A Discussion About Theatre" (1910); "On a Purely Literary Topic" (1940); "About Jack London" (1912); "Reflections on a Provincial" (1931); "Solveig"* (1916); "The Spielberg Palace" (1931); "On Fathers and Sons"

---

* available in English. This is not a complete listing.

(1902); "Women's Intelligence" (1923); "Tractate of Fools" (1931); "One of the Cities" (1911); "My Small Village" (1928); "After the Tunnel" (1933); "Flatten the Iron!" (1905); "The Rigan Hanmonean" (1926); "Caught in a Lie" (1926); "The Boers" (1931); "In South Africa—the Negroes" (1931); "The Jews in South Africa" (1931); "The East" (1926); "Strikes in the Land of Israel" (1934); "Social Redemption"* (1934); "The Crisis of the Proletariat"* (1932); Notes.

Poems: a) Everyday Poems, b) Songs of Zion.

*Samson** (a novel).

2.   *Selected Writings*: Tel Aviv, 1946, 3 Vol. (A significant number of articles also appear in *Writings*.) The volumes include:

Exile and Assimilation, Tel Aviv, S. D. Salzman, 1946 "The Story of My Life Part One" (1936); "On National Education"* (1903); "The Jewish Revolt" (1906); "In the Days of Mourning" (1906); "Your New Year"* (1908); "Four Sons"* (1911); "A Letter on Autonomy"* (1904); "The Jews and Russian Literature" (1908); "From the Frying Pan into the Fire" (1910); "The Chirikov Incident" (1909); "The Bear From His Lair" (1909); "The Russian Caress" (1909); *Homo Homini Lupus* (1910); "I Do not Believe" (1910); "Might and Right" (1911); "An Exchange of Compliments"* (1911); "Phenomena of Our Existence" (1910); "A Strange Phenomenon" (1912); "The Wrong Way" (1912); "In Place of a Defense" (1911); "Dialogue" (1912); "The Obscurantist" (1912); "Greater Albania" (1913); "Race"* (1913); "The Language of the Enlightenment" (1913); "The Truth"* (1916); "Popular and National Language" (1916); "A Lecture on Jewish History"* (1933).

When the World Was Born, Jerusalem, T. Kopp, 1943. "The Story of My Life, Part II"* (1936); "Turkey and the War"* (1917); "The Story of the Jewish Legion"* (1926); "Twenty-four Hours: An Interlude in the Life of the Acre Prisoners"* (1929); "The Alexandrian Battalion" (1915); "The Mule Drivers" (1919); "Tel Hai"* (1920); "So the Banners of the Legion Were Passed On" (1925); "The Regiment"* (1932); "Commander Patterson" (1929); "Joe Katz"* (1923); "When the World Was Still Young"* (1931); "Chivitta Vecia"* (1935); "Court Jews" (1923); "On Militarism"* (1933); "A Jewish Legion" (1924); "Flatten the Iron!" (1905); "Two Traitors" (1905); Notes.

Zionist Policy, Jerusalem: Eri Jabotinsky, 1946. "Majority" (1923); "The Iron Wall: We and the Arabs"* (1923); "Ethics of the Iron Wall"* (1923); "Islam" (1925); "The East" (1926); "The Seventh Dominion" (1928); "It Was Not Said About Us" (1928); "The Crisis of the Land of Israel"

---

* available in English. This is not a complete listing.

(1931); "A Round Table With the Arabs" (1931); "Cantos" (1932); "The 'Picturesque' East" (1932); "*Affen Prippacheck*: The New A B C"* (1937); "Evidence Submitted to the Palestine Royal Commission"* (1937); "Sunk Without Trace"* (on partition) (1937); "The War and the Jews"* (1940).

3.   *A Hebrew State: A Solution to the Question of the Jews*, Tel Aviv: T. Kopp, 1936.
"Introduction to the Polish Edition"; "The Absorptive Capacity of the Land of Israel"; "Small-Scale Zionism and Greater Zionism"*; "Why We Do not Want the Exile"; "Anti-Semitism of Man and Anti-Semitism of Circumstances"; "The Settlement and The Government"; "Building the Land and its Problems"; "A Mosaic on the Mandate"; "The Danger of Islam"; "The Arabs of the Land of Israel"; "The Court Jews and the Legions"; "The Class Question in the Settlement"; "The Ten-Year Plan"; "A Helping Storm, A Typhoon, and Evacuation"; "Around the Polish Initiative"; "Two Petitions."

4.   *The Jewish War Front*,* Jerusalem: T. Kopp, 1941.
Part I: "Is this the Aim of War?"; Part II: "Anti-Semitism of Things"; Part III: "The State of Mass Exodus"; Part IV: "Max Nordau's Plan for the Land of Israel."

A comprehensive listing of Ze'ev Jabotinsky's writings, in all languages, may be found in *The Writings of Ze'ev Jabotinsky 1897–1940, a Bibliography*, ed. Israel Yevarovitch (Tel Aviv: The Jabotinsky Institute in Israel, 1977).

Works on Ze'ev Jabotinsky's Thought:
a Selected Bibliography

Avineri, Shlomo. *Varieties of Zionist Thought*. Chapter Sixteen: "Jabotinsky: Monism, the Integral Nationalist Theory." Tel Aviv: Am Oved, 1980.

Axelrod, Abraham. *Ze'ev Jabotinsky's Social Thought*. Tel Aviv: *HaVaad HaPoel* of the *Histadrut* (the National Labor Federation), 1962.

Bar-Nir, Dov. *From Jabotinsky to Begin: the Profile of a Movement*. Tel Aviv: Am Oved, 1983.

Benari, Yehudah. *Ze'ev Jabotinsky's Politics*. Tel Aviv, 1964.

Benari, Yehudah. *Ze'ev Jabotinsky*. Tel Aviv: M. Neuman, 1971.

Benari, Yehudah. *Ze'ev Vladimir Jabotinsky: A Biographical Sketch* (in English). Tel Aviv: The Jabotinsky Institute, 1977.

Gepstein, Solomon. *Ze'ev Jabotinsky: His Life, His Wars, His Achievements*. Tel Aviv: The Tel Hai Fund, 1941.

Jabotinsky, Eri. *My Father, Ze'ev Jabotinsky*. Jerusalem: Steimatzky, 1980.

Nedava, Joseph, ed. *Ze'ev Jabotinsky: The Man and His Thought*. Tel Aviv: The Ministry of Defense, 1980.

Nedava, Joseph, ed. *Jabotinsky's Perception of the Image of Women*. Tel Aviv. 1963.

Remba, Isaac. *The Shield and the Prisoner*. Tel Aviv: Steimatzky, 1960.

Schechtman, Joseph. *The Life and Times of Vladimir Jabotinsky* (2 vols) (in English). Silver Spring, Maryland: Eshel Books, 1956.

Schwartz, Sholom. *Jabotinsky, Warrior of the Nation*. Jerusalem, 1943.

Shavit, Jacob. *The Mythologies of the Right*. Tel Aviv: Emda, 1986.

Vainshel, Yaakov. *Sketches of Ze'ev Jabotinsky*. Tel Aviv: Hamatmid, 1944.

Vainshel, Yaakov. *The Last of the Giants*. Tel Aviv: Makada Press, 1961.

For Jabotinsky's centennial birthday, in 1977, the Jabotinsky Institute in Tel Aviv published an expanded and detailed bibliography of his essays and articles: *The Writings of Ze'ev Jabotinsky 1897–1940, A Bibliography*, ed. Israel Yevarovitch.

INDEX

About the Author

Dr. Raphaella Bilski Ben-Hur is a member of the department of Political Science, the Hebrew University of Jerusalem. She received the Jabotinsky Prize in 1992 for the Hebrew version of *Every Individual, A King*.

She has published as well, on the subjects of the influence of ideology on policy the principles of the welfare state, the concept of social justice and social policy. She held a number of public positions. Among them: Chairman of the National Council for Health and Society; Co-chairman of the Council for Social Planning, reporting to the Prime Minister, adviser on social and welfare policy to the government.